Gun Culture or Gun Con

Why do attitudes to firearms differ so markedly in the UK and USA?

Can greater gun availability actually lead to a safer society?

The sh~~~~~~~~ killing of sixteen young children in a Dunblane primary school in 1996 ~~~~~~~~~~~~~ing p~~~~mentary reform to gun laws in the United Kingdo~ ~~~~~~~~~~~~~~~~~~~~~~~~~~~~~~~~~ ~ed handguns had been outlawed. *Gun* ~~~ *~~ ~~l?* p~~ ~~~~~~~~~~~~~ ~ analysis of the social and political reactions to events in Dunblane and also examines many of the wider issues relating to gun control in the UK.

Rigorously comparative throughout, Peter Squires provides a non-partisan exploration of the differences between attitudes to firearms and their control in the UK and in the United States of America. Among the topics the author considers are:

- the social history of firearms on both sides of the Atlantic
- the differing policy directions adopted in the UK and the USA
- media coverage of the gun question
- the future of the gun in society

This book brings a combination of sociological, criminological, historical and political analysis to bear upon a wealth of fascinating new material.

Peter Squires is Reader in Criminal Justice Studies in the School of Applied Social Sciences at the University of Brighton.

Gun Culture or Gun Control?

Firearms, violence and society

Peter Squires

London and New York

First published 2000
by Routledge
11 New Fetter Lane, London EC4P 4EE

Simultaneously published in the USA and Canada
by Routledge
29 West 35th Street, New York, NY 10001

Routledge is an imprint of the Taylor & Francis Group

Typeset in Baskerville by Taylor & Francis Books Ltd
Printed and bound in Great Britain by St Edmundsbury Press, Bury St
Edmunds, Suffolk

British Library Cataloguing in Publication Data
A catalogue record for this book is available from the British Library

Library of Congress Cataloging in Publication Data
Squires, Peter
  Gun culture or gun control: firearms, violence and society / Peter
Squires.
    p. cm.
  Includes bibliographical references and index.
  1. Gun control–Government policy–Great Britain. 2. Gun control–Law
and legislation–Great Britain. 3. Dunblane Massacre, Dunblane,
Scotland, 1996. 4. Firearms and violence–United States. I. Title.

HV7439.G7 S68 2000
363.3'3'0941–dc21
                                                      00-032185

ISBN 0–415–17086–9 (hbk)
ISBN 0–415–17087–7 (pbk)

For Matthew

Contents

Figures

Preface

When I first began researching the firearms question back in 1995, there was some scepticism about the relation of this issue to British social and public policy. After March 13th 1996, however, few people entertained any doubts that this was an important policy issue. My initial approaches to British 'guns and gun culture' debates led to studies of the representation of firearms in the film industry and of the debates concerning the upgrading of the armed response capacity of the British police. Unfortunately, for reasons of space, neither of these two fairly substantial studies made it into the present book. In the event, the study of 'culture and control' issues, which unfolded to form the present book, echoed many of the political and ideological issues (individual freedom, citizenship rights and social discipline) with which I had been preoccupied in an earlier book.

That earlier book, *Anti-Social Policy*, was primarily concerned with the disciplined 'welfare collectivism' established throughout British social policy and a series of rather conditional citizenship rights. The final sections of the book anticipated the fragmentation of that welfare regime and its replacement by 'post-fordist' forms of welfare delivery and more coercive forms of order maintenance. Such themes very much underlie the present book. After all, Britain's response to Dunblane, the prohibition of all handguns on the mainland, can be seen as a classic instance of 'disciplined collectivism'. The conditional rights of shooters assumed a markedly lower priority than the claims of public safety, a fact much bemoaned by shooters themselves.

In the USA, however, things are somewhat different. There, republican traditions, a presumption about the 'right to bear arms', an accumulated gun stock nearing 250 million and almost 50 per cent of households admitting to ownership of at least one gun, make for a rather different context. Most significant of all, however, are the laws passed in over thirty states permitting private citizens to carry concealed self-defence firearms. Doubting the capacities of police and criminal justice agencies, many Americans have 'tooled up' and purchased a little post-fordist insurance from the local gunstore. Inevitably, self-defence firearms are only one facet of this 'post-modern law and order' yet they are one of the most obvious, immediate, and emotive – especially when they are misused. Following the tragedy of Dunblane, the UK clearly rejected the private ownership of firearms, although other aspects of post-fordist law and order, like surveillance technologies and private security services, have been adopted enthusiastically. Even so, it remains to be seen whether the future shape of law and order will be dominated by market forces (particularly market-driven technologies, such as firearms) exploiting popular anxieties about crime and disorder. Perhaps safer, less damaging and ultimately more sustainable policy solutions will be devised.

A number of people have shared their time and ideas with me as this book was being written. My colleagues at the University of Brighton, Lynda Measor and Bob Skelton, were kind enough to read and comment upon some earlier chapters. And, at a time when few in Britain seemed to be researching firearms, Ian Taylor was always encouraging. Equally, following a symposium on gun control at the BSC conference in Belfast in 1997, Pat Mayhew was kind enough to impart some very useful information and advice. Sarah Marshall began a very useful collection of news reports on firearms issues and Alison McLoughlin of the Scottish *Daily Record* kept me supplied with her paper's own firearms debate material.

Peace was maintained on the domestic front, despite the rigours of proof-reading. Fortunately, Matthew was frequently on hand to take me off to the park to play football. Last, but by no means least, Mari Shullaw at Routledge, in the nicest possible way, urged a greater economy with words – something which has never come naturally to me.

Peter Squires,
Brighton 2000

1 Introduction

Why guns?

Opening shots

Guns are an unusual subject for a British social scientist and a fairly infrequent topic among British criminologists. Things are obviously quite different in the USA. My exploration of the 'sociology of the gun' began somewhat by chance. I was actually researching in the crime prevention field, but noticed a headline: 'Home defence choices' on the front cover of the American *Guns & Ammo* magazine at a newsagent. An article in the magazine profiled a number of handguns said to be particularly suitable for guarding your home against intruders and a companion article ran through a number of tips on 'defensive handgun combat tactics'. Included here was advice on weapon availability and access, speed and accurate shooting, and concealment and cover.

Although the article carried advice on safe storage of guns in the home, particularly homes containing children, none of the weapons pictured in the photographs accompanying the text were shown in any way locked or disabled. One was in a bedside cabinet, another in the half-open drawer of a coffee table. There is, clearly, something of a dilemma here. A gun which is locked away, disabled, or perhaps just unloaded, is not as rapidly available as one left loaded and ready. According to critics, the American firearms industry exploits fear, which stimulates gun purchases in the first place (Diaz, 1999) and then, fear of an immediately life-threatening worst case scenario disinclines many American gun owners from paying very much attention to gun safety advice (Weil and Hemenway, 1992). The results are fairly predictable. Proponents of handgun control in the USA argue that fifteen children and young people are killed by guns each day, most of them in or around their own homes. An episode of the American syndicated *Court TV* series broadcast by the BBC during 1996 illustrated the dilemma. The programme was devoted to a 1992 case in Jacksonville, Florida, in which a 3-year-old boy had shot his 2-year-old sister with a handgun he had found in his parents' bed. Florida state law requires that gun owners store their weapons safely and beyond the reach of children. However, central to this case was not just the 3-year-old's easy access to the .357 revolver in the bed, but the nine other guns in the household, four more of them (two loaded) in the bedroom alone. Taken together, the prosecution argued, so many firearms left lying around the house suggested wanton negligence on the part of the otherwise respectable, white, lower-middle-class, church-going parents. The case was apparently the first of its kind in which parents were successfully prosecuted for their culpability in a homicide. It was something of a test case in the developing gun control debate.

The reason an article on the cover of an American gun magazine caught my eye had to do with some very domestic issues. I had recently been involved in a research project investigating burglary, harassment and victimisation on a 'problem' social housing estate. The very first interviewee told of how she had had to take her cat to the vet after it had been shot by an air rifle. A number of other interviewees told of how 'kids up here' play with air guns and a couple pointed out to me the small round holes that air pellets had made in the glass of their doors or windows. Later I conducted an interview over the kitchen table with a man and his partner. Leaning against a corner kitchen unit was an air rifle. A few interviews later a man in his thirties gave the following, candid, response to my question about whether he had any fears or concerns about crime on the estate. 'I've got a gun cabinet back there, you know. Two shotguns and a .22 rifle. And if anybody breaks in here, they can have some of that.'

Not long afterwards, another man explained how he had bought a plastic replica, semi-automatic pellet pistol because, 'it didn't cost much, and I thought that, you know, if anyone, got in here, I could threaten them with it because, you know, unless you look very close, it looks quite real'. Replica weapons do look quite real, they now feature in a significant percentage of opportunist 'armed' robberies at post offices, building societies and similar business premises (Matthews, 1996). Certainly, the staff working in such businesses and at whom such weapons are pointed often think them to be real. These 'lethal looks' were what prompted a woman interviewed on a TV documentary about 'road rage' to purchase an imitation handgun. She had previously been attacked while driving and bought the blank-firing revolver to point at any would-be assailants in the future. Unfortunately for her, the police confiscated the gun and the woman faced prosecution for carrying it in her car. A similar fate befell the householder who had detained two men with an imitation firearm after he discovered them burgling his home. Having called the police he was promptly arrested when they arrived and charged with a firearms offence. Coincidentally, new legislation, in the shape of the Firearms Amendment Bill 1994, strengthening the law in cases where an imitation firearm was used to threaten or intimidate, was currently before parliament. *Guns Review* claimed that both the incident and the proposed new legislation were typical of a British tendency to punish the innocent in matters of firearms control (*Guns Review*, August 1994: 579).

In 1995, reacting to a growing concern about individuals using weapons for self-defence purposes, the Home Office minister, David MacLean wrote that, 'tackling crime and protecting citizens are primarily jobs for the police. … I would discourage anyone from keeping an imitation firearm to ward off intruders. This could well increase the risk of violence' ('Cadmus', 1995a: 670). Shooting commentators were outraged and saw the Home Office position as yet further evidence of British society 'gone soft' by allowing criminals to walk all over the law-abiding with impunity. Instead, they argued, the right to own a firearm within one's own home and to use it against an intruder when the householder feels endangered ... is a right at common law and a right in common decency. The current trend in sympathising with the criminal and penalising the victim must end. It is now time to start exerting pressure on Parliament to state the law clearly so that we may all sleep more soundly in our beds.

('Cadmus', 1995b: 751)

The gun question

But what does this all add up to? What processes might have been driving this apparent resort to weapons, even replica weapons? What did it say about our fears, our sense of personal security or our confidence in the public institutions of criminal justice and law enforcement? The word from the streets of New York, according to Geoffrey Canada was that 'it is better to be judged by twelve than carried by six' (Canada, 1995). Is that it? Is society becoming more dangerous and are guns part of the solution or part of the problem? Has sports shooting served primarily as a cover for many people who really wanted – or even believed in their inherent right – to own firearms for other purposes? If the choice of public protection firearms pointed to a lack of confidence in the existing political authorities to deliver public order, is this best interpreted as further evidence of an individualistic, libertarian strain of thought eating its way through our traditional 'social contract'? Is it evidence of an increasingly marke-tised and individualised conception of personal security as a consumer good? (Christie, 1993; Taylor, 1999).

Alternatively, does widespread firearms ownership represent a positive shift in modes of governance, delegating authority over fundamentals of life, death and personal security to the citizenry at large. As Law and Brookesmith would have it, 'modern fighting handguns' have three main groups of users, the police and the military use them in the course of their work, 'while the ordinary citizen, *in civilised countries*, keeps them to defend his home and his person ... in recognition of the fact that the police cannot be everywhere to protect everyone all the time and that the citizen has to take some responsibility for his own safety.' (Law and Brookesmith, 1996: 159, 170; emphasis added). It is sometimes suggested, usually in respect of the USA (though somewhat in the face of American homi-cide statistics), that 'an armed society is a polite society'. So might gun ownership be seen as a positive, socially disciplining influence? After all, such a relationship, originating alongside the post-revolutionary notions of the 'citizen-militia' has often been asserted. Handling the responsibility of lethal firepower, it is suggested, builds character and teaches respect. Is this, now, simply another part of a world we have lost? Finally, might we interpret these changes in the light of post-modern discourses: the fragmentation of confidence in political systems and the disconnectedness of social values, policy objectives and institutional achieve-ments?

Raising such dilemmas some years ago in a discussion of the future of crime prevention, British criminologist Tony Bottoms laid his emphasis on the strand of virulent individualism he saw 'invading' Western societies and concluded in the following terms: 'I profoundly hope that this … interpretation of our own situation is an over-pessimistic one. For if individualism really is unstoppable, the end result, or nightmare, could ultimately be a society with massive security hardware protecting individual homes, streets, and shops, while all adult citizens would carry personal alarms, and perhaps guns, for individual protection while moving from place to place' (Bottoms, 1990: 20).

Emerging issues

The issues raised here have their parallels on either side of the Atlantic. Despite elements of convergence, however, the UK and the USA do tend to approach firearms rather differently. Yet during recent years, both cultures have seen firearms assume centre stage as major problems of public policy. The USA saw the sharpening of a long-running debate on firearms in American life in the wake of the political assassinations of the 1960s. More recently, the growing toll of gun homicides has combined with a series of confrontational debates about guns in the USA. These debates, often arising following particularly harrowing shooting incidents, have concerned: civilian ownership of military-style 'assault weapons'; proposed bans on small cheap handguns ('Saturday night specials'); school shooting incidents; waiting periods and national firearms registration (the Brady Bill); particular types of ammunition, such as the so-called 'cop-killer' bullets or other expanding 'injury-maximising' rounds, and the emergence of a number of right-wing, anti-governmental paramilitary militias 'tooling up for Armageddon' for whom the 'right to bear arms' seems nothing short of a sacred creed. The emergence of such issues and concerns have provided lobbying opportunities for a number of recently established gun control campaign organisations such as Handgun Control Inc., the Coalition to Stop Gun Violence and the Violence Policy Center (Carter, 1997).

On the other side of the coin, however lies the USA's history and 'gun-culture' (Hofstadter, 1970), a civilian gun stock exceeding 200 million (Kleck, 1991), and the influential National Rifle Association, the staunch defender of what it believes to be the USA's Second Amendment rights. Despite the American gun lobby being kept somewhat on the defensive by the series of issues referred to earlier, the Reagan and Bush administrations provided a more sympathetic climate for shooters' rights. In 1986, in a victory for the gun lobby, the Firearm Owners Protection Act was passed, dismantling somewhat a number of controls set in place almost two decades earlier in the 1968 Federal Gun Control Act. Then, in a development of potentially greater significance, the early 1990s saw an increasing number of states, now numbering over thirty, adopting what are known as 'shall issue' concealed carry laws. The new laws entitle ordinary citizens to apply for a permit to carry a concealed handgun outside their home or business. The laws have been passed in reaction to epidemic-level fears about violent crime and insecurity across the USA and as a direct response to gun lobby pressure at the state level. The laws have also provided a lucrative market for gun manufacturers, and it is this confluence of interests, the gun lobby, gun owners and the gun industry, that is now coming under increasing scrutiny.

The concealed carry laws are the focus of a sharp debate between the pro-gun and anti-gun lobbies. The gun control lobby, on the other hand, finding the political route to policy change often blocked in a stalemated political process, has recently turned to the courts. Rather like the cigarette industry a decade ago, the gun industry now faces a host of product liability, public health and safety law suits brought by, among others, crime victims, gun control groups, municipal authorities and police departments. Some commentators argue that the cases have been brought less with a realistic aim of winning and more with a view to keeping the gun control issue high up the political agenda. However if the gun manufacturers and distributors lose these actions they are likely to cost them millions (Diaz, 1999: 12–14).

For all the hostile words comprising the slow war of attrition on the American gun debate, relatively little has really been achieved. The NRA and it allies are, above all, defending a principle and see the thin end of a long wedge in almost every gun control measure proposed. By contrast the pro-control groups are struggling for apparently fairly marginal and, it seems, often easily circumvented, policy measures (waiting periods, 'one gun per month' purchasing limits). Yet in these practical details lies the gun controllers' deeper motive. They too are fighting for a principle, the principle that society should take responsibility for the effective regulation of an item as dangerous as a firearm. It is, they claim, not an issue that can simply be left to the good sense of individual citizens. Indeed, at the very heart of the gun control debate there lie some fundamentally opposed conceptions of citizenship. Neo-liberals argue that the 'right to bear arms' is an essential precondition of free citizenship, whilst more left-leaning and 'social democratic' commentators insist upon gun regulation as a means of protecting the wider 'social' interest.

Opposing camps

The slow grind of the American gun control debate contrasts markedly with the British experience. Seven months after the terrible shootings at Dunblane Primary School during March 1996, in which sixteen young children and their teacher were killed and ten further children and three teachers wounded, the government resolved upon a ban on the private ownership of all large calibre handguns. Even this did not satisfy the UK's newly established gun control movement and, a few months later, implementing a manifesto pledge introduced to capitalise upon a wave of public outrage, the recently elected Blair government extended the ban to virtually all privately owned handguns of any calibre. (Exceptions applied in the case of certain antique or historic weapons, muzzle-loaded weapons and gas-powered handguns.) The British gun lobby, notwithstanding initial denials that there even was a British 'gun lobby', were caught on the back foot.

Once thought powerful and well-connected, the gun lobby had successfully blunted the political momentum on gun control which followed the Hungerford massacre of August 1987. Even amidst the controversy following the killing of sixteen people and the wounding of a further twelve by a man dressed in paramilitary fatigues and carrying, among other weapons, an AK47 military assault rifle, members of parliament with shooting connections were able to secure important amendments to what became the Firearms (Amendment) Act of 1988. Semi-automatic rifles, burst-firing weapons and 'pump-action' shotguns all became prohibited weapons but no additional measures to restrict the availability of the type of semi-automatic pistol, with which half of the Hungerford victims were shot, were proposed. Amendments to the new legislation also established a new advisory body, the Firearms Consultative Committee, comprised of shooting sports, firearms industry and policing interests with whom the Home Office were expected to consult over any future firearms control proposals. As we shall see later, while many commentators from within the shooting fraternity came to see the FCC as 'their' committee, critics came to view the FCC as playing a more effective role in representing shooting interests than in promoting the cause of public safety (Mills and Arlidge, 1996).

Despite the relative success of the shooting lobby's rearguard action after Hungerford, this 'victory' rather obscured certain divisions appearing within the representative bodies of the UK's different shooting 'disciplines'. After Hungerford, a series of 'un-British' weapons were prohibited and the more traditional shooting disciplines protected. Strenuous efforts were made to associate the shotgun, in particular, with rural tradition and nature conservation – agricultural pest control and the 'glorious twelfth'.

Handgunning, however, had no similar pedigree to draw upon, but had become a recognised sport (using .22 calibre single shot pistols) in the Olympic and Commonwealth Games where valuable personal qualities of concentration, discipline and precision were said to be tested. Although the overall number of firearm certificates (rifles and handguns) issued had fallen significantly since the 1960s, handgun shooting was becoming an increasingly popular participation sport, the number of certificates issued beginning to rise, once more, in the early 1990s. However, as we shall see later, the growing popularity of the handgun was not based upon enthusiasm for the .22 calibre single-shot pistols such as used in the Commonwealth Games but rather it reflected a growing interest in the larger, more powerful, higher calibre, revolvers and semi-automatics increasingly popular across the Atlantic. Newer shooting competitions placed rather less emphasis upon the disciplined aesthetic of single-shot precision and more upon what was known as 'practical shooting' or 'police pistol' competitions. Targets were often humanoid silhouettes and the competitions might simulate combat-style conditions where speed and firepower, rather than simple accuracy, were called for.

Enthusiasts of the newer shooting disciplines were less content to try to shield their sport behind the more traditional forms of shooting. Rifts began to appear in the 'shooting lobby'. After Hungerford, a fairly new organisation, the Shooters' Rights Association (first established in 1973 to lobby against gun control proposals floated in a government Green Paper of that year) roused itself once again. Although directing its criticisms specifically at the Firearms (Amendment) Bill, then before parliament, the SRA's true objective appeared to lie in the restoration of a British 'right to bear arms'. This ancient right, it argued, was not simply a component of true democratic freedom but, equally, a legitimate form of sporting self-expression and a positive national asset in the event of military mobilisation. 'Our fear [of firearms]' opined the authors of the SRA report, 'has emerged, not from growing risks, but from a changed philosophy' (Yardley and Stevenson, 1988: 124). The appearance of an American-inflected discourse on firearm rights in the British context need not be too surprising; after all, one of the authors of the SRA report was himself American. Nevertheless, the SRA's argument went further than many in the shooting fraternity, especially those in more 'traditional' shooting disciplines, either wanted or felt particularly wise.

Facing intense media and public pressure following the Dunblane shootings, such disagreements on philosophy and tactics – between damage limitation and taking shooting's case to the public – led the shooting fraternity to dissolve in a series of rifts and recriminations, tactical blunders and public relations disasters. Only too late in the day did it begin to pull together, establishing a new Sportsman's Association, attempting to present a united front for the shooting sports. In the event, however, it is doubtful whether the eventual outcome would have been any different, even if the gun lobby had played a more effective role. A much fuller discussion of these issues is to be found in later chapters of the book.

The SRA were right about one issue, however – the importance of 'political philosophy' and culture to the determination of a society's particular stance on the gun question. The centrality of contrasting conceptions of the relationship between individual and society – that is, contrasting notions of citizenship – have already been remarked upon in relation to the pro- and anti-control lobbies in the American gun debate. In the UK, however, where the libertarian tradition has scarcely found an effective foothold, a far more paternalistic and collectivist attitude has prevailed in respect of firearms. In former times, or perhaps in several former times, competence with arms has been considered a public duty and a condition of citizenship (Malcolm, 1994). In more recent times, and certainly since the passage of the 1920 Firearms Control Act (which effectively eliminated the 'right' to bear arms in the UK) the control of firearms has been construed as necessary for the maintenance of public safety. Furthermore, although the themes are to some extent inter-linked, it has been from under a public order and public safety agenda rather than one of 'crime control' that the greater proportion of British gun controls have emerged. In the USA, the dominant gun control discourse has historically been one centred upon crime control or violence control and, as we have already implied, it has been rather unsuccessful. More recently, the focus of American gun control advocacy has begun to shift to embrace a public health perspective (Zimring and Hawkins, 1997).

Although the shooting sports have the dubious distinction of being one of the few (if not the only) sports regulated by the criminal law, both Hungerford and Dunblane were regarded less as 'crimes' than as gross failures of public safety policy. The enormity and exceptional nature of the two events lifted them beyond the scale of mere 'crimes'. Men had run amok with guns in the UK before, but never had they left such devastation or so many victims in their wake. However, just as the American gun control debate was beginning to incorporate elements of an alternative philosophical perspective, articulating a collective 'social' interest in the regulation of firearms so, equally, in the British context, it was becoming difficult to ignore the growing use of firearms in crime.

Gun owners and commentators from within the shooting fraternity have repeatedly expressed profound dismay when any link is drawn between the use of firearms in crime and legal firearm certificate holders. Gun owners, they argue, are invariably honest and responsible and seldom misuse their firearms. The vast law-abiding majority, they complain, should not be tarred by the brush of the criminal minority. They have a point. The same point is strenuously reiterated in the USA: legal gun owners, it is said, do not present a law and order problem. However, particular legal gun owners undoubtedly do present problems. The atrocities at Hungerford and Dunblane were both committed by persons holding firearm certificates. Similarly, about a thousand firearms a year are stolen from certificate holders (suggesting that some gun owners have had insufficient security) and, finally, it is irrefutable that a small proportion of firearm owners do come to use their weapons in unlawful ways. For instance during 1992–1994, 14 per cent of homicides were committed with a legally owned handgun. During this period, of the twenty-two homicides committed with a legally held firearm, eighteen (82 per cent) were classed as 'domestic' homicides (Home Office, Research and Statistics Directorate, 1996) a figure which rather confirms a number of American surveys which suggest that a firearm in the household is considerably more dangerous to the occupants of the household than any potential external aggressor (Kellerman *et al.*, 1993). Nevertheless, on the whole, existing research in the UK does tend to confirm that legal firearm certificate holders and armed criminal offenders generally form two distinct groups of people (Greenwood, 1972).

However, there are two aspects to the relation between legal gun ownership and firearm-related offending. If the issue is considered as a problem of gun owners themselves committing crimes – the 'bad apple' theory – then the policy response becomes one of controlling – or punishing – the deviant individuals. If the question is rephrased to incorporate a more social and collective interest, however, policy-makers have to address the collective consequences of widespread gun ownership or widespread gun availability. In the USA, a sizeable number of people (and especially gun owners themselves) subscribe to a version of the bad apple theory. One saying goes 'there are no bad guns, only bad men.' In the UK by, contrast, a more paternalistic attitude prevails, with gun availability regarded as inherently problematic. As the British gun control debate which followed Dunblane revealed, this is a hotly contested issue involving the comparison of complex international statistics. Yet even the best available quantitative data can seldom do justice to complex qualitative factors such as culture, tradition, prosperity, cohesion and community, factors which are known to have significant influences upon rates of crime and violence. High rates of gun ownership alone do not necessarily imply high rates of firearm offending. Switzerland, a high gun ownership, low crime, society, provides the shooting lobby's own 'best case' here (Munday, 1996a). That said, however, the international research does tend to suggest that the more guns there are in a society, and the more freely available they are, then the higher the rates of firearm-related offending will be (Killias, 1993). In this sense, the USA provides the gun controllers with their best case (Zimring and Hawkins, 1997).

Contrasting philosophical perspectives and diverging conceptions of neo-liberal versus social democratic citizenship animate the world views of the pro- and anti-gun control camps. Likewise, these markedly different world views inform the discourses of individual rights or collective 'social' responsibilities which form the ideological mainstays of the two traditions. However, these philosophical differences are also reflected in a third area of dispute that is rather less often remarked upon. The two traditions subscribe to differing epistemologies concerning notions of truth, evidence and causality in respect of the connection between levels of firearm availability and rates of firearm involvement in crime. For the neo-liberal tradition, subscribing to the freedom of the individual to bear arms, the only meaningful evidence is that of direct causality. The test of any evidence suggesting a link between legal guns and criminal acts is essentially juridical, rather than social scientific. Any other evidence is merely circumstantial. The epistemological question reverts to the individualist frame of reference, we have to have someone to blame. In order to be blameworthy they have to be proven to be responsible; in order to be responsible, standards of proof and notions of direct causality have to be met. We call this model of truth and proof a juridical one although, intriguingly, in product liability test cases in the USA, the courts have already moved way beyond it (Diaz, 1999).

An alternative 'social scientific' understanding of the relationship between gun availability and firearm-related offending is less concerned with direct causality and more concerned with aggregate social factors and statistical correlates. Widespread gun availability does not in any meaningful sense 'cause' criminal gun use, but firearms are seen as 'facilitators' of certain kinds of criminal choices. The more guns there are and the more persons with access to them the greater the 'facilitation effect'. Gun lobby commentators often misrepresent this argument to claim that it purports to show that guns – inanimate objects, after all – can 'cause' crime or, in a psychological variation of the same claim, that 'the trigger pulls the finger', however both suggestions deliberately misconstrue the issue. A social scientific perspective does not seek to hold anyone responsible for gun crime, it is concerned exclusively with explaining, at the societal level, the relations between aggregate social phenomena – in this case, rates of gun availability and rates of gun crime. As opposed to the type of juridical interventions against individual firearm offenders outlined earlier, social scientific findings are more amenable to policy level interventions to address 'problematic' conditions – in effect, 'gun control' strategies. The claim that few legal gun owners actually misuse their weapons is no argument against such policies, for the latter are (in rationalist models of policy-making at least) meant to be informed by objective evidence of 'risks' and seek, accordingly, to achieve aggregate harm reduction.

Unfortunately, two major weaknesses are to be found in this way of viewing the issue. First, many gun control policies adopted in the USA have been so ineffectual, so poorly enforced or so easily avoided that it is often very difficult to show reliable harm reduction effects (Kleck, 1991). Second, many recent bursts of gun control activism on either side of the Atlantic, and in Australia, New Zealand, France and Germany as well, have not been informed by a rationalist policy process (or, at least, not such a process alone) but rather they have also been highly political responses to horrific shooting incidents, attempting to bring some closure and derive a public benefit from tragedy.

Trends in firearm-related offending

Returning to the British case, it is no argument against tighter gun control policies to point out that, throughout the 1980s, the rate of firearm-related offending was rising while the number of firearm certificate holders was falling. This is so in two senses. First, objective evidence of a problem, for instance the UK's increasing rate of firearm-related offending (see Figure 1.1) would ordinarily suggest the need for policy responses strengthening firearms controls, if only to reduce still further the slippage from legal to illegal gun stocks (as we have seen already, around a thousand legally owned firearms are stolen each year) and scrutinise more closely those to whom society has granted the privilege of gun ownership. (Evidence suggesting the unsuitability of both the Hungerford and Dunblane killers to be firearm certificate holders came to light after both incidents.) Second, accurate measures of 'gun availability' are extremely difficult to produce. While we may have good information on the number of legally owned firearms, estimates of the size and scale of the illegal gun stock have varied wildly from one to four million weapons. And as we have already noted, it is from the illegal gun stock that the vast majority of our crime guns come. For instance, during 1992–1994, none of the forty-three firearms used in homicides connected to organised crime, the drug trade, or so-called 'contract killings' had ever been licensed or legally held (Home Office, Research and Statistics Directorate, 1996). Finally, in the UK, over the past decade, the difficulty of making an accurate assessment of the scale of the illegal gun stock has been compounded by the widespread availability, quite legally, of replica or imitation firearms. The use of these in 'armed robberies' has significantly inflated the reporting of this offence.

So, while the USA leads the developed world by a wide margin as far as firearm-related crime is concerned, over recent decades the UK too has been having to wake up to this aspect of the late-modern condition. There is, of course

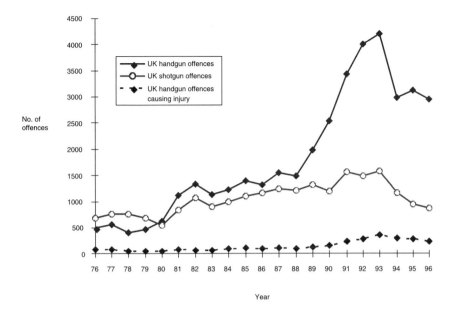

Figure 1.1 Notifiable offences involving handguns, shotguns and handguns causing injury in the UK: 1976–1996

a number of other senses in which the British public have become more accustomed to firearms over recent years. On the one hand, the past three decades have experienced a continuing backcloth of terrorist and paramilitary activity associated with the 'Troubles' in Northern Ireland and even more recently the 'Peace Process' faced various difficulties over the question of the surrender and decommissioning of the paramilitary weapons. There is, undoubtedly, a genuine dilemma here, rooted in the *realpolitik* of Northern Ireland, but it is compounded by the failure to extend the handgun ban, introduced after Dunblane, to Northern Ireland itself. A peace process founded upon the surrender of only some of the weapons might appear rather incomplete. Of course, as a result of terrorism's escalation of the security risks in the UK as a whole, another avenue by which the British public has become more accustomed to the sight of firearms has concerned the arming of the police, and the media attention given to armed policing incidents (these issues are discussed in more detail later). A diverse range of media influences have also provided a channel by which a 'gun culture' has been brought to the UK. Nevertheless, it is in the crime statistics themselves that one obtains a particularly clear sense of the increasing involvement of firearms (especially handguns) in crime and violence in the UK.

The decade and a half before 1993 saw a steep climb in the number of offences recorded in which handguns were reported to have been used. Furthermore, in 1980, handguns overtook the far more prevalent shotguns (in 1996 shotguns outnumbered handguns by a ratio of almost four to one) as the criminal firearm of choice. Since then the sharply rising trend of handgun use in crime has pulled away from the shotgun figures, especially after 1988. The steepest rise in handgun use, between 1988 and 1993, is shadowed by an increase in the number of incidents in which handguns used in crime have caused injury. The fact that the injury rate also appeared to rise during this 5-year period tends to confirm that the apparent increase in the use of handguns was not only due to an increase in the use of replica weapons. Data we examine elsewhere does suggest that between a third to a half of recorded 'armed robberies' involve only imitation or replica weapons (Morrison and O'Donnell, 1994), whereas a rising injury rate clearly suggests that a number of these weapons will be real. Before 1980, approximately 10 per cent of criminal uses of handguns resulted in injuries; throughout the 1980s the percentage of handgun crimes resulting in injuries varied between 4.5 and 8 per cent, but climbed back to 10 per cent in 1994.

After five years of steep increase, the number of offences recorded fell sharply during 1994, remaining fairly stable in 1995 and 1996, the year of the Dunblane shootings. The sharp fall in crimes involving handguns after 1993 reflects both a sharp fall in all robberies (especially of shops, banks, garages and post offices) during that year, and a declining proportion of robberies in which firearms were carried. According to the Home Office these changes reflected a number of developments in crime prevention, policing and in crime itself, including: improved situational crime prevention measures especially security screens and CCTV, proactive policing strategies regarding armed robberies in a number of areas, a shift on the part of 'professional' offenders towards 'softer' targets where firearms were not needed to undertake the robbery and a diversion of criminal activity from robbery to the drugs trade (Home Office, Criminal Statistics, 1996). In view of the falling numbers of handguns involved in crime, opponents of the handgun prohibition introduced in 1997 have continued to dispute whether a handgun ban was necessary. The longer view, however, of apparently rising levels of armed violence, might suggest a different perspective (see Figure 1.2).

Figure 1.2 presents a percentage index for the three firearm crime trends represented in Figure 1.1. The figures are indexed back to 1976, and each subsequent year is represented as a percentage of the 1976 figure. The figures are then tracked over two decades, the advantage of using a percentage index is that it allows the trends to be clearly represented and directly compared. It is immediately apparent that the seventeen years between 1976 and 1993 witnessed something of an eight-fold increase in recorded offences involving handguns (although a proportion of these will undoubtedly involve replica or imitation firearms) and over a four-fold increase in handgun offences resulting in injury (not all injuries will result from the weapon being fired but, perhaps, from the weapon being used as a blunt instrument). In 1986, shotguns were responsible for almost four times the number of fatal injuries as compared to handguns (thirty-seven compared to ten) whereas, ten years later, these figures had reversed with handguns responsible for thirty homicides and shotguns seventeen.

Overall firearm violence has also been rising – although over a somewhat longer period – in the USA also. However, as Figure 1.3 shows, the trend for firearm homi-

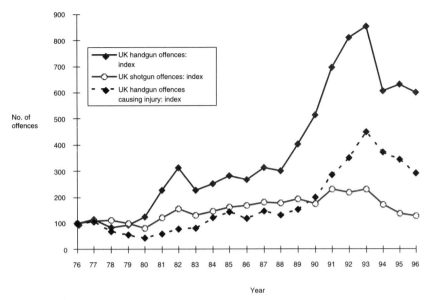

No. of offences

UK handgun offences: index
UK shotgun offences: index
UK handgun offences causing injury: index

Year

Figure 1.2   Percentage indices for notifiable offences involving handguns, shotguns and
handguns causing injury in the UK: 1976–1996

cides has tended to fluctuate. Separate figures for handgun homicides in the
USA became available after 1968. Despite the fact that the American gun stock
comprises more long guns (rifles and shotguns outnumber handguns by about
two to one) handguns are responsible for significantly more firearm homicides.
Handguns were employed in some 70 per cent of firearm homicides in the early
1990s. Figure 1.3 shows the overall number of firearm homicides (rifles, shotguns and handguns) and the figure for handguns alone.

Overall, firearm homicides have risen over the entire 32-year period depicted
in Figure 1.3. However the graph shows three phases during which firearm
killings rose fairly rapidly and two periods during which they fell back somewhat.
The first phase during which homicides rose includes the entire 1960s and the
first half of the 1970s. Between 1974 and 1976, gun homicides fell by around 15
per cent, before rising again, beyond their earlier peak, between 1977 and 1980.
After 1981, the figures fell sharply by over 20 per cent during the next two years,
then stabilised for two further years before rising sharply to record levels in 1991
and 1993. In explaining these trends, many criminologists have looked no
further than the increasing availability of guns – especially handguns – in
American cities. According to McCaghy and Cernkovitch the evidence on causes
of death in the USA shows that the increase in the number of homicides
between 1960 and 1975 was largely the result of an increase in firearm homicides (McCaghy and Cernkovitch, 1987). Likewise, according to Diaz, the sharp
increase in handgun homicides from the mid-1980s is attributable in part to the

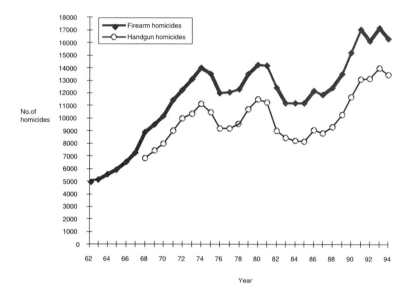

Figure 1.3   Firearm homicides in the USA: 1962–1994

increasing number of semi-automatic pistols, especially the newer 9 mm weapons, produced and marketed and available on the streets after 1985 (Diaz, 1999).

Figure 1.3 looks only at firearm homicides in the USA. The data are enough to indicate trends, though these figures are dwarfed by the Justice Department statistics on all violent crimes involving handguns. In 1992, handguns were used in a total of 931,000 murders, rapes, robberies and assaults, a figure almost 50 per cent higher than the annual average of the previous five years.

In many ways, the UK and the USA are thought to be closely related, but they are sharply contrasted when questions of guns and gun control are raised. However, the fact that, during the latter part of the 1980s and the early 1990s, both societies appeared to be experiencing (relative to their own contexts) sharply escalating trends with respect to the criminal use of firearms, suggests another comparison. This is the subject of Figure 1.4, below.

The percentage indices in Figure 1.4 compare the British trends depicted in Figure 1.2 with the USA's handgun homicide index. By contrast to the acutely rising trends in the UK, the chronic problem of firearm violence and firearm-related homicide appears to be almost stable. In truth, between 1988 and 1993 handgun homicides in the USA rose by 50 per cent, although these are dwarfed by the percentage increases in firearm-related offending, during the same years, in the UK. It is, above all, the absolute number of firearm homicides in the USA which has, over the years, provoked continuing concern (a concern heightened by the fact that the trend has risen sharply over more recent years). In the UK,

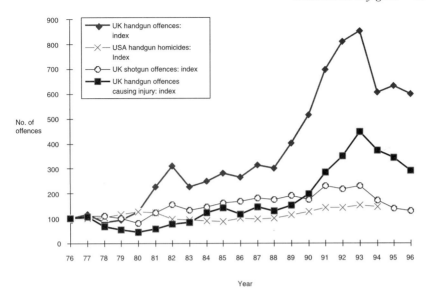

Figure 1.4 Comparative indices for firearm offences in the UK, handgun offences
causing injury in the UK and handgun homicides in the USA: 1976–1996

although the absolute numbers of firearm killings and firearm-related offending
remain fairly low by international standards, the increases over the past two
decades and, above all, the sharp rise between 1988 and 1993 would, in themselves, seem worthy of a greater degree of attention than they have received in
British policy circles. That is, until 1996.

With the banning of all privately held handguns in mainland Britain
following the Dunblane shootings, there is a temptation to consider the British
gun question largely closed. The fact that handgun offences fell sharply during
1994 and have continued to fall after 1996 might add confirmation that the most
acute moment of the UK's handgun crisis has now passed. While the factors
which produced the rapid increase, after 1988, in firearm-related offending
might be seen as exceptional and context specific, it is unlikely that it had much
of a direct relationship with the legal ownership of handguns by virtue of the
fact that very few crime guns come from the legally held stock. On the other
hand, the fact that firearm offending now appears to be falling does not amount
to a reason for reconsidering handgun prohibition. For one thing, the abolition of
a legal trade in handguns may have freed up enforcement resources to concentrate upon the illegal trade and, by eliminating the opportunities for firearms to
slip from legal to illegal hands, may have helped frustrate a criminal supply
route. As a number of commentators have noted (Hallowes, 1999), virtually all
guns begin life as legal commodities and closing off the points at which they
might be diverted into criminal hands is likely to mean that fewer of them end
up there. However, just as we have only a limited understanding of the reasons

for the increase in firearm-related offending before 1994, we have very little information on the effectiveness of the policy measures introduced in 1997 or the gun control enforcement strategies pursued by the British police and customs, either in the UK alone or, in conjunction with our European Union partners, across the continent as a whole.

Combat ready

Addressing this lack of basic information on firearms, firearms control and society in the UK was one of the motivations for writing this book. Another reason, this of a rather more political and ideological flavour, lay in the attempt to open out the hitherto rather truncated debate about firearms, their signifi-cance and their control, in British society. Another factor, again somewhat cultural in tone, involved a comparative dimension, in this case comparing British orientations to firearms with those of a society with whom we share many superficial similarities. It is often remarked, in humour, that the UK and the USA are two societies divided by a common language. Now, one might also want to add that they are divided too by a sense of personal risk in a dangerous world, by a lack of confidence in public order which fuels an instinct for armed self-preservation, justifies the 'right to bear arms', and equips the threatened citizen with the hardware, the legal frameworks and the mental attitudes to confront and, if necessary, to shoot a potential aggressor. A wide range of specialist commentators and firearm industry magazines (*Combat Handguns, Guns & Ammo*) appear to proffer advice to Americans on how to live life in combat-ready mode (Cooper, 1989; Gibson, 1994; Bird, 1997).

In the rest of the book we go on to explore a series of questions pertaining to firearms, society and firearms control. These involve questions concerning indi-viduality and citizenship and the nature and significance of a right to armed self-defence. The existence of this 'right' is considered in relation to the social contexts of risk and insecurity in which it is considered a solution. A range of discourses, both establishing and interpreting these rights to and social relations of the gun, are considered. First there are historical and cultural discourses, establishing particular relationships to firearms as part of a legitimate (but now fragmenting and increasingly contested) tradition. Second, there are discourses emanating from the film and media industries which deploy firearms within a range of believable scenarios where their potency and utility are plain to see and which anticipate the potential personal defence dilemmas of a dangerously armed future world. For reasons of space, these issues will not be fully developed in this work but taken up in further work. Third, there is a related discourse, particularly associated with the British news media and the way they have tended to report on firearms as a kind of dangerous, alien, American invasion. Fourth, there are discourses about and within policing, particularly concerning the uniquely unarmed and consensual model of British policing as it has had to come to terms with the criminal use of firearms and its own developing armed response capacity (again, these issues will not be fully developed in this work but taken up elsewhere; see Squires, 2000). Fifth, there is a discourse of tragedy examining how the media, society and the British political process came to terms with and developed a response to the UK's worst-ever shooting tragedy. Finally there is a criminological discourse on gun control, not itself a major aspect of the British debate, but a means by which proposals regarding the reform of the UK's gun laws might be contextualised and rationalised. In developing these issues, the remaining chapters focus upon the following issues.

Chapters 2 and 3 explore a range of cultural and historical issues relating to firearms in the UK and the USA. We attempt to supplement the often exclusively technical approach to firearm history by giving attention to the social and cultural roles associated with firearms and the rights, duties and privileges with which they were associated. Particular attention is given to hunting, duelling and the military relations which firearms helped sustain. Bringing the focus up to date we consider twentieth-century trends in firearm-related offending and parallel efforts at gun control during the century. In the American context, in Chapter 3, we give attention to the firearm's close links with the foundation of the American Republic and the history and mythology of the western frontier. We consider the debate about the Second Amendment to the American constitution and then turn to consider the related crime control and gun control debates in the USA. Whereas much historical writing on both crime control and gun control has been versed in a broadly progressive tradition regarding the coming of modern order and linking the onset of democratic citizenship with peace and disarmament, the chapter closes by asking a few rather more revisionist questions about violent crime and handgun proliferation in late-modern disorder.

Chapter 4 acts as a bridge between the preceding cultural and historical chapters and the more contemporary debates. It examines the dominant themes which have emerged within British news-media reporting of firearms issues during recent years. Central to the dominant media discourse is a repeated reference to the alleged perils of an 'alien' American gun culture said to be infiltrating the UK. The analysis explores a number of issues defining different aspects of the UK's 'gun problem' such as rising rates of armed robbery, the arming of the police and the question of self-defence. Furthermore, the British media's reporting of American firearms incidents and the American 'shooting scene' allows the media to firm up a particularly British outlook. The British media, in setting themselves so resolutely against the notion of an armed society appear, above all, to be reiterating their commitment to ideas of 'safe' British community, supposedly the complete opposite of the dangerous 'new' world across the Atlantic. And yet, no sooner are these safe 'gun free' cultures and communities drafted into existence than they too become prone to the seemingly inexorable expansion of gun power.

Chapter 5 considers the public and political events which followed the shooting tragedy at Dunblane Primary School in March 1996. Drawing upon contemporaneous reporting and commentary, an attempt is made to describe the initial reactions of all concerned to the awful incident. The chapter then turns to the response to Dunblane, orchestrated through the British political process, as a campaign began to develop in favour of tighter firearm controls and eventually a complete prohibition on the private ownership of handguns. The chapter attempts to account for the incredible success of the gun control campaigners as, supported by a large section of the British press, they created a wave of pressure that caught the established British policy processes completely by surprise and easily overturned, first, the findings of Lord Cullen's public inquiry into the event, second, the parliamentary scrutiny process and, third, the government's own carefully concocted political compromise.

Chapter 6 turns to consider the criminological questions largely neglected in the British gun control debate of 1996. The chapter examines the international evidence about gun availability and crime and explores the ensuing debate in the light of the arguments from gun lobby commentators in the UK and from both pro- and anti-gun control perspectives in the USA. From the available criminological evidence on gun control the chapter considers the ways in which the reform of the British gun laws (embracing the wider social and cultural perspectives pertaining to the nature of British society, the preservation of order and the regulation of firearms) came to be rationalised.

The British gun control debate was nothing like the kind of stalemated war of ideological attrition with which the USA has become familiar. In the UK, however, it was not criminology which enabled us to avoid this fate. Even so, it remains the ambition of British criminologists and policy-makers (and gun controllers the world over) that a revisionist and realist criminology, sensitive to the social, cultural and ideological relations within which our concepts of society, citizenship, safety and justice are construed, will help provide us with a basis for both crime control and gun control strategies. By way of a conclusion, an attempt is made to draw together the several disparate issues from the earlier chapters, considering the notion of the 'gun culture', in order to derive some important and enduring lessons about firearms and safety, society and gun control.

2 The spectre of the gun

Historical and cultural perspectives

Mechanical and ballistic discourses

Most historical examinations of firearms and their development devote themselves to the detailed and technical examination of innovation in weapon design and manufacture. Sometimes this also extends to questions of weapon use and, for instance, the impact of weapon innovation on military tactics. Such studies generally treat the weapon simply as a piece of machinery. The properties and capacities of firearms are dispassionately examined almost entirely divorced from any reference to the social purposes embodied in a weapon's design, the uses to which it may be put or, indeed, the consequences of its use. Firearms and ballistics are pure science. Typically, attention is given to the nature and developing efficiency of a weapon's firing mechanism, the speed, reliability and frequency of reloading and the type and composition of ammunition used. Attention might focus upon the range and accuracy of a weapon, the propellant power of the charge used, the barrel pressure in a weapon when fired, the muzzle velocity of the bullet and the extent of weapon recoil.

Consideration of such issues, especially when addressing the technological innovation contributing to the design and production of serviceable firearms, necessarily involves a wider range of factors such as the production of stronger, more durable, metals capable of withstanding the temperatures and pressures of repeated firearm operation, the accumulation of experience and expertise in the gunsmith's craft and, somewhat later, the increasing sophistication of production processes allowing the mass production of weapons. In the emerging science of ballistics the qualities of differing types of metals, of propellant charges and of bullets and other projectiles could all be traced back to basic principles of physics, chemistry and metallurgy. Only later does forensic science combine with ballistics to produce a tripartite division of ballistics into 'internal', 'external' and 'terminal' ballistics (Heard, 1997). Respectively, internal ballistics concerns itself with what happens inside a gun when it is fired, up to the point when the bullet exits the barrel; external ballistics is concerned with the factors influencing the flight of a bullet and the rather ambiguously named 'terminal' ballistics deals with the impact of bullets upon their targets and the factors influencing bullet performance upon reaching a 'target'. In all of this, beyond the essentially clinical discussion of issues such as entry wounds, bullet expansion and wound cavities, bullet deceleration, penetration and exit wounds, consideration of the 'target', for whom the bullet impact may indeed be terminal, seems almost entirely neglected. A target is simply a series of physical properties in humanoid form and rather less reliable than the ballistic gelatine used for weapon and ammunition testing in the firearms industry. The idea that firearms might be used by people to shoot and kill other people seems hardly worth a mention in many of the texts examining the history of firearms development. Even so, reflecting the priorities emerging from the law enforcement and civilian self-defence contexts in which handguns might need to be used, a growing preoccupation with weapon and ammunition efficiency has surfaced in the USA. This quasi-scientific discourse of lethality, focusing upon 'stopping power', 'bullet penetration', 'wound channels', 'double-tap accuracy' and 'one-shot knock-downs' has recently become quite central to American firearms marketing and, like everything else concerning firearms in the USA, it has become a highly controversial subject (Firearms Tactical Institute, 1998).

Given the great extent of the literature on bullet impacts and 'wound ballistics' one could be forgiven for wondering why the human consequences of gunfire have received so little attention (except, perhaps, in the literature on trauma medicine). One explanation might be that the primary purpose of firearms is so obvious as not to require much further elaboration. A more plausible explanation might be that the integrity of this scientific discourse on firearms would not stand too close a scrutiny if the human (or perhaps anti-human) implications of all this scientific discourse were made more explicit. A lack of understanding about the factors brought into the equation when weapons or bullets are designed has allowed firearm manufacturers – and the shooting fraternity at large – to evade the kind of public scrutiny which might have made the shooting sports safer and more responsible.

For instance, during the 1980s, the commercial production in the USA of the teflon-coated armour-piercing pistol bullet depended upon developments of an essentially technical nature and firearms industry marketing decisions. However, when media and political correspondents began to refer to these rounds by a rather different name – 'cop-killer bullets' – a wholly different perspective on the social utility of the new technology was opened up (Vizzard, 1997: 138–140). Subsequently, as a controversy developed about whether the bullets should be prohibited for civilian use, the police chiefs and policing unions and the National Rifle Association found themselves on opposing sides of the debate. In turn, opposition on this and a number of other issues (for instance the proposed 'assault weapons' ban) hastened the break-up of the political alliance between the police and the NRA as allies in traditional 'law and order' politics (Larson, 1994; Spitzer, 1995). Hence a great deal might follow if we could penetrate the 'technical curtain' surrounding the firearms industry and shooting in general. Later in the book, a number of similar issues are considered in the course of our discussions of weapon use in law enforcement, the American gun control debates and the British firearms control debate which took place after the Dunblane killings.

The tragedy at Dunblane, in particular, undoubtedly exposed shooting in the UK to the kind of public scrutiny it had never previously received and which, arguably, was long overdue.

However, the technical histories alluded to above are not my chief concern here. This is not to say that these discourses are not themselves interesting for what they tell us about our orientations towards violence, personalised killing and a certain kind of human interaction, it is simply that my main focus is somewhat different. That said, of course, it often has been the case that technological developments in firearm design and production have impacted fundamentally upon the social relations of firearm use – typically, giving an advantage in any conflict to the adversary with the more powerful, most portable, more accurate, most rapidly reloaded or, perhaps more recently, most concealable weapon. However, these wider social relations of firearm use (including production issues, distribution issues, wider cultural factors and, above all, their use in human interactions) are almost entirely absent from the historical and technical literature. The purposes of this and the following chapter, by contrast, are to examine precisely the social and historical discourses relating to firearms with a view to drawing out the social, cultural and political significances of firearms for human beings and human societies. John Ellis in his fascinating, if paradoxically titled book, *The Social History of the Machine Gun* (if ever there were a technology that merited an 'anti-social' history, the machine gun is probably it) describes his objective as, 'a study of what the history of the machine gun tells us about society' (Ellis, 1976: 20). In this chapter, as a prelude to the more contemporary and focused chapters which follow, with certain caveats, my purpose is essentially similar.

Social and historical discourses

This sociological and historical examination of the impact of firearms upon society is approached by considering the ways in which a variety of commentators have themselves pronounced upon the social and historical significance of firearms. In this sense, the chapter's focal concern is with the ways in which historical discourses concerning firearms have interacted with established perspectives on society and individuality. The range of the chapter is rather wider and provides more of an overview than Ellis's work in that it attempts to embrace all firearms rather than just those of a single type and it develops less of a 'history of' firearms than a study of the ways in which firearm-related discourses interact with a range of sociological themes and issues. These themes concern civilisation and citizenship, authority, safety and order, masculinity and tradition, and violence, crime, risk and disorder. In a related sense, I am much less interested in the military applications of firearms and far more concerned with firearms as carriers, mediators, facilitators and, it has to be said, terminators of social relations.

Firearms and the 'firearm question' are seldom approached in this fashion. Even in the USA where more column inches have been devoted to discussions of firearm-related issues than probably anywhere else in the world, this is not an especially familiar approach. Within American criminology an entire academic speciality is now given over to increasingly partisan discussions of 'gun control' (considered later). More recently a public health discourse has also joined this debate, but both sets of arguments are preoccupied above all by a regulative politics in which, depending upon the side of the argument one takes, the significance of guns themselves is largely given. They are either a right and a positive social benefit (self-defence) or a cause of untold social harm and misery.

For those subscribing to the former viewpoint, the USA throws up another key firearms discourse, which celebrates the firearm and its contribution to American culture and tradition: hunting, 'winning the West', 'taming the wild frontier' and 'making the man' as it were. These are themes that, as we shall see, the USA's cultural industries have exploited to the full. More recently, a range of authors largely within the American shooting fraternity has also attempted to enhance the intellectual credibility of this interpretation (Tonso, 1982; Kopel, 1992a). These cultural and traditional discourses overlap with anti-gun control discourses on the civil liberty and constitutional issues raised by the Second Amendment, the so-called 'right to bear arms' to which, over many years, a considerable investment of legal scholarship has been devoted (Cramer, 1994; Bijlefeld, 1997). This is a complex and specialist field to which, despite its relevance to the nature of the American firearms discourse, we can hardly do justice in a single chapter. Even so, at least one recent commentator has argued that the Second Amendment has been rendered largely obsolete, it survives now only by virtue of being frequently invoked in public debate – usually by firearms lobby spokesmen. However, Spitzer continues, while 'the desire to treat the Second Amendment as a constitutional touchstone by gun control opponents is understandable, given the "rights talk" that pervades American political discourse … such claims are without historical, constitutional or legal foundation. More problematic, this misplaced invocation of rights only serves to heighten social conflict, cultivate ideological rigidity, and stifle rational policy debate' (Spitzer, 1995: 43, 48–49).

Again, however, any immersion in the supposedly traditional cultures of the American 'Wild West' leaves us with another dilemma: when did the gun turn bad? What is the relationship between the 'civilising firepower' of those early pioneers who, according to the received history (Slotkin, 1992), laid the foundations of a great society, and the indiscriminate, destabilising violence of an illegal automatic weapon fired from the window of a passing car in a 'drive-by' shooting in the suburbs of San Diego? (Sanders, 1994).

Questions such as these are closely related to one of the more insistent themes of recent social scientific discourse, concerning either the crisis of modernity or the coming of post-modernity. If, especially in an American historical imagination, firearms played their part in some epic civilising process whereby law, order and authority were established, security was guaranteed, individual rights and citizenship were underpinned by notions of democracy and social justice, safety was enhanced and violence, risks and fear diminished as influences in modern human life, then how might we account for today's unprecedented rates of firearm-related violence – and the fear and disruption these bring? (Zimring and Hawkins, 1997). Moreover the distribution of firearm violence is especially uneven. Patterns of criminalisation and victimisation are highly concentrated within socially deprived inner-urban and suburban neighbourhoods and among young African-American males. In this fashion, Courtwright, writing about 'violent America', describes a broadly cyclical process whereby the conditions of the 'ghetto' dictate a life on society's new frontiers. 'It is possible to think of the urban ghettos as artificial and unusually violent – vice-ridden combat zones in which groups of armed, unparented, and reputation-conscious young bachelors, high on alcohol, cocaine and other drugs menace one another and the local citizenry, undeterred if not altogether untouched by an entropic justice system' (Courtwright, 1996: 272).

One need not subscribe to Courtwright's entire 'demoralisation' thesis even though his depiction of violent, gang-related and gun-driven armed conflicts is widely shared. His observations upon the 'entropic' nature of the criminal justice system in a number of socially disorganised urban areas are intriguing. In the old frontier settlements during the nineteenth century it was said that men had to make their own justice with the gun because authority, law and order were in scarce supply. Yet in many socially disorganised and fragmented neighbourhoods of the USA's conurbations it still is. Rates of criminal victimisation, always high in poorer areas, have risen inexorably but police and crime prevention resources remain unresponsive and inaccessible (Canada, 1995). Worse, the residents of entire neighbourhoods are written off or further alienated by aggressive, or operationally racist, policing initiatives which fail to distinguish between victims and violators (Tonry, 1995; Currie, 1996; Miller, 1996). Davis likewise describes the quasi-military approach to policing adopted by the LAPD in seeking to impose order on troubled neighbourhoods (Davis, 1991). For residents, safety and security plummet as fear and danger assume a dominant position in the organisation of daily life. Because police support cannot be relied upon, residents arm themselves. The promise of collective security, central to the mission of the modern interventionist state which sought to harness the civilising process to a democratic and universal conception of citizenship, falters as residents look increasingly to their own interests (Bauman, 1993). In turn, its legitimacy and authority already damaged through non-performance and further detached from recognisable notions of justice, the police, their supposed monopoly of force further diminished, find their role increasingly difficult and hazardous among a community of the armed and dangerous.

Modernism appeared to link law to order and democracy in the pursuit of justice in the service of all citizens. Upon these foundations rested the legitimacy and authority of society and the state (Hunt, 1996). In the post-modern world, however, justice is replaced by contingency, having little or no relation to order while law and democracy are considered little more than manipulable resources at the disposal of those citizens fortunate enough, powerful enough or affluent enough to access them. Individual citizens should rely upon no-one. To expect to do so not only runs contrary to the ethic of personal responsibility but is also a risky and ill-advised personal strategy. No-one will look out for you. In this sense, the unravelling of modern social democratic criminal justice is first and foremost the reassertion of an individual's own responsibility for his or her personal safety and security (Morrison, 1995). This means minding your own business and taking appropriate precautions to safeguard your possessions. In the UK it might mean joining a local neighbourhood watch group or purchasing a burglar alarm (in any event elements of voluntarism or individualism in crime prevention). For an increasing number of Americans it might involve a trip to a local gunshop.

While the UK has nowhere near the same levels of armed violence, in many comparable urban areas British rates of property crime are noticeably higher than those in the USA (Zimring and Hawkins, 1997). British commentators have also pointed to a similar combination of factors – multiple deprivation, drugs, unemployment, under-qualified and aggressive young men, and racism – driving the criminalisation and victimisation trends in socially disorganised and marginalised communities in the UK's larger towns and cities (Campbell, 1992). In turn these factors both forestall the development and inhibit the success of policing and community safety strategies designed to tackle these several dimensions of social exclusion. Such communities remain, rather like the young people within them, subject to public policy's own inverse law of policy justice, that is: over-controlled and under-protected, under-resourced and least consulted.

While firearms have not played so central a social or cultural role within the UK as a whole, compared with the USA, the UK shares a common armed ancestry with the USA. Many commentators cite the 1688 Bill of Rights as a vital constitutional foundation for the American Second Amendment (Malcolm, 1994). Even during the 1996 British gun control debate, gun lobby commentators frequently began their submissions of evidence to either the Cullen Inquiry or the Home Affairs Select Committee by reference back to seventeenth-century legal principles (Greenwood, 1996). As we shall see, hunting with firearms and duelling with firearms have both formed part of an essentially common European heritage but neither appear to have assumed the kind of broad social and cultural significance that they would later acquire in the USA. In the European context, access to firearms was certainly mediated by social class (true in respect of both hunting and duelling) such that although, in the UK, firearm manufacturing was widespread, gunsmithing remained essentially a craft profession serving the requirements of either local elites or the military. This explains, in part, why, outside military action, the UK has little real tradition of fighting with handguns or of handgun use in criminal activity. Even later, during the nineteenth century, with industry developing the capacity to produce larger numbers of firearms, most of these were destined for military service around the expanding Empire. A combination of elite restrictions, concentrated land ownership, the absence of suitable game and an urbanisation of working-class residential patterns conspired to keep firearms out of the hands of those perhaps more likely to employ them in criminal activities. In such ways a variety of contingencies influenced the 'civilising process' and, by the second half of the nineteenth century, a largely unarmed civilian policing system underpinned the increasingly collectivist character of the urban social order.

Given these emerging themes within the social and historical discourses on firearms, society and culture, the remainder of this chapter will now attempt to develop some of the more important themes and issues a little further. The central themes to be covered will include:

- first, questions concerning firearms, state formation, the monopolisation of violence and civilising and decivilising processes;
- second, questions concerning firearms, culture and social development, including the uses to which firearms are put within society (questions of legitimate and illegitimate uses of firearms and the varying cultural traditions to which firearms give rise);
- third, questions regarding efforts at gun control (including police activities – armed or not) and questions concerning firearms, the law, individual and citizenship rights, and,
- finally, questions concerning crime, fear, and the risks associated with post-modernity centring upon firearms and the 'gun question'.

Throughout the chapter the prevailing emphasis will remain upon the social and historical discourses through which firearms are discussed and, variously, posed as problems or presented as solutions for individuals and societies. As is perhaps already clear, a strong theme linking these separate discussions concerns a particularly 'special' Anglo-American relationship. In the course of developing these core discourses on firearms, culture and society we lay the foundations for the issues covered later in the book.

Civilisation, authority and violence

The role that firearms have played in the establishment of modern nation states is often overlooked. Almost two decades ago Giddens complained that the almost complete neglect of studies of the role of violence and war in the rise of capitalism was one of the 'most extraordinary blank spots in social theory in the twentieth century' (Giddens, 1981: 177). Yet during the period to which Giddens's observation applies – the rise of capitalism – firearms were chief among the tools of violence. In turn, during the nineteenth century the process of industrialisation reinforced the growing power of European imperialist states by equipping their enlarged armies with the firepower to subdue the world. The power of the state in the West was to rest for many years upon its relative monopolisation of access to weapons.

Yet if the growing power of the modern nation states rested upon their capacity to deploy organised violence in the pursuit of national objectives, a characteristic of the post-industrial world has been the prevalence of disorganised violence within contemporary societies. We could never claim violence to be a neglected feature of the contemporary social sciences. From international relations, through to criminology and gender studies, violence is a recurring theme and fear of violence a central factor in contemporary culture and politics (Furedi, 1997). Even so, the broader role of disorganised violence in the context of 'post-modern' social fragmentation has not yet received the kind of sustained theoretical attention given to organised collective violence in the context of state formation. Likewise, the broader significance of the gun in human affairs is seldom considered and (notwithstanding the considerable literature directly devoted to the American gun control debate), outside the USA, relatively little developed sociological attention has been paid to the social significance of one of the principal instruments of contemporary violence – the handgun. Yet, where handguns proliferate (especially where access is unregulated) in civilian owner- ship they appear to exacerbate social tensions, increase homicide and suicide rates while finding ready employment in criminal hands and laying the founda- tions of a new kind of violent havoc. These issues are developed further in the course of a review of the British gun control debates later in the book.

It is said that the distinctive feature of the modern form of liberal governing has been the effective monopolisation of legitimate force in the hands of the state. There is, no doubt, something of a tautology here for, as Walter Benjamin observed, echoing Shakespeare, 'legitimacy' is one of the spoils that usually accrue to the victor. Inevitably, there is often far more to it in practice. Nevertheless, consolidation of the means of violence and the establishment of collective security certainly rank among the first foundations of liberal governing. One need not accept the central premises of contract theory, it is enough to acknowledge its powerful ideological legacy. Thus, for Hobbes, singular authority was to bring to an end the war of all against all. For Locke this now legitimate authority established the order of life, liberty and property and, later, for Blackstone, it also encompassed the doctrine of personal security without which all other rights were meaningless.

Blackstone's *Commentaries upon the Laws of England*, published in England during the turbulent 1790s has been an influential source of traditional legal authority upon the right of self-defence in the UK and the USA. In his writing, Blackstone affirmed, 'the natural right of resistance and self-preservation' in order to 'restrain the violence of oppression' (Blackstone, 1793). According to Malcolm, the notion of the Englishman's right to be armed within civil society had its heyday in the eighteenth and early nineteenth century. 'Blackstone's pronouncement in 1765 that an armed public was essential to protect the consti- tution as well as the individual seems to have been readily and generally accepted' (Malcolm, 1994: 165). In the conflict-ridden years following the French Revolution and the return of soldiers from the Napoleonic War, yet before the first steps in proto-democratic state formation during the late 1820s and early 1830s (in turn, the establishment of a modern system of policing for the capital, electoral reform and the creation of a more efficient system for the regulation of pauperism), English authorities appeared genuinely concerned about the prospect of armed insurrection in England. E.P. Thompson has provided a definitive account of this period in his study of *The Making of the English Working*

Class (Thompson, 1963) but a rather neglected aspect of this history has been the concern about the armaments available to the people. For instance, the Peterloo Massacre of 1819, during which mounted yeomanry had charged a crowd of protesters killing eleven, was followed by angry debates in parliament and demands for emergency legislation to prohibit civilian carrying of firearms. When the organisers of the illegal Peterloo demonstration were prosecuted for organising an illegal and armed assembly their defence lawyer, citing Blackstone, developed an argument about the necessity of arms for civic protection – a right to safeguard all others. The judge, while apparently uncomfortable with arguments from Blackstone, nevertheless conceded the right to arms for self-protection, but drew the line at the carrying of arms at a public demonstration where they might be likely to provoke 'terror and alarm' (Malcolm, 1994).

The legislative response to the crisis lay in the infamous 'Six Acts' discussed by Thompson (1963). Two of these, the Unlawful Drilling Act of 1819 and the Seizure of Arms Act of 1820 specifically addressed the question of civilian access to firearms. The Act of 1819 sought to prevent the training of persons in the use of arms and military exercises while the Act of 1820 empowered Justices of the Peace, in counties affected by disturbances, to confiscate arms they considered 'dangerous to the Public Peace'. Despite the perceived emergency, the legislation was fiercely contested and, as a compromise, it was agreed that the Seizure Act would continue in force for only two years unless renewed. Even so, opponents still described the legislation as, 'a violation of the principles of free government and utterly repugnant to our constitution' (Malcolm, 1994: 168–169). Malcolm also draws upon the speeches of other members of parliament, recorded in *Hansard*, bitterly regretting the necessity for such seemingly draconian legislation. The principles upon which the Seizure Act was founded, it was said, appeared at variance with the free spirit of England's venerated constitution, and contrary to the right of subjects to retain arms for the defence of themselves, their families and their property. Equally, it was said, possession of arms was vital for the protection of a man's liberty, for the ability to possess arms was the factor which distinguished a freeman from a slave (ibid.). In the event the Seizure of Arms Act was allowed to expire. Subsequently, reinforcing the connection between social class and disarmament, section four of the Vagrancy Act made it an offence to be in possession of an offensive weapon 'with intent' to commit a crime.

Even as late as 1850, some twenty years after the introduction of a professional system of policing in London, the liberal historian Thomas Macaulay continued to insist that the right to bear arms for self-defence represented 'the security without which every other is insufficient' (Macaulay, 1850). In the UK at least, however, this view rapidly became eclipsed by a more collective conception of security under the 'Queen's Peace' maintained and administered by an unarmed civilian police. While the law continued to permit the use of weapons as a means of 'last resort' self-defence it has, especially following the 1920 Firearms Control Act, prohibited the carrying of firearms with that express purpose. From around the mid-twentieth century onwards, self-defence has not been considered an acceptable reason for the granting of a firearms licence. In the USA, as we shall see, the right to armed self-defence fared differently. Even in the UK, some members of the shooting fraternity cling to a view that, by virtue of never being formally repealed, the 'right to bear arms' still exists in the UK or, that, even if it doesn't, it ought to. These views surfaced once again, in 1996, during the British gun control debate following the Dunblane shootings.

The different evolution of the Common Law right of self-defence in English and American circumstances is worth noting. In the latter context, the conditions of frontier society, and a mixture of individualism, egalitarianism and republican resistance sponsored a much stronger 'right to self-defence' than was tolerated in England (Brown, 1991). These contrasting resolutions of the authority and order problem gave rise to a series of questions about individual rights and collective security and in recent years these have been much debated. In different parts of the world the issues have emerged in a variety of forms and they have been addressed in different ways. For instance, in the USA, the strong republican-individualist presumption about the right to bear arms has met with sustained criticism following a series of shootings which have politicised the gun control debate and led many to question the supposed 'Second Amendment' right. The question remains far from resolved and, in federal legislative terms, something of a political stalemate has been reached. Though it is fair to say that the right to private possession of handguns is probably more controversial now than ever before (McDowall and Loftin, 1983; Spitzer, 1995; Bruce and Wilcox, 1998). In the UK, it would no longer be true to say that the right to own a handgun is controversial, because, following Dunblane, the 'right' no longer exists. Some commentators have gone further, arguing that, since the 1920 Firearms Control Act, the 'right' was really only a privilege. The speed with which handguns were outlawed throughout most of the UK during 1996 and the enthusiasm with which, during the preceding decade, most of the UK had embraced the notion of town centre CCTV systems monitoring public spaces, points to the UK's far more collectivist tradition in matters of law, order and security.

Nonetheless, in many parts of the world the idea of security, law and justice as public goods which cannot be rationally and efficiently allocated by private market mechanisms has already been challenged. On both sides of the Atlantic, 'transition societies' in Eastern Europe and post-apartheid South Africa (Cohen, 1994) have seen a considerable expansion in the provision of private policing and security services. It is becoming increasingly necessary to speak of a mixed economy of law and order. In the USA and South Africa and in large third world cities, such as Rio de Janeiro, perimeter security cordons, 'psychological stockades' and armed private police with state-of-the-art access control systems guard both down-town business districts, tourist-rich locations or up-market residential enclaves (Poole, 1993). In the UK, where the commitment to collective security has been more enduring, private sector security has still been one of the fastest growing industries (South, 1988), though it has not yet made such dramatic inroads into more conventional policing tasks. The signs are, however, that this may be likely to change.

More generally, we have witnessed an emerging neo-liberal critique of collective security and centralised authority as concepts. In the USA as the dangerous flip-side to the renewed emphasis upon small-scale 'communitarianism' in civic life, this critique has been closely linked to debates over Second Amendment rights to own and carry firearms. More recently these debates have expanded to include the post-Vietnam, anti-federal, 'survivalist' groups and the variety of right-wing, paramilitary organisations which, since the Waco siege and Oklahoma bombing, have been an especial focus of concern (Coates, 1987; Flynn and Gerhardt, 1989; Gibson, 1994). The advocates of this 'new republicanism' drew upon the neo-liberal, even libertarian, arguments that 'social justice' is a mirage (Hayek, 1976), 'society', no more than an aggregate of individuals (Nozick, 1974) and 'collectivism' a dangerous, passive and stultifying form of unfreedom (Letwin, 1983). An alternative, suggested in 1974 by the libertarian philosopher Robert Nozick, involved the idea of policing and security functions being provided by private protection agencies, supported by subscriptions, and flourishing or failing according to sound, tried and tested, market principles. In place of the single social contract of authority, Nozick substitutes a multitude of, as he sees it, individual contracts of choice (Nozick, 1974: 12–15). An irony for Nozick was precisely the likelihood that such protection agencies would amalgamate, ultimately to monopolise the exercise of coercive force and thereby establish a new (and legitimate) basis for the minimalist state.

A conquest of violence or a new form of power?

Aside from questions of the legitimation of authority, an important feature of the exercise of liberal governing power in the modern age was, as Foucault noted, the efficiency of its exercise. Power is most effective when most economic, invisible and least reliant upon the use of overt force. For Foucault the most efficient applications of power were those which established the docile and malleable bodies upon which democratic models of governing could safely be conferred (Foucault, 1977). Even so, the attainment of this 'civilised hegemony' frequently relied upon quite explicit forms of violence and warfare. In this respect, as Mestrovic has suggested, following Foucault and others, 'there is no reason for assuming that civilisation, by itself, is a humanising force' (Mestrovic, 1993: 41). Such arguments run quite contrary to the more familiar liberal histories which equate the achievement of modern democratic civilisation – the 'civilising process' – with the 'conquest of violence' or the 'demand for order' (Critchley, 1970; Elias, 1982; Silver, 1967). Indeed, this supposed conquest of violence – or, at least, its expulsion to the margins – might provide an answer to Giddens's earlier question about sociology's lack of interest. If violence really had been defeated, what interest would it hold for us?

Critchley's book *The Conquest of Violence* is an English contribution to the debate about the containment of violence in modern Britain. Furthermore, Critchley also celebrates this 'conquest of violence' as a great British achievement. Violence is represented negatively, as a pathology of the social condition and Critchley's account tells of how the UK's violent and 'ungovernable' past came to be subdued, largely during the latter part of the nineteenth and early twentieth centuries.

Critchley proposes a three-fold classification of the forms of violence to which societies are prone. The first form of violence is described as primitive, elemental and small scale. It is said to result from the petty jealousies and rivalries of normal social interactions. While such violence may be overlain by racial, familial, cultural or other differences it is seen as largely unorganised (maybe even disorganised) and unpolitical. By contrast, two further forms of violence are political and organised. Critchley labels these either 'reactionary' or 'forward-looking' violence. The labels themselves may be contested, according to one's view of the progressive or reactionary 'causes' in whose name the violence was exercised. Among the reactionary forms of violence lie attempts by groups to win back former rights and privileges. The Peasants' Revolt or the activities of the Luddites are taken as examples. By contrast, progressive forms of violence, championing modern and democratic ideas, might encompass the activities of the Chartists and Suffragists and, more recently, the activities of civil rights demonstrators. Published in 1970, Critchley's typology had no place for the several concerted paramilitary, 'terrorist' or 'freedom-fighter' campaigns emerging during the three succeeding decades – nor is it immediately obvious where such activities would fall in his typology.

Accepting, for the moment, Critchley's classification, we need to look at the reasons he put forward for the conquest of violence during the century before 1970. If, as some commentators appear to argue, society has become more violent (or at least more preoccupied by violence) since 1970, we need to ask what may have caused the restraints to appear to lose their grip. Critchley suggests a number of key factors: the flowering of a 'native self-discipline' among the British; the gradual political and economic incorporation of the lower classes (removing the political and economic motives for violence); the diminishing influence of religion (and religious conflict) in British life; the absence of racial conflict; the establishment of a professional, unarmed civilian police force 'policing by consent'. Finally, the development of trade unions and other institutions providing for the organised representation of working-class political interests have removed somewhat the need for strikes or other more confrontational forms of industrial action (Critchley, 1970: 25). Taken together, according to Critchley, these factors account for the diminishing significance of violence as an issue in social affairs over the preceding century. Yet if violence has apparently made something of a comeback, we need to ask what has changed – or, at the very least, interrogate his claims a little more closely.

The violence-restraining factors identified by Critchley reflect a markedly parochial British perspective. Nevertheless, they point to a range of material and cultural processes which established the social and economic basis for the relatively homogenous and deferential character of the British working class. In more recent years, each of Critchley's factors would seem to have been switched into reverse and the 'native self-discipline' of the British – surely an effect rather than a cause – would appear rather less in evidence. Economic dislocation, widespread unemployment, social exclusion, social and cultural diversity, racism and ethnic conflicts, the diminishing significance of trade unions, rising consumerism and related processes of desubordination, further question the extent of our 'conquest' of violence. The institutional measures for containing organised and political violence may have remained strong, but even here there is evidence of a shift from 'consensual' to more coercive management styles (Hillyard and Percy-Smith, 1988; Jefferson, 1990; Waddington, 1991). The question of disorganised, non-political and individual violence, by contrast, raises different problems. With growing numbers lacking the means of achieving mainstream consumer satisfactions through mainstream economic opportunities and with an apparently diminishing commitment to mainstream values, rising levels of individual and instrumental violence began to appear. Here, two qualifications need to be introduced.

First, increasing levels of recorded violence are to some extent attributable to policy shifts in recent years which have prompted criminal justice agencies to give a higher profile to certain patterns of violence (sexual violence, racially motivated violence, 'domestic' and 'acquaintance' violence, and violence against children). In turn, more victimisation of these kinds is reported, resulting fairly naturally in heightened concerns about it. Second, despite the increasing attention afforded to violence, it still represents only a small minority (around 5–6 per cent) of all crime recorded. The point suggests the need for caution in the interpretation of the evidence. A significant increase in the propensity for violence among certain more disadvantaged or criminalised subsections of the population is undoubtedly a cause of concern but it should not lead us to misunderstand the phenomenon as a whole. A small but growing number of people resorting to violence – and perhaps also to weapons in the furtherance of particular criminal activities – is not the same as a general increase in violence or weapon use. In fact criminal violence and especially weapon use in violence is, like many forms of criminal victimisation, quite markedly patterned (Mawby and Walklate, 1994).

Critchley does not mention weapon availability as a factor in the 'conquest of violence' except to applaud the ethic of unarmed policing. However the strict controls on and licensing of handguns in the UK since 1920 have undoubtedly played some part in keeping weapons out of the hands of those who might use them for criminal purposes. Firearms controls are certainly not the whole of the story. Like Critchley we have to take account of the broader social and economic factors which shape the opportunities, perspectives and motivations of those who might seek to use firearms (and violence) for criminal advantage. Even so, it remains the case that societies with higher rates of firearm ownership tend to have higher rates of illegal firearm violence. In the UK too the upturn in firearm-related offending during the 1960s most commonly involved the UK's most available firearm – the shotgun (Ball *et al.*,1978). In more recent years, the widespread and largely unrestricted availability of replica, imitation or deactivated firearms has led to their use in up to 50 per cent of reported 'armed' robberies (Morrison and O'Donnell, 1994; Matthews, 1996). Likewise, the apparently increasing resort to firearms by 'organised' or 'professional' groups of criminals, terrorist groups and those involved in illegal drug dealing reflects a number of fairly instrumental factors relating to the type of criminal activity, the ease with which weapons can be obtained and the risk of encountering the police. Cultural orientations to firearms within certain offender groups, the power and status a gun confers, may also be influential. Certainly a number of well-placed commentators have pointed to a developing 'gun culture' among certain criminal groups in the UK (Silverman, 1994; Davison, 1997).

It would seem that Critchley's announcement of the 'conquest of violence' may have been a little premature. Ironically, he wrote about this 'conquest', the political and ideological consensus to which it closely related and the 'social contract' tradition of liberal governing from which both derived, just at the point that all three began to unravel somewhat. This has, in turn, entailed problems for the value base of liberal governance and its relation to power and violence. As we have argued, the very essence of the contractual model of civil society implied that explicit force and violence were to be expelled to the margins. Since 1970, of course, liberal democracies have found ample reasons to resort to force and violence at their margins but they have also appeared incapable of restraining increasing violence within. Both sets of developments point to social changes extending beyond the capacities of certain styles of modern liberal governing or beyond the limits of a certain type of power founded upon industrial production and collective social discipline.

According to Foucault,

> If the economic take off of the West began with the techniques that made possible the accumulation of capital, it might perhaps be said that the methods for administering the accumulation of men made possible a political take off ... in fact the two processes – the accumulation of men and the accumulation of capital – cannot be separated. ... Each makes the other possible and necessary, each provides a model for the other.
>
> (Foucault, 1977: 218–221)

Absolutely central to the political and economic power of the West has been its military prowess (Mann, 1986: 453–455, 490). In turn, this was particularly dependent upon new ways of exerting military force and, especially, upon new forms of deadly technology – in short, firearms. As Kiernan has argued, 'firearms were essential to the rise of the modern state' (Kiernan, 1967: 136). In due course, new and remarkably 'industrial' methods of first producing, and then deploying, the power of the gun established the 'military industrial complex' which sustained the power of the West. According to Foucault again:

> The Classical age saw the birth of the great political and military strategy by which nations confronted each other's economic and demographic forces; but it also saw the birth of meticulous military and political tactics by which the control of bodies and individual forces was exercised within states ... Historians of ideas usually attribute the dream of a perfect society to the philosophers and jurists of the eighteenth century; but there was also a military dream of society.
>
> (Foucault, 1977: 168–169)

This 'military dream' of the disciplined society was also in some senses progressive, democratic and contractual, for it related closely to the idea of the citizen-militia. Soldiers of the modern liberal state would also be citizens, bearers of rights but equally accepting of military duties (Haswell, 1973). According to Ellis, Frederick the Great, the eighteenth-century soldier king of Prussia had argued that the most important duty of the military commander was to prevent desertion (Ellis, 1976: 171). Yet, in the modern age, the efficient conduct of war could no more rely upon reluctant conscripts than a developing capitalist economy could rely upon slavery. As *The Times* had argued in 1857, while urging for the establishment of a British 'Volunteer Army': 'We must popularise the Army, and martialise the population. The gulf must be narrowed between the soldier and the citizen' (Cunningham, 1975: 97–98). Similar sentiments, though expressed for a contrary purpose, had surfaced in the USA almost a century earlier. There they had played a crucial role in arguments about the importance of local militia forces and the maintenance of colonial independence. The American colonies' experience of British governmental authority, resting upon the power of its large standing army, had tipped the ideological balance in favour of the localised militia system. Unlike in the UK where the volunteer militia served as a relay of central governmental authority, in the USA it was established precisely in opposition to it. Thus, James Madison, one of the architects of America's Second Amendment, spoke of the 'impious doctrine [of] the Old World, that the people were made for kings, not kings for the people' (Madison, 1788, in Bijlefeld, 1997: 4). When early American commentators spoke of 'every citizen [being] a soldier and every soldier [being] a citizen', the methods of military discipline envisaged may have been similar to those adopted by the old country even though their immediate political purpose was quite the opposite (Edel, 1995: 26–39).

Although nineteenth-century Britain's attempt to establish a 'Volunteer Force' was not without problems, it served a number of valuable social functions: defraying the expense of training men in marksmanship, embodying patriotism, helping familiarise the middle classes to leadership and the working men to military discipline and inculcating a degree of working-class loyalty towards established institutions. At a time of heightened imperial tensions brought on by the Boer War, key political figures threw their weight behind renewed efforts to improve the military utility of the British working man. In 1900, the Prime Minister, Lord Salisbury, declared that he would, 'laud the day when there was a rifle in every cottage in England,' while key political figures including the Lord Mayor of London, The Duke of Westminster and the Archbishop of York attended a meeting in London to promote the establishment of a Society of Working Men's Rifle Clubs for facilitating the practice of rifle shooting (Stevenson, 1996: 148).

Taken together, such Victorian initiatives in militarising the working class complemented the capitalist reorganisation of the UK's industrial army. Despite the political turmoil of the early part of the nineteenth century, training in arms began in the mid-century intended to discipline the worker-soldiers for the defence of the realm. It continued into the twentieth century right up to the eve of the First World War. Central to the disciplined citizenship of the modern age, therefore, was an idea that the cannon-fodder go willingly when their country needed them – or at least that they accept the legitimacy of their conscription. And so, by and large, they did. And when, a little over a year after the ending of the war, Parliament passed an Act requiring police certificates for all pistols and rifles and registration of firearms dealers, the disciplined citizenry largely complied. Some commentators have seen the shift from official encouragement of working-class shooting sports in 1900 to the restrictive framework of firearms controls established only twenty years later as something of a surprising reversal of philosophy. Yet those twenty years comprised both the First World War and, more importantly, the Russian Revolution, which the British establishment regarded as a dire warning about the dangers of an armed and mobilised working class. However, there is a marked continuity of collective class discipline here. The British working class were armed and militarised to facilitate collective disciplining when it suited the national purpose and they were disarmed and demilitarised later for precisely the same reasons.

Furthermore, the philosophical vindication of the soldier-citizen developing at this time also had its materialist foundations. At the very least, the waging of modern warfare required that far more people be involved. In turn, widening involvement implied the value of every person's contribution laying a foundation of collective sacrifice upon which notions of citizenship might rest. Keegan, in his *A History of Warfare*, documents, in particular, the factors which contributed to the increasing lethality of war during the nineteenth and early twentieth centuries, as evidenced in the lengthening casualty lists (Keegan, 1993: 359–361). Many of the crucial changes were of a technical nature. A century earlier the development of the musket had contributed to new methods of aggregating fire-power and training it upon an enemy by using troops in block or 'square' formation, rather like mobile fortresses or battering rams to engage an enemy line. Such complex manoeuvres demanded well-disciplined troops (Delbruck, 1990). They also demanded plenty of them, as many as the growing populations of the industrialising nations could spare. The armies of the modern era were typically much larger than any which had gone before. They had to be. The methods of warfare in the modern era were particularly wasteful of manpower.

As technical improvements in the available weaponry exceeded the ability of military leaders to assimilate these into their battle planning, war became an increasingly costly enterprise. The new, more rapidly reloaded Springfield rifle, for instance, available to Union forces at the battle of Gettysburg, played an important role in enhancing the firepower of the Union troops, enabling them to repel repeated Confederate advances. Few technical developments, however, had quite the impact of the machine gun on the Western Front during the First World War. The German army's Maxim guns effectively ended an entire, attrition-based, strategy of military campaigning, although it took the best part of the war for the allied generals to realise this (Ellis, 1976). In due course, there-fore, the military dream of disciplined society turned into a series of nightmares as nineteenth-century and twentieth-century wars brought a rationalised indus-trial efficiency to the task of mechanised slaughter (Pick, 1993).

Mass firepower or, later, mechanised firepower, created the conditions for the erasure, not just of individuality but of the collectivity too. A few well-armed men could command an entire battlefield. For Bauman, this potential power, the inhu-mane violence ultimately represented by the Holocaust, or Hiroshima, was not an aberration of our industrialised and civilised modernity but very much a direct product of it (Bauman, 1989). And now, in a 'post-industrial' age, the gun, once the instrument of a new form of social, political and military stability in Europe and the West, wreaks a new kind of havoc at home. Where modern forms of social disciplining have lost their hold, replaced by competitive individualism, a war of all against all resumes. In such a war weapons become the only commodity worth having. The gunman, only recently transformed into modernism's disciplined and responsible citizen, bearer of rights and carrier of military duties, changes once again, becoming now like a sniper, the king of a new post-modernism – albeit a rather nervous one. The master of all he surveys – through his gunsight.

Armed violence no longer stalks just the frontiers of liberal politics, but it has come to play an increasing role in domestic politics. Society, ever the junior partner in the social contract (notwithstanding the claims of the theory) has come to play the role of the sorcerer's apprentice. And this citizen-apprentice has run off with some of the state-sorcerer's guns, establishing a new power in the land. In nineteenth-century America, firearms manufacturers liked to present their weapons as adjuncts to the democratic and civilising process, firearms were 'Equalisers' or 'Peacemakers' but, at least in the longer term, the opposite seems the case. In a first scenario, the lone gunman had no need of democracy and no place in society. He was, in this sense, forever an outlaw. In a second scenario, with everyone armed to the teeth and equally dangerous to one another, there was no such thing as society, merely the effective accurate range of one's weapon.

The criminally inclined find a use for firearms just as military technologies come to be employed in the developing 'war' against crime. The rise of the indus-trial West was accompanied by the production of firearms and now its late-modern crisis seems marked by problems concerning the consumption – and use – of firearms, especially by those groups in society for whom the industrial-democratic systems of mass disciplining appear to have broken down. Either way, for the criminally inclined (lacking mainstream economic opportunities or motiva-tions) or for the vulnerable (potential victims of the former and lacking faith in the responsiveness of official law enforcement), a gun might appear to offer access to a vital currency of power and freedom. Power to act or freedom from fear; an armed short-cut to the 'American' dream or self-defence in an 'American' nightmare.

Having entered these reservations about the so-called 'conquest of violence' and raised the spectre of the gun as a dangerous element in unstable social rela-tionships, it is now time to examine the particular histories of weapon regulation as they evolved differently in the UK and the USA, the two societies upon which this analysis is primarily centred. At the outset, it should be borne in mind that any discussion of firearms control is not just a question of the deployment of restrictive governmental power. In both societies the issue of firearms control is, in reality, a positive, political and distributional question, as much concerned with the rights, privileges and opportunities of those to whom firearms are allowed as with the prohibitions or restrictions placed upon others. In this sense, historical discussions of firearms control are as much concerned with the creation of rights and duties as with their removal. The important questions, therefore, revolve around the ways in which certain cultural ideals or certain societal and group interests are constructed, deployed or otherwise mobilised within these legislative histories. A similar point, though made for different reasons, is apparent in the work of the American writer David Kopel whose two substantial studies, *The Samurai, the Mountie and the Cowboy*, published in 1992 and *Guns: Who Should Have Them?* published in 1995, both explore the social and cultural significance for US society of a range of more or less restrictive firearms control policies.

The earlier book, having reviewed the gun control policies and firearm-related crime problems of a range of societies, including Japan, the UK, Australia, New Zealand, Switzerland and Jamaica, concluded that the prevalence of guns in the USA and the entrenched character of the USA's 'gun culture' means that, 'a gunless America is not possible … the American gun is here to stay'. The implications of this, he argued, for the future development of rational gun control policies in the USA are that, 'instead of a futile attempt to erase gun culture, there must be a conscientious effort to mold gun culture for the better … to encourage social control and civic virtue in gun ownership'. The only realistic policy option, therefore is to promote responsible gun ownership (Kopel, 1992a: 422). The later book examined the operation of a number of recent gun control measures and considered the issues relating to the access of a variety of social groups: women, African-Americans, even children, before answering its own title's question to the effect that any responsible citizen should be allowed access to guns because 'disarming non-criminal citizens is no part of the solution to the crime problem'. Blanket gun control policies are even compared to 'quack' medical remedies purveyed by unscrupulous entrepreneurs (Kopel, 1995b: 413). Even children's rights to possess weapons are at issue, 'because children are not necessarily as responsible as adults … many anti-minor laws strip young people of their right to self-defence'. Yet, according to Kopel, there could be no constitutional argument 'for completely abrogating the self-defense rights of minors' (Kopel, 1995b: 376).

The reason for drawing such examples from Kopel's writing is to illustrate the ways in which notions of citizenship and individual rights are creatively framed within firearms regulations. Because these conceptions of autonomy and citizenship relate directly to fundamental ideas about personal security and self-defence – those rights without which all others are said to be worthless – they remain bitterly contested. In the British case, despite a Common Law right to self-defence, the carrying of weapons in anticipation of the need to exercise this right is deemed contrary to prevailing collective and paternalist notions of 'good order': the Queen's Peace. The disarmament of the public has facilitated a tradition in which a largely unarmed police have been able to establish a philosophy of policing through collective consent. However, more recent enhancements of the police's armed response capacity raise questions stretching beyond individual civil liberties. The interests of a more collective conception of order have sustained civilian disarmament in the UK, albeit this has been a rather hierarchical form of collectivism which has typically privileged certain established class interests. Collective as this order may be, it is sometimes less than consensual and often less than democratic.

Firearms and social control in the UK

In the UK the essential foundations of the British approach to firearms were set in place in the period immediately following the Civil War, although the process can scarcely be said to have been concluded until well into the nineteenth century. And it was not until 1920 that the (albeit qualified) British 'right to bear firearms' was legislated out of existence by the Firearms Control Act (Greenwood, 1972; Malcolm, 1994).

The consolidation of monopoly control over firearms which began in the middle of the seventeenth century proceeded via the establishment of further restrictions upon who was allowed to possess firearms and use them; how they were to use them; and where they were permitted to use them. The restrictions, imposed gradually during the seventeenth century, overturned former arrangements in which access to and ownership of firearms had been both a privilege and a duty. Firearm ownership had been restricted by religious affiliation (no Catholics), or according to a property qualification, or required as a duty by virtue of membership of the local militia. Militia members, as ratepayers, had to contribute to the cost of civic defences, support town 'watch' schemes and, when required, assist in raising 'hue and cry' to bring outlaws and felons to justice whenever the peace of civil society was threatened. Such were the costs and duties associated with the privileged access to firearms enjoyed by a minority of Englishmen (Greenwood, 1972: 7–11). Militia organisation largely disappeared over the course of the next century, although in the eighteenth and early nineteenth century some militia functions were taken over by the private associations for the prosecution of felons which grew up in many areas of the country (Little and Sheffield, 1983; Shubert, 1980).

Hunting

Amidst repeated concerns with 'popish plots' and fears of rebellion, leading to periodic forays into disarming, first Catholics, then Protestants, and then Catholics once more, a major firearm control measure was passed in the form of the Game Act of 1671. This Act substantially tightened the property qualification attached to the right to hunt game and effectively outlawed the simple possession of firearms by any person not so qualified. Blackstone noted that, under the Act, the property qualification required to hunt was fifty times the amount needed to permit a man to vote (Malcolm, 1994: 71; Hay, 1975: 189). The immediate result was that less than 1 per cent of those living on the land were entitled to hunt game, even on their own land. The 1671 Act created a new structure of law enforcement and gave a 'new class of gentry-appointed officials ... direct power over the sport. It gave them a kind of "private game police"' (Malcolm, 1994: 70). Gamekeepers or other appointed persons were empowered to search premises on a warrant and seize all 'illegal' weapons or other 'engines of destruction' (Hay, 1975: 194). Malcolm's conclusions about the primary purposes of the game legislation are unequivocal.

> The Game Act of 1671 made it no longer necessary to prove that guns and bows had been illegally used; it simply included them in the list of prohibited devices, thus depriving nearly the entire population of a legal right to own them. There can be no doubt that this prohibition was intentional. ... [The Act] lowered the standard of proof ... [leaving] much to the discretion of the individual justice, and put more emphasis on confiscating the weapons of tenants on country estates rather than locking up poachers.
>
> (Malcolm, 1994: 72–73)

Later criticism of the Act saw it as class legislation restricting the conditions of subsistence of the rural poor (Thompson, 1975). Yet the Act 'circumscribed arms ownership more than ever before or since.' The aristocracy's control over the distribution of weapons was substantially tightened, 'the use of an act for the preservation of game was a customary means to curb lower class violence ... [it] effectively transferred nearly exclusive control of the power of the sword to the country gentry.' (Malcolm, 1994: 74–76). While enforcement of the Act was rather mixed, with poaching offences reflecting the bulk of the cases, the major significance of the Act lay in its establishment of a system for the regulation of access to weapons by class and religion in the turbulent political context of seventeenth-century Britain.

Duelling

If the control of access to weapons for hunting was one of the avenues by which firearms control was advanced in the UK, the decline of the duel after the seventeenth century, first in Britain and later in the rest of Europe, marks another of the apparently 'civilising paths' to the present. For centuries the practice of settling disputes with swords had been regarded as obvious, necessary, civilised, skilful and honourable – something central to the masculine qualities demanded of the military men who appeared the most enthusiastic duellists (Spierenburg, 1998). Furthermore, as Kiernan observes, duelling was itself an expression of elite privilege, 'an assertion of superior right, a claim to immunity from the law such as a ruling class is always likely to seek in one field or another ... the ultimate hallmark of gentility was the right of gentlemen to kill one another'. It was also part of a 'gentleman's code', testing and thereby defining the moral fibre of the man (Kiernan, 1988: 53, 107, 160).

When duels were conducted with swords and governed by a civilising ethic of chivalry the death rate was comparatively low. A simple cut marking an opponent was enough to give 'satisfaction' to an aggrieved party. When, during the sixteenth and seventeenth centuries, firearms began to replace swords as the duellists' weapons of choice the lethality of duels initially increased only marginally. Early firearms were inaccurate, under-powered and often misfired. Indeed, in due course, it was the growing power, reliability and accuracy of pistols (and therefore the heightened lethality of duels) which, according to Kiernan, served, far more than religious or legal condemnation, to bring the practice to an end (Kiernan, 1988). Karl Marx was himself something of a beneficiary of the limited accuracy of early under-powered pistols. In 1836 he accepted a challenge to a duel from a young officer of the Borussia Korps but received only a small wound above his left eye (Wheen, 1999). As duelling pistols became more powerful, reliable and accurate, many other duellists were not so lucky.

Another factor, initially responsible for the democratisation of the duel and later for its decline, concerned the 'deskilling' process that firearms brought to duelling. Reflecting its military origins, early duelling depended upon a certain proficiency with a sword. In turn, swordsmanship was a skill that every young officer and gentleman had to master. The sword was the weapon of a gentleman (Billacois, 1990). By contrast, a pistol simply had to be pointed and its trigger pulled. The exclusivity of the duel, once confined to traditional military elites, was thus breached. In the eyes of contemporaries, any young upstart with a grudge might challenge his peers and, given the lottery that duelling had become, stand a fair chance of winning. As the lethality of duels increased and their exclusive social basis began to diminish, leading opinion began to turn against the practice. The church began to criticise the barbarism of duelling, writers lampooned the self-destructive stupidity of the duellists and the military began to regret the losses to its promising, if rather impetuous, young officer class. In the UK, the early nineteenth century saw a number of duellists and their seconds facing criminal charges and, around the same time, parliament began to consider the prohibition of the duel – but only after the practice was already well in decline. Duelling persisted for rather longer in France, its anachronistic alliance of patriarchal masculinity and notions of bourgeois honour coming to grief on the barbed wire and machine guns of the 1914–18 Western Front (Nye, 1998). European military thinking had been dominated by elitist notions of individual heroism. The very characteristics nurtured in a duelling culture, personal courage, fortitude, calmness under pressure, were the very attributes thought necessary to command men in battle. The First World War changed all that, military strategy began to rely less upon valiant individualism and more upon technology and tactics (Ellis, 1976).

Self-defence

In the UK, although the Common Law regards the use of 'reasonable force' as permissable in cases of self-defence, civilians are effectively denied firearms for self-defence purposes. Yet there are circumstances in which a firearm, held for some other purpose, might lawfully be used for self-defence. Equally, police officers might lawfully apply lethal force (an issue we consider later), even 'shooting to kill', within the terms of section 3 of the 1967 Criminal Law Act. There is some dispute about exactly when the Common Law right to self-defence with firearms was eclipsed in the UK. Greenwood contends that the provisions of the 1920 Firearms Act did not eliminate the right (Greenwood, 1972) but that the 1920 Act was very much the first step 'along the one-way traffic system which [the government] planned for gun control' ('Cadmus', 1995a). In 1920, Home Office guidance issued to Chief Constables had accepted that, 'it would be a "good reason" for having a revolver if a person lives in a solitary house, where protection against burglars and thieves is essential' ('Cadmus', 1995a), a principle with rather obvious class specific overtones.

In 1937, the Home Office advice to the police began to shift. 'As a general rule applications to possess firearms for house or personal protection should be discouraged on the grounds that firearms cannot be regarded as a suitable means of protection and may be a source of danger' (in 'Cadmus', 1995a). However, answering a parliamentary question in 1946, the Home Secretary made it clear to the House of Commons that personal protection no longer amounted to a satisfactory reason for requiring a firearm. Law and Brookesmith argue that 'the British citizen's right to a firearm for self-defence was administratively terminated in 1954 by a change in government policy and, while the common law right to defend oneself still exists, various statutes make it an offence to carry any weapon in anticipation of the need to exercise that right' (Law and Brookesmith, 1996: 170). In 1962 the presumption against gun ownership for self-defence had strengthened still further.

> It should hardly ever be necessary for anyone to possess a firearm for the protection of his house or his person. Such applications should be discouraged on the ground that firearms cannot be regarded as a suitable means of protection in this country and may be a source of danger. This principle should hold good even in the case of banks and firms who desire to protect valuables or large quantities of money; only in exceptional circumstances should a firearm be held for protection purposes' (in 'Cadmus', 1995a). By 1989, however, when the Home Office was required to make the advice they issued public, the guidance had hardened still further. As the author of the *Guns Review* piece angrily concluded, 'the right to keep arms for the defence of one's home has not been removed by law but by an on going conspiracy between the police and civil servants, doubtless fully supported by some politicians. It has never been the subject of debate, study or consideration beyond the corridors of Whitehall.
>
> ('Cadmus', 1995a)

Yet if and when the right to armed self-defence actually disappeared, the issue still surfaces from time to time and the courts have been known to take a lenient view of those who have used firearms for self-defence purposes. Somewhat more controversial, as we shall see, have been court decisions in respect of police officers or security personnel who have employed lethal force. A case which achieved particular notoriety in 1988, however, was not some dramatic sounding 'vigilante' whose actions could be equated with those of a Hollywood hero. It rather concerned an elderly Derbyshire gardener defending the shed on his allotment. Tired of thefts and vandalism inflicted upon his allotment, the man concealed himself in the shed overnight armed with his shotgun. When two young men attempted to break in he fired at them through the door, seriously injuring one. The case temporarily excited national attention in a context of rising concern about police effectiveness. Newspapers were reporting an increase in localised vigilantism and those who boldly took the law into their own hands drew some tacit approval from the popular press. Although the allotment holder was prosecuted, he was cleared of intentional wounding. Throughout the trial public opinion seemed squarely on his side.

Eight years later, the judge at his trial was interviewed in a TV debate about the limits on citizen self-defence. The former judge commented that he thought a firearm could be a useful protection against burglars, and that the best and most effective method of self-defence might be a gun (*Guardian*, 20.5.1996). Outcry followed, requiring the Lord Chancellor's intervention to restate the current legal position. Two years earlier, however, the editor of *Guns Review* had drawn precisely the same conclusion as the judge: 'Juries, thank God, still show some sense and in cases where householders have used firearms against intruders, they have invariably acquitted – as indeed they should' (*Guns Review*, July 1994: 499). Later, the same magazine devoted a substantial article to the question of using firearms for self-defence, concluding that 'the right to keep arms for defence is now a necessity and the arguments must be addressed' ('Cadmus', 1995a; 1995b). Likewise, during a post-Dunblane shooting sports lobby of Parliament in November 1996, a Tory MP rather rashly commented to a reporter that 'people in his Bristol NW constituency felt safer with a gun in their homes' (*Guardian*, 5.11.1996). Warming to a similar theme towards the end of their book *The Fighting Handgun*, Law and Brookesmith also argue that, 'there are numerous examples of victims of crime who suffered or were killed without having any chance to defend themselves … the official thinking refuses to recognise that an enormous number of crimes … would be prevented when criminal predators find themselves facing an armed citizen instead of a helpless victim' (Law and Brookesmith, 1996: 170–171). This advocacy for a more 'American' right to armed self-defence and the 'net benefit' to be derived by society through widening gun ownership marked a hardening of pro-gun rhetoric and a more forceful assertion of shooters' rights in the UK. Taken together they signalled a number of changes occuring within the British shooting community.

The Bill of Rights

Two centuries earlier, when duelling was still at its most popular among the landed military elites and the control of the hunting weapons of the lower classes only recently begun, the UK's broader internal political tensions were thought to be settled with the ascendancy of William and Mary. This so-called 'Glorious Revolution' not only ensured the establishment of Protestant dominance, but also promised the restoration of the 'traditional' rights and liberties of Englishmen. Among these fell the Englishman's 'traditional' right to arms. In due course, following substantial drafting and redrafting of clauses, article 7 of the Bill of Rights spelled out the right of Englishmen to have access to weapons in the following terms: 'The Subjects which are Protestants may have arms for their defence suitable to their condition and as allowed by Law' (Malcolm, 1994: 119).

Absent from this final formulation was any reference to the militia or any reference to principles of 'common' or 'collective' defence. The statement remains very conditional. It specifically excludes all bar Protestants, and it refers to 'Subjects' not citizens. Effectively the article implies an individual right to be armed to repel burglars, that is to say, an individual right for personal defence. And finally, with the phrase, 'as allowed by Law' the statement anticipated the need to further limit the right to arms whenever the government might see fit (Malcolm, 1994: 119–121). In subsequent years, the government went on to do just that.

As we have seen, the unsettled political situation at the turn of the nineteenth century saw the introduction of temporary restrictions on the right of access to firearms. Even so, during the greater part of the nineteenth century – even after the establishment of police forces – it was still asserted that 'any person could purchase and keep in his possession a firearm without any restriction'. By the early twentieth century, however, this 'right' had vanished. By this time, the problem of highway robbery had been long since resolved and the practice of duelling as a means of resolving disputes had first fallen into abeyance and then been outlawed (Kiernan, 1988; Gilmour, 1992). Finally, after 1856, with the establishment of police forces in all areas, the private prosecution societies largely disappeared. The consolidation of coercive force had been substantially achieved in mainland UK. But what of the right to firearms?

As allowed by law

The English right to arms had always depended upon what was 'allowed by law' and, in the latter part of the nineteenth century, pressure for change began to mount. First, rather nominal controls were introduced but later proposals addressed the carrying of firearms outside the home. Later still, widespread concerns arising during the 1890s, about armed robberies and urban violence in London, led to the introduction of parliamentary bills seeking to restrict access to concealable pistols and revolvers (Greenwood, 1972; Pearson, 1983). None of these Bills were successful until 1903 when the Pistols Act was passed to prohibit the sale of pistols to minors and felons and to require all purchasers who were not householders to obtain a ten shilling licence from the post office. The explicit justification for the 1903 Act, according to its sponsor, was not crime but accident prevention. Nevertheless, increasing concern about rising armed crime in London appeared to be among the factors prompting parliament's speedy introduction of comprehensive new firearms controls at the end of the First World War. Domestic crime, however, was only part of the story.

In response to the turbulent domestic and international post-war politics, Parliament passed the 1920 Firearms Control Act. It was described as a 'comprehensive arms control measure'. The Act repealed the right to be armed by requiring a firearm certificate, eligibility for which was to be decided upon by a senior police officer, for anyone wishing to 'purchase, possess, use or carry any description of firearm or ammunition for the weapon' (Greenwood, 1972). According to Malcolm, 'while the reverberations of the French Revolution left the English right to keep arms intact, the repercussions of WW1 and the Bolshevik Revolution did not' (Malcolm, 1994: 170).

The Act was based upon the recommendations of the Blackwell Committee established in the face of fears concerning political militancy and the threat of revolution following the First World War. The Committee comprised senior Home Office officials and representatives from the police and prison service, Customs, the War Office, Board of Trade and the Irish Office. The Committee met in secret and its report was never published, although the now declassified documents record that 'the acquisition of semi-automatic pistols and bombs, by "the anarchist or intellectual malcontent of the great cities", was a special concern to the government of the time' (Yardley, 1996). According to Stevenson, 'the committee proceeded on the assumption that controls were desirable and that they would be effective' (Stevenson, 1996: 157–158). Police evidence suggested that armed crime, although at a relatively low level, began rising even before the First World War (123 incidents during 1911–1913). During the war itself, wartime restrictions were thought to have kept the number of armed incidents low, but the Committee took the view that, with the ending of the war and the expiry of the temporary Defence of the Realm firearm controls, armed crime would soon rise again.

More pressing than the fear of crime, however, according to Malcolm, was a fear of growing political unrest and disorder – even of revolution. Cabinet meetings during early 1920 reflected the sense of urgency and alarm. 'The Great War had been preceded by industrial unrest and had been waged with appalling ferocity. Demobilisation brought back to the UK thousands of soldiers brutalised in a savage and senseless conflict. The Bolshevik revolution was in full swing ... the Communist Party of great Britain and the Trades Union Congress [were forming] ... wages were low and a general strike threatened ... [and] Ireland was in a state of virtual civil war' (Malcolm, 1994: 171–172). In London and Liverpool even the police had been on strike, though a planned national strike had faltered (Uglow, 1988). In this turbulent political context, and with the Defence of the Realm firearm controls due to expire, the government were anxious that the weapons being brought home from the war as souvenirs by returning soldiers be rapidly brought within a system of control. The intended mechanism of control involved a decentralised licensing system which conferred a considerable degree of discretion upon Chief Constables and local police action.

According to Malcolm, 'the manner in which the government attempted to slip its arms bill by parliament betrays its anxiety about the reception it would receive'. The Home Secretary attempted to claim the proposed measure was 'non-controversial', and that it addressed only the need to keep weapons from criminals and dangerous persons (Greenwood, 1972). Although the Bill was passed comfortably with a large measure of cross party support, a few members expressed their concern about the loss of ancient rights and the preservation of the field shooting sports. The inadequacy of the Bill as a response to the criminal use of firearms was also asserted (Malcolm, 1994: 173). Interestingly, only one speaker (Jameson) referred to the question of weapons for purposes of self-defence and he addressed himself specifically to the Irish context where, 'very many peaceful, law-abiding people have [need of] firearms with which to defend themselves against murderers and rebels. ... The danger is that if you pass a law like this it will be obeyed by the peaceable subject, but not by the murderers and criminals' (Mr Jameson MP, cited in Malcom, 1994). Still deeper political motives became apparent, for just as it was proposing legislation to curtail the general population's access to firearms in England, Scotland and Wales, the government was either tacitly condoning or even directly assisting in the supply of firearms to loyalist paramilitary organisations in Ireland (Farrell, 1983). In due course, after Partition, political factors have continued to influence the firearms control regime prevailing in Northern Ireland.

In the years after its passage, the enforcement of the 1920 Firearms Control Act appears to have been subject to much local variation. Early complaints about over-zealous enforcement led to the Home Office issuing revised instructions to the police in late 1920 but by then the tone of complaint against alleged police interference into the rights of legitimate sporting shooters had been set (Greenwood, 1972; Stevenson, 1996: 158–160). In the years which followed, although deficiencies of the 1920 legislation became apparent, the relatively low salience of the problem of firearms use in crime largely kept the issue off the political agenda. The apparent problem of firearms or imitation firearms being used in crime was tackled in an act of 1933, while a Firearms Act the following year raised the age at which firearms or ammunition could be bought or hired from fourteen to seventeen. These were scarcely controversial matters however. The, by no means insignificant, fact that participation in 'shooting and field sports' remained an activity largely frequented by the rural land-owning upper classes meant that firearms were seldom a live political issue. As we have already seen, this largely privileged access to firearms is very much part of an English tradition – indeed, it is a large part of the explanation for why smooth-bore shot-guns remained outside conventional firearms control until the late 1960s.

The Report of the Bodkin Committee in 1934, continued this reassuring tone. The Committee had been established to review existing firearms control legislation and advise the Home Office (Home Office, 1934). Discussing the effect of the 1920 Firearms Control Act, the Committee remarked that the Act, and its enforcement, had been remarkably successful, not least because of the stalwart attitudes shown by 'manufacturers of and dealers in firearms [who] have borne their losses with resignation and have loyally co-operated with the authorities in the measures for the restriction of firearms during the past 14 years'. The Committee concluded,

> We recognise that no scheme of controls can make it impossible for the determined criminal to obtain possession of firearms. ... [But] so far as it is reasonably possible by legislative and executive measures to reduce the risk of such evils, we think that the statutes already referred to and the efforts of those concerned in their enforcement can be regarded as highly successful, and we are of the opinion that, in view of 14 years' experience of the working of the Statute, no alteration of substance ... is required.
>
> (Bodkin Committee, in Greenwood, 1972: 60)

The Committee also applauded the work of the police in operating the system of controls introduced in 1920. The Bodkin Committee's mainly rather detailed recommendations (prohibitions on civilian machine guns, regulation of the length of shotgun barrels and firearm silencers and regulations for the firearm trade) were enacted in the Firearms (Amendment) Act of 1936. Finally, a 1937 Firearms Act consolidated into a single statute all existing firearms legislation.

The 1937 Act stood for twenty-five years without repeal or significant amendment. Before the Second World War the UK apparently had no major firearms problem. There appears to have been no systematic collection of data on firearms offences in the years preceding the war. Nonetheless, Greenwood cites evidence given in a parliamentary answer revealing that, during the eighteen months between July 1936 and December 1937, only twenty persons arrested in London were found to be in possession of firearms and, of these, twelve were air weapons and another a toy pistol. 'This can only be considered a very satisfactory state of affairs ... [the firearms control legislation] appears to have been largely accepted by the shooting community and liberally applied by the police' (Greenwood, 1972: 70). Things were to change and disturb this conservative consensus, but its persistence is worthy of note. After the war a consensus of a different kind has been said to have prevailed, this time based upon peace, growing prosperity, party-political compromise, full employment and the welfare state (Kavanagh and Morris, 1989). Although crime rates leaped upwards during the war, mainly the result of offences against wartime restrictions (Morris, 1989), the post-war era is said to have marked the high-watermark of 'policing by consent' (Reiner, 1992). After 1955, however, rising crime rates began to perplex and preoccupy academics, politicians and criminal justice system personnel alike.

During the war, one consequence of the disarming of the British public became apparent in the shortage of weapons available for domestic 'home defence'. An American Committee for the defence of British Homes was formed urging Americans to collect their firearms together to be sent to the UK to 'aid in the Battle of Britain.' At the time the initiative appeared an essentially pragmatic measure, adjusting the distribution of weapons according to pressing wartime needs but, rather later, in a Shooters' Rights Association publication of 1986, the initiative takes on a deeper ideological significance, providing evidence of the dangerous folly of disarming the public (Yardley and Stevenson, 1988). At the end of the war the more familiar low key and consensual British firearms control procedures resumed. Fearing that 'souvenir' firearms had been brought home by returning troops the Home Secretary authorised a six-week amnesty during 1946 when the 'illegal' weapons could be surrendered without fear of prosecution. In all the exercise netted over 75,000 weapons including 59,000 pistols and 1,580 machine guns.

In addition to the amnesty, the years following the war saw evidence of a tightening up of police policy in relation to the issue and renewal of firearm certificates. In 1946, the Home Secretary had commented in Parliament that, 'I would not regard the plea that a revolver is wanted for the protection of an applicant's person or property as necessarily justifying the issue of a firearm certificate.' (Home Secretary, 17th October 1946, quoted in Greenwood, 1972: 72). The implication was clear – outside of wartime, armed protection of persons and property was a collective task to be carried out by the police and the state, not a responsibility to be discharged by individuals acting in their own interest. The collective providential state had taken upon itself the task of safeguarding the last liberty of individuals, in this sense the British tradition differed significantly from the American.

Yet as crime began to rise in the 1950s, the UK's relationship to firearms began to change. Media reports and a number of infamous shooting cases (1952: Bentley and Craig, 1955: Ruth Ellis) began to excite concern about a growth in 'American-style' gun violence with armed tearaways, apparently quite unlike our own more patriotic and deferential working-class villains (Mannheim, 1941: 108) spreading panic and alarm in London and our larger cities. These issues began to exercise British politicians in the 1950s, not least as they debated proposals to abolish the death penalty. During the debate on the Second Reading of the Murder (Abolition of Death Penalty) Bill in 1965 Sir Peter Rawlinson MP remarked: 'We wondered in 1956 and 1957 whether this country's crime and criminal activities would develop as they have overseas; into the use of gangs and gangsters armed with guns. Would there be increased danger to the public and would the police have to be armed?' (cited in Greenwood, 1972: 261). The documentary-style introduction to the 1949 film *The Blue Lamp*, in which PC George Dixon was shot and killed, also sought to depict the cavalier violence of a new generation of delinquents more than willing to use firearms and violence to get what they wanted (Richards, 1997). The film's portrait of the unarmed policeman, advancing upon the gunman, firmly established the definitive image of British policing. In later years commentators returned frequently to this image in debates about the future of policing and/or the value of the death penalty. On the one hand 'Dixon' epitomised a tradition of unarmed policing by consent that many sought to preserve. On the other hand, critics noted, Dixon was shot and killed.

Outside the cinema, in 1950, firearms were known to have been used or carried in only nineteen robberies in the Metropolitan Police District (31 per cent of total robberies). During the late 1950s, however, the number began to increase, rising still faster during the 1960s. By the end of the 1960s over 300 robberies by persons carrying firearms (or supposed firearms) were recorded in the Metropolitan Police District, although firearm-related robberies were still dwarfed by the number of robberies carried out by offenders carrying other weapons.

While firearm robberies began to grow after the early 1960s, commentators have suggested that firearm robberies only grew as a reflection of more generally rising rates of armed robbery. Even so, the twenty years between the late 1940s to the late 1960s saw a threefold increase in the proportion of robberies committed with firearms. In the mid-1950s the proportion of robberies committed with a firearm stood at around 14 per cent, by 1969 it had doubled to 28 per cent (Greenwood, 1972: 170–172).

Against a backdrop of rising concern about crime – and armed crime in particular – during the late 1950s and early 1960s, Parliament returned to debate the question of firearms control. In 1962, a private member's bill introduced further controls on the possession and use of shotguns and air-powered weapons. Three years later, the 1965 Firearms Act established a number of new firearm offences and increased the penalties for many existing offences as Parliament attempted to forestall criticism that the impending abolition of the death penalty would lead to an upsurge in violent crime.

During the 1960s the number of firearm fatalities began to rise. Between 1960 and 1967 firearm homicides rose from nineteen to forty-eight per year, suicides rose unevenly from 177 to 193, and a fairly stable trend in firearm accidents peaked at eighty-three in 1961 falling back to sixty-three by 1967 (Greenwood, 1972: 177). In 1967, amidst continuing concern about violent crime, a Criminal Justice Act extended the licensing system to shotguns after three police officers were shot and killed in London. The following year the 1968 Firearms Act brought all the existing firearms legislation together in a single statute. Barring minor changes, this statute formed the legal basis for British firearms control policy for the twenty years until 1988 when the Firearms (Amendment) Act was hurried through Parliament after the Hungerford shootings.

Greenwood argues that the shooting of the three London police officers in 1966 shattered a seeming consensus on keeping shotguns outside of the main firearm licensing system. Even in 1965, both the Home Secretary and the police were still resisting the imposition of additional controls to restrict shotguns in line with other firearms. Yet, it is sometimes claimed, this apparent consensus also obscured a more fundamental continuity in British firearms control. In recent years, commentators from within the British firearms lobby have begun to challenge the ideological underpinnings of these policies and the assumptions upon which they have been based.

As we have already seen, after the First World War and, less dramatically, after the Second World War, British governments extended firearm controls or pursued civilian disarmament strategies in the interest of collective security and the protection of social and political order. To the firearms lobby, however, such initiatives appeared simply as the state pursuing its own illiberal agenda. The Criminal Justice Act and the Firearms Act of 1968, which brought shotguns into the British licensing system, followed an incident in which police officers were shot with illegally held handguns. The 1960s did witness an increasing resort to shotguns in armed crime (Ball *et al.*, 1978; Harding, 1979) but the 1966 shootings were said to have had a broadly symbolic effect, allowing the government to take another restrictive step. Rather perversely, however, no additional restrictions were proposed for handguns. Nor were additional restrictions placed upon handguns after the Hungerford killings in 1986, even though half the victims died after having been shot with a semi-automatic pistol.

The basis for the firearms lobby's perception that government has always been pursuing its own hidden agenda on firearms control rests in large part upon the unpublished (hence 'secret') report of Sir John McKay's Working Party, commissioned by the Heath government in 1971, on the control of firearms in the UK. In turn the Working Party Report led to a Green Paper, *The Control of Firearms in Great Britain: A Consultative Document*, published in 1973. No legislation resulted from the Green Paper but, to shooters, the philosophy behind the Green Paper was especially revealing. The core problem was defined as one of increasing use of firearms, particularly shotguns, in crime. The solution was seen to lie in society arranging its firearms controls in order to make it as difficult as possible for criminals to gain access to weapons. The most effective and reliable means of achieving this was by substantially reducing society's total gun inventory (Harding, 1979). Responsible politicians, it was implied, could do no other.

The evidence upon which the Green Paper based its arguments is discussed at greater length elsewhere but, for shooters, the importance of the document lay in the brief glimpse it provided of what they had always suspected: the government's 'draconian' long-term aim was complete civilian disarmament. Unfortunately, the fact that successive governments failed to extend controls over, let alone prohibit, handguns until after Dunblane literally forced their hands, however, rather weakens the shooters' argument. If government really had been pursuing an implicit policy of complete civilian disarmament, one might have expected tighter handgun controls following serious shooting incidents in 1966 and 1986.

Concealed weapons and armed responses?

In 1966 an armed man killed three police officers with a handgun. The incident had enormous social and political significance and proved the catalyst for a number of important changes, but no proposals for the tighter regulation of handguns followed. The penalties for firearm-related offending were increased. Likewise, the Home Office, concerned for some time about an apparent increase in offenders using shotguns (the sawn-off variety), seized the opportunity to bring shotguns into the established licensing system within its consolidating 1968 Firearms Act. Finally, the police recognising many inadequacies in their armed response capacity went on to establish a specialist firearms, training and tactical deployment unit, then known as D.11 (next PT17, now SO.19) (Waddington, 1988). This unit also undertook the specialist training of officers for airport and diplomatic protection duties. During the following decade the deployment of armed officers came increasingly to be seen as a necessary component of a graduated police response in the context of growing concerns about domestic and international terrorism (Hoare, 1980).

The 1980s saw a series of abrupt reversals in police armed response strategies. The underlying policy involved the use of fewer but more highly trained police 'authorised firearms officers', however, it appeared that these officers were being called upon more frequently (Gould and Waldren 1986; Josephs, 1993; Sargent *et al.*, 1994). The decade began with politicians and senior police officers articulating a robust response to criminal and terrorist activities. The ending of the 1980 Iranian Embassy seige, when hooded and black-clad SAS men stormed the building, killing the gunmen holding the hostages, was said to epitomise a tough, new, no-nonsense approach to peace-keeping (Newsinger, 1997). At the same time, growing unease began to surface in some quarters regarding allegations of a 'shoot-to-kill' policy adopted by police and security force personnel in Northern Ireland (Asmal, 1985; Jennings, 1990; Urban, 1992). Furthermore, a number of incidents on the mainland in which innocent citizens were shot and killed in armed police operations, most notably the case of Stephen Waldorf in 1983, suggested that this was an issue of rather wider significance (Benn and Worpole, 1986).

The Waldorf incident and a series of further cases in which unarmed and innocent civilians were killed by armed police forced a rethink in police strategy. The Home Office undertook a review, completed in 1986, of police armed operations. The importance of these issues for policing in the UK is hard to over-estimate. On one side, the idea that the police were 'tooling-up' was regarded with something akin to horror, an acknowledgement that the 'Dixon image' had gone for ever and 'policing by consent' a thing of the past (Mainwaring-White, 1983; Northam, 1988; Jefferson, 1990). On the other hand the view that the police were under-protected for the roles they had to perform had gained increasing currency, especially among police rank and file, in recent years and senior officers were forced to respond (Waddington, 1991).

The underlying principles of the Home Office Working Party's 1986 Report, reiterated much of the existing official guidance upon the police use of firearms. It stressed the appropriate and minimum use of force, emphasising incident containment, the avoidance of confrontation and, where possible, the resolution of armed incidents without shooting. These principles were essentially continuous with existing police policy (Home Office, 1986). The Working Party specifically rejected a more aggressive philosophy involving training and equipping specialist armed officers to confront and engage armed offenders (Yardley and Eliot, 1986). Furthermore, the Working Party Report also rejected a submission by the Association of County Councils that rapid weapon-carrying response vehicles (ARVs) be deployed around constabulary areas (although it soon became clear that some police forces still had them) (Waddington and Hamilton, 1997). True to form, no sooner had the Working Party formulated its conclusions than an incident occurred which swept its cautiously constructed guidance away.

A man dressed in combat fatigues and armed with an AK47 assault rifle, a carbine and a Beretta semi-automatic handgun killed sixteen people in the Berkshire town of Hungerford. Michael Ryan was the UK's first 'spree killer' (Josephs, 1993). In the immediate aftermath of the incident, a number of commentators voiced serious criticisms of the police response. It was, indeed, a cruelly ironic fact that, less than a year earlier, the Working Party had bowed to political pressure and rejected a proposal to establish ARV patrols in each police force area. Rapid response ARVs, it was argued, might have enabled the police to intervene more quickly and more effectively, perhaps stopping Ryan's killing spree (Edwards, 1988). In the event, the HM Inspector's report into the incident concluded that the most likely outcome of such an intervention would have been that the lightly armed ARV crews would have been shot, heavily outgunned by Ryan's Kalashnikov (Josephs, 1993: 174; Mason, 1988; Waddington and Hamilton, 1997: 98).

Nevertheless, although the HMI report expressed severe doubts about the use of ARVs at Hungerford, it still went on to recommend ARV deployment in other force areas. Subsequently, many police forces did introduce ARVs. Waddington and Hamilton conclude that Hungerford offered a 'window of opportunity' for a policy change in the police deployment of firearms which was actually desired on other grounds. Reactive deployment of firearms officers, the politically cautious policy settlement articulated in 1986, could be held up as a demonstrable failure in Hungerford. In turn, the incident 'allowed the police to take a decision that was justified on operational grounds while minimising the threat to police legitimacy. It [allowed the police] to portray the policy change as something forced upon them' (Waddington and Hamilton, 1997: 105). Of course, as we have already seen, the tendency to explain innovations in armed or paramilitary policing by reference to external threats – increasing violence, increasing resort to firearms by criminals – is a familiar if not always accurate explanation of policy changes. In recent years the phrase 'event driven' has been in rather frequent use (Squires, 2000).

Hungerford led to a number of other, rather paradoxical outcomes. Media attention had focused on Ryan's 'Rambo-like' appearance and, above all, his Kalashnikov assault rifle, virtually ignoring the semi-automatic handgun he used to kill half of his victims. The police, likewise, still concerned about the availability of shotguns (although Ryan had not used one), seized the opportunity to argue for an urgent change in the law concerning shotguns. The legislation which followed the Hungerford incident reflected these apparent priorities. Accordingly, when the government hurriedly pulled together its new firearms control proposals after Hungerford, fourteen of the nineteen clauses in the original 1988 Firearms (Amendment) Bill were drawn from the Green Paper of thirteen years earlier. Hungerford appeared to be an opportunity to resurrect a series of gun control proposals of over a decade earlier. However, there were no proposals to restrict the availability or lethality of handguns. Even Yardley and Stevenson, in a critical review of the 1988 Firearms (Amendment) Bill, noted that 'the logical inconsistency of the Government proposals was inescapable' (Yardley and Stevenson, 1988). Rather strangely, in the light of subsequent events, after Hungerford, both the Police Federation and ACPO had come to the conclusion that additional controls on section 1 firearms (rifles and handguns) 'would be unproductive' (Yardley, 1988).

In the event, although the shooting lobby was able to win some important concessions as the Bill passed through Parliament (one of these, the establishment of a Firearms Consultative Committee, we will discuss later) the resulting legislation satisfied almost no-one. For gun control campaigners the legislation had not gone far enough and completely overlooked the handgun problem. In the view of the shooting lobby the Act achieved no social purpose by imposing an irrelevant and irritating series of controls upon legitimate sports shooters. For Kopel (1992b) however, one positive result of the 1988 legislation had been the way it had galvanised the British shooting organisations into becoming a more effective political lobby. Increasingly they sought to take the initiative in arguing a case for limiting the existing restrictions upon civilian access to 'sporting' firearms (Jackson, 1988). Likewise a rather more thorough and ideologically driven critique of the Firearms (Amendment) Bill was compiled by Yardley and Stevenson on behalf of the resurrected Shooters' Rights Association. This document covered the history of the UK's firearm legislation. It discussed a number of philosophical issues relating to firearms in society, drawing attention to the English origins of the 'right to bear arms' (Munday, 1988a) and articulating a more contemporary case for 'shooters' rights'. The publication concluded with the SRA's own alternative recommendations, including the suggestion that research be commissioned to consider the effectiveness of the systems of firearm regulation practised in the UK. Such proposals might well be considered fairly mild by comparison with others floated at the time (Yardley and Stevenson, 1988).

Civilian disarmament and social change

Despite the ambiguity of the evidence concerning successive governments' long-term plans for firearms, this has not tempered the frequency with which claims about 'civilian disarmament' have been made. As more restrictive licensing and higher fees have contributed to a fall of nearly one-third in the number of firearm certificates on issue between 1968 and 1992, shooters' resentment against 'civilian disarmament by stealth' has grown. Indeed, Greenwood claimed to have identified an implicit 'civilian disarmament process' operating before 1968. The subsequent Green Paper of 1973 merely served to confirm his suspicions. The thrust of Greenwood's analysis, having added up the hours devoted to the firearms control and inspection process while dealing with largely law abiding sports shooters, was to question whether this was an appropriate or efficient use of police time – or even a job for the police at all (Greenwood, 1972: 226–233). Complaints against the firearm control system have continued. Reading the commentaries in many of the UK's gun and shooting magazines during the early 1990s a definite impression is conveyed of a seemingly beleaguered minority defending their rights and their sport against the uncaring, alien, heavy-handed central state. After 1993, however, the number of firearm certificates issued began to rise once again as newer shooting disciplines began to take hold in the UK. A more extensive discussion of these issues, arising once more during the UK's most recent firearms control debate, following the Dunblane shootings, is undertaken in the penultimate chapter.

Greenwood concludes his study on firearms control in the UK, essentially the only comprehensive study of this question, with a seeming paradox:

> Half a century of strict controls on pistols has ended, perversely, with a far greater use of [firearms] in crime than ever before. ... No matter how one approaches the figures, one is forced to the rather startling conclusion that the use of firearms in crime was very much less when there were no controls of any sort and when anyone, convicted criminal or lunatic, could buy any type of firearm without restriction.
>
> (Greenwood: 1972)

But then, he adds, 'we do not know how much worse this would have been if there had been no controls' (Greenwood, 1972: 243). Greenwood then proceeds to explore this question and the potential consequences of dismantling existing firearm controls by reference to the criminal use of shotguns before 1968 (when they were first brought into the licensing system). Greenwood argues that, although shotguns were unrestricted until 1968 they were only used in a small number of offences. Although he criticised the statistical evidence available, he argued that, 'legislation has failed to bring under control substantial numbers of firearms, and it certainly cannot be claimed that strict controls have reduced the use of firearms in crime'. Finally, he concluded, 'it is possible to build up a sound case for abolishing or substantially reducing controls' (Greenwood, 1972: 245). And for good measure, he adds that much police time and effort is wasted in processing and licensing firearm applications, while seemingly pointless controls antagonise the law abiding, discredit the law and increase the risk that gun owners will flout the regulations or seek to obtain weapons illegally.

A contrary perspective to Greenwood's conclusion finds support from an unlikely American source. First, though, it is worth noting that Greenwood's attempted rebuttal of the efficacy of firearms controls begins by consideration of the specific case of shotguns but then extends to embrace all other firearms as well. This shift in the argument appears invalid for a number of reasons. To begin with, when shotguns were the most numerous and the least restricted, they were the type of firearm most often turned to criminal uses, but they are, being much larger and less concealable (even when 'sawn-off'), far less suitable for many criminal purposes. The firearm most often involved in criminal activity during the past two to three decades has been the handgun, a weapon subjected to strict control for well over half a century. Furthermore, increasing criminal resort to handguns over the past twenty to thirty years has occurred independently of British firearms controls. Even so, by regulating the gun trade, the strict controls operated in the UK have substantially curtailed the size of the British gun stock. This has ensured (though obviously rather imperfectly) that access to weapons has been tightly circumscribed thereby limiting the leakage (through theft or fraud) of firearms from the legal to the illegal pools. Each measure obviously plays a valuable public safety function. Though shooters have often voiced complaints about the ways in which firearms controls have impinged upon themselves and their sport, legal gun owners in the UK have overwhelmingly tended to responsibly comply with the firearms licensing system. Reflecting the largely collective and 'consensual' culture which has prevailed in issues of weapons control policy in the UK, shooters clearly ignored the urgings of their more militant colleagues to defy or boycott the regulations emerging after Dunblane. In one sense they had to, defying the new legislation might have implied that shooters were not the civic-minded and responsible group they had always claimed to be.

Raising these more cultural and contextual issues, in response to Greenwood, however, we encounter an unlikely source of support. Greenwood's argument makes the point that firearms have moved from a context of limited controls to tighter and tighter control regimes – while armed crime has continued to rise. The case of shotguns is clearest, they were unrestricted before 1968 but then became subject to licensing and inspection arrangements. As we have seen, Greenwood tends to run the argument concerning the alleged ineffectiveness of shotgun controls along with a more general observation about ineffective firearm controls. But it is not the case that, over recent decades, the social control of firearms has become simply and one-dimensionally more restrictive. In fact there are grounds for suggesting that, in more recent years, the crucial shift might have been in another direction. Legal controls might have tightened, fees increased and criminal penalties extended but, certainly during the early 1990s, more people were taking up pistol shooting and more shooting clubs were opening. Likewise, the Home Office were considering the adoption of more streamlined procedures for the licensing and inspection of shooters and their clubs, including the delegation of a greater responsibility for regulating the sport to shooting club officers themselves.

In a second sense, the demographic context of shooting has also been changing significantly. It is not that there were no social controls – or even weak social controls – upon firearms, just that the most significant ones might have been 'extra-legal' in character. Kopel, in his expansive cross-cultural study of firearms controls, makes the point that in the UK there has been a prevailing assumption that firearms, and shotguns in particular, were a 'toy of the landed gentry' (Kopel, 1992b: 78). Statistically, he notes, this perception is not actually borne out by data on weapon ownership, although shotgun ownership has traditionally been much more widespread in rural areas, where the gun has played a role in agricultural pest control aside from its more exclusive involvement in game shooting. Armed crime, by contrast, was much more common in urban areas, although the nature of firearm ownership was changing. As the pattern of firearm ownership began to shift away from its traditionally 'landed-privileged' and/or 'rural-occupational' bases so the cultural exclusivity of firearms and shooting also began to change. Alongside this 'quasi-democratic' influence affecting firearm ownership came an equivalent consumer pressure reflected in the media representation of firearms as powerful cultural commodities. We discuss some of these issues in a later chapter but, for the UK, the issue might be seen in terms of the apparently growing attraction of firearms, as components of a culturally mediated hegemonic masculinity (Sparks, 1996). At a time when community and familial controls (especially a number intrinsically linked to the 'productive-citizen' status of men) were said to be weakening and fragmenting, firearms – legal or illegal – might have seemed to offer access to a type of masculine power to men whose orientations to firearms embraced both the criminal and the non-criminal and included both psychological and ontological motivations (Connell, 1995).

A further indication of changes in the British attitude to firearms arose in respect of the burgeoning markets in imitation, replica and deactivated firearms. Even in the 1970s, controversy had surrounded incidents in which offenders carrying replica weapons had been shot and killed by armed response officers. During the 1980s, ACPO and the Police Federation began to press for the prohibition of such 'imitation weapons' (Fry, 1989, 1991). As has been argued already, a significant proportion of 'armed robberies' appear to be committed with 'replica' handguns (Morrison and O'Donnell, 1994, 1997) and, at least until tougher specifications were introduced covering the deactivation of firearms, police were beginning to uncover evidence of a thriving illegal cottage industry reactivating deactivated weapons. Ironically, the sudden expansion of this illegal cottage industry stemmed directly from the 1988 Firearms (Amendment) Act, which had declassified deactivated weapons. As a concession to the shooting lobby, section 8 of the Act 1988 allowed for the approved deactivation of (now prohibited) automatic and semi-automatic weapons (Home Office, 1989). Appropriately deactivated weapons were no longer classed as firearms, hence they did not require a firearm licence at all. In time, however, police commentators became concerned that criminals were exploiting this 'loophole' in the regulations. A deactivated machine gun might cost only £300 but some could be returned to working order. Between 1993 and 1995 fourteen incidents were reported involving deactivated weapons including two killings, three woundings and two further cases where shots had been fired (McSmith, 1994). Police and a number of opposition MPs stepped up their pressure for a toughening of the regulations on deactivated weapons and, in due course, tougher specifications (but no overall prohibition) were introduced for deactivated weapons during 1995 (Millward, 1994; Bowditch, 1995).

However, defending their corner, shooting correspondents continued to reject the need for any prohibition on replica firearms (Maybanks and Yardley, 1992). Proposing to leave open this 'supply-side' of the firearms equation, they argued that there were already so many illegal weapons in circulation that prohibiting replicas would have little effect. Unfortunately, Morrison and O'Donnell's evidence suggested otherwise. And controversy is still ignited every time police officers shoot persons later found to be carrying only replica firearms.

Against the general context of the series of seismic cultural and demographic shifts referred to earlier, legal regulation alone may have a rather limited purchase. We have already noted changes in British shooting sports, changes in firearms industry marketing, alleged security deficits resulting from European integration and the impact of the ending of the Cold War upon firearm trafficking. In such a context, liberal thinking often tends to regard the effort to 'make people good by law' as generally doomed to failure. To coin a phrase, 'fraternity cannot be created by Act of Parliament' (Joseph and Sumption, 1979: 121). And so it may be with firearms control. Even so, firearms controls have certainly restricted the size of the British gun stock and regulated routine firearm dealing and possession. However, aside from severely restricting the supply side (obviously an issue of no small significance), they have had relatively little to do with and have exercised little control over the growing use of *illegal* firearms by offenders. Equally, they can never have been expected to have much bearing upon the wider cultural influences relating to firearms. These are, by and large, different social control questions. Kopel (an American gun rights advocate) concludes his examination of British firearms control in broad agreement with Greenwood. He issues a caution to his fellow citizens who might be 'misled' into thinking that strict gun controls in the UK have anything to do with low rates of violent crime in the UK. Firearms controls, he says, have had 'little net impact upon crime prevention. … Internalised social controls, rather than gun controls, seem to better explain the low crime rate, because changes in social controls more closely parallel the changes in the crime rate' (Kopel, 1992b: 106–107).

In other words, strict gun controls do not necessarily imply low rates of criminal violence or even diminishing rates of gun-related offending (such claims remain controversial, however, and we consider the evidence in more detail later). Nevertheless, it need not follow that an opposite claim holds true, that liberal gun laws mean low rates of gun crime. The cultural, regional and demographic variations within the USA are enormous but liberal gun laws have certainly not brought diminishing criminal violence. Furthermore, the social, cultural and situational factors associated with a high incidence of firearm violence in the USA (Zimring and Hawkins, 1997) are also the factors associated with the UK's own emerging firearm problems. Social and cultural factors contributed to the climate of disciplined collectivism which paved the way for the UK's rather unique relations of 'consensual' social control – or 'policing by consent' – but now, given the apparent relaxation of a range of these cultural restraints pertaining to masculinity, violence and tolerance (Reiner, 1992b) it would seem a rather reckless experiment in public safety to propose the relaxation of existing British firearm controls. After Dunblane, of course, any such proposal would seem politically quite untenable, notwithstanding the broadly 'American' discourse on individuality, rights and guns coming to influence the British firearms debate. We now turn to consider the firearm question in its American historical and cultural contexts.

3 The making of the American 'gun culture'

In 1970, Richard Hofstadter began his seminal article on the USA as a gun culture with the observation that the USA 'is the only modern industrial urban nation that persists in maintaining a gun culture'. He commented upon the extent of firearm ownership in American society and noted a disposition toward violence in American life which was then (as now) causing acute concern. Then he added, 'and yet [the USA] is apparently determined to remain the most passive of all the major countries in the matter of gun control. Many otherwise intelligent Americans cling with pathetic stubbornness to the notion that the people's right to bear arms is the greatest protection of their individual rights and a firm safeguard of democracy'. Moreover, it appeared, many Americans seemed to hold to this belief whatever the costs (Hofstadter, 1970: 4).

Hofstadter was by no means the first to reach such a conclusion. A British journalist, resident in Washington, commented in 1966, that 'however much I may love and admire America, its gun laws come near to ruling it out of civilised society' (Harris, 1968). This was very much a dominant liberal perspective on the gun question at the end of a decade which had seen three high profile political assassinations, rising crime and violence, increasing racial conflicts and the passing of the first federal gun control legislation for three decades. Other commentators replied that the problem was not guns, as such, but a supposed propensity to armed violence, detectable throughout American history and which, in more recent years, had distilled into the modern American 'gun culture'. Yet, while concerns about violence have fuelled the immediate policy question, American attachments to firearms obviously go much deeper.

Hunting, history and frontier culture

An enthusiasm for hunting as a leisure pursuit is a vital aspect of the cultural legacy of firearms in the USA. Hunting is one among a wide range of issues discussed by Slotkin in the context of an all-embracing idea of 'frontier culture'. Hunters are said to undergo a spiritual and emotional replenishment through their immersion in the wilderness where skill and ingenuity (distinctly masculine ideals) enable them to overcome the challenges of nature (Slotkin, 1996). Other writers have come to understand the American 'attachment to firearms' from a more phenomenological perspective. The deep cultural legacy, with its orientations to the frontier and manhood, is crucial but, for Tonso, there were also questions concerning technological mastery and geography, also questions of subsistence and self-defence, which faced settlers at the point of rapid westward expansion. This combination of factors – as well as the vast expanses of remaining 'wilderness' containing game large enough to merit hunting and shooting – help explain the grip this great American pastime has continued to exert on many sections of American manhood (Tonso, 1982).

Even so, things may be changing and, writing in the November 1995 edition of *Texas Parks and Wildlife*, Bigony anticipates a change in the American psyche. Beneath an attractive, soft focus photograph of 'father and son' hunting together, wearing identical check shirts, huntsman pants and accessories, runs the following caption: 'Traditionally, youngsters learned the joys and rewards of hunting from their fathers and grandfathers. But due to changing demographics and changes in family structures, many of today's families do not have the male role-model to pass along the hunting tradition' (Bigony, 1995). Perhaps the family that shoots together, stays together, although the article went on to develop an argument that more women ought to take up hunting in order to help preserve the tradition.

A fear that hunting might be dying out – squeezed, on the one hand, by environmental, animal rights and gun control pressures and, on the other, the loss of habitats or animal species deemed worthy of hunting – has begun to surface in recent years (Diaz, 1999: 92). This has brought some rather mixed blessings. With a shrinking market for hunting weapons (rifles and shotguns), firearms manufacturers, fearing for their profits, began to promote handguns far more vigorously while shifting the orientation of their advertising from sport, leisure and the rural environment towards self-defence on the streets. It is difficult to regard this shift, from a traditional, even civilising, rural firearms culture to an armed and dangerous urban gun culture as anything but deeply problematic.

Even so, a superficial examination of American orientations to firearms might suggest a fairly seamless transition here – just as a generation of Hollywood's maverick cowboys slipped effortlessly from their western landscapes into identical roles as tough city cops in a later film genre. Likewise the USA's media industries have undoubtedly played a major role in sustaining the imagery, values and characters associated with America's western frontier by constantly recycling America's western traditions. Thus the wider debate on firearms in American society reverberates with the history, folklore and political philosophy of the USA's past. The debate draws upon complex constitutional debates about citizens, freedom and citizen militias from the late eighteenth century, through to the more practical considerations of personal safety in the wilderness of the early settlers. Patterns of life on the frontier of the developing nation added their own particular emphases and justifications to American attitudes to firearms and violence (Einstadter, 1978). As Brown puts it, 'A cluster of beliefs mentally programmed westerners to commit violence: the doctrine of "no duty to retreat"; the imperative of personal self-redress; the homestead ethic; the ethic of individual enterprise; the Code of the West; and the ideology of vigilantism' (Brown, 1994: 393). Subsequently, the distorting and glamourising lenses of Hollywood added their own unique gloss to this 'cowboy culture'.

The modern firearms industry also plays a major role in sustaining the gun culture. Gun industry advertising seldom misses an opportunity to invoke the past. As Diaz notes:

> despite the colder realities of the business, the gun industry packages firearms in the sepia tint of nostalgia, conjuring up the Western frontier, fathers and sons hunting at the turn of the century, and grand moments of martial history. … For decades, the gun industry has portrayed itself as a repository and guardian of fundamental US cultural values.
>
> (Diaz, 1999: 85)

The briefest glance at mainstream American gun magazines reveals many images of the cowboy culture and the western frontier – even alongside the most sophisticated modern semi-automatic handguns and articles on contemporary firearm issues. A particularly interesting example of firearm publishing's ability to interweave fact and fiction came in 1995 when *Guns & Ammo* magazine offered its readers the chance to purchase a 'special edition' of the Colt revolver 'as used by John Wayne in his cowboy films'. Yet this continuous invocation of the past and of traditional values obscures a crucial shift in the production, marketing and purchase of guns and, ultimately, in the uses to which guns are put in the USA. While tradition plays a vital role in legitimating contemporary patterns of firearm ownership, for many of the new urban-dwelling handgun owners, contemporary orientations to firearms seem driven by uniquely modern anxieties.

Firearms and violence

Notwithstanding the significance of firearms in American history and culture, it has been the continuing problem of firearm-related violence that has kept the gun close to the forefront of the USA's contemporary political agenda. However, one of the particular ironies of the gun control debate in the USA is the way in which traditional political positions become reversed. Many liberals support gun control policies conferring powers upon the state to regulate personal choices while conservatives become advocates for individual freedom (Kleck, 1991).

The modernist premise of a society founded by the gun was that, ultimately, it could dispense with the gun. By contrast, the uncertainty currently facing many Americans precisely concerns whether 'banning weapons will make their lives more or less dangerous' (Malcolm, 1994: 165). At the moment, many seem to be hedging their bets. According to McCaghy and Cernkovitch, 'a large segment of Americans want something done *about* guns; in the meantime they keep guns in case they have to do something *with* them' (McCaghy and Cernkovitch, 1987: 141).

In 1991 Kleck produced estimates suggesting an accumulated weapon stock of almost 200 million firearms in the USA. Long guns, shotguns and rifles accounted for around two-thirds of the civilian weapon stock but handguns constituted a fast growing proportion (Kleck, 1991: 17–21). Reviewing the available data on firearm ownership in the USA in 1978, Williams and McGrath found that a recent National Opinion Research Survey had suggested that almost a half of sampled households contained at least one firearm. This figure conformed to the rates of 43 to 50 per cent discovered in subsequent surveys and is consistent with Kleck's findings that 49 per cent of households owned guns. Furthermore, in households with guns, the mean number of guns owned was four, while the average handgun owner tended to have at least two (Kleck, 1991: 21). Interestingly, in view of much recent concern and press speculation about firearm distribution and violence, in 1978 the rate of legal ownership of firearms by blacks (32 per cent) fell significantly below that of whites (Williams and McGrath, 1978: 51–56). Of course, evidence such as this raises further questions about the extent of illegal possession of firearms. In any one year over 100,000 guns are stolen from private citizens, with a Police Foundation study suggesting that 'approximately 25 per cent of the criminal arsenal is made up of expensive handguns that were stolen from private citizens' (DeZee, 1978: 42).

The following comparisons are revealing, although they relate to a time *before* the rapid increase in American handgun offences. In 1983, while there were eight handgun killings in the UK, and thirty-five in Japan, there were a grand total of 9,014 in the USA (Bromhead, 1988). Subsequently, Justice Department statistics have shown that, in 1992, violent crimes involving handguns broke all previous records, rising almost 50 per cent above the annual average of the past five years. Handguns had been used in a grand total of 931,000 murders, rapes, robberies and assaults in 1992. This rising trend in firearm-related crime continued into 1993, a year in which the FBI Uniform Crime Reports recorded over 23,000 homicides, some 16,189 undertaken with firearms, of which no less than 13,252 were shootings with handguns (Davis and El Nasser, 1994). Firearms are used as the murder weapon in 96 per cent of killings of policemen. Morris and Hawkins earlier concluded their own review of grim statistics with the observation: 'Since the beginning of this century, some three-quarters of a million people have been killed in the United States by privately owned guns, 30 per cent more than in all the wars in which this country has been involved in its entire history. In sum and in short, the populace is armed with a dangerous weapon' (Morris and Hawkins, 1970: 65).

McCaghy and Cernkovitch show that in the USA in 1985 approximately 60 per cent of all homicides (including suicides) were firearm related, while in 43 per cent of murders the cause of death is a handgun, in 7 per cent a shotgun and in 4 per cent another form of firearm. Figures we have already considered showed that handguns were responsible for 70 per cent of American firearm homicides. However, some proportion of these shootings will involve the defensive use of firearms and the figures will include shootings by police officers and other security personnel. The authors conclude, however, that the evidence on causes of death in the USA points to the clear conclusion that, 'from 1960 to 1975, the increase in the number of homicides was largely the result of an increase in firearm homicides' (McCaghy and Cernkovitch, 1987).

More recent work by Diaz goes further and becomes more specific: the increasing lethality of high capacity semi-automatic pistols, vigorously marketed by the firearms industry since the mid-1980s, was largely responsible for a surge in firearm violence on the streets. 'The street-level effect of the so-called "nines" was evident in Chicago where more people were murdered with 9-mm pistols during 1992 than were slain with the same gun during all of the 1980s' (Diaz, 1999:104). Furthermore, a new trend was observable. When the weapon was a semi-automatic pistol, victims were often shot several times.

> In short ... pistols began killing more people than revolvers had, and their enhanced firepower (especially more rounds) was directly reflected in more lethal injuries on US streets. The number of pistols manufacturers made increased by 92 per cent from 1985 to 1992, and deaths by handguns increased by 48 per cent, from 8,902 to 13,220. The number of juveniles arrested for weapons violations more than doubled between 1985 and 1993.
>
> (Diaz, 1999: 103–104)

Moreover, during the 1990s, firearms manufacturers have continued to ratchet-up the calibre, power and lethality of the semi-automatic handguns destined for both the law enforcement and civilian concealed-carry markets. This has resulted in what Diaz has called a 'spiral of lethality' fed by gun industry marketing and a recurring argument, typically surfacing whenever police officers are shot, that the police are being 'outgunned' by offenders. The irony is, however, that any newer and more powerful weapons (even those originally designed for military or law enforcement markets) invariably find their way very quickly onto the civilian market to become, in turn, part of the USA's law and order equation which the police are often left to solve. In this sense, the 'spiral of lethality' is very much market driven. While firearm manufacturers like the credibility which comes from selling their guns to the police, their real objective is the much bigger and more lucrative civilian market (Diaz, 1999: 89–141).

Attempting to account for such widespread inter-personal lethality, Brown has argued that, since the American Revolution, violence has been a constant feature in American social and political life. He argues that the frequent resort of Americans to violence has to be understood as the result of a long process of historical and cultural conditioning. He explains this in the following terms. 'Repeated episodes of violence, going back into our colonial past have imprinted upon our citizenry a propensity to violence. Our history has produced and reinforced a strain of violence which has strongly tinctured our national experience' (Brown, 1975: vii). A great deal of American violence has comprised socially conservative forms of vigilante resistance.

Armed vigilantism, according to Brown:

> arose as a response to a typical American problem: the absence of law and order in a frontier region. On the frontier, the normal foundations of a stable orderly society – churches, schools, cohesive community life – were either absent or present only in rough makeshift forms. The regular, legal system of law enforcement often proved to be woefully inadequate. ... In frontier states, law and order was often a tenuous thing. Outlaws ... took every advantage they could of the social disorganisation stemming from the newness of the settlement and the weakness of the traditional institutions of state, society and church.
>
> (Brown, 1975: 94)

Geographical difficulties, transportation problems and the cost of financing law and order were also part of the equation – self-motivated vigilante action was cheap, informal and highly flexible – but also rather arbitrary. Even late in the nineteenth century when systems of law enforcement had been established in most areas, Brown shows how vigilantes often established parallel systems of community justice alongside the official system and sometimes with the open collusion of law officers (Brown, 1975: 122–159).

Following the War of Independence and alongside the 'frontier culture', which Slotkin (1992) shows to be deeply embedded in the American psyche, attitudes towards armed violence and the deployment of force within society were largely laid down throughout a particular series of violent conflicts: (1) the American Civil War, (2) the wars against the American Indians, (3) the conclusion of the 'war in the west', otherwise known as the Western Civil War of Incorporation, which saw the victory of conservative urban and industrial interests and the consolidating authority of capital (Trachtenberg, 1982; Brown, 1991) and (4) the rapid development, in the 1880s, of the National Guard and allied policing methods throughout the northern industrial states to combat growing labour militancy (Weiss, 1978). Subsequent twentieth-century influences might include: (5) the USA's unfortunate experiment with prohibition in the 1920s, the crimogenic consequences of which – gangsterism, mob-violence and the use of machine guns in criminal activity – outlived the Volstead Act itself (Helmer, 1970; Vizzard, 1997; Behr, 1997) and (6) American experiences of two world wars and the more uncertain reaction to perceptions of defeat and betrayal in Vietnam (Hellman, 1986; Gibson, 1994). A final influence, and still a very live issue, concerns the question of racialised violence in the USA. As a number of commentators have noted this question is itself linked intimately to the contrasting 'frontiers' encountered within key phases of American history (Slotkin, 1992). In some ways patterns of racial violence, now involving firearms, have become more pressing problems in many of the USA's sharply divided cities – the new 'killing fields' (Wright *et al.*, 1992). A crucial feature of contemporary racial violence, however is not its historical inter-racial dimension but, on the contrary, the concentration of firearm violence and patterns of lethal victimisation (gun-related homicides) *within* African-American communities (Canada, 1995; Zimring and Hawkins, 1997; see Figure 3.1).

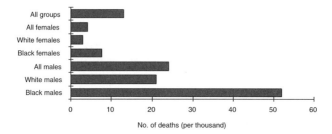

Figure 3.1   US gun-related deaths by sex and race in 1988: deaths per thousand of the population

Sources: Zimring and Hawkins, 1987; US National Center for Health Statistics

However such arguments about the inherently violent character of American culture can be rather double-edged. A society like this might be one in which a measure of firearms control would be considered prudent. This, at least, was the general tenor of the conclusions reached in the majority of the criminological and policy-relevant research undertaken during the 1960s.

The report, *Firearms and Violence in American Life* (Newton and Zimring, 1968) submitted to the US National Commission on the Causes and Prevention of Violence drew the following, quite unambiguous, conclusions. The bottom line was, the more firearms there were, the more firearm violence there tended to be. The proportion of gun use in violence appeared to rise and fall with the level of gun ownership in a community. The distribution of handguns was a particular problem. While less than a third of American civilian-held firearms were handguns, these weapons were used in over three-quarters of firearm homicides. Cities with a high proportion of gun use in one crime tended to have high proportions of gun use in other crimes. While many people appeared to place their faith in firearms for self-defence, householders seriously over-estimated the effectiveness of guns for home defence purposes. Ownership of a gun might have offered a degree of reassurance but this was largely illusory. Firearms kept at home were most likely to be used against other members of the household – even excluding the additional suicide and accident risks they posed. On the other side of the coin, widespread availability of firearms made it easier for extremist groups and offenders to gain access to guns because there was significant 'leakage' of firearms from legitimate to illegitimate owners. Finally, firearms appeared to facilitate violence and increase the lethality of confrontations. In response, the authors proposed a comprehensive catalogue of firearm control proposals (Newton and Zimring, 1968: xi–xv).

The authors of the National Commission Report voiced their alarm about the sharp increases in civilian firearms ownership (in the ten years after 1958, 30 million firearms were added to the civilian stockpile, annual sales of rifles had doubled while handgun sales had quadrupled). All this occurred during a decade characterised by sharp increases in crime and violence, race riots in major cities and increasing firearm involvement in crime. While rifles and shotguns might be purchased for 'sporting purposes' – essentially hunting – handguns were not thought to be 'sporting guns' thus the sharp increases in handgun ownership raised a number of pressing criminal justice and public health policy questions.

Accordingly, the National Commission went on to propose a four-tiered strategy of controls. This involved, firearms registration, prohibition of gun ownership by certain classes of people, increased penalties for the use of guns in crime and more restrictive firearm licensing. No one set of measures was thought likely to succeed in isolation, but the central plank of the strategy was thought to lie in the restrictive licensing of handguns: 'We believe, on the basis of all the evidence before us, that reducing the availability of the handgun will reduce firearms violence' (National Commission, 1969: 170–179). A series of more specific policy measures were then put forward designed to achieve these aims. The National Commission was broadly supported in its gun control ambitions by the recommendations of the 1967 Report of the President's Commission on Law Enforcement (President's Commission, 1967) and by the work of Morris and Hawkins in *The Honest Politician's Guide to Crime Control* (Morris and Hawkins, 1970). Such texts, key positional statements of a social democratic American criminology, were taking on the American gun culture. Above all they sought a reduction in the country's overall gun inventory, particularly its stock of civilian-owned handguns. They refused to acknowledge there were any social benefits to be derived from a society in which citizens were armed and potentially lethal to one another.

The development of this pro-control academic culture, the passage of the 1968 Federal Gun Control Act and opinion polls indicating broad popular support for yet further controls, were enough to convince Kennett and Anderson that the USA's attachment to the gun was beginning to wane (Kennett and Anderson, 1975). Even in 1981, Franklin Zimring, one of the USA's foremost pro-control academics, attempted to predict the future of gun control into the next century. His optimistic analysis suggested that, 'if history is an appropriate guide, the next thirty years will bring a national handgun strategy' (Zimring, 1981). The strategy, he claimed, would comprise three elements: (1) federal restrictions on handgun transfers and a de facto national licensing system, (2) tighter gun controls in many localities with an increasing number adopting handgun bans and (3) increasing federal law enforcement assistance in states and cities where gun violence problems were especially acute and where attempts were being made to enforce gun control policies beyond the 'national minimum' (Zimring, 1981). Above all, Zimring hoped that a growing body of popular opinion would continue to support more restrictive firearms controls. However, there were signs that the tide of opinion might be beginning to turn.

The politics of guns

In the mid-1970s, the USA's National Rifle Association, the country's foremost pro-gun political lobby began to mobilise to resist the developing climate of gun control. By 1974, two newly formed pressure groups, The National Coalition to Ban the Handgun and Handgun Control Inc. (known as the National Council to Control Handguns until 1978) were lobbying for federal legislation to extend the handgun controls contained in the 1968 Gun Control Act (Gottlieb, 1986: Vizzard, 1997). The Act had banned mail order sales of firearms and the importation of foreign-made, cheap, low-quality handguns – the so-called 'Saturday Night Specials' – although such weapons could still be manufactured in the USA. The gun control groups wanted an end to the production of 'Saturday Night Specials' and an outright ban on the sale of handguns to civilians. Handgun Control Inc. later came to regard this position as politically unwinnable and retreated to a position favouring much stricter controls on handgun sales, registration, licensing and waiting periods (Carter, 1997). Concurrent with the development of the new lobby groups, legislation was being proposed in Washington to outlaw the 'Saturday Night Specials' and prohibit private ownership of handguns.

For most of its history, the NRA, formed in the early 1870s, had played two principal roles. It began, according to Davidson (1993), as a quasi-governmental league devoted to rifle-training and military preparedness. The organisation was given access to surplus military firearms which were discounted to its members and constituent organisations. This direct governmental subsidy was one of the chief reasons for the organisation's growth in the early years. Later, the NRA evolved into a more broad-based membership support organisation catering to the needs and interests of a wide range of hunters and sporting shooters. In the 1970s it adopted a further role and, alongside a concerted effort to boost its grassroots membership, became a hard-nosed political lobbying organisation standing for 'the right to bear arms'. Following an internal coup which significantly altered the political complexion of the organisation's leadership, the NRA established a lobbying organisation (the Institute for Legislative Action), a Political Victory Fund and a Firearms Legal Defense Fund and began to adopt a more belligerent approach to the defence of shooters' rights. For some time the NRA had been able to maintain a close alliance with the 'law enforcement community' (police officers unions, associations of police chiefs, criminal justice pressure groups) because of its tough positions on 'law and order' – in particular, firearm-related offending. Unfortunately for the NRA, however, its increasingly inflexible position on the right to bear arms – all arms, any arms – caused this alliance to fragment when it lobbied against proposals to outlaw so-called 'cop-killer' bullets and assault weapons. Not unreasonably, many police officers objected to the NRA's support for weapons and ammunition which, they felt, placed themselves in greater danger (Spitzer, 1995; Vizzard, 1997).

Within this increasingly politicised environment of the American gun control debate, came an increasingly sceptical academic commentary on the apparent ineffectiveness of firearms controls. Where the social democratic criminology of the late 1960s seemed to have few doubts – more guns, especially more handguns, meant more gun crimes – the newer wave of academic commentators seemed rather less convinced. A new chapter in the debate had opened. Many of the standard assumptions about gun control received serious critical attention for the first time. An article by Murray, in 1975, attempted to examine the relationships between access to handguns, the existence of varying types of gun control laws and levels of gun-related violence. Reviewing existing research findings and examining data relating to all fifty American states he argued: 'Gun control laws do not have any apparent effect on a large enough proportion of the population or on those critical elements of the population who are associated with violent acts to effectively limit access to handguns by those who want them … the relationship between gun laws and crime rates is non-existent' (Murray, 1975: 90). Confronting one of the central planks in the gun control argument, he added that, 'it seems quite unlikely that the relative availability of handguns plays a significant part in explaining why some states have higher rates of acts of violence associated with firearms than others'. And then he concluded, 'these findings are a direct contradiction of the widely held opinion concerning the relationship of firearms, gun control laws and crime rates; although, of course, more research is needed in this area' (Murray, 1975: 91). The academic community soon began to respond to this call for further research.

The emerging new generation of gun control research differed in respect of the level of complexity it brought to the analysis. For a start, 'gun control' appeared a much oversimplified concept. There were many different types of gun control. Measures varied in their effectiveness and may have many intended and unintended consequences. Research began to throw light onto some of these complex issues. Take, for instance, Cook's cautious conclusions on the findings of research into the impact of gun availability on violent crime patterns:

> If robbers could be deprived of guns, the robbery-murder rate would fall, the robbery-injury rate would rise and robberies would be redistributed to some extent from less to more vulnerable targets. The assaultive murder rate would decline, with the greatest reductions involving the least vulnerable types of victims. The overall assault rate might well increase. [However] none of this evidence is conclusive.
>
> (Cook, 1981)

And, he might have added, much of it is contested. The general point was that any gun control measure faced policy-makers with difficult choices, choices they might have to take with incomplete knowledge and facing unforeseen consequences. Moreover, much as in any other sphere of policy-making, interventions would, at best, be only partially successful and there would invariably be opportunity costs. A simple faith in an all or nothing, 'gun control' solution appeared misplaced. Reviewing Washington DC's 1975 Firearms Control Regulations, allegedly the toughest gun control laws in the USA, Jones was forced to agree, gun control 'is no panacea for crime control' (Jones, 1981).

Researching American gun control

There is now an enormous body of empirical and statistical gun control research exploring the issues involved. In the following few paragraphs my objective is simply to review some of the main themes and issues emerging in the developing debate. More extensive surveys of the literature (incorporating a range of perspectives) might be found in Wright *et al.* (1983) Kates and Kaplan (1984), Zimring and Hawkins (1987), Kleck (1991, 1997), Spitzer (1995, chapter 5), and Zimring and Hawkins (1997).

There are many different types of gun control laws of greater or lesser restrictiveness in relation to different types of guns or different types of would-be gun owners. These laws might be more or less easily circumvented and, in different localities, the police might enforce these laws with greater or lesser enthusiasm. Factors such as these might all have a bearing upon whether a law achieves its stated aim of restricting legal ownership of certain types of weapons. Other factors might then influence whether any changes in the availability of legal firearms had any impact upon those weapons most likely to be employed in crime – illegal firearms. The laws themselves would be implemented in differing contexts where different attitudes to firearms prevailed – the urban/rural divide was particularly significant. Next, a whole host of contextual factors might limit the effectiveness of gun controls. For instance, tough controls in one area might be undermined by more relaxed controls in neighbouring jurisdictions and, however tough the controls might be on paper, criminal justice agencies would find it hardest to enforce the controls among the most determinedly criminal populations. Many years of a 'war against drugs' did not prevent the emergence of a thriving drug culture in many areas causing Kaplan (1981), among others, to consider the potential costs of gun control strategies. General disarmament might indirectly concentrate gun ownership among the criminal, or particular offenders, while disarming robbers might simply displace robbers onto 'softer' or more vulnerable targets (Skogan, 1978) or require robbers to actually use more violence (rather than simply pointing their guns to intimidate) against victims (Kleck, 1991).

Proponents of gun control have replied that the effectiveness of much firearms control was compromised by a variety of factors, that the laws were easily evaded, poorly enforced or, in any event, inherently rather weak (DeZee, 1978; Larson, 1994). Commentators coined a phrase, 'the politics of ineffectiveness' (Leff and Leff, 1981) to describe early American gun control strategies, but there remains a strong sense among supporters of gun control that this notion still applies. Many states strengthened their basic screening programmes for would-be handgun buyers but, as the market for handguns was expanding rapidly during the 1970s and 1980s, there was a recognition that without a more comprehensive national registration system such controls would remain limited (Cook and Blose, 1981). However, existing law forbids the ATF (the Bureau of Alcohol, Tobacco and Firearms, the agency responsible for enforcing federal firearms laws) using its database to construct a federal firearms register, so the possibility for further progress on that front appears unlikely (Larson, 1994;

Vizzard, 1995). The long-awaited federal 'instant check' system, introduced in 1998, was thought to offer some benefit in regulating gun purchases, keeping handguns from offenders and other unsuitable persons, but research had already shown that offenders purchased their weapons from a wide range of unregulated sources (Moore, 1981). The new checking system simply does not apply to the vast array of legal gun sales between private persons or sales at gun shows and similar events – let alone an unspecified number of illegal gun sales in the USA's 'grey' or 'black' gun markets (Diaz, 1999).

Finally, for all of these reasons, different gun control laws might appear to be more or less effective against certain types of armed offenders or certain types of firearm-related offending. For instance, Deutsch and Alt examined the effectiveness of a new gun control law in Boston, Massachusetts. In view of Massachusetts' own relatively more stringent gun purchase controls, 87 per cent of crime guns were acquired outside of the state. Therefore, the new law sought to target unlawful firearm possession by imposing a mandatory one year prison sentence for anyone carrying a firearm without an appropriate licence. The research attempted to assess whether any deterrent effect had been achieved. While the researchers found evidence of a 27 per cent reduction in armed robberies in the months after the implementation of the new law, there were no reductions in homicide. In the short term, the researchers noted, the new law and its rigorous enforcement had achieved some deterrent effect but they recommended further evaluation in the future to see whether the deterrent effects were sustained (Deutsch and Alt, 1977). Studying the impact of the law over a longer period, however, Pierce and Bowers confirmed the short-term reduction in armed robbery but also found some evidence in weapon and offence displacement. They also found some evidence of a decline in gun homicides but concluded, nonetheless, that 'it was the publicity about the law's intent rather than the severity or certainty of the punishments actually imposed … that was responsible for the observed reduction in gun-related crimes' (Pierce and Bowers, 1981).

The impact of gun control laws upon offenders' behaviour has been equally unclear. Loftin and McDowall examined the impact of a new mandatory sentencing law on firearm violence in Detroit (Loftin and McDowall, 1981). The law, introduced in 1977, established a mandatory two-year prison sentence for any felony committed with a firearm. A slogan, 'one with a gun gets you two' accompanied the introduction of the legislation which, according to Loftin and McDowall, was politically popular because it did not infringe legitimate firearms ownership and the burden of the penalty fell directly upon offenders. Unfortunately, the legislation appeared to have very little impact upon violent gun-related offending in the city. The authors discovered a number of factors which tended to limit the effectiveness of such laws. They concluded that, despite the clear aims of the new legislation, there was still a great deal of scope within the enforcement, prosecution and sentencing processes for moderating the impact of such laws, a point later confirmed by Lizotte and Zatz (1986). Furthermore, the Detroit law was both narrow in its scope (applying only to the commission of offences with firearms and not the unlawful carrying or possession of firearms) and limited in its effect (proposing only a 2-year sentence enhancement). Kleck has also reviewed the effectiveness of sentence enhancement and mandatory sentencing for firearm-related offending. While confirming their popularity, some thirty-nine states had sentence enhancement provisions in 1980, he rather doubted their efficacy. During a period in which the USA was investing heavily in 'custodial solutions' and average sentence lengths were growing, sentence enhancements became overwhelmed by a more general 'toughening up'. In particular, sentence enhancements might seem relatively meaningless for the growing number of 'life' sentenced offenders. Anyway, according to Kleck, the USA simply did not have the prison capacity to incarcerate every firearm-carrying offender. 'We could empty the prisons of every killer, rapist, drug dealer, and other offender who did not use a gun in the crime for which they were imprisoned, make each weapons violator serve just one year, and still not have enough prison space to make each violent gun crime arrestee serve even three years in prison. Legislative intent is obviously impossible to implement, so criminal justice agencies are forced to subvert that intent' (Kleck, 1991: 339).

However, in addition to these more practical and empirical considerations relating to the evaluation and statistical modelling of the effects of firearms control law, other, rather more partisan, commentators began to enter the debate. Noting that any measure of law enforcement was typically the least effective against those likely to be the least inclined to obey the law, these commentators attacked gun control for its tendency to most effectively disarm the law-abiding. This was something of an oversimplification, but it had a basis in fact. According to Wright, gun control could be looked upon as a slur upon the responsibility and integrity of the USA's many millions of gun owners, the overwhelming majority of whom would only ever use their firearms for a legitimate sporting purpose (Wright, 1995). Although Wright himself eschewed a partisan approach to gun control research, many of his findings on the apparent ineffectiveness of gun control laws have been eagerly taken up by the gun lobby (Wright and Marston, 1975; Wright et al., 1983).

Likewise, while the pro-control lobby have continued to press for bans on 'Saturday-Night Specials' (small, cheap handguns) or, more generally, for the prohibition of the civilian ownership of any handgun, researchers closer to the gun lobby have argued that such laws could be self-defeating or counter-productive. Extending the 1968 Gun Control Act's prohibition on the import of 'small, cheap handguns' to include a ban on the domestic production of weapons would not, according to some commentators, constitute a feasible policy option (McClain, 1984). First, there is a degree of ambiguity about the definition of the 'Saturday Night Special'. (How small or how cheap is such a gun?) Second, small, cheap handguns do not appear to represent a distinct crime threat, more expensive weapons produced by some of the USA's prestige handgun manufacturers are just as likely to feature in the ATF's annual listings of top-ten crime guns (Diaz, 1999: 27–29). Finally, prohibiting small and cheap handguns might simply encourage offenders to obtain larger, more powerful and ultimately more lethal weapons. As Kleck argues, such a development could not be seen as a public policy gain (Kleck, 1991: 84–85). In any event, with the production of new weapons for concealed-carry and female customers, the market in firearms is shifting in a contrary direction. 'Stopping-power', compact size and concealability, magazine capacity, speed and simplicity of use are now the key selling points in a personal defence handgun. Moreover, Kates and Kleck have drawn similar kinds of conclusions in respect of proposals to ban the ownership of all handguns. Kates draws an analogy between a handgun ban and the USA's experience with alcohol prohibition and questions the value of a law which he believes likely to achieve the least compliance among the most criminally inclined while simultaneously preventing the law-abiding from defending themselves (Kates, 1984). A well-known NRA slogan and bumper-sticker puts the point most succinctly: 'When guns are outlawed, only the outlaws will have guns'. Kleck refers to handgun-only gun controls as a 'policy disaster in the making' expecting handgun owners (and offenders) to switch to more powerful, more accurate and more lethal long guns. According to Kleck, 'long guns are eminently substitutable for handguns in virtually all felony killing situations' (Kleck, 1984: 195) and he concluded his 1991 discussion of this issue with a paradox. It was just as well that handgun only controls had not been very effective. 'Fortunately, existing handgun-only policies ... are not very effective, and have not reduced handgun availability enough to stimulate much gun substitution among violence-prone people' (Kleck, 1991: 93–94).

Such a conclusion, coming at the end of a period of intense and ideologically charged, though ostensibly 'scientific', social research into the impact of particular gun control laws and policies, where some reference back to 'evidence' might seem essential, serves to underline the sharply partisan character of much of this debate. Yet if the interpretation of the research evidence has proven to be an ideological minefield, the debate on the Second Amendment – where philosophy, ideology, culture and historic intention all come together – seems even more polarised.

The Second Amendment

Although the US Supreme Court has considered the issue constitutionally settled for at least half a century, the status, meaning and implementation of the Second Amendment to the American constitution is probably more hotly contested now than at any other time in its history – including its original drafting. An American Bar Association Report from 1975 on the Second Amendment concluded that there was 'less agreement, more misinformation, and less understanding of the right of citizens to keep and bear arms than on any other current controversial constitutional issue' (Miller, 1975).

Malcolm, in the course of her researches into the English origins of the Second Amendment, argues,

> the American Bill of Rights, like the English Bill of Rights, recognised the individual's right to have weapons for his own defence rather than for collec-

tive defence. The ... intention was to guarantee citizens the means for self-defence and to ensure that when, in the course of time, it was necessary to raise standing armies, they would never pose a danger to the liberties of the people.

(Malcolm, 1994: 161, 164)

As the film director John Milius is said to have commented, the Founding Fathers 'weren't worried about your ability to shoot burglars – they wanted to make sure you could shoot cops as well' (quoted in Smoler, 1994). As Smoler notes in a review of Malcolm's book, it is a rather brutal joke, 'but pretty good, if largely forgotten, history' (Smoler, 1994). Essentially the same point was made by Newt Gingrich, Republican Party spokesman, in 1995. For Gingrich, standing by the Second Amendment was part of the Republican Party's new 'Contract with America' but it was also a stand on basic traditional values and a component in the Party's tough anti-crime agenda. Urging for tougher sentences and promoting the right of law-abiding citizens to possess firearms for their own personal protection were related elements of a moral and material rearmament. He went on to wrap his argument in the fabric of constitutional history. 'The Second Amendment is a political right written into our Constitution for the purpose of protecting individual citizens from their own government. ... If the American colonists had not been trained in how to shoot and fight, they could not have become American citizens' (Gingrich, 1995: 201). One can only speculate on the public reaction to a suggestion that the British people arm themselves against the police or the government.

Whereas the 1689 English Bill of Rights had exploited the fiction of an Englishman's 'ancient and indubitable rights' to carry into law a qualified and conditional 'permission' regarding access to firearms, the early American colonists were no less creative in establishing a rights claim regarding firearms suitable to their own circumstances. The form of words eventually adopted by the US Congress and sent to the state legislatures for ratification as the Second Amendment to the constitution of the United States declared: 'A well-regulated militia being necessary to the security of a free State, the right of the people to keep and bear arms shall not be infringed' (Malcolm, 1994).

Second thoughts on the Second Amendment

There is an enormous body of historical and legal scholarship concerning the Second Amendment which it would be quite impossible to do justice to here. At the same time there are those commentators who regard the Second Amendment itself as something of a red-herring in the firearms debate – albeit a deeply symbolic one, a touchstone of the entire gun debate in the USA (Spitzer, 1995). Levinson, on the other hand, undertakes a more 'relativist' reading of the Second Amendment. He is interested rather less in the 'truth' – the 'correct' or 'incorrect' interpretation of the Amendment itself – and more concerned with the ways in which differing interests have, at different times, sought to reinterpret the meaning of this most contested sentence. At the time that he wrote his article, Levinson felt that many American legal scholars regarded the Second Amendment as 'embarrassing', not least because *they* feared that its 'true meaning' would not square with contemporary notions of citizenship in a modern liberal society. As a result, the legal establishment had tended to ignore the Amendment (Levinson, 1989). This is no longer the case, not least because of the NRA's constant reiteration of Second Amendment 'rights talk' (Glendon, 1991). Furthermore, because, sociologically speaking, those things which people believe true become true in their consequences, a few words on the Second Amendment are called for. Even so, discussion of this most controversial sentence itself is not my chief priority here.

First, however, it is important to recognise the entrenched political significance of a belief in the 'right to bear arms' among large numbers of Americans – a belief undoubtedly bolstered by the substantial lobbying efforts, especially since the mid-1970s, of the National Rifle Association (Davidson, 1993). For example Davidson, writing in 1969, commented that 'the course that many seek in firearms control legislation is really prohibition, as total, blighting and morally stupid as was the attempt at Prohibition of alcoholic beverages from 1919 to 1933 ... the disarmers, while priding themselves on liberal and humanitarian motives, are pretty much theoretical heirs to the Puritanism that consumed the [advocates of alcohol prohibition]' (Davidson, 1969: 14–15). Second, we need to acknowledge the starkly contrasting perspectives adopted with regard to the Second Amendment by commentators from both sides (and none) in the 'great American gun war' (Kates, 1983; Bijlefeld, 1997).

On one side the Second Amendment is viewed as a gross, 'embarrassing,' mistaken, historical anachronism and, on the other, as a vital, even indispensable, foundation of republican freedoms and American virtues currently imperilled by a liberal conspiracy to disarm and enslave the people. There is little moderation in this debate. The issue now fills volumes with both academic, social and political commentary and arguments prepared for litigation. Even so, recent historical research by Malcolm (1994) and others on the derivation of the American right from the English Bill of Rights and on the drafting of what became the Second Amendment attempts to suggest a fair degree of clarity of intent regarding the purpose of the clause.

The individualist interpretation

According to Malcolm, the Second Amendment guarantees an individual right to bear arms that stands as a fundamental guarantee of a citizen's civil liberty in a free society. She concludes:

> the American Bill of Rights, like the English Bill of Rights, recognised the individual's right to have weapons for his own defence rather than for collective defence. The decisions taken together make the task of deciphering the framers' intentions much surer ... the intention was to guarantee citizens the means for self-defence and to ensure that when, in the course of time, it was

necessary to raise standing armies, they would never pose a danger to the liberties of the people.

(Malcolm, 1994: 161, 164)

The NRA and its members and supporters are pledged to protect this legacy. The title page of its magazine, *American Rifleman*, bears the message, 'every law abiding citizen is entitled to the ownership and legal use of firearms'.

Legal historian Stephen Halbrook who has written extensively on the significance of the right to bear arms in American history endorses the 'individualist' interpretation of the Second Amendment, the concept of 'the people' found in the Second Amendment, he asserts, 'meant the same as it did in the first, fourth, ninth and tenth amendments, i.e., each and every free person' (Halbrook, 1982). He has consistently reiterated this argument in two further books (Halbrook, 1984, 1989) and in a variety of articles, one published in the journal of the Second Amendment Foundation. 'The framers, supporters and opponents of the original Constitution all agreed on the political ideal of an armed populace, and the unanimous interpretation of the Bill of Rights in Congress and by the public was that the Second Amendment guaranteed the individual right to bear arms' (Halbrook, 1994).

Clearly central to Halbrook's academic analysis is an attempt to unearth the 'original intentions' of the framers of the Second Amendment, and he is far from alone in this (Hays, 1960; Sprecher, 1965; Kates, 1983; Cramer, 1994; Van Alstyne, 1995). Likewise, Shalhope's 'ideological' analysis endorses the individualist interpretation of the Second Amendment by reference to the ideological and political ambitions of those who framed it. Shalhope, however, appears ideologically uncommitted to the retention of the Second Amendment in contemporary American public policy-making, for 'whether the armed citizen is relevant to late twentieth century American life is something that only the American people ... can decide' (Shalhope, 1982). As a historian, however, Shalhope shares even with his academic critics the belief that 'we must not allow today's needs, however urgently they are felt, to obscure our understanding of the origins of the Second Amendment' (Shalhope and Cress, 1984).

Other commentators, whose area of scholarship remains the Second Amendment, seem rather less convinced that it is now outdated or anachronistic. Kates, for instance, notes that a Second Amendment right to firearms for personal self-defence may be just as relevant today as 200 years ago (Kates, 1983). Furthermore, Levinson cites the remarks of a number of firearm enthusiasts in the USA who have argued that the disarming of citizens is little more than a prelude to totalitarianism implying that the massacre at Tianamen Square or even Stalin's purges and the Nazi Holocaust might not have occurred if the citizens against whom these acts of oppression were committed had been armed (Levinson, 1989; Defensor, 1970). The extreme nature of such claims underlines the intensity of the gun control debate in the USA and why, for instance, critics of the enforcement activities of the Bureau of Alcohol, Tobacco and Firearms (ATF) have courted controversy by referring to ATF agents as 'jack-booted thugs' (Anderson, 1996).

Other more 'prudential' commentators (Levinson, 1989) appear to care less about unearthing the intentions of political actors of two centuries ago than with developing the legal framework they believe the USA needs today (Zimring and Hawkins, 1987; Freedman, 1989; Spitzer, 1995). These more 'consequentialist' commentators hardly endear themselves to Halbrook who, in his 1989 book decries the fact that academic scholars have tended to overlook the original debates when presuming to comment on the 'right to bear arms' in the contemporary USA. The sense that, from his perspective, all is not well is conveyed in his observation that the American courts 'have rarely, if ever, relied on original sources to construe guarantees for the right to bear arms under the state bills of rights' (Halbrook, 1989: viii). Cramer makes a similar point, 'the history of the right to keep and bear arms is disappointing. In spite of overwhelming evidence concerning original intent, much of the judicial interpretation of the Second Amendment ... has been repeated efforts to avoid the original intent ... In this century especially, original intent has increasingly been formally abandoned by the courts as a basis for constitutional interpretation' (Cramer, 1994: 269). Gardiner agrees, arguing that the US Supreme Court, in one of the few cases where it might have ventured an interpretation of the Second Amendment (the 1939 'Miller case'), it studiously avoided doing so and, by ignoring history and common law, proceeded to set an unjustified restriction upon the individual right to bear arms (Gardiner, 1982). Barnett goes even further, 'the Constitution is being wilfully interpreted in a politically partisan way by those who disagree with the merits of the Second Amendment' (Barnett, 1995: 451).

The collectivist interpretation

On the other side of the debate, however, lie those who have argued for a more collectivist interpretation of the Second Amendment or, relatedly, those who argue that the Amendment applies only to the federal government and has no bearing upon the individual states. Arguing the collectivist position effectively amounts to the claim that the Second Amendment is now largely obsolete. The reason for this is that the collectivist argument ties the 'right to bear arms' to the performance of militia service. The notion of a 'citizen militia', while vital at the time that the Amendment was first debated, has no real relevance to contemporary USA. Military and police functions have changed enormously over the course of 200 years in response to the changing needs of American society (Cress, 1984; Ehrman and Henigan, 1989; Edel, 1995; Spitzer, 1995). As Henigan, then a director of the Handgun Control Inc. Legal Action Project argued in uncompromising terms in 1989, 'the NRA's version of the "right to keep and bear arms" is, in short, nothing more than a constitutional illusion created by mass advertising to further a political objective. However strong this constitutional fantasy ... it remains a mirage nonetheless, which disappears when approached by real judges faced with deciding the constitutionality of real laws'

(Henigan, 1989: 11). Williams has developed the point, linking the notion of a 'universal citizen militia' to Rousseau's notion of the 'general will':

> The right to bear arms belonged to all ... but as a collective right, a right of the universal militia and not of separate private individuals. Republicans feared government and sought to give the people ways to resist it, but they also feared the self-interest that lurked in each individual's breast ... they identified the militia with the body of the people – a rhetorical construct that by definition could not betray the common good because the common good was its good. That construct was utopian and artificial at the time, but [it] ... offers a guide to interpreting the Second Amendment.
>
> (Williams, 1991: 615)

Thus the amendment embodied the aspiration that a monopoly of force in society could be vested in those who represented the common good. For Williams there are no modern equivalents of this embodiment of the common good in today's sceptical, pluralistic and divided USA.

Among those who have argued for the collectivist interpretation of the Second Amendment are commentators such as Emery who, as early as 1915, voiced his concern about the 'evolution of a distinct class of criminals, known as "gunmen", who carried small concealable firearms' (Emery, 1915). Other commentators, especially – but not exclusively – those advocating more restrictive gun control legislation, have tended to subscribe to the more collectivist reading of the Amendment (Haight, 1941; Feller and Gotting, 1966; Rohner, 1966; Weatherup, 1988). On most occasions the American courts have done likewise. As the New York Bar Association argued in its Report of 1982, the view that the Second Amendment guaranteed an individual right to possess firearms, 'has never found judicial favour. The federal courts have long regarded the Second Amendment as concerned only with the "organised militia" maintained by the states' (Bar Association of New York, 1982).

The last words here on this issue go perhaps to Spitzer who has noted that the Second Amendment has generated relatively little constitutional law. Between 1876 and 1939, only four Supreme Court cases have ruled directly on the status of the Amendment. In two further cases, in 1972 and 1980, the Second Amendment did receive a brief mention but the court's earlier judgments were unaffected. With the last substantial case decided in 1939, however, long before the ideological reactivation of Second Amendment politics in the mid-1970s, it is difficult to claim that pressing legal dilemmas or judicial activism are responsible for pushing the issue up the political agenda in recent years. On the contrary, 'the inescapable conclusion is that the Supreme Court has settled this matter and has no interest in crowding its docket with cases that merely repeat what has already been decided' (Spitzer, 1995: 42). Furthermore the process of constitutional incorporation (the extension to the individual states of the guarantees in the Bill of Rights) has been completed without including the Second Amendment. Thus, 'even if the Second Amendment did protect an individual right to bear arms outside of service in a militia, it would still not apply to the states because it has not been incorporated, and thus would not be a right citizens could claim in their daily lives' (Spitzer, 1995: 43). In short, therefore, there is nothing in the Second Amendment to prevent individual states (and other jurisdictions below the state level), using what are known as their 'police powers', to introduce gun control regulations in order to prevent crime and promote health and safety. Indeed, on this reading of the Second Amendment, there is nothing to prevent the federal government from doing likewise. Of course, as we have seen, this is a hotly contested issue, though the barriers to further gun control seem political and ideological rather than legal and constitutional.

A mountain of paper controls

Further evidence of the legal obsolescence of the Second Amendment comes from the fact that there are estimated to be some 20,000 laws, regulations, city ordinances and the like regulating or controlling the sale, transfer, ownership, possession and use of firearms. Aside from any overall observations about the net effectiveness of all this law, it still amounts to a substantial mountain of 'paper gun control' for a society that, allegedly, acknowledges a 'right to bear arms'. Despite the existence of so many legal enactments controlling guns, however, most commentary tends to concentrate on just a few of them. In the next section I will consider four of the most well known and contentious of these. Before that I will look briefly at the, often rather limited, attempts at federal (nationwide) gun control. Although, on the whole, it is difficult to regard attempts at federal gun control as anything but weak and ineffectual, measures discussed in the national political arena do attract the lion's share of political commentary so it seems appropriate to begin there.

Federal gun controls

A federal ban was introduced in the 1920s on the purchase of weapons by mail order. In contrast to many twentieth-century gun controls, the 'mail order sales' ban achieved some unexpected support from the likes of Smith & Wesson because it helped cut out the downmarket competition.

Smith & Wesson had plenty to be concerned about, for until about 1870 they had monopolised the manufacture of revolvers, through their ownership of a revolving cylinder design patent. When this patent expired dozens of other manufacturers, who had not hitherto specialised in firearms, tried to enter this lucrative market, producing what came to be known as 'Saturday Night Special' pistols destined for an unsophisticated market and sold at a low price, placing the handgun within reach of all. New mass markets opened up made possible by new methods of industrial production, the advent of mass popular advertising in newspapers and magazines and a cheap and efficient national postal service. This was to have important social implications in urban America (Sherrill, 1973; Kennett and Anderson, 1975: 98–99).

Subsequent federal gun controls include the National Firearms Act of 1934 and the Federal Firearms Act of 1938 which, following concern about violent gangster activity during the alcohol prohibition years, sought to ban the private possession of machine guns and regulate the interstate transfer of firearms. These pieces of federal firearms regulation followed a great deal of gun control activity at the state and local level prompted by concerns about rates of violent and gun-related crime. No further federal legislation followed, however, until the assassination of President Kennedy prompted the submission of several separate firearms control bills to Congress. A protracted debate between pro-gun and anti-gun lobbies followed, leading to a familiar political stalemate. In this context, in one of the first systematic analyses of the USA's gun-crime problem, former US Attorney General, Carl Bakal, published a savage attack on the fatal consequences of widespread gun ownership in American society (Bakal, 1966). His book began with a fascinating account of the fifty or so fatal shootings which, he claimed, happened on any given day in the USA. These 'routine and unremarkable' killings tended to secure a few lines in local newspapers. Within a few days they would be forgotten by all but those most directly involved as new days brought new killings. The largely anonymous killings described by Bakal all came from the same day. Towards the end of the chapter he revealed the date from which they were all taken: November 22nd, 1963, a date on which gun shots killed a much more prominent victim as he toured Dallas in a presidential motorcade (Bakal, 1966).

Between 1965 and 1968 new gun control measures were introduced in several states including, Connecticut, Illinois, New Jersey and New York, and in cities such as Chicago and Philadelphia, though it took the killings of Robert Kennedy and Martin Luther King to break the national political deadlock. In October 1968 the Federal Gun Control Act was signed by President Johnson. Although this Act was described as 'sweeping' and 'comprehensive' by many commentators, this is, perhaps, only by contrast with the limitations of previous legislation. Essentially the Act established tougher licensing and revenue control powers to regulate the trade in firearms. It restricted the traffic in imported weapons, increased the federal firearm dealer's license fee (but only to ten dollars) and established stricter regulations on the access of young people to firearms and ammunition. Heavier military weapons, such as anti-tank guns and bazookas, were brought within the legislation and federally licensed firearms dealers could not knowingly sell weapons to known criminals. Finally, anyone caught using a firearm in the commission of a federal felony risked an extra year's imprisonment. The 1968 Act, the eventual product of much negotiation and manoeuvring, was clearly no panacea for the firearms problem. Furthermore, no sooner had the Act reached the statute book than anti-control groups began mobilising to undermine it. After almost eighteen years of campaigning, lobbying and political manoeuvring and the relentless reassertion of 'Second Amendment rights', the gun debate was eventually pushed to centre stage and the gun lobby began to score some political successes.

In 1986, a decontrol measure, the Firearm Owners' Protection Act, was passed (Patterson and Eakins, 1998). The 1986 Act weakened the already modest controls imposed in 1968. In particular, the rules on interstate sales of guns and upon certain categories of lawful owners were relaxed. In addition the Act sought to facilitate the purchase of ammunition, ease the record-keeping requirements facing firearm dealers and curtail the inspection powers of the ATF (the Bureau of Alcohol, Tobacco and Firearms). The wider significance of the 1986 Act may have been symbolic, however, for it suggested that the advantage in the great gun war had now passed to the gun lobby. Further evidence of this shift in the balance of power, during the Reagan presidency, came when the ATF, having first faced a tighter legal, fiscal and political scrutiny of its enforcement activity was itself almost disbanded (Vizzard, 1997; Martinek *et al.*, 1998).

However, while the Reagan presidency proved a hostile environment in which to pursue national gun control initiatives, the attempt on Reagan's life in 1981 inaugurated the most recent, though certainly protracted, phase of gun control policy-making at the federal level. The President's press secretary was severely injured in the shooting, and he subsequently became very much 'a symbol of the evils of unfettered handgun ownership' (Patterson and Eakins, 1998: 55). His wife, Sarah Brady, became an active gun control campaigner, later becoming a key spokesperson for Handgun Control Inc., the leading American pressure group working for gun control. In due course a legislative initiative championed by Mrs Brady, proposing 'waiting periods' during which it would be possible for the authorities to conduct background and criminal record checks on would-be gun purchasers came to preoccupy opposing camps in the 'gun war'. The waiting period was sometimes referred to as a 'cooling off' period on the assumption that some would-be killers bought firearms in the heat of the moment intent on avenging themselves.

The bill, which soon became known as the 'Brady Bill', attracted the staunch opposition of the NRA and its supporters who interpreted it as an intrusion upon what they saw as their inalienable right to bear arms. However, gun control supporters argued that without appropriate background checks even the limited safeguards of the 1968 Federal Gun Control Act were unworkable. Under the 1968 Act it was an offence to sell a firearm to persons guilty of felony offences – even gun lobby commentators such as Kopel (1995b) recognised the need to exclude offenders and persons suffering mental illness, for instance. Yet without the background checks proposed in the Brady Bill, there was no means of excluding such persons. Furthermore, argued gun control supporters, the right to bear arms could never be regarded as an 'absolute' right, any more than the right to free speech was absolute. As Reynolds argued, 'just as the demand "your money or your life" is not protected by the First Amendment [right to free speech] so the right to arms is not without limits' (Reynolds, 1995: 461). In other words, the requirements of public protection necessitated some limit to the enjoyment of potentially anti-social rights. Ensuring that the wrong people could not legally purchase guns might be one means of achieving this.

However, nothing is quite so straightforward where American gun control is concerned. Although a version of the Brady Bill was first introduced early in

1987, despite the fact that a good deal of the Bush presidency was devoted to passing tough new crime control legislation, it was not until 1993 during the Clinton presidency that the (Brady) Handgun Violence Prevention Act was passed establishing a five-day waiting period for gun purchases. It was the first significant piece of gun control legislation for twenty-five years even though, by the time it was passed, it had acquired a symbolic value far greater than its likely impact on gun crime or gun owners really merited.

Despite this, in the first full year of the law's operation over 15,000 handgun purchases were denied (out of over 400,000), 4,365 being attempted purchases by persons with felony records (Schwarz, 1999). In any event, the legislation was due to lapse after five years *whether or not* the Justice Department had put in place a nationwide instant-check system for vetting gun buyers (such a system, managed by the FBI, came into operation in November 1998). The practical impact of the interim Brady legislation was further undermined by court cases which ruled that local police departments could not be compelled to run the gun control checks on behalf of federal authorities when no resources were identified for this purpose. Nevertheless, with the Brady Bill passed, gun control groups attempted to press home their advantage introducing a further bill – Brady Two. This sought: (1) to make the waiting period permanent, (2) to require all states to establish handgun licensing systems and register all transfers, (3) to limit handgun purchases to one a month, (4) to require all gun owners to pass safety training courses, (5) to ban small handguns, (6) to limit the capacity of ammunition clips to six rounds and (7) to require persons owning several firearms to obtain an 'arsenal licence' and agree to random police inspections (Kopel, 1995b).

The NRA and the gun lobby have continued to resist the Brady/Handgun Control Inc. inspired legislation, regarding the new Bill (Brady Two) as something of a 'transitional law' attempting to shift American gun control policy towards a system of 'needs-based' licensing. In turn, this 'needs based' licensing is seen as granting enormous operational discretion to the police in determining access to lawful handguns (such as in New York) and making, according to the gun lobby, handgun ownership a privilege rather than a right. This they see as a first step towards handgun prohibition. As the debate has unfolded a developing propaganda war has resulted with gun lobby commentators citing cases in which law-abiding citizens have used firearms to protect themselves (Kleck, 1991; Lott, 1998) and gun control groups emphasising the fatal consequences of widespread and easy access to firearms (Larson, 1994; Zimring and Hawkins, 1997).

Two final strands of federal gun control, once again prompted by tragedies, have been, first, the passing of the Youth Handgun Safety Act of 1994 following growing concern about shootings involving young people and, second, the series of 'assault weapons' bans first ordered by the Bush administration and further developed by President Clinton after 1993. In January 1989 a man carrying an AKS assault rifle (a Chinese version of the infamous AK47) had entered a school-yard in Stockton, California and opened fire upon the teachers and students gathered there. Five people were killed and twenty-nine injured. This and similar incidents led to a number of state legislatures, following California, to adopt their own state-wide bans on the sale, ownership or possession of 'assault weapons' (Godwin and Schroedel, 1998). Following a year of particularly intense political manoeuvring, the Violent Crime and Law Enforcement Act, containing an assault weapons ban, was passed in September 1994. Rather like the debate over the Brady Bill, the assault weapons issue became a contest of immense ideological and symbolic significance for the two sides in the debate. Firearms enthusiasts saw the proposed ban as, yet again, the thin end of a long wedge and disputed what an 'assault weapon' actually was. They regarded it as irrational to arbitrarily select certain features of some weapons with a 'more military appearance' on the dubious grounds that these were somehow more dangerous and they claimed that 'so-called assault weapons' only appeared very infrequently in the crime statistics (LaPierre, 1994; Kopel, 1995b).

Data from the ATF, however, indicated that, between 1986 and 1991, over 20,000 assault weapons were traced to crimes, including 1,300 murders, in the USA (Brady, in Bijlefeld, 1997: 204). Gun control campaigners have simply questioned why, outside of military service, anyone would want an assault rifle. After all, they argue, such weapons were not intended or designed either for accurate target-shooting or for hunting, the two forms of civilian rifle use regarded as legitimate.

On this issue, as in so much of the recent American gun control debate, the contending parties occupy antagonistic and apparently irreconcilable positions. This is not so unusual, campaign or 'pressure' groups often take more extreme positions than mainstream public opinion. Despite a number of ambiguities, American public opinion has generally shown itself both more willing to compromise and more willing to accept an additional degree of gun control in return for a promise of greater public safety (Wright *et al.*, 1983; Kleck, 1991; Bijlefeld, 1997). Regardless of this the two sides continue to slog it out, committing enormous political resources in pursuit of often marginal symbolic advantages. In Spitzer's terms the federal gun control battle represents 'elephantine political forces' battling over 'policy mice' (Spitzer, 1995: 181). Only at the state or municipal level do the heated ideological interchanges recede somewhat to allow more pragmatic or instrumental considerations to come to the fore. We have earlier noted that there are some 20,000 gun control laws currently in existence and, by way of illustrating something of the diversity of these laws and some of the issues and controversies they raise, I propose to mention just four.

Localised gun controls

While the balance of power in gun control debates at the federal level has swung in different directions at different times, gun controls at the local level – states, municipalities, counties – represent a confusing mosaic of contrasting regulations, restrictions and entitlements concerning firearms. Although only the most compromised control measures have become part of federal law, at the local level gun control laws can be strict, specific, enforceable and even, in their own terms, effective. In particular jurisdictions, gun control measures introduced can reflect a range of social, cultural and political factors relevant to a given area. Even so, local gun controls can often be related to the national agenda. Taken together the cumulative activity of local law making and law enforcement can throw up national trends indicating groundswells of public opinion which might later impact at the national level. Equally, as in the case of California's 'assault weapons' ban, local gun control measures can serve as the precursors for later national initiatives. In the following discussions, I briefly consider four localised gun control policies which came to have national significance.

Sullivan and the 'usual suspects'

One of the earliest and most significant pieces of 'localised' gun control legislation was the Sullivan Law (named after the New York politician who sponsored the bill) introduced in the state of New York in 1911. The law was introduced following the near-fatal shooting of the city mayor in 1910 and an upsurge of concern about armed criminal gangs and immigrants.

During the later part of the nineteenth century, New York City had introduced legislation to outlaw 'concealed weapons' carried by the 'criminal classes' but these restrictions had not covered handguns, even though actually firing a weapon within the city limits without good cause was a misdemeanour offence. The laws governing the possession of firearms within municipal areas were many and varied and subject to highly variable (often discriminatory) enforcement. The laws were used rather selectively to disarm residents of working-class, immigrant or African-American communities. The typically discretionary character of such early efforts at citizen disarmament serves to reinforce arguments about the racist nature of many gun control initiatives and, relatedly, the rather selective interpretation of the Second Amendment (Cottrol and Diamond, 1995). In fact, the build-up of cheap 'two-dollar' pistols in the poorer districts is perhaps far better understood as a supply-side issue resulting from the range of new manufacturers cashing in on what they saw as a lucrative domestic market. In the process the 'niggertown Saturday Night Special' was born (Sherrill, 1973) creating a gun culture in the low-rent inner-city areas which has preoccupied city law enforcement ever since.

The Sullivan Law was a mixture of old and new controls. For instance it confirmed existing bans on the carrying of firearms by aliens and minors, but introduced a licensing system for concealable firearms, making unlicensed carrying of concealable firearms a felony and unlicensed possession a misdemeanour. It required firearm dealers only to sell to persons who had already obtained a permit and required them to register all sales. The penalties for non-compliance with the firearm control laws were also increased. By all accounts the new laws were at first vigorously enforced in the city, especially against immigrants and suspected aliens (Kennett and Anderson, 1975: 182–184). Over the years, opponents of gun control have continued to criticise the New York gun controls as both 'unconstitutional' and 'un-American,' and a step towards firearm prohibition. Likewise they have tried to show that the controls have been largely unsuccessful in reducing levels of violent and gun-related crime. Supporters of gun control have replied that the controls are limited, inadequate and easily circumvented. Accordingly, Larson describes a number of ploys adopted by unscrupulous and unlicensed firearms purchasers and dealers to avoid interstate firearm trading controls. He notes that a majority of the firearms seized in connection with crime in New York tended to come from southern states, such as South Carolina and Virginia, both with significantly more liberal firearms laws. Much more recently, both states have adopted laws restricting buyers to one gun purchase a month, a policy (introduced in the face of strong firearm industry and NRA opposition) which has, apparently, significantly altered the flow of crime guns into New York (Larson, 1994). Such experiences clearly demonstrate to gun control campaigners that effective control strategies – whatever merits they may have in particular localities – cannot be effectively pursued in isolation. After 1911 many other states, cities and municipalities adopted a wide range of firearms regulations many of them very similar in nature to the New York law.

To have or have not

While the New York law introduced a measure of gun registration and licensing a law passed seventy years later in Morton Grove, a small town in Illinois, went much further by completely banning the sale and private possession of hand-guns. In 1983 an Illinois District court rejected a claim that the law was unconstitutional and the Supreme Court declined to intervene.

If Morton Grove represents one end of a wide spectrum of locally based American firearm regulation, Kennesaw, in Georgia, represents the other end. In Kennesaw firearm ownership became compulsory in 1982. The head of every household (with certain exemptions – felons and the mentally ill, or conscientious objectors) was required to maintain a firearm and suitable ammunition. Both laws were widely regarded as symbolic and neither was expected to have much influence on rates of firearm possession in their respective localities. For instance, Morton Grove was a small community with low rates of crime and low rates of handgun ownership and the Kennesaw ordinance was conceived and carried by an essentially pro-gun community largely in response to the Morton Grove ban, though it carried no penalties for non-compliance. Even so, when passing the law, Kennesaw's mayor voiced the hope that the fear of encountering an armed citizen might deter offenders. Early research evidence appeared to confirm just such an effect, comparing periods before and after the passage of the law, as burglaries were reported to have fallen by over 50 per cent. Other evaluations put the figure even higher as Kennesaw became something of a *cause célèbre* for the gun lobby, contributing a concrete example to a growing body of academic research into the utility and effectiveness of 'private armed force' in crime control (Wright, 1984; Polsby, 1986; Stell, 1986; Kleck, 1988, 1991). Later research, however, found no significant reduction in the Kennesaw burglary rates when the figures were re-examined over a longer time period (McDowall *et al.*,

1989). The more general debate about firearms for citizen self-defence, however, we take up shortly.

While local ordinances, such as those at Morton Grove and Kennesaw, do allow us an insight into the extremely diverse range of firearm regulations that local authorities in the USA appear willing to enact – and the attitudes that underpin them – they tend to offer relatively little in the way of reliable conclusions. The communities themselves are often fairly small, they are rather untypical and they tend to have fairly low rates of crime. Nevertheless, in the ideologically charged and intensely fought arena that is American gun control politics, even the findings of much larger-scale 'gun control' or 'crime control' projects seldom escape fierce critical contestation. Studies, too numerous to mention, let alone adequately review, have examined at exhaustive length the evidence, the reliability of evidence and the interpretation of evidence produced by research on a variety of differing firearm control strategies. Alternatively, communities with differing gun control strategies have been compared in a search for insights into the types of laws or policies which will deliver the greater public benefit. Yet even framing the question in such obviously utilitarian terms meets an objection that firearms ownership is a fundamental right that should not be surrendered on claims of public utility. As Spitzer has argued, the 'rights talk' surrounding any discussion of gun control is a political tactic employed by the gun lobby 'to blunt criminological analysis that supports stronger gun control' (Spitzer, 1995: 65). Having already discussed the more philosophical issues pertaining to the Second Amendment, the coming discussion of 'what works' in American gun control will confine itself to the findings produced by criminological and public-health research. Before this, however, we need to consider a final series of local gun control ordinances which have lately prompted a degree of controversy in the USA: the 'concealed-carry' laws.

Concealed carry

The NRA's magazine *American Rifleman* and other publications such as *Guns & Ammo* or *Combat Handguns* regularly feature articles and stories of the 'it happened to me' variety, recycling the tales of those who used a weapon to good effect in deterring an aggressor. At the time of writing over thirty American states have introduced laws allowing those civilians in possession of a state-wide concealed-carry permit (issued either by the police or other municipal licensing departments) to carry a concealed firearm. In some cases the laws expressly reverse older laws which made the carrying of concealed firearms an offence, now the laws create a presumption that the authorities 'shall issue' a concealed-carry permit to qualified persons. Most states have adopted these laws since 1990, four adopted them in the 1980s, Alabama adopted its law in 1936, New Hampshire in 1923 and Vermont has never regulated concealed-carry weapons. The precise licensing arrangements vary from state to state, fees are charged for the issue of the permit and then for subsequent renewals. In the different states, permits are awarded for between one and five years and age limits apply with most states only issuing permits to persons over 21-years-old (though some issue at age 18). Sixteen states require the applicant to undergo some shooting practice, legal and/or safety training (usually of less than ten hours' duration) but eleven states require no training of any kind (Lott, 1998).

During 1994, for example, Arizona enacted its own concealed-weapons law. There is no requirement for the applicant to prove a need to be able to carry a concealed weapon, any legal resident with no criminal record can obtain a permit. Applicants have to undergo a sixteen-hour training course covering such topics as safe gun handling, firearms law and the safe way to carry a concealed gun. Also as part of the course, a number of 'shoot/no shoot' scenarios are set up to test the applicant's judgmental skills. The course concludes with a marksmanship exercise but, 'failure to make a minimum score will not be reason enough for the police to refuse issuing the permit'. In any event, so great was the demand for concealed weapon permits in Arizona that in only the first month of their availability there had been over 10,000 applications to join the classes (Walker, 1994: 14).

Arguments about concealed-carry firearms and citizen self-defence, are the point at which claims based upon individual rights relating back to the Second Amendment directly encounter more collectivist conceptions of safety and *public* order. However, according to Spitzer, both common law and criminal law accepted the legitimacy of the use of force for self-defence long before the Second Amendment. Considerations of self-defence 'supersede even constitutional guidelines' (Spitzer, 1995: 46). At issue in the concealed-carry debate, therefore, are rather more ancient concerns: the gravity of the threat facing victims, the availability of alternative means of defence, such as retreat (although Brown [1991] argues that American law, in contrast to British, imposes no 'duty to retreat'), the proportionality of the force applied to effect a defence, and the reasonableness of any lethal force employed (Uniacke, 1994). Beyond the level of individual encounters, however, considerations of public safety would suggest that attention must be given to the social consequences of individuals' self-defence choices. In the USA this translates into a question about whether increasing or widening firearm availability prevents or encourages crime and violence. Specifically, does allowing law-abiding citizens to have guns contribute to the prevention of crime and violence or do more guns mean more homicides, suicides and accidents?

Given their fairly recent origin, there has been relatively little evaluation of the impact of the new laws. Lott's conclusion, boldly signposted in his book's title *More Guns, Less Crime* and frequently reiterated throughout the text is that, 'allowing citizens to carry concealed handguns reduces violent crimes and the reductions coincide very closely with the number of concealed-handgun permits issued'. Furthermore, he continues, 'mass shootings in public places are reduced when law-abiding citizens are allowed to carry concealed handguns' (p. 19). Ultimately, he adds, such laws 'are the most cost-effective means of reducing crime' (p. 159). In view of this conclusion his research prompted an angry reaction from the gun control lobby when it was first published. Decontrol, not more control, was being proposed.

There is no doubt that Lott's research was ambitious – the study draws upon an enormous array of data relating to crime rates, demographic characteristics, arrests rates, sentencing patterns and information about the numbers of concealed-carry permits issued for all 3,054 American counties over a seventeen-year period from the beginning of 1977 to the end of 1992. Subsequently, additional data, relating to 1993 and 1994, were added. Yet despite the impressive looking findings produced by Lott's quantitative criminological modelling, his research raises a number of more basic questions. First, Lott presents evidence indicating that the proportion of American citizens owning or with access to legal firearms has grown significantly during the past decade, from around 27 to 37 per cent. However, the limitations of surveys in researching gun ownership have been comprehensively demonstrated by Kleck (1991) and it is difficult to link the more general information on gun ownership to the specific county-level data on the issuing of concealed-carry permits. Extra permits do not necessarily mean extra guns. New permit holders might simply be carrying their already acquired weapons, or just carrying them legally having obtained a permit. Given highly variable patterns of local firearms law enforcement, we are unable to tell whether Lott's central assumption, that concealed-carry laws deter offenders by increasing the likelihood of potential assailants encountering an armed and dangerous victim, actually holds true. The significance of the new laws may be rather more symbolic.

A second dilemma concerns the timing of the study. Even though incorporating some additional data relating to 1993 and 1994, the research covers a period *before* the adoption of the non-discretionary concealed-carry laws in most of the states which now have them. Only a handful of states adopted their laws before 1994. The characteristics of those states tend to set them apart – they are typically pro-republican, rural and with, by American standards, relatively low but rising crime rates. Such states already tend to have higher rates of gun ownership and, by all accounts, more permissive attitudes towards firearms regulation. Even though, in Lott's analysis, it appears that the urban and more densely populated parts of such states achieved the most significant reductions in violent crime, it is not clear that conclusions drawn from such a narrow selection of states hold any obvious lessons for other quite different areas. Ultimately, a rather more considered assessment, when the concealed-carry statutes passed in the mid-1990s have had time to register their longer-term effects, would seem a priority.

Finally, Lott tells us nothing about the illegal gun stock, the size, scale and distribution of which represents the other side of the coin to the arms carried by 'law-abiding' citizens. The deterrence model adopted by Lott regards the weapons of the 'honest citizen' as a crime-deterring factor but disregards the weapons of the 'predatory criminal' as crime-facilitating. Even if the new permits have added to the number of 'good guns' on the streets, the marginal difference in a country of over 200 million firearms (over 65 million concealable handguns) seems unlikely to be responsible for the scale of the falling trend in violence that he claims. As Zimring and Hawkins' recent study (1997) shows, while lethal violence represents, statistically, a relatively small percentage of American crime, a willingness to use guns in the commission of violent criminal acts represents a distinctly American pattern, the geography of which is highly concentrated. Fearful citizens 'tooling up' in the suburbs and rural areas may, despite Lott's findings, have relatively little to do with the chronically high patterns of criminal violence in deprived and socially disorganised inner-city areas. Likewise, critics have accused Lott of working from an NRA script which insists, 'guns don't kill, people do', and it is true that he has concerned himself exclusively with 'good guns' owned by 'good people' in areas with strongly established and 'civilising' gun cultures. Advocates of gun control, on the other hand, who claim that there is no such thing as a good gun, are often accused of over-looking the fears and insecurities of those millions to whom firearms seem to offer a promise of personal protection.

Lott's book contributes to a growing body of work which, since the early 1980s, has begun to focus upon the question of citizen self-defence. The issue came to a head, in New York, in 1984, with the so-called 'subway vigilante' incident, when Bernhard Goetz shot four black men he believed were about to rob him. Almost inevitably, following the 1976 film *Death Wish*, the case – the white, middle-class fight back against victimisation – took on racial overtones and polarised New York opinion. After a high profile trial, a jury found Goetz not guilty of attempted murder but guilty of illegally carrying a concealed firearm (Brown, 1991: 134–135). Unfortunately for Goetz, the end of his short period in custody was only the beginning of his further troubles as legal fees and the loss of a multi-million dollar civil case to one of the men he shot, now permanently disabled, brought him to bankruptcy. Despite Goetz's rather mixed fortunes, many states now regard 'concealed-carry' as a personal security solution. Many Americans do defend themselves with their own personal defence firearms (though there is much controversy about exactly how many) and 'armed citizen' self-defence anecdotes abound in the shooting press. Whenever shooting atrocities occur, such as the 1993 New York subway shoot-ings or the killings in 1999 at the Columbine High School, near Denver, gun lobby commentators are usually to be found arguing how the incident might have been prevented if other passengers or, in the case of the school shootings, the teachers themselves, had been armed. Other commentators are clearly taken aback by the incongruous idea that school teachers need to carry firearms.

Given the intensity of this issue, therefore, it is highly unlikely that Lott's find-ings will close the debate. The concealed-carry question poses many fundamental dilemmas about public order and law enforcement, about the extent to which citizens can rely upon police protection and, above all, about people's sense of vulnerability and fear in the face of apparently rising crime. Equally, the issue raises questions about safety, deterrence, crime causation and crime reduction – all of which are hotly contested (Green, 1987). For Kates, however, writing in 1983, the public's fear of crime and the right to self-defence were the central issues:

It is regrettably the case that enormous increases in police budgets and personnel have not prevented the per capita incidence of reported robbery, rape and aggravated assault from rising by 300, 400 and 300 per cent respectively since 1960. Increasingly police are concluding, and even publicly proclaiming, that they cannot protect the law-abiding citizen, and that it is not only rational for him to choose to protect himself with firearms, but a socially beneficial deterrent to violent crime.

(Kates, 1983: 268)

Furthermore, Californian statistics for 1981 appeared to show armed citizens responsible for twice as many 'justified shootings' of felons than the police, in Chicago and Cleveland citizens justifiably killed three times as many as the police (Kleck and Bordua, 1983). As Spitzer has put it, 'those who acquire guns for self-protection are reacting to the perceived and real threats of modern American life' (Spitzer, 1995: 75).

The queue at the gunstore

The reasons people have for purchasing firearms speak volumes. As Sherrill noted in 1973, 'after any serious riot gun sales are said to jump fourfold in that locale'. He added that, 'doubtless there is some connection between the rise in crime and the increase in gun sales, but there is no way to know to what extent the teetering mound of arms causes crime and to what extent it is simply there as a defensive response' (Sherrill, 1973). Two years later, Kennett and Anderson drew their own conclusion, from an avowedly more cultural and 'sociological' perspective. For them, the purchase of guns by American citizens,

reflects the persistent view that the ultimate defence of the individual American, his final, back-to-the-wall recourse, is his gun. It was a sentiment that was felt in frontier log cabins and in isolated farmhouses and lingers today in city and suburb. The ultimate fear is not that government will tyrannise, but that it will fail to protect. That fear persists; it causes lines to form in front of gun stores after every major riot or atrocity.

(Kennett and Anderson, 1975: 253–254)

Similarly, Richard Raynor, discussing the Los Angeles riots in the wake of the first Rodney King trial verdicts, commented: 'The riots began on Wednesday, 29th April 1992. Monday, 4th of May, was the first day – the first of many – that gun sales topped 2,000 in Southern California, twice the normal figure, a gun sale every forty seconds' (Raynor, 1992). However, having reviewed a range of research projects during the 1970s examining the links between fear of crime and the demand for security devices – alarms, locks *and handguns* – Wright was unable to establish such a clear and simple relationship (Wright, Rossi and Daly, 1983). Far more important, according to McDowall and Loftin were the ways in which individuals responded to three determinants of collective security: high violent crime rates, civil disorders and assessments of police strength. They concluded, 'the demand for legal handguns is positively related to riots and crime rates and negatively related to a measure of resources devoted to collective security, the number of police per capita. We interpret this as evidence that legal handgun demand is responsive to evaluations of the strength of collective security' (McDowall and Loftin, 1983: 1,147; Kleck, 1991: 27–33).

Other commentators have investigated the psychological motivations expressed by gun owners. Research on the reasons given for gun ownership by a variety of groups (for example, householders, offenders or young people) throws up relatively few surprises. As we have seen, the personal protection motive is a consideration for many gun-owning householders although many incarcerated felons and young people emphasise essentially similar reasons (Wright and Rossi, 1986).

Surveying the motivations for gun carrying among juvenile offenders, Sheley and Wright noted that, 'the evidence suggests that among the juveniles studied, the odds of surviving in a hostile environment were seen as better if one were armed' (Sheley and Wright, 1993: 386–387). Most of the respondents, typically residents in high crime, high violence, socially deprived urban neighbourhoods, had themselves been victims of violent crime and their choice to arm themselves became understandable in this context. Guns were also status symbols, they were 'cool' to own, giving their owners a real macho 'power buzz' but, overall, these were secondary considerations. Homicide is the leading cause of death for black males in the age range 15–24 and DuRant *et al.*'s 1995 survey found that previous exposure to violence and victimisation was the factor most strongly associated with gun carrying. The youths' attitudes to gun use appeared to be determined by their situations, over a third agreed with the statement that, 'it would be okay to shoot someone if that's what it takes to get what you want' and almost three out of ten said they thought it 'okay to shoot someone who doesn't belong in your neighbourhood'. While the juveniles indicated that personal protection may have been their primary motivation for gun acquisition, it is difficult to avoid the conclusion that they also saw guns as '*potentially* instrumental in committing crimes' (DuRant *et al.*, 1995).

Sheley and Wright concluded that the results of such surveys are not especially encouraging. 'The perception that one's very survival depends on being armed makes a weapon a necessity at nearly any cost. Attempts to reduce juvenile gun-related crime through threat of criminal justice sanctions can hardly be expected to produce results if a juvenile "must" have a gun to survive and crimes are committed with guns because they happen to be in the youth's possession' (Sheley and Wright, 1993: 387). Similar to Canada's own conclusions on juvenile gun possession, the prospects of disarming the USA's inner-city youth appeared remote in the face of such a powerful motivation as their own sense of insecurity. As Canada noted, he began to understand the scale of the problem, 'when I heard young teenagers saying they'd "rather be judged by twelve than carried by six"' (Canada, 1995: 68). The changing political economy of American cities and the marginalisation of large numbers of inner-city residents from mainstream economic activity has brought widespread informal drug dealing with high rates of gun ownership and gang membership (Short, 1996). Fagan has commented that the increase in rates of lethal violence within such communities reflects the increasing number and firepower of weapons available to gang members (Fagan, 1996: 41). Equally, Huff cites evidence suggesting that most gangs have members, 'with weapons more powerful and more lethal than the standard weapons issued to law enforcement officers' (Huff, 1996b: 91).

Furthermore, conventional policing interventions in such high-crime, deprived communities can apparently cause as many problems as they solve. The first episode of Roger Graef's 1998 TV series *In Search of Law and Order* described a police initiative which had effectively disarmed a local gang only to leave that gang and the community and territory it defended at the mercy of other gangs whose guns and key members had not been removed by the police. According to Canada, young people living under such vicious, mean, and violent circumstances form a new generation: 'the handgun generation, growing up under the conditions of war ... too many guns, too much crack, too few jobs, so little hope' (Canada, 1995: x). The violence itself is not new, 'violence has always been concentrated among the poor. The difference is that we have never had so many guns in our inner cities' (ibid. p. xi). For Canada, the problem demands a multi-layered response: reducing the demand for drugs, reducing the prevalence of poverty, domestic violence, child abuse and neglect, reducing the amount of violence on television and in the movies and also reducing and regulating the possession of handguns. The evidence is undoubtedly contested, but while firearms certainly appear among the proximate causes of crime and facilitate the commission of violent offences, few gun control proposals offer anything even remotely approaching a quick fix. Gun availability and gun control are but two factors among many (including poverty and economic inequality, racism, social disorder and drugs – in effect, indicators of social division) which help sustain chronic levels of firearm violence (Kleck, 1991: 445).

Armed and dangerous to one another

The firepower in private hands in the USA is truly awe-inspiring. Given the propensity of contemporary Americans to use these weapons against others and against themselves, a number of questions arise. What is the significance of widespread private firearm ownership and widespread firearm use in the context of modern insecurities and uncertainty about the role of government in delivering, fostering or facilitating public order? In what ways might widespread resort to firearms announce the arrival of a new stage in liberal governing consequent upon the seeming collapse – or at best the weakening – of a social commitment to collectivist principles of public safety and order? To appropriate Foucault's own metaphor of the 'great confinement' in eighteenth-century Europe, might our post-modern insecurities prefigure the great (American) 'tooling-up'? A corollary of this 'tooling up' might, according to Mestrovic, be the coming of a new 'barbarian temperament'; an intolerance of others and an insensitivity to suffering (Mestrovic, 1993). Furthermore, as the civilian population has expanded its weapon stock, so have the police and law enforcement agencies. The language and tactics of warfare have long been used to describe efforts to 'fight' crime but the future of policing, as depicted in journals like the *International Police Review*, begins to appear increasingly militaristic, driven increasingly by technology and weapons.

Kleck has made a particular study of the defensive use of firearms by law-abiding citizens (Kleck, 1986, 1988, 1991). The real gun control question, he argued in his 1986 article, concerned precisely *whose* guns a policy sought to control. In his 1991 book Kleck estimated that gun-owning citizens employ their own firearms in a defensive capacity as many as a million times a year (1991: xiii). Such figures are vital to the debate – a large number of defensive uses (whether or not a gun is fired) suggests a widespread public benefit to off-set the numbers of lives lost to firearms. If firearms are being used so often in self-defence (or to prevent or deter other criminal activity) it would certainly provide important evidence of a considerable 'net benefit' to society of widespread firearm availability. Not only would those individuals with firearms be defending their own civil liberties and improving their own life chances (LaPierre, 1994) they would also be contributing to the common good as well. Arguments about individual welfare maximisation appear entirely in tune with notions of collective welfare maximisation. Free market economics has found its direct parallel in unrestricted citizen gun ownership for rational economic man. Armed pursuit of rational self-interests makes society as a whole safer and more secure, though this is not so much a case of the 'hidden hand' at work than the hidden trigger finger. Again, using language more familiar in economic debates, Lott also implies criticism of those citizens who refuse to carry firearms themselves but benefit from the 'umbrella of security' provided by concealed gun carriers (Lott, 1998: 110). In such an equation, not owning a gun is no longer a sensible public safety choice but a form of 'free-loading' on the efforts of others.

The findings produced by commentators such as Kleck and Lott emphasising the social value of handguns for self-defence or revealing the crime deterring effect of concealed-carry weapons have contributed significantly to recent gun control debates. If a net benefit can be discerned from widespread firearms ownership the arguments about gun control might need reconsidering. However, we have already considered some of the limitations of Lott's research findings and other commentators have similarly raised questions about Kleck's own 'estimates' of the frequency with which handguns are used for self-defence. Indeed, Kleck himself has acknowledged his evidence to be somewhat speculative. There may be little doubt about the advantage to an individual citizen who employs a firearm to protect him or herself and his or her family. However, for many, the real question of the 'net social benefit' to be derived from widespread gun ownership depends not upon successful self-defence by individuals, or even by particular groups of once-vulnerable individuals, but rather upon the aggregate balance sheet. In other words, the question is whether more lives are saved by, or lost to, firearm violence. Posing the question this way, firearms as contributors to aggregate population mortality, a new group of commentators joined the debate.

The public health agenda

Many recent contributions to the American gun debate have come from a public health perspective. Reviewing data on the prevalence of firearm-related deaths in the USA, researchers from the public health community have argued that firearms are now the cause of a public health emergency of epidemic proportions (Koop and Lundberg, 1992). From within this perspective, a number of analyses have emerged centring upon firearms as 'risk factors' and suggesting that guns kept at home are more dangerous to family members and other occupants or acquaintances than they are to would-be criminal assailants or strangers. A study in the 1970s drawing upon FBI statistics concluded that 'self-defence guns' kept at home were six times more likely to be used in the deliberate or accidental killing of friends or relatives than used against burglars or other unlawful intruders (Drinan, 1990). Particular concern has been voiced about the numbers of children and young people killed or injured in firearms accidents at home. The absolute numbers may be relatively low in national terms but the prevailing interpretation of such tragic deaths is that they are all entirely preventable (Wintemute, 1987; Schwarz, 1999).

A later study of firearms at home, by Kellerman and Reay (1986) examined all the gunshot deaths in King County, Washington from 1978 to 1983. There were 743 in all. Acknowledging that a large number of gun owners kept weapons at home, partly for self-protection, they concluded, 'keeping firearms at home carries associated risks. These include injury or death from unintentional gunshot wounds, homicide during domestic quarrels, and the ready availability of an immediate, highly lethal means of suicide' (Kellerman and Reay, 1986: 1,557). Thus, guns were involved in the deaths of friends or acquaintances twelve times more often than in the case of strangers. Even excluding suicides, guns kept at home were eighteen times more likely to be involved in the death of family members than in the deaths of strangers. Most firearm deaths in the home occurred during the course of arguments or altercations, hence easy access to firearms seemed to be especially problematic in volatile households prone to domestic violence. Overall, therefore, Kellerman and Reay's study found forty-three suicides, criminal homicides or accidental firearm deaths involving a gun kept in the home for each case of homicide for self-protection. Later studies have also confirmed that guns kept in the home increase the risk of homicide while providing little help in resisting criminal assailants (Kellerman *et al.*, 1993). McDowell and Wiersma also found relatively few instances of successful self-defensive use of a firearm and concluded their own study in the following terms. 'Coupled with the risks of keeping a gun for protection, [our] results raise questions about the collective benefits of civilian firearm ownership for crime control' (McDowell and Wiersma, 1994).

Firearms lobby commentators reject the attempt to equate firearm ownership and gun control with an epidemiological model of disease control and point to a range of weaknesses in the evidence offered by public health analysts in support of gun control (Kates *et al.*, 1995). In particular, they tend to dispute the inclusion of suicide data within equations examining the numbers of lives lost or lives saved by firearms, arguing that suitably motivated would-be suicides will always find other reliable methods of killing themselves. Guns, they conclude, do not 'cause' suicides. While this may be true, however, it is certainly the case (as we shall see in a later chapter) that firearms certainly facilitate the realisation of suicidal intent.

Second, firearms lobby commentators dispute the calculations employed in studies by researchers such as Kellerman. It is claimed that Kellerman only considered the lethal use of firearms excluding all the occasions on which a gun may only have been pointed to deter a would-be assailant (or where a gun was fired but the results were not fatal). This methodology, it is claimed, significantly undercounts the number of lives saved by firearms (Blackman, 1994). However, such an argument cuts both ways, the data tell us nothing about the unwarranted defensive use of firearms. Sloan's comparative 1988 study found that only some 4 per cent of gun homicides between 1980 and 1986 were judged to be justifiable or in self-defence (Sloan *et al.*, 1988). Armed Americans seem very quick to go for their guns, but 'shooting first, and thinking later' (precisely the advice in self-defence handgun manuals – Tanner, 1995) brings some rather anti-social and enormously damaging public health consequences.

A variant of the foregoing argument claims that the true measure of a self-defence gun's effectiveness is not just derived from lives saved or lives lost but from the confidence and sense of ontological security of one's self, one's rights, one's family and one's property to which a firearm contributes (Schulman, 1994; Waters, 1998). On the other hand, a community in which firearms are freely available and in which citizens are armed and dangerous to one another also tends to be a community in which violent, firearm-related deaths are more commonplace. Furthermore, the risks attached to widespread firearm availability are not borne equally by all members of the community. Responding to the paradigm 'innocent victim' cases of children shot and killed while playing with their parents' loaded and unlocked 'self-defence handguns' which had been left in readiness in a bedside cabinet, gun lobby commentators express the ambition that training programmes in responsible gun-ownership will educate the public and reduce the frequency of preventable domestic firearm accidents. As Suter has argued, 'the responsible use and safe storage of any kind of firearm causes no social ill and leaves no victims' (Suter, 1994). Likewise, NRA speakers argue that 'good' gun owners in the USA are 'safe, sane and courteous in the use of firearms'. Unfortunately, research evidence suggests a rather more ambiguous picture. A significant proportion of gun owners disregard basic safety procedures. Over one-third of gun owners surveyed kept their guns loaded and over a half left them in unlocked drawers or cupboards. People who owned guns for defensive purposes were most likely to keep firearms loaded and unlocked – in readiness. The presence of children in a home did tend to increase the likelihood that some safety procedures were followed but whether a gun owner had undertaken a course in safe gun handling appeared to make no difference (Weil and

Hemenway, 1992). Findings such as these, suggesting that gun owners themselves cannot be relied upon to handle guns safely, have led to increased calls that firearms manufacturers should include additional safety features into firearm design (Diaz, 1999). However, firearms manufacturers have proven difficult to regulate and they have had their own agendas to pursue.

Women and guns

Much of the political commentary on the politics of firearms in the USA is taken up with discussing the political lobbying of the National Rifle Association (NRA). Rather less is said about the political influence of arms manufacturers in the USA. However, many commentators have drawn important conclusions about the capacity of American firearm manufacturers to affect the determination of public policy by their political and economic influence.

Recently, however, commentators have drawn attention to the role of firearm manufacturers in developing new marketing strategies which, they argue, ride roughshod over committed public health strategies and anti-crime policies. As Canada has put it, 'greedy handgun manufacturers and lax government regulations have helped precipitate in this country a crisis of unimagined proportions' (Canada, 1995: 67). Likewise, Diaz comments at length on the success the firearms industry (and its political allies) had in exempting firearms from the USA's consumer product safety regulations. For over thirty years, the country's most dangerous consumer product has been exempted from the scrutiny of consumer safety law. Equally, firearm manufacturers, keen to keep overheads down and profits up, have bitterly resisted the pressure to install additional safety features into their mass-produced handguns (Diaz, 1999: 13–14). Diaz also refers to a Justice Department Survey suggesting that the proportion of households in the USA owning firearms is now declining significantly and that firearms ownership is concentrated in fewer hands. For instance, only one in six Americans admits to owning a handgun (the operative word here may be 'admits'). However, even as the number of gun owners may be falling, the number of guns sold increases. 'Fewer and fewer Americans own more and more guns', and this, in particular, has prompted the industry to look for new markets (Diaz, 1999).

The past decade has seen firearms manufacturers coming to regard women (and young people) as relatively under-exploited markets. For many women, self-defence has come to include training in the use of handguns. The NRA runs its own handgun shooting programmes for women under the 'Refuse to be a Victim' banner (Quigley, 1989). More recently feminists have also taken up the issue of guns for self-protection and, in the words of Naomi Wolf, are being urged to 'fight fire with fire'. 'Guns', as Cindy Hill argued, adopting Second Amendment rhetoric to a liberal feminist cause, 'are the tools by which we forge our liberty' (Hill, 1997: 389). Whether such developments are best described as the effective 'empowerment of women through self-defence choices' or just clever marketing ploys by the firearms industry, will remain open questions (Wolf, 1994; Stange, 1995).

In 1983 American firearms industry market analysts predicted that the primary market for firearms sales – white males – was close to saturation point. Accordingly, the industry was encouraged to diversify its product range and seek sales among sections of the population not traditionally associated with firearms ownership (Canada, 1995: 123; Pogrebin, 1989). Zimring and Hawkins make an essentially similar 'demographic' point connecting the increasing proportion of female-headed households and the growing popularity of handguns for domestic self-defence. They even suggested (perhaps rather controversially) that women's self-defence would become the crucial ideological battleground in the developing American gun control debate. 'The American woman of the 1990s will thus be the first and most important leading indicator of the social status of self-defense handguns in the more distant future. If female ownership of self-defense hand-guns increases dramatically, the climate of opinion for drastic restriction of handguns will not come about' (Zimring and Hawkins, 1997: 196–197).

Perhaps indicating the way this issue will be resolved, a new firearms industry product range emerged including the Black Widow – 'a real manstopper' – and Smith & Wesson's 'Ladysmith' .38 revolver, available in pink or pearl-handled grips and designed for concealment in a handbag or purse. This new marketing venture was backed by a major advertising initiative selling fear, concealed-carry weapon solutions and an 'attractive' range of accessories. In 1989 the marketing exercise was complemented by an industry-backed, Second Amendment lobby publishing venture, the magazine, *Women & Guns*. The same year, Paxton Quigley a writer and advocate of armed self-defence for women, published her book *Armed and Female*. Certainly the media have latched onto the 'women and guns' angle, it is overloaded with ideological symbolism and makes a good feature story although, as we shall see, some commentators find the actual evidence of a rising trend in firearms ownership for self-defence among women both unreliable and overstated (Smith and Smith, 1995).

Although explicitly rejecting suggestions that her book might be considered a feminist treatise, Quigley neverthless drew attention to cultural and demographic changes which have both influenced and reflected the fortunes of feminism in the USA. Thus, 'More women [are] living alone and working outside of the home and having more disposable income. In turn, women have become acces-sible targets, not only for rape, but for robbery and assault, and the need for personal protection has become acute' (Quigley, 1989: 7). Recognising that there are some fairly sharp ideological contradictions between feminism (the voice of urban, upwardly-mobile, professional women) and the politics of the gun lobby (south-western, rural, red-neck masculinity) Lentz comments on how Quigley builds her case on an assertion that society has changed, not women (Lentz, 1993: 383). Society is represented as having become more dangerous. Living and working arrangements are such that men can't always be around to protect women. Carrying a gun need not be a matter of feminism, but a question of common sense. Women are not so much becoming frighteningly autonomous new aggressors (that might be more than a crisis-ridden masculinity could take) rather they are just seeking to defend themselves more effectively.

Quigley's book is based upon a conception of women's vulnerability – not unlike traditional views of femininity in patriarchal culture. Here we can never know how much security is enough. For those women who lack male protection, guns are but a second best option. As Zimring and Hawkins note, 'President Reagan was not alone when he justified a gun in the dresser drawer as particularly suited for periods when he would be away from the ranch. Generations of men who are not themselves supposed to be afraid in their own households, have kept handguns "for the little woman"' (Zimring and Hawkins, 1997: 196). However, armed women face the same dilemmas as armed men – carrying a gun raises the stakes.

By contrast, the enthusiasm of certain strands of contemporary feminism for guns and armed defence is predicated not upon women's vulnerability but upon their strength and a symbolic rejection of victimisation (Wolf, 1994). Labelled 'power feminism' or, connecting with an older American tradition, 'pioneer feminism' this argument articulates a liberal 'equal rights' approach to women's safety. While fear of crime has encouraged millions of American women to take up self-defence classes, the power feminists urge women to break free from the shackles of convention, from 'victim status' and the assumption that men – or the police – will protect them. Instead, the power feminists urge women to fight fire with fire.

Perhaps it goes without saying, but the gun question has become a hotly contested issue within American feminism, often degenerating into hyperbole, stereotypes and a cross-fire of statistics (Stange, 1995). Opponents of the gun lobby point to increased rates of fatality in households with a firearm, and to the fact that women are five times more likely to be shot dead by a spouse or family member. They conclude that the NRA's 'Refuse to be a Victim' armed self-defence training programme simply adds to the overall quantity of risks faced by women in particular and society more generally (Hemenway *et al.*, 1995).

Advocates of armed self-defence for women reply with figures on the number of women reporting having defended themselves with firearms. Likewise, all the major gun magazines, but especially *Women & Guns* and *Combat Handguns* feature regular stories, the 'true-life' experiences of women who have used their weapons to prevent or deter an attack – or to kill an attacker. It is difficult to gauge the extent to which such gun advocacy – or, depending upon how you look at it, gun marketing – has been successful as there are a number of ambiguities in the research evidence and the firearms industry has not been keen to allow academic researchers access to its own polling data. A 1988 Gallup poll found that 15.6 million American women owned a firearm, and 81 per cent of women sampled in a survey by *Women & Guns* said that their principal reason for owning a gun was self-defence. However, 'contrary to the heavy media emphasis on handguns, many of the weapons owned by women are long guns,' less obviously associated with a self-defence motive (Smith and Smith, 1995). Similarly, the existing figures may run together women reporting guns within their households with women who actually own the guns themselves. Finally, evidence of a rising trend of female firearms purchasing seems overstated, the gender gap in firearms ownership appeared not to have closed between 1980 and 1994 and, contrary to the media hype, 'gun ownership is higher among married women living outside large cities, and it is associated more with hunting than with either fear of crime or past victimisation' (Smith and Smith, 1995). None of this is to deny that a trend may be developing, or that the politics of fear and firearms industry marketing will not combine to carve out a new niche market for concealed-carry firearms among younger, single, female city dwellers, but it seems that they are not yet buying them in sufficient numbers to impact upon more traditional patterns of ownership or existing trends in firearm acquisition.

Saturday night's alright for fighting

In view of the intensity of the American gun debate, any discussion of the firearm question, whether it concerns the use of guns in crime, gun control strategies, or even the interpretation of the Second Amendment, tends to become rather all-consuming. What the debate often lacks is a wider context taking on board questions of society, culture and citizenship in contemporary society. This wider perspective seems important in order to reconnect the particular discussion of the gun in society and gun control to policy questions concerning individuality, state and society; law, order and safety and the effective governance of contemporary societies.

Blumberg embarked upon such a discussion in 1973. Discussing the wider politics of the American crime problem he identified the roots of the USA's contemporary law and order crisis. Not only had what he called the 'law and order ideology' fashioned an exclusive and essentially defensive consensus around a supposedly beleaguered (white) middle class, insulating their values and protecting their institutions from attack, it had also led to unprecedented levels of fear and some seemingly drastic forms of self-protection. 'In cities of over 500,000 inhabitants, the percentage of respondents who feel unsafe rises to 80 per cent. Ominously, 30 per cent indicate that they keep a gun for "self-defence". Small wonder, then, that the "law and order" and "crime in the streets" themes have such incredible appeal as knee-jerk exclamations of patriotic fervour' (Blumberg, 1973: 2). Things have moved on. Now he would have to add the frequent assertion of a 'right to bear arms' among those knee-jerk exclamations.

The politics of firearms intersects with many other social issues in contemporary America, throwing up many intriguing paradoxes. For many republicans and NRA hardliners the right to bear arms – any arms, all arms – defines a particular type of commitment to civil rights. Yet at the same time, it is precisely the fear of the 'gun in the wrong hands' that sustains and, from time to time animates the more philosophical versions of republican idealism. In particular, the alleged relationships between firearms, race and class and the idea of the violent ghettos, fuel an especially hard-edged cocktail of racist and reactionary values linking the break-down of family and community, with drug-dealing, rampant criminality, benefit dependency and firearms. As Freedland noted in January 1995, in a critical commentary upon the rising influence of a new right-wing republicanism in the USA, these issues go to the heart of middle-class, white America's preoccupation with the 'underclass'. Many right-wing opinion leaders, he noted, appear to be in agreement that, 'something [does] have to be done about the offspring of the (mainly black) underclass, who, raised by teen-moms, grow into gun-wielding, benefit draining, drug-dealing hoodlums' (Freedland, 1995a).

Writing at a perhaps more optimistic time, Kennett and Anderson concluded their wide-ranging study of attitudes towards the gun in the USA in the following terms. 'The gun [in the USA] is part of a whole series of traditional attitudes about government, society and the individual. They run, like so many threads, through the tapestry of the national past. In its essence, the gun controversy is a struggle between these attitudes and new ones' (Kennett and Anderson, 1975: 254). And they continued, consistent with the 'conquest of violence' thesis we have examined earlier in relation to the UK:

> But in the long run, time works against the gun. Increased social consciousness finds its excesses intolerable, whereas they were once accepted without thought. The era of thermonuclear war [sic] has made the citizen soldier harder to defend. The war against crime has mobilised the computer and other sophisticated techniques. Moreover, the police have come to regard the armed citizen more as a hazard than an ally. The city is the enemy of the gun, and the city is growing ... In megalopolis the gun as necessity seems doomed.
>
> (Kennett and Anderson, 1975: 255–256)

Optimistic thoughts for the future of modern civilisation, no doubt. But, as we have already seen, the conquest of firearm violence seems far from completed. If anything, the gun may be even more popular (Wright *et al.*, 1983; Kleck, 1991). A raft of recent gun control measures notwithstanding, the spectre of the gun has in no way been exorcised. The citizens of Kennett and Anderson's megalopolis have, more recently, been buying their guns in droves. Equally, the concealed-carry permits issued by over two-thirds of American states permit citizens to go about their daily business 'armed and dangerous'. Every night has become a Saturday night.

4 Discovery and construction
Media coverage of the 'gun question'

Guns in the news

Having considered a range of social, cultural, historical and political themes driving debates about firearms on either side of the Atlantic, this chapter turns to consider a series of contemporary themes developed in the British news media concerning firearms, crime and society. The significance of this focus upon the media lies in the way that press coverage given to firearms-related news items during an extraordinary period in British social, political and cultural life appeared to articulate a broadly shared set of ideas connecting concerns about firearms and violence with policing and public safety policies with an emerging popular 'common sense'. During a few short years, firearms-related issues came to preoccupy the UK as never before. In this period the UK witnessed a number of critically defining moments when British politicians, the British police, the British media and an overwhelming section of the British public (as canvassed in a series of opinion polls) came to position themselves against firearms and against the notion of a British 'gun culture'. The present chapter will explore a series of issues in which this British outlook is constructed. The following chapter will explore more directly the issues arising from the reactions to the tragedy at Dunblane.

The central objective of this chapter is to review the media coverage given to firearms – and firearms-related matters – in the UK, and to reflect upon its significance. However, there is more to this than just a review of media reporting. Rather, issues surfacing in the media are simply taken as the most public manifestations of a series of discourses to which a much wider range of commentators, most notably politicians, criminologists, firearms lobbyists and gun owners, police and criminal justice system personnel and even ex-offenders, has contributed and which define a British perspective on the 'gun question'.

Guns and gun cultures

The following two chapters treat the firearms questions and discourses emerging in the UK in recent years as social, political and cultural phenomena. Media reporting is central to the developing analysis but is not the entirety of it. By the end of a particularly turbulent period concerning British society and the gun question, a question gathering in intensity over recent decades but coming to a head during the years 1993–1997, the UK formally declared itself against the gun and against gun culture. How sustainable this commitment will be, remains to be seen.

The two positions arrived at – opposition to guns and opposition to gun culture – are closely related, though not the same. Our attitudes towards firearms themselves have been sustained, in recent years, by concerns about the apparent increase in firearm-related offending during the 1970s, 1980s and early 1990s (Weatherhead and Robinson, 1970; Morrison and O'Donnell, 1994, 1997) reflected in media reporting. Particular concerns have been voiced about 'terrorists' (Schlesinger *et al.*, 1983) armed robbers (Ball *et al.*, 1978), armed drug gangs (Silverman, 1994; Small, 1995; Davison, 1997) and a series of incidents in the early 1990s in which police officers were shot at or killed by armed offenders. Illegal weapons were thought to be less and less the exclusive preserve of the 'professional' career criminal and, instead, were thought to be falling into the hands of a young, amoral and dangerously unstable class of offenders for whom firearms meant power and respect. Guns could be drawn for the most trivial of provocations (Mungo, 1996).

As a result of the perceived increase in the frequency of attacks upon police officers (Gould and Waldren, 1986; Ingleton, 1997), the years 1994 and 1995 witnessed the beginning of a protracted debate within police and government circles concerning the provision of better defensive equipment for police officers (stab and bullet resistant vests, new batons, CS sprays), the enhancement of the police's 'armed response' capacity and concerning the question of the more routine arming of the police (Waddington, 1991). By the end of the period under consideration, then, at least an interim position 'against the gun' had been achieved, with rank and file police officers themselves voting by over four to one against the routine arming of the force. An important backcloth to these ongoing issues involved the attempts to maintain momentum on the Northern Ireland peace process and the vexed question of the 'decommissioning' of the paramilitaries' weapons.

The rejection of the gun in routine law enforcement activity relates to a rejection of a wider 'gun culture'. Above all, however, the wholesale rejection of this gun culture itself followed directly from the sense of national outrage and distress which followed the killings at Dunblane Primary School in March 1996. In the ensuing months, the anger at a firearm licensing system which had allowed Thomas Hamilton to legally own the weapons with which he perpetrated his atrocity, bolstered by key sections of the popular press, developed into an effective and unstoppable campaign against handgun ownership. As the campaign gathered momentum, first the firearms lobby and then Lord Cullen's official report into the incident were easily bypassed. A number of significant Conservative politicians were summarily discredited and the starting positions of ACPO, the Police Superintendents' Association and, not least, the Cabinet's own preferred compromise rapidly became politically untenable. Only Blair's 'New Labour' were adept enough to ride the tidal wave as opposed to being swept aside by it. Even so, as the episode closed with the passing of the Firearms (Amendment) (Number 2) Act 1997 by the new Labour government, it was clear that Labour's final position on the gun question was some way from the position indicated by the initial utterances of its spokespersons in opposition in 1996.

Gun cultures and contemporary Britain

The banning, in 1997, of the private ownership and possession of virtually all handguns and the tightening of the licensing regimes for all other firearms draws the period covered in this and the following two chapters to a close. By the end of this unique episode in British history something of an apparent consensus against guns and gun culture had been achieved. Along the way, aside from the banning of all handguns, firearm ownership, the design and characteristics of different guns and the shooting sports themselves had been subjected to hitherto unheard of critical attention. For instance, the psychological motivations of shooters had been questioned; sceptical inferences had been drawn about the wearing of camouflage and so-called 'combat' gear in association with shooting. Such was the concern that a dress code banning camouflage, quasi-military dress or belt holsters 'likely to cause alarm to the public' was introduced by the shooting associations at the British national pistol championships at Bisley. Weapons were only to be carried in the competition arena unloaded and concealed.

Similarly, handgun shooting contests, known as 'practical shooting', popular in the USA, which simulated combat or 'police training' conditions often involving 'humanoid' targets, were especially criticised for bringing an undesirably 'macho' element into the British shooting fraternity. Practical shooting stressed speed, agility and firepower as opposed to the more disciplined aesthetic of single-shot marksmanship and advantaged shooters employing rapid-fire weapons capable of being quickly reloaded. Larger calibre semi-automatic handguns, a far cry from the single-shot .22 handguns used in Olympic pistol shooting competitions, came into their own in such contests. The increasing popularity of such competitions and rising ownership of larger calibre handguns led some commentators to point to what was to become the 'worst case' scenario, a growing 'Americanisation' of British shooting sports and the worrying rise of an American style 'gun culture' in the UK. Always compounding such concerns was the experience of the 1987 Hungerford killings and a deeply held fear that the British firearms licensing system was incapable of screening out some of the more unreliable applicants. Inadequate boys, so the argument ran, needed powerful toys to fend off their own masculine insecurities. In a wider sense, concerns were also raised about the shifting motivations of other firearms owners. While 'self-defence' is no longer considered an acceptable reason for granting a firearm certificate (Greenwood, 1972) more people were claiming to keep real or imitation firearms to deter potential attackers, and the 1990s also saw a number of incidents in which crime victims used firearms, occasionally to deadly effect, to defend themselves. In this, the trend among the wider public was thought to reflect a growing tendency among those operating outside the law, to carry guns for protection while drug-dealing, enforcing deals, asserting authority, demanding respect or guarding one's 'turf'.

While the central debate homed in upon handguns, a range of other issues connected to the broader 'gun culture' also emerged. The sale of toy guns to children became an issue during 1996, in part reflecting the entirely plausible claim that resisting the development of a gun culture required a multi-layered response (Squires, 1996b). However, any parent witnessing a child (though usually boys) pick up a stick, point it and shout 'bang', knows there is rather more to it than simply preventing the sale or purchase of gun-like toys in toy shops. Even this issue had an American reference point. The US-based marketing chain 'Toys R Us' agreed to cease selling and promoting toy or imitation firearms. The decision apparently followed a spate of incidents involving children mistakenly shot and killed by police or neighbours while playing with toy guns or killing one another while 'playing' with their parents' real firearms (Larson, 1994). No such general policy appeared in the British following Dunblane although some stores (no doubt reluctant to lose their share of a market estimated to be worth over £9 million per year) claimed to be reviewing the types of toy firearms they stocked (Ball, 1996b). Only after the British government announced its handgun control package in October 1996, Selfridges, the London department store, issued a press release declaring that it would no longer be selling toy or imitation firearms (Ball, 1996a) although other stores, for instance the Early Learning Centre, have made explicit their refusal to market war or weapon based toys over many years. Rather endorsing ELC's approach, some American research first published in 1999 suggested that, among other factors, young people who had played with toy guns as children were more aggressive as adolescents (McVeigh, 1999).

Yet if toy firearms were one cause of concern, then so were a range of leisure pursuits from computer games to the wide range of 'shoot-em-up' combat simulations in amusement arcades. Meanwhile, the debate about the influence of guns and violence in films and on TV was reprised (seldom to any conclusive effect) each time a film was alleged to have crossed some hitherto established threshold (*Reservoir Dogs*), or when real criminal events were said to have been influenced by events depicted on screen (*Natural Born Killers*).

For adults, paintball contests, popular in the USA where they were even seen as useful to the cultivation of an effective business ethos – reducing stress while promoting teamwork, assertiveness and competitive instincts (Gibson, 1994) – also spread to the UK. Interestingly, the more instrumental rationalisations of paintball (those that do not rely upon the idea that men find shooting to be simply 'fun') bear an uncanny resemblance to the justifications offered up for pistol shooting itself. In a couple of articles which must qualify among the most untimely events in recent magazine publishing, the men's magazines *Maxim* and *Men's Health* featured articles on the merits of pistol shooting in their April 1996 editions – available on the news stands during late March 1996 – just days after the tragedy at Dunblane.

In *Maxim*, Ndidi Nkagbu offered pistol shooting as a therapy for relieving executive stresses. Apparently, 'a growing number of young professionals are bringing a gruelling day to a close with a stress busting session at their local gun club … the sense of well-being that comes after shooting a gun is claimed to have a calming effect similar to meditation'. Many men, and a few women, appear to gain a great deal from 'chilling out with a 9 mm semi-automatic'. Something about the precision, care and concentration needed to repeat the mundane activity of making a hole in a cardboard target 15 to 25 metres away is 'great for releasing your aggression'. But the author then continues in a different vein, for care, concentration and precision sit rather uneasily with the idea that your time at the gun range might be 'half an hour pretending to be Mel Gibson in *Lethal Weapon*' (Nkagbu, 1996). Likewise, while Michael Bracewell's article in *Men's Health* attempts to offer some insights into what he calls men's emotional and psychological fixation for guns, it is ultimately the 'man-making' qualities of handguns that he cherishes. Handling firearms, he argues, encourages discipline, responsibility, concentration and insights into the self. Shooting a gun becomes a form of healthy and responsible mental training for manhood (Bracewell, 1996).

However, the suggestion that gun clubs might be attracting the 'stressed out' and volatile, perhaps even encouraging these to own their own firearms, caused a degree of alarm on public safety grounds. Gun clubs had an important delegated authority to police their own memberships (subject to Home Office rules and police inspections and the requirement that all prospective members undertake safety training and undergo a probationary period). Furthermore, while all clubs had an obvious incentive in weeding out unsuitable persons, the idea that shooting might offer the stressed and unstable some form of therapy had an uncomfortable degree of ambiguity about it. Of course, not all commentators agreed that, in the UK, masculinity needed firearms, or that other traits and values thought to be connected with shooting, particularly those forms of shooting associated with the USA (large calibre handguns, 'macho' guns used in the movies, combat-style shooting or paintball contests) had anything much to offer to society, personnel management or British business culture.

A very British gun culture

But if it was, in part, the supposedly American influence that caused questions to be asked about male psychology, guns and gun clubs, the assault on the UK's nascent gun culture during 1996 exposed even the very British shotgun to a barrage of criticism. The shotgun was closely associated with a more elitist variety of sports shooting, or 'field', 'game' and 'country' sports. One of its leading lobby organisations – the British Association for Shooting and Conservation (BASC) – had been established precisely to present a very responsible, rural and environmentally friendly public image (Taylor, 1997). However, the shotgun itself had a rather more chequered past.

For a start, and partly because of a historically rather more permissive licensing system, there were considerably more shotguns in circulation, roughly seven legally owned shotguns for each legally owned handgun (1.4 million shotguns compared to just over 200,000 handguns in 1996). Furthermore, a legitimate case for the use of shotguns in agricultural pest control, aside from their role in a rather more diverse rural economy, had been established for many years. Yet precisely because of the shotgun's greater availability, it was a weapon which – in its illegal 'sawn-off' form – had become associated with a particular stage in the escalating British crime war: armed robbery (Weatherhead and Robinson, 1970; Ball *et al.*, 1978; Harding, 1979).

Ball *et al.* (1978) argue that bank or 'security' robberies, more than any other serious crimes, reveal a specific ancestry very closely reflecting the security measures and policies adopted by financial institutions such as banks and building societies. As security systems improved to present an effective barrier to stealth robbery attempts, the point of attack in robberies shifted to the staff working within the public areas of the banks, and then to the customers or to the security guards transporting the money. In other words, Ball *et al.* argue, during the 1960s the 'security war' gave way to a 'pavement war' and, on the pavement or the floor of the bank, the sawn-off shotgun was a particularly effective frightener, carried, according to John McVicar, more to intimidate than to shoot. Later, as banks and building societies invested in greater security, opportunist armed robbers were displaced onto 'softer' targets, such as post offices, off-licences and petrol stations (Matthews, 1996). Many of these opportunist robbers (perhaps as many as 50 per cent) carried only replica or imitation weapons that were incapable of firing. To the offenders such 'guns' had many of the advantages sought in a real weapon but fewer of the risks. One can only say fewer of the risks – there have been occasions when offenders armed with replica weapons have been shot by police armed response teams. We examine this question of police responses to armed incidents in later chapters.

According to McVicar, 'The arms used in armed robberies [in the 1960s] were mostly sawn-off shotguns, chosen because they looked nasty and made a lot of noise. They weren't really used to kill anyone; they were used for intimidation … even loaded with rice' (McVicar interviewed, Mungo, 1996). During the late 1960s and early 1970s, 'armed robberies in the metropolitan area of London were running at the rate of one every five days, mostly in broad daylight and during business hours' (Ball *et al.*, 1978). While Ball *et al.* attribute the increasing resort to firearms by criminals in terms of what was needed to carry out the robbery, others have pointed to the significance of the abolition, in 1965, of the death penalty for murders committed in the course of a robbery (Waddington, 1988; Ingleton, 1997). 'Before this change', according to Waddington, 'robbers frisked each other before going out on a job to ensure that their partners in crime carried no weapons, lest they all be hanged for the murder committed by anyone of them' (Waddington, 1994). The increasing rate of armed robberies, particularly in the capital and against which the police were having only limited success, led eventually to the formation of the specialist Metropolitan Police robbery and flying squads. The flying squad, in due course celebrated on TV as *The Sweeney*, portrayed a new rougher, tougher style of policing relatively unfamiliar to British TV audiences brought up on a diet of *Dixon*, *Z-Cars* and *Softly, Softly* (but also an increasing number of imported American 'cop shows'). Either way, whether on the streets in the 'pavement war' or on the TV screens of the nation, the 'sawn-off' established an unenviable place for the shotgun in post-war British criminal history.

As we shall see, an intriguing combination of voices – former armed robbers, retired and serving police officers, journalists and criminologists – argue now that the character of armed robbery – and of armed robbers – has changed. Although the number of incidents recorded show a fairly dramatic increase since the late 1960s (almost 500 armed robberies recorded in England and Wales in 1970, nearly 6,000 in 1992), the proportion of these committed with shotguns has fallen significantly. Police records indicate that the handgun is now the weapon of choice among armed robbers. The reliability of the figures is open to question, however. If witnesses do not actually see a weapon it may not exist; if it is not fired – and they seldom are – it may not be real, hence the interpretation of the figures has become a matter of specific criminological debate (Maybanks and Yardley, 1992; Morrison and O'Donnell, 1994, 1997; Matthews, 1996).

The fortunes of the shotgun took a turn for the worse in 1968 with the passage of the Firearms Act. Until 1966 the Home Secretary and the police had been resisting the imposition of additional controls to restrict shotguns. Yet a dramatic shooting incident in August 1966, in which three police officers were killed, shattered the apparent consensus. While the officers were killed with handguns, Roy Jenkins, as Home Secretary, mindful of the growing concern about the use of shotguns in armed crime went on to propose further controls on shotguns. Two years later, the consolidating 1968 Firearms Act was passed followed, the same year, by a tough new Criminal Justice Act as the government looked for a firm response to the seemingly growing threat of violent crime (Greenwood, 1972). Another incident, nineteen years later, in Hungerford, led to the production of a hastily drafted and rather compromised Firearms Amendment Bill, banning the American style 'automatic' or 'pump-action' shotguns and restricting a shotgun's breech or magazine capacity to two shots. The resulting act, the Firearms (Amendment) Act 1988, (discussed more fully in chapter 2) satisfied almost no-one and did nothing to address the question of the handguns with which Michael Ryan had killed half of his victims. Subsequently, smaller but rather less dramatic incidents with, fortunately, lower death tolls have seen men armed with shotguns embark upon 'spree' shooting events (Timmins, 1996). Even so, no further shotgun control proposals emerged until 1996. Nonetheless, by the time of the inquiry into the Dunblane killings and the emerging national debate about firearms control, it is fair to say that the image of the shotgun had become somewhat tarnished.

Labour members of the unfortunate Home Affairs Select Committee which reported, controversially, on the possession of handguns in August 1996, had published their own rejected proposals including tougher licensing arrangements for shotguns and a ban on the issue of shotgun certificates in urban areas (Mullin, 1996). In the late 1980s even spokesmen for sports shooting had themselves raised similar concerns. Arguing the case for the 'sporting gun' in 1988, Jackson quoted the remarks of the Director of the British Field Sports Society to the effect that 'the growing number of weapons being held in urban areas' appeared to have little to do with sports shooting (Jackson, 1988: 83; Kopel, 1992b). By 1996, however, when the call for tougher control of shotguns was taken up by the 'Snowdrop' gun control campaign and adopted by some newspapers any such reservations had disappeared. In October the *Sunday Times* reported that ACPO were to press the government to include shotguns within the tougher licensing arrangements which applied to 'section one' firearms and to subject all applicants to a more restrictive 'good reason' test (Grey *et al.*, 1996). Commentators from the shooting associations replied that such proposals were a part of what they had feared all along, a politically motivated attack upon 'country sports' and rural ways of life culminating in generalised disarmament. For the 'countryside lobby' the proposal to restrict shotgun ownership came on top of recent proposals to ban fox hunting and other hunting with dogs and in the midst of British farming's BSE crisis. Commentators in the *Times* cautioned against proposals which would further alienate the 'rural community' and a countryside campaign developed which appeared to throw into sharp relief a number of important cultural differences between the UK's rural and urban communities.

While the shotgun had acquired a reputation as the quintessentially English and socially exclusive firearm, many aspects of the recent debates about its usage or control echo themes from the American gun control debate. Thus, cultural and regional differences were compounded by misunderstandings and mutual distrust. Just as the weapons themselves had spilled beyond their particular cultural niche, so the supporting discourses of, on the one hand, rights, rural tradition and economy and, on the other, social control and public safety became somewhat ideologically overstretched. In the arguments of the shotgunners (similar to those of the NRA in the USA) any further controls were seen as irreversible steps towards their eventual disarmament culminating in the elimination of their lifestyles and livelihoods. For the pro-control lobbyists an insufficiently tough regulation of the shotgun was itself a dangerous folly, a loophole in our gun laws allowing the slippage of weapons into criminal hands and the first foolhardy step on the slippery slope towards an American style gun culture. While something of a consensus appeared to prevail in respect of the handgun – which many commentators were willing to describe as somehow 'unBritish' – the shotgun was a rather more complex proposition. Contrasting national stereotypes – the UK as consensual, peaceful and unarmed and the USA as culturally diverse, conflict-ridden and armed – came to appear rather inadequate.

Even as journalists and commentators invoked the Anglo-American contrast with unerring regularity during the period covered by this analysis, it became increasingly clear that this image of peaceful, consensual, the UK besieged by an encroaching American gun culture required some qualification. It is fair to note at the outset that the contrast drawn perhaps tells us more about the values underpinning the political culture subscribed to by many UK journalists and, probably, most of their readers, than it describes the firearm problem.

'Bang!' goes the neighbourhood

Central to the UK's denial of the gun was, as we have seen, the attempt to associate it with things American – American culture, American society, American cowboys, gangsters or cops and American film or television. Yet even as we tried to deny the gun any purchase in British culture and society we also began to acknowledge that it was not quite so simple. While some areas were thought to be far removed from the sound of gunfire, we were not quite so sure about a number of others. And yet, firearm incidents were being reported 'out of place'. Shootings were occurring where journalists and the public had not expected them. The argument that firearms were essentially American, fundamentally un-British, faltered the moment it was implied that there were parts of the UK where shootings were less unexpected. Even so, shootings were being reported in the most unexpected places.

At 8.30 p.m. on April 18th 1995, a Metropolitan Police officer was shot following a call, described as 'routine', to a house in Ilford, east London. The officer later died as a result of gunshot wounds to the chest and stomach. A neighbour, who heard the shots fired and witnessed the aftermath, commented, 'I can't believe it's happened in this area. It's full of respectable people' (*Guardian*, 19.4.1995). Another neighbour, quoted in the *Daily Mail* added, 'It is all horrifying. This is a quiet neighbourhood' (*Daily Mail*, 19.4.1995). A Meridian TV news report echoed the theme almost exactly a year later after a police informant was shot and killed at his home in Southampton in what police later acknowledged had been a drugs-related professional hit. A local woman interviewed commented: 'It's all a bit scary really, this is not the sort of thing you normally expect around here' (Meridian TV News, 15.4.1996). Likewise, Duncan Campbell, writing in the *Guardian* about a dispute within London's Kurdish community in Islington which had escalated to shootings and firebombings, interviewed residents who described the area thus: 'This is not a street that is used to shoot-outs [it] is mainly residential, [we have] never had any trouble before' (*Guardian*, 29.4.1994). In August 1994, it was a 'running gun battle' in 'a quiet residential area in leafy suburbia' which caused the alarm. 'For a few minutes of terror, residents of a leafy London street found themselves in the front line of a gun battle … as a quiet street in suburban London exploded into violence' (Twomey, *Daily Express*, 4.8.1994b).

In 1995 newspapers carried reports of an 'armed raider' shot and killed in an 'ambush' by armed police at a social club in Tyneside. The police had received a tip-off that the social club was to be raided and took a decision to station a tactical firearms unit within the club. In the confusion when the intruders were challenged, police officers opened fire, killing one man. The *Guardian* rounded off the story by noting that local residents had been startled that 'armed criminals had come to the generally quiet area'. Adding emphasis, a neighbour's comment was recorded. 'It is frightening to think that people have been using guns so close to our homes, [this] is normally a quiet place' (*Guardian*, 25.4.1995). However, following the case of a five-year-old boy mistakenly shot and killed in Bolton in August 1997, as rival drug dealers attempted to shoot his step-father, a central theme in the media reporting was that 'the horror of drugs related violence is spreading from the inner city' (*BBC Nine O'Clock News*, 6.8.1997, *Guardian*, 7.8.1997). Although occurring in the 'home of the gun' – the USA – such themes were equally prevalent in the British media's reporting of the 'Jonesboro massacre' in March 1998. Two embittered Arkansas schoolboys with a substantial arsenal of automatic weapons and 3,000 rounds of ammunition had opened fire upon a playground full of their classmates after one boy had apparently been rejected by a girlfriend. Several pupils were killed and injured, mainly girls. Writing in the *Guardian*, Vulliamy noted the irony that such shooting incidents, four in as many months in the USA's rural Bible belt, were happening in quiet, community towns, 'places people thought of as safe' (Vulliamy, 1998). Understandably, such themes and images also dominated the early reporting of the Dunblane tragedy. Only a few weeks later, precisely the same issues emerged as journalists sought to come to terms with the massacre in Port Arthur, Tasmania. As Wilson, writing in the *Daily Mail*, put it, the peculiar horror lay not just in the number of people killed, 'but that it should have happened not in some crime ridden city but in a place remarkable only for its tranquility' (Wilson, 1996).

Such press reports make use of a kind of 'residential closure' by way of returning to the supposedly exceptional nature of the event which established the 'news worthiness' of the incident in the first place. There is a basic symmetry to the press reports. Guns obviously seem unwelcome and intrusive in 'quiet' neighbourhoods. This appears so whether they are carried, and fired by criminals or by the police. Each time the story communicates surprise that firearms have been used 'out of place' in some quiet, respectable, leafy, residential community in the UK, we are less and less able to console ourselves with the myth that the problem is one of exclusively American origins. This is undoubtedly a problem for our discourses of law and order, for the notions of 'community' and 'neighbourhood' are frequently employed as supposed antidotes to problems of crime, public disorder and the social fragmentation from which they are often said to spring. It can come as something of a shock to discover how vulnerable the peace can be.

Staring down the barrel

This idea of unarmed Britain staring down the barrel of the American nightmare formed a dominant theme in the firearms news reporting in the British press during the period 1994 to 1997 (Appleyard, 1996). During June 1994, David Leppard, writing in the *Sunday Times*, described a recent arrest of armed robbers in London.

> A suspected armed robber lies spread-eagled on the pavement. A second man is handcuffed face down in the road. Stunned passers-by watch as plain-clothes detectives stand over them brandishing machine guns. It could have been a scene from Los Angeles or New York. It wasn't. This was London's Regent Street last week. The detectives were from Scotland Yard's flying squad, they had just completed another successful armed arrest. Welcome to the face of modern Britain.
>
> (Leppard, 1994a)

Perhaps our American nightmare had already arrived.

Alternatively, our American future could be the USA's own past. Peter Waddington, wrote a background piece in the *Daily Mail* following an exchange of shots between robbers and police following an attempted smash and grab raid at a Putney jewellery shop. (The incident was featured on most front pages the following day: 'Gun battle in leafy suburbia', *Daily Express*, 3.8.1994, 'Jewel bandit shoots himself after blasting two cops', *Daily Mirror*). Waddington described the scene: 'A quiet street in suburban London explodes into violence. Two armed robbers flee from their car firing at police as they run. Three officers fall to the floor with gunshot wounds, while others return fire from an arsenal of high-powered weapons ... but this is not Chicago in the 1920s but Britain in 1994' (Waddington, 1994). A witness, quoted in the *Daily Mirror* made a similar connection, 'It was just like something out of a western'.

Moore, Leppard and Waddington are by no means the only journalists or commentators to pose the UK's firearm question in this fashion. Articles of this type typically come in three stages. First the enormous differences between the UK and the USA with respect to the gun are emphasised. Next, the risks entailed by the 'distorted' American ideal of armed citizenship are described and, finally, we are led to fear the worst about the emergence of an American style 'gun culture' in the UK. Thus, writing a background article – 'Mean Streets' – drawing upon findings from a *Sunday Times* survey of British Chief Constables about the police use of firearms and the deployment of armed response vehicles in their force areas, Ellis and Foster noted that, while drugs were at the heart of the rising crime and violence, the new threat apparently came from the availability of guns. 'London, Manchester, Birmingham and Glasgow and our other great cities are not yet exactly like New York, Chicago, Los Angeles or Miami, but they are getting there. And the peace of rural England is being similarly disturbed' (Ellis and Foster, 1994). However, developing a theme that was to be voiced repeatedly during the next two years, the authors argued that greater protection for, or the arming of, the police would only address some of the worst symptoms of the seemingly growing 'tidal wave of crime' and drug-related violence, but not the underlying causes.

Writing in the *Sun* two months later, John Capers, introduced as the former head of the NYPD's drug-homicide squad, took up the issue of what the UK needed to do to avoid the 'horror of New York'. He noted that commentators were drawing parallels between Moss Side, in Manchester, and New York but argued that while the problem of firearm violence in Moss Side was getting worse it hadn't yet reached New York proportions. 'Your gun problem is not as acute as America ... but what scares me about Britain is that it is becoming easier for criminals to get guns while your police are armed only with a small truncheon' (Capers, 1994). His immediate concern, however, was less about the fact that arming the police would increase the number of guns on the street and risk escalating levels of violence, and more about the better protection of police officers. 'It is insanity for society to expect to maintain law and order without equipping police officers adequately'. He went on to specify different projects offering some purchase on the problem – early intervention projects for children and young people deemed 'at risk' and specific strategies for tackling the growing problem of armed drug gangs.

Nevertheless, he argued, the immediate problem facing the British police was a generation of young people with dangerously American attitudes towards drugs, guns, gang membership and the police and who were now active on the streets.

> These people have no fear and know they can do anything they like if the police are not armed. You don't know what you're up against … your police are going to be up against hoods carrying guns more and more – and a lot more cops are going to get killed and hurt. … It is not a question of if it will happen in Britain, but when.
>
> (Capers, 1994)

The same line of argument, that changing circumstances will require the British police to adopt firearms, had been developed by a Metropolitan police officer in an article in *Police* magazine on his return from a visit with the NYPD. Facing tougher and apparently more determined offenders, he argued, the police will find themselves powerless to act if unarmed (Shaw, 1989). By contrast, Waddington has argued how arming the police could significantly increase the hazards of much routine police work.

> Since the gun in the holster poses the danger of it being snatched, many [US] cops take the view that in any kind of confrontation they might as well hold it in their hand and use it as a means of intimidation. The result is that much earlier resort is made to firearms than is strictly necessary. … [Yet] dealing with a pub brawl is bad enough, imagine doing so while hanging on to a gun with one hand.
>
> (Waddington, 1989)

While particular responses may have differed, the idea that the UK was being sucked, inevitably, into the horrors of the American gun culture was becoming common ground. Less than a month after Caper's dire warnings came news of two Metropolitan police officers shot in the street by masked men riding a motorbike. According to David Rose, writing in the *Observer*, the incident established 'a new benchmark of peril'. The incident came only a month after two police officers had been killed while responding to apparently innocuous disturbance calls from the public. During 1993–1994, according to Rose, more police officers had been killed in London than in Los Angeles (Rose, 1994). These incidents, and particularly a meeting between Commissioner Paul Condon and colleagues of the murdered officers, were said to have had a profound effect on Condon and he asked one of his Deputy Assistant Commissioners to prepare a report on the issues relating to both the arming and the better protection of the police. This developing debate regarding the arming of the police will be considered later.

Yet while a former NYPD chief could draw upon American lessons to advocate arming the British police, Simon Jenkins, writing in the *Times* the following month, derived an opposite conclusion. He drew attention to one particular area of criminal activity 'blighted by guns', the crack cocaine trade, itself an American and Jamaican import. Drawing upon American experiences, he argued that a general arming of the police to deal with this specific crime threat would bring foreseeable disadvantages. He claimed that many police officers knew this too.

> More sensible policemen do not want an armed police force. They know it would encourage arms among criminals and not save police lives. … [Guns] encourage the "Hollywood cop" police image at the expense of community policing. After ten painful years the police have begun to recover from the disaster of the macho "hi-tech" SPG era, an overarmed and insensitive paramilitary approach to law and order.
>
> (Jenkins, 1994)

Furthermore, an armed American police system had not prevented the emergence of criminal drug gangs. On the contrary, when the demand was high and the trade lucrative enough, such gangs were almost bound to flourish, bringing with them their own armed enforcement culture. Such gangs did present a specific policing problem but, Jenkins continued, 'it is fantasy to believe an armed police will do anything to counter these threats'. Furthermore, the one country with wide experience of attempting to use a heavily armed police and paramilitary force to stamp out the cocaine trade is the USA, but 'the result has been a disaster for the American police and especially for its relations with black people' (Jenkins, 1994). Essentially similar conclusions were drawn in *Guardian* editorials of April 14th and August 4th 1994. 'The lessons of America cannot be ignored. Arming the police only increases violence … worse still is the way the gun drives a wedge between the police and the public' (*Guardian*, 4.8.1994).

The USA, the destination to which we were moving ever closer, and the destiny we should seek to avoid, became a source of quite contrasting lessons, depending upon the perspective of the writer. And if former American cops could offer their words of wisdom about how the UK might respond to apparently rising levels of armed crime, British journalists could also cross the Atlantic seeking other lessons. Peter Hitchens, corresponding from Washington for the *Daily Express* ventured into the developing debate on the arming of the police. Indirectly he responded to issues raised by Capers, noting that a society can quickly get used to armed policemen and, 'once they strap on [their guns] they will never get rid of them' (Hitchens, 1994). His particular fears centred upon the immediate increase in risk resulting from the presence of additional guns on the street (during 1993 in excess of one thousand civilians were killed by police shootings in the USA and a further three thousand were injured) and upon problems of violence escalation. Hitchens reported growing concern in the USA about an apparent 'arms race' developing between the police and criminal gangs and noted the growing pressure for permissive 'concealed-carry' laws emanating from residents wanting guns for self-protection.

Hitchens declared his American evidence as sufficient proof that the UK had better find another solution to the growing problem of firearm violence rather than arming the police. Yet his own preferred solution was no less dramatic and, in the light of American evidence, no less dubious. His argument was both cultural and constitutional. 'Britain with its deep reserves of civilisation and restraint, may still have a small chance of putting back the clock to the days when every policeman was armed with the willing support of every citizen – a far better protection than a 9 mm automatic. [Yet] the weaponless constable also had one other invisible safeguard which was wantonly thrown away.' While Parliament, allegedly preferring to 'keep its own hands clean and let the police dirty themselves with death and revolvers', had debated the death penalty many times it had 'never properly debated arming the police'. He attacked successive Home Office administrations for concealing and massaging the statistics which could show that 'armed crime began to sprout like a weed a few weeks after the death penalty was abolished'. The 1960s were depicted as a period when an older criminal culture sustained, in part, by factors such as the death penalty, was itself transformed. Thus, 'the 1963 Great Train robbery was committed without firearms but the prison raid which sprang many of them from gaol was carried with the full modern panoply of firearms' (Hitchens, 1994).

Ultimately, Hitchens argues, the nation has never been offered, 'a simple choice between capital punishment for murderers, or gun law for all of us'. His final image – allegedly the result of politicians having mishandled the real gun question for so long – is both dramatic and depressing. Only the gun-driven nightmare of the USA awaits us. 'Not many years hence the last bobby in the last shire will buckle on his magnum and transform himself into just another cop. Will we ever forgive those who, without any mandate, brought Dodge city to Britain? Should we?' (Hitchens, 1994).

As a debate on the supposed 'routine' arming of the police heated up during 1994, Paul Condon, drew his own American parallels in the course of a press conference to launch his first Annual Report as Commissioner of the Metropolitan Police. As we have seen, Condon had earlier voiced his concern about firearms-related crime in the capital. He had commissioned a review of police firearms deployment and of the defensive equipment available to police officers. These issues were foremost among the questions raised by journalists attending the press conference. Responding to questions Condon had noted, 'we are not in a gun culture like the USA ... we still have the opportunity to sit on top of it in this country. Better legislation on the acquisition and distribution of guns was an alternative to an armed police service'. He continued that it was time for a review of these questions, adding that this was essential to ensure that the UK did not 'adopt the gun culture of the USA' (Tendler, 1994f; Bennetto, 1994; Twomey, 1994b). Condon's further comments, particularly his suggestion that dishonest firearms dealers were the most likely source of 70 per cent of the illegal firearms recovered by the police, provoked an angry reaction from sections of the gun trade.

Bent dealers?

According to Condon,

> Seventy per cent of firearms used in crime have not been stolen and recycled they've been recycled through legitimate dealers through a variety of scams involving legitimate use of guns ... [and] things like the deactivation of guns.

There's a whole range of clever things that can be done to recycle deactivated guns brought in from Eastern Europe, deactivated, reactivated and recycled.

(Tendler, 1994f)

Condon's comments, particularly the point about 'scams' involving licensed dealers adding to the supply of illegal firearms, were widely reported.

The following day spokesmen representing the gun trade retaliated, challenging Condon to produce any evidence he had linking licensed dealers to the underworld. The issue rumbled on for some months in shooting magazines where the Commissioner's remarks were taken to be indicative of his allegedly broader gun control ambitions. In January 1995's edition of *Guns Review*, editor Colin Greenwood returned to a favourite theme. 'If Sir Paul Condon, or anyone else, thinks that the problem [of armed crime] can be solved or even reduced by attacks on law abiding shooters he is mistaken ... It will never be solved by attacking the gun which is no more than a symptom of the disease of lawlessness' (*Guns Review*, January 1995: 12). The day after Condon made his statement, the Gun Traders Association, representing some 400 firearms dealers, wrote to him expressing 'grave concern' about his comments and requesting clarification, while the British Association for Shooting and Conservation expressed their fear that his comments would lead to further restrictions on recreational shooters 'but which would have no effect on armed crime'. Michael Yardley, spokesman for the British Field Sports Society, accused Condon of attempting to engineer 'a policy change by innuendo'. Yardley claimed he had earlier been involved in a survey which showed 'only 1 per cent of guns used in crime had ever been within the licensing system'. The onus was on the police, he said, to prove their allegations.

Despite the heat generated by this particular interchange, it has to be said that as a comment on the sources of illegal firearms it was rather much more ambiguous than it might at first have seemed. For instance, while firearms might make their way into criminal hands by a variety of routes including: theft, illegal manufacture, illegal importation (smuggling), reactivation of deactivated weapons and diversion from the legal trade, the (admittedly) limited evidence available does suggest that one source of supply dwarfs all the others. There is virtually no evidence of the illegal manufacture of working firearms in the UK although, during the early 1990s evidence emerged of a thriving but localised cottage industry reactivating previously deactivated weapons (especially weapons deactivated prior to 1995 before the more rigorous deactivation specifications were introduced). Around a thousand firearms (handguns, rifles and shotguns are reported stolen each year) while Customs and Excise records show a fairly stable, if slightly rising pattern of illegal weapons seized at points of entry into the country (333 handguns, 174 rifles and 362 shotguns seized in 1997) (Customs and Excise, *Annual Report*, 1997). The remaining criminal supply line is diversion from the legal trade which, again, is a rather less than clear description of the actual source of illegal weapons. As a number of commentators have pointed out, other than those illegally manufactured, arguably all firearms begin life as legal weapons – in the factory – the real policy question concerns where, precisely, they leave the legitimate supply chain.

In response, Scotland Yard insisted that the figures were based upon intelligence sources and, in order not to compromise existing investigations, they had not been published. However, it was confirmed that for the past year the National Criminal Intelligence Service (NCIS) had been conducting an inquiry into the origins of criminal firearms. Although no official results or statistics had been disclosed, a police spokesman interviewed said he would not argue with Condon's figures (Darbyshire, 1994). Subsequently police sources confirmed that a number of proactive intelligence-led operations had taken place against individual firearms dealers who had drawn suspicion upon themselves by virtue of dubious transactions or levels of purchasing seemingly incompatible with their legitimate trade or business. There were some 243 licensed firearms dealers in the Metropolitan Police area yet only a handful had been the subject of proactive police operations. According to police sources, the problem had to be seen as one involving a few questionable dealers occasionally venturing into the 'grey market' in the context of an otherwise legitimate and responsible trade. Police evidence, contrary to claims made by supposedly informed sources within the shooting fraternity, was that there were nowhere near one million unlicensed firearms in the UK. 'The idea that there may be as many as one million unlicensed guns is hugely hyped and probably wrong. There is no evidence of wholesale smuggling or circulating of illegal handguns … the UK is not awash with illegal guns' (Hallowes, 1999).

Despite this, no hitherto published evidence or independent confirmation of the sources of firearms used in crime came up with figures anywhere approaching the 70 per cent cited by Condon. This, in itself, is not surprising given the fundamental access problems in researching the matter and the fact that it has anyway been a somewhat neglected area in British criminology. Morrison and O'Donnell found most of their armed robber interviewees acquiring (buying or renting) their weapons from 'friends' with few demonstrating any knowledge or interest in where the guns actually originated. Occasionally they mentioned criminal black-marketeers, but 'under the counter' deals by licensed dealers did not feature (Morrison and O'Donnell, 1994). Likewise, Maybanks' study in 1992, although having found that only 2 per cent of the 'criminal firearms' recovered by police had ever been licensed, noted that only eight weapons were known to be stolen whereas nearly two-thirds did not have serial numbers rendering it almost impossible to trace them further back. Even so, no reference was made to licensed firearm dealers as a source of weapon supply (Maybanks, 1992). Corkery's 1994 study on the theft of firearms noted a link between guns stolen and their eventual use in crime – particularly robberies – but the conclusion, admittedly drawn upon the relatively small proportion of weapons actually recovered by the police, could say little about the origins of the remainder. Based upon this sample of weapons recovered (which might not be representative) criminal firearms appeared to come from a range of sources with no one source of supply obviously predominating (Corkery, 1994).

In the manner of much police 'operational intelligence', however, it may be the case that Condon's information was of a more anecdotal nature. Rather later some forensic evidence produced by the police strengthened Condon's claims. This evidence revealed the lengths gone to by illegal dealers to erase identifying marks and serial numbers from unlicensed firearms. One person who had the most to gain by 'sanitising' an illegal firearm in this fashion, to prevent it being traced back to him, would be the bent dealer. Crooked dealers, as it were, had both motive and opportunity and the technical knowledge to make a good job of obscuring the origin of an illegal gun. It did not amount to proof that Condon was correct but it rather strengthened his claim (Hallowes, 1999).

There was further support for the Commissioner in a case which came to trial in 1995. Five defendants who ran a registered firearms dealership were initially found guilty of illegally distributing some 200 handguns. The particular 'scam' at the centre of the case involved fictitious sales of firearms. Some of the weapons were said to have actually been sold to 'active' offenders. In the event, the convictions were overturned in the Court of Appeal on a somewhat technical legal point. Nonetheless, the case was certainly evidence of registered firearms dealers illegally trading in weapons and, to police eyes, it might well seem that this was a legal loophole which needed to be filled (*Times*, 'Law Report', 14.8.1996).

An editorial in the *Daily Telegraph* expressed its general support for Condon's efforts to win the battle against armed criminals by cutting off their supplies of weapons. But regarding the trade in licensed firearms, it concluded, somewhat complacently as it turned out, that there was little to be gained from further regulation of the legitimate trade. 'The law on firearms is probably as tight as it can be' (*Daily Telegraph*, 8.3.1994).

Cautious official pessimism

Not all police officers appeared entirely satisfied with the Commissioner's responses to the UK's apparently growing gun problem. Despite having announced a firearms policy review, Condon continued to describe his stance on firearms – and that of the Metropolitan Police – as 'event driven'. While, in one sense, this official stance alludes to the traditionally responsive nature of much police action against crime, in another sense, it implied that the stakes might at any time be raised by criminal elements (and any ensuing media or political outcry). Above all, however, the notion of 'event driven' pointed to a doctrine of 'cautious official pessimism' which implied that the routine arming of the British police, if not absolutely inevitable, was beginning to look a distinct possibility.

For Caroline Nicholl, a chief superintendent from Milton Keynes who had just returned from a study tour of the USA examining police responses to armed incidents, being 'event driven' implied ceding the initiative on crime control to the criminal. Writing in the *Observer* she called for a more robust response on the part of the police and implicitly criticised Condon's decisions. 'Arming more officers just puts more guns on the street', she commented, 'we do not want to follow the bad example of America … we have a choice of either being reactive in a way that will escalate the violence, or dealing with the problem in ways that will reinforce the values and culture that have made Britain a comparatively safe gun free society' (Nicholl, 1994). She supported her argument with figures which purported to show the dangers of a routinely armed police; in New York the majority of shootings were, apparently, by police officers. 'In 1993 the New York police shot dead twenty-two and injured fifty-eight, but nine out of ten police bullets miss their targets'. Arming the police would reduce neither the risk nor the threat, she concluded. To be 'event driven' was to be driven down a slippery slope where the stakes were constantly raised,

> for if every increase in violence or gun use is met by a police response to have more guns this will take us to a point at which citizens will start to believe there are only two options: arming the police or arming themselves ... we need a much wider debate rather than allowing the situation to slip too far. ... The issue of firearms is not one for the police alone. It is a challenge for society to get the guns off the street.
>
> (Nicholl, 1994)

David Leppard, writing in the *Sunday Times*, echoed the point:

> The rapid rise in drug related crime, a growing black market in automatic weapons, and the rise of a new breed of criminal who resorts to gratuitous violence, have all raised the stakes. It may only be a matter of time before another police officer is killed prompting renewed public outcry ... moving matters further down the slippery slope. The sight of machine gun carrying officers in busy London streets could be an avoidable evil. But isn't it time for parliament to decide?
>
> (Leppard, 1994b)

Being 'event driven' was also no solution to spokesmen for the Police Federation, which represents police constables and all ranks up to and including inspector. Fred Broughton, chair of the Federation, called for a clearer position to be adopted. He argued that many of his colleagues linked the abolition of capital punishment to the increasing use of firearms in crime. David French, chair of the constable's section of the Police Federation, raised the question of whether the decision on arming the British police might ultimately be decided by a European court. He noted, 'we are being driven by events and those events might lead to a decision taken in Europe on whether we eventually carry arms'. But then he added, as if by way of attempted reassurance, that there was no possibility of gun battles on British streets because 'this is not America where the right to own a gun is ingrained in history' (Campbell and Travis, 1995). Since shots had already been exchanged on British streets and since many commentators – journalists, police officers and academics alike – had already drawn parallels with the 'American gun culture', then this 'reassurance' had a somewhat hollow ring to it.

Lessons from the USA

During the twentieth century the USA has frequently been regarded as a leading influence upon British social and economic developments. This tendency to look to the USA, however, certainly has a much longer historical pedigree in the way the old European societies looked to the 'New World' and its new frontiers as a means of rejuvenating and enriching themselves (Slotkin, 1973). In the twentieth century, however, one of the more critically perceptive attempts to examine the phenomenon of 'Americanism' has been Gramsci's essay 'Americanism and Fordism' written during the early 1930s while its author was incarcerated (Gramsci, 1971). In his essay Gramsci attempted to determine whether the development of new systems of industrial production (principally the scientific rationalist methods pioneered by Taylor in Henry Ford's new car factories) and related systems of distribution, communication and mass consumption prefigured the coming of a new type of culture and, ultimately, a 'new type of man'. Central to Gramsci's analysis was the question whether American civilisation represented a new culture which would 'invade' Europe. True to his own interpretation of progressive historical materialism he concluded that the USA was not so much a new culture but rather an advanced development of European traditions – 'an intensification of European civilisation' (a condition towards which Europe was already heading) and which would, in due course, overturn European culture and society 'by the implacable weight of its economic [and cultural] production (Gramsci, 1971: 316–317).

For Gramsci, Fordist industrial production methods became the crucial foundations for a depiction of modernist order. Ironically, however, Gramsci described a time when the criminological consequences of prohibition in the USA and, especially, the perceived threat of the distribution of automatic firearms among a criminal population ('gangsters' and 'tommy guns') were sowing the seeds of a particular kind of disorder. Yet irrespective of the quality of the social order achieved under American industrialism, the proliferation of personal firearms in an armed society (and the growing fears and insecurities both contributing to and resulting from this) came, by the end of the century to be the cause of a uniquely American form of disorder: as Zimring and Hawkins put it, a third world homicide rate in a first world society (Zimring and Hawkins, 1997). Hence, looking again to the USA, interpreting its late-modern or even 'post-modern' social relations, we might ask once again whether a new kind of culture (the gun culture) or a new kind of man is emerging. This man, surrounded by a complex range of fears and insecurities characteristic of our late modern condition, apparently seeks safety neither in numbers nor in the social contract and its collectivist promise of justice, security and citizenship. In this sense, firearms and a new lethal individualism bring with them a potential to unravel the relationships between civilisation and the rule of law in modern liberal-democratic political discourse (Hunt, 1996). Whether this represents a completely new individualism or, as Gramsci suggested, simply the acute intensification of a kind of competitive individualism which is already familiar may be less important than its implications. Lacking confidence in democratic collectivism, firearms and armed self-defence may be the new man's solutions. But, as we have seen, these bring their own consequences.

An early indication of the dominant perspective on the USA adopted by British journalists discussing firearms issues came in late 1993. The occasion for the piece was a report of the ninth foreign tourist shot and killed in Florida during the year. Writing in the *Guardian*, Suzanne Moore noted that tourists venturing abroad now had much more to contend with than foreign food and upset stomachs. In Florida at least, they had to dodge the 'crack-crazed murderers who roam the sunshine state gunning down innocent tourists'. Florida, she concluded, had become 'a shooting gallery for crooks with tourists as targets' (Moore, 1993). Recalling an earlier period, while resident in Miami, she noted how the closing line on media crime reports invariably had the police suspecting that the killings were 'drug related'. The fact that such crimes were also gun related was apparently thought unworthy of a comment, prompting Moore to reflect upon the meaning and significance of guns in contemporary America. Her starting point echoed the 'civilising thesis' discussed in an earlier chapter. 'Guns may once have represented something great in this country, but what do they mean now? They mean you shoot someone for something. Their watch, their wallet. Or for nothing. They switched TV channels. They disagreed. They haven't got a gun and you have. Because it is exciting, glamorous, deadly'. To the British, she argued, there will always be something profoundly alien about American gun culture. The USA was confused about guns, she continued, and incapable of addressing 'the powerful fantasies that the culture continues to foster about what, exactly, possessing a shooter might do for one's self-esteem'. The journalist's characterisation of the effects of firearms upon a person's capacity, autonomy and status – and upon the social relations that such persons are able to establish and/or sustain – was very similar to the simultaneously 'king-making' yet risk driving qualities of firearms depicted in the cinema. She ended on a cautionary note. We might read about street muggings, armed drug dealers in South London and Moss Side and think that the UK was becoming like the USA, 'but it's not, not yet anyway' (Moore, 1993). And there was both the nightmare and the paradox, the evil we had to avoid at all costs was precisely where we seemed to be heading.

Freedom, fun, farce, fear and commerce

As we have seen, the nightmare of the American gun culture was often the backdrop against which the UK media began to discuss the firearm question during the period 1993 to 1995. However, Suzanne Moore was not the only British journalist to bring an outsider's eye to bear upon the dangerously mixed blessings of an armed society. Early in 1994, the *Daily Mirror* ran a story entitled 'Dirty Harriet' relating an incident in which a female police officer in a New York hair salon intervened by pulling a gun when three would-be robbers barged in. 'Like any good cop', the officer had her gun concealed under her hairdressing smock and shot the three robbers. 'It was classic Dirty Harry stuff', an admiring colleague is said to have quipped to journalists. It may have been good public relations for the NYPD, but more by luck than judgment. Later in the article it was noted that 'Dirty Harriet' may have been killed or seriously injured herself were it not for one of the robbers' guns misfiring (Hall, 1994).

When the British press turned to report on the politics of the American gun control debates, particularly President Clinton's attempts to extend various aspects of US federal gun control legislation, journalists adopted a familiar stance. The USA's apparent obsession with guns was presented as dangerous and perverse and, above all, deeply alien to British common-sense. Clinton's successful ban on nineteen types of 'military assault rifle', carried in Congress by only two votes during May 1994, was the subject of an article in the *Guardian* (Walker, M. 1994). Readers were allowed to draw their own conclusions about the apparently responsible politicians who had mobilised against the ban, voicing constitutional, civil libertarian and even socially utilitarian arguments in favour of AK47s, and Uzi sub-machine guns. As a gun control – let alone a crime control – measure, most non-partisan commentators agreed that the ban would have only a limited effect (most killings are perpetrated with handguns) but this did little to temper the arguments made.

One side heralded the changes as a 'dramatic strike against deadly weapons and the criminals who used them', and a major setback for the National Rifle Association (NRA) which had hitherto been seen as a lobby too big and powerful for politicians to ignore. Their opponents (at least those in the mainstream) described the measure as an attack upon the US constitution and upon the innate freedoms of Americans. In some of the more remote areas and among the survivalist and separatists sects organising there – the semi-underground militias and 'redneck' racist organisations of the USA's far right – such legislation was simply further evidence of a great governmental conspiracy against the people (Coates, 1987; Flynn and Gerhardt, 1989). Ed Vulliamy's reporting from the 1994 'Soldier of Fortune' rally at Las Vegas helped enrich this picture of strange gun-obsessed USA. He found many examples of gun-related rhetoric; posters urging 'Ban Clinton, not guns' and an interviewee who described gun control as 'the ultimate betrayal of American civilisation'. This was followed closely by distrust of the 'commie conspiracy' running the federal government, intolerance of homosexuals – especially in military service – and opposition to American troops being placed under UN command when serving overseas (Vulliamy, 1994b). Taken separately such issues may appear rather peripheral and unconnected, undoubtedly somewhat paranoid but, equally, quite esoteric. However in his important book on the diverse manifestations of the USA's paramilitary sub-cultures, *Warrior Dreams*, Gibson goes some way towards constructing the composite mind-set of the anti-government 'new age warriors', militia-men, survivalists and sect members, some of them not so far from the USA's political mainstream after all (Gibson, 1994).

In view of recent events in the USA – the Waco siege, the Oklahoma bombing, the increasing visibility of militia and racist organisations, the

Montana township siege, even a revival of KKK activity in some areas – a good deal of which has been reported upon in this country by Ed Vulliamy and Jonathan Freedland (see for example Freedland, 1994, 1995a, 1996; Vulliamy, 1995, 1998), it would appear that Gibson's analysis is not far from the mark. As Freedland has written, 'the world inhabited by Tim McVeigh [the Oklahoma bomber] is not some alien madscape, but one utterly in step with mainstream American thinking. Its core beliefs are not eccentric ramblings but dominant themes in US politics ... they overlap not only with the respectable right, but even with the liberal left' (Freedland, 1995a). The Oklahoma bomb polarised the USA, but to the camouflage clad militia patriots, 'Waco was the most visible example of a federal grand plan to attack God loving Americans whose only crime is to be well armed. ... In this view Clinton's gun control measures are part of a long term assault on American freedoms'. Federal agents, the FBI and agents of the Bureau of Alcohol, Tobacco and Firearms (ATF) are construed as the enemy, 'soldiers of some remote superstate bent on depriving ordinary Americans of their basic liberties' (Freedland, 1995a). G. Gordon Liddy, a former Watergate conspirator and now right-wing commentator, caused uproar during 1995 when, in the course of a radio talk show, he argued that because ATF agents often wear bullet-proof vests 'into action' the best way to kill them would be to shoot them in the head.

In the immediate wake of the assault weapon ban but before the Oklahoma bombing the National Rifle Association had distributed a fund-raising circular to members and supporters hoping to capitalise upon the 'angry white backlash' against federal enforcement agencies. The ATF agents, to whom the task of regulating the American male's three favourite things falls, bore the brunt of the NRA's anger. ATF agents were described as 'jack-booted thugs' in 'nazi bucket-helmets and black stormtrooper uniforms'. Federal agents were described as 'harassing, intimidating and even murdering law abiding citizens' (Freedland, 1995b). From the point of view of the NRA, the timing of the circular, distributed just before the bombing, was especially unfortunate. Former President, George Bush, who had relied heavily upon NRA financial support during his presidential campaign, declared himself appalled by the NRA's allegations and invective and resigned from the organisation. Subsequently, wiser counsels appeared to prevail within senior republican and NRA circles, leading the republicans to defer their proposed repeal of Clinton's assault weapons ban in an effort to diffuse the populist rhetoric fostering the growth and influence of the radical right and militia movements. In 1997, following a power struggle within the NRA, a number of hard-liners were ousted from office and the organisation began to pursue a more mainstream campaigning strategy, rejecting the fringe ideologies of the radical anti-government militia groups (Bruce and Wilcox, 1998). The implicit warnings in such British press reports from the USA are worthy of serious consideration. They are aspects of American culture seldom presented to the UK. Judged from the relative safety of the latter's more consensual and collectivist shores, the peculiar diversity of American culture and, not least, the centrality of the firearm within it, are clearly invoked as something different, dangerous and best avoided.

Weaving a little more local colour into the issues raised by the assault weapons ban, Ed Vulliamy writing in the *Observer*, considered some reactions to the new legislation in an independent firearms manufacturing firm located in the alcohol-free Tennessee Bible belt. Among other lethal product lines, the Daniel family-run firm were responsible for the first commercial production of the Ingram sub-machine gun, later marketed in the USA as the Cobray, a weapon similar in design to the Israeli-produced Uzi machine pistol. The Daniels also manufactured a weapon known as the 'street sweeper' – a large semi-automatic shotgun capable of firing four rounds a second (Vulliamy, 1994a). Mrs Daniel, the 'first lady of fire-power' was apparently a keen collector of machine guns. Interviewed on her private shooting range cradling a Mac 11 silenced machine gun, she argued, 'ownership of guns is a god-given right, it's part of America and they're trying to take it away from us'. Then, she added, 'I like guns because of the power.'

The Daniels defended their trade with familiar anti-federalist, NRA and republican arguments: guns were not to blame for rising crime and violence, the real problems started within discipline in the family and declining moral standards. However, according to Larson (1994), it was not family breakdown and declining moral standards that led 16-year-old Nicholas Elliot to take a Cobray pistol to school with him and there open fire upon teachers and fellow pupils. Rather, it was a morbid fascination with the American gun culture itself. Having researched the production and marketing of the firearms in the USA, 'I discovered', he relates, 'that the story of Nicholas Elliot's gun was the story also of the forces that infuse the gun culture … that makes guns … all too easy to come by and virtually assures their eventual use in the bedrooms, alleys and school-yards of America. Reach out, the culture cries, and kill someone'. And people do (Larson, 1994: 5).

Later, with the impending federal ban on nineteen types of 'assault weapons', the Daniel firm increased production to sell as many as possible before the prohibitions cut in. Such were the compromises struck over the passage of the legislation, that only new production and further sales of the weapons were to be prohibited – assault weapons purchased before the ban were unaffected by the legislation and did not have to be surrendered by their owners. Thus, such bans could be particularly good for short-term trade and might really inflate the price. 'When the Reagan administration banned some fully auto weapons', commented Mr Daniel, 'we had ten days before Reagan could get back from a tour and sign the Bill … we put out 70,000 machine guns in those days and as the stocks got lower the price went up' (Vulliamy, 1994a).

The Daniel firm's other business options lay in selling gun parts for self-assembly by purchasers. Despite the debate generated by the Clinton Bill, the legislation comprised a number of loopholes. The regulations only covered the nineteen named assault weapons but not their constituent parts and in many states the sale of self-assembly firearms was not unlawful. The firm was also considering the production of a small double-barrelled revolver aimed at the 'domestic self-protection' market – it was, apparently, not a very accurate weapon, it just had to be pointed in the right general direction and fired – 'we think its going to be a big seller', they noted.

Vulliamy's article, like many of those covering aspects of American gun culture and appearing in the British press, conveys its message by virtue of the contrasts and juxtapositions it establishes. The central contrast, as we have seen already, lay between an external British perspective and the strange, even incomprehensible, values and ideologies to which Americans seemed susceptible. Central to our failure to understand are those peculiar American constructons: a seeming affinity for, the right to, the need for, a reverence towards and even a love of firearms. A culture, apparently so similar to our own, with which we have enjoyed a special historical and political relationship, seems in fact so far away. And yet, although we fear and fail to understand this American gun culture, a central feature of our own cultural constitution seems to involve the belief that we were being drawn almost inevitably towards it. As we have already seen, this is a perspective shared by almost all commentators on firearms issues in the British press.

The contrasts established in Vulliamy's article involved the links established between the Daniel firm's commercial interest in firearms manufacture (a 'dry' economic motive), Mrs Daniel's evident enthusiasm for machine guns (an emotional appeal) and the constraints of public safety policy (bringing social policy to bear upon a social pathology). The final section of the article suggests that public opinion might, at last, be turning against the gun and the violence wrought by guns. Recent skirmishes over the Brady Law during 1993 and over the assault weapons ban may not result in many lives being saved but they might prefigure a sea-change in public opinion. Although fully automatic weapons are thought to constitute only around 1 per cent of the civilian armoury, proponents of the assault weapon ban 'estimate that they account for 8 per cent of guns used in violent crimes and the FBI refers to them as the "weapons of choice" for gangland street fighters and drive-by killers' (Vulliamy, 1994a).

However the central juxtaposition established by the article occurred in its final paragraphs. The story switches abruptly to the trauma unit of a Washington DC hospital. We are immediately thrust among the tangible human consequences of the gun culture and the direct personal costs occasioned by a finger pulling a trigger. Two young people had been shot in their car as they stopped at traffic lights – the man survived, but lay in a coma after being hit twelve times. Unfortunately fourteen bullets killed the girl. The head trauma physician commented that he had only seen 105 cases so far this year, and explained 'it's been too cold to shoot properly and so the killing season hasn't really started yet … the rise in deaths and multiple wounds from semi-automatic weapons has been so new and so fast that our injury scaling system hasn't really caught up with it. I have the biggest number of Uzi patients outside the state of Israel' (Vulliamy, 1994a).

While British newspaper articles on firearms in the USA often invoke the idea of the gun as an American social pathology, they no less frequently tend to imply that individual gun ownership is influenced by less than strictly rational motives.

Recognising this helps to explain the 'news worthiness' of an item about a novel gun exchange programme established during 1994 in Los Angeles and syndicated from the *Los Angeles Times*. This gun exchange programme offered three hours of free counselling therapy for anyone who turned in a gun (Paddock, 1994). Previous gun exchange programmes have featured cash, food, shoes, toys, concerts and even sports tickets but this one was apparently designed to address the personal factors which may have prompted people to purchase guns in the first place – gun owners who might be angry, depressed or suicidal. 'Many people who own guns because of fears may be open to trying to find other ways of dealing with their fears', commented the scheme's originator. However, given the fact that firearm death had risen by 247 per cent in the area during the past decade, many people may have needed some convincing of the merits of a gun withdrawal programme based upon the denial of external risks. Finally, despite the fact that gun withdrawal schemes across the USA net thousands of weapons annually, the programmes are compared by critics to attempts to empty the ocean with a thimble (Paddock, 1994).

Critics of gun surrender programmes also argue that those least likely to give up their weapons are precisely those most likely to use them for criminal purposes. 'In violent neighbourhoods social arrangements have evolved that resemble a state of war … and if one is to believe the residents, just about everybody keeps a gun' (Vergara, 1994). In precisely those – typically inner-city – areas where gun withdrawal schemes would achieve the greatest direct benefits, the marginalisation of large numbers of inner-city residents from mainstream economic activity means that drug dealing is widespread and gun ownership and gang membership are high (Short, 1996).

Whatever their particular motivations for gun ownership, British journalists described these well-armed young gang members as 'shooting down the American dream'. Edward Stourton, writing in the *Sunday Telegraph* argued that gang activity, drug dealing and shooting was percolating down the age range. There had, apparently, been a major increase in violent offending by 10– 14-year-olds. 'Police sources confirmed a 600 per cent increase in gang murders in the four years to 1993', and identified both adolescent hitmen and 'executions' of 11-year-olds, who had offended gang leaders (Stourton, 1994). Moreover, if the age of the new gang members was the concern of the *Sunday Telegraph* it was the apparently changing sexual distribution of gang activity which concerned the *Guardian*. The picture accompanying an article in November 1995 showed a teenage girl, her face scarred by a gang initiation ritual, carrying a large semi-automatic handgun. The picture's caption ran: 'Girls shoot, rob and sell drugs in another nightmarish distortion of the American dream' (Nicoll, 1995). The accompanying article described how female gang membership had been growing over the past decade as the girls began to discover that their status in their communities increased through their assumption of 'auxiliary' gang membership. 'If these girls want something they are now just as likely [as their male counterparts] to kill you for it'. The wider social context for this shift of adolescent girls into gang activity was said to be the American government cutting back on welfare payments and thereby increasing the pressure on teenage girls trapped between a lack of job opportunities, broken homes and early pregnancy. Amidst such bleak prospects, gang life offered a kind of comfort and security. The new female gang members were now 'willing to fight, stab, carry guns and shoot them'. Furthermore, while 'it did not fit easily with the American idea of femininity', the changing pattern of gang involvement is reflected in the crime figures. A Brooklyn law enforcement official commented, 'many have progressed to the killings carried out by the male gangs [and] the number of girls arrested for serious felony offences has increased 10 per cent annually since the mid-1980s' (Nicoll, 1995).

If the gang phenomenon is represented to the UK as the 'shooting down of America's dreams' and consistent with the version of the USA that we ought to be avoiding at all costs, other British press commentaries illustrate some wider dimensions of the firearms culture. In their own ways these examples perpetuate the 'America to be avoided' theme of much British press commentary while also exploring the social and economic relations which underpin the gun culture.

Responsibility, ricochets and repercussions

A particularly intriguing characteristic of the American gun culture (though by no means entirely unknown on this side of the Atlantic), reported upon by British journalists, concerns the complex and frequently convoluted legal repercussions which may ensue when a gun is fired. Perhaps the most well-known case has been that of Bernhard Goetz who, in December 1984, shot and injured four black men he thought were about to rob him. The media had a field day, drawing parallels between Goetz's case and the *Death Wish* films and referring to Goetz as the 'subway vigilante'. Goetz was acquitted of attempted murder in 1987 following a very controversial trial which polarised much of New York – to many he was a hero, to others a trigger happy racist – though he later served eight months in custody for illegal possession of a firearm. Yet twelve years after the original incident, lawyers acting for the man most seriously injured in the shooting (suffering partial brain damage and paralysis) were still suing Goetz for $50 million. The situation was not unlike the more recent predicament of two New York 'subway cops' who were forced, following a civil action, to pay large compensation sums to a robber they shot. The court found that the robber was shot 'without just cause' by virtue of the fact that he was not actively endangering anyone's life or attempting to escape when the police officers opened fire (Hitchens, 1994).

Goetz, rendered bankrupt by virtue of having to finance a series of legal actions following the incident, declared himself perplexed but fairly philosophical when interviewed, during 1996, by Ian Katz of the *Guardian*. Most people had commended his actions, he said, seeing it very much as a 'good guy – bad guy situation' – 'and people like the bad guys to get shot. ... In the old west, if someone had shot four outlaws, why would they bother to try and catch him?' (Goetz interviewed, Katz, 1996).

Equally complex but, so far, less protracted repercussions followed a different kind of shooting which occurred, also on a New York subway train, in 1993. The shooter, exhibiting many of the solitary and embittered characteristics of the modern 'spree-killer', was a black man said to have a grudge against white people. He had walked along the coach of a subway train arbitrarily shooting passengers with a semi-automatic handgun. He was eventually charged with six murders. Amy Federici, whose parents later took out a legal action against both the manufacturers and distributors of the weapon and ammunition used, was one of the victims. Central to the plaintiffs' legal action was an issue of product liability in relation to the production, marketing, advertising and distribution of the weapon and ammunition (Jefferys, 1994). The case also reflected the influence of a growing public health discourse within American gun control campaigning which emphasised the epidemiological factors in weapon and ammunition design contributing to increased death and injury rates (Karlson and Hargarten, 1997).

The handgun used by the killer, a Sturm Ruger P89 had been highly publicised in the firearms press. The advertisements called it 'light' and 'high-performance' even suggesting that its price would leave competitors gasping for breath. Using his reloading clip the killer was able to fire, reload and fire a total of thirty rounds in under two minutes. The weapon itself, the high-capacity magazine and the ammunition were also factors in what Diaz has described as the 'lethality spiral' in handgun marketing during the later 1980s and 1990s. This 'spiral' worked as follows. Increasing concern about armed criminals, led many American police forces to switch to 9 mm semi-automatic handguns during the 1980s. In turn, the weapon manufacturers made similar weapons available to the civilian market, often advertising their wares as 'approved by the FBI' or 'first choice for the LAPD'. As criminal elements began to use the more powerful semi-automatics against the police, the argument developed that the police needed greater firepower, higher capacity magazines, bigger bullet calibres and more effective 'man-stopping' ammunition. Although the evidential basis for such claims was often highly questionable, the police invariably got their new weapons and new ammunition which were, in due course, also made available on the civilian market, and the whole cycle began again. Drawing on firearm industry publishing Diaz even argues that one of the main reasons that weapons manufacturers sought a law enforcement contract was often not primarily about direct profits but rather about product credibility and leverage on the more lucrative civilian market (Diaz, 1999).

The ammunition used in the 1993 subway train killings, Black Talon hollow-point bullets (their penetrating and flesh-cutting qualities also prominently advertised), had themselves been the subject of a congressional review. The basis of the legal claim against the manufacturers was that both gun and ammunition were designed and promoted in a way that would particularly appeal to criminals. Drawing a parallel with recent successful actions against the tobacco companies, lawyers acting for the plaintiffs argued that the manufacturer ought to bear some responsibility for deaths and injuries resulting from their product's use. The lawyers alleged that the companies knew exactly what they were doing.

'Their advertising plays up to the bloodlust of psychopathic personalities. The defendants have a duty to design their products so they avoid unreasonable risk of harm, [they have] behaved with a wilful and wanton disregard for public safety' (Jefferys, 1994).

Help for the plaintiffs had come from the NYPD. A police spokesman commented that, of the 1,400 firearm homicides occurring in New York in 1993, a disproportionately high number involved semi-automatic handguns such as the Ruger, firing deep-penetration bullets like the Black Talon. In other words both gun and ammunition were consistently used for criminal purposes. It was this issue of alleged 'consistent use' which the plaintiffs hoped might make the manufacturers responsible under the product liability laws. In response, Winchester, the bullet manufacturer argued that the bullet had been withdrawn from the civilian market in November 1993:

> The Black Talon was … a high performance bullet created for law enforce-ment officers but we developed a commercial version because we believe every law-abiding citizen has the right to the best self-defence … our tests showed it would penetrate to around 12 inches. That is perfect for law enforcement and self-defence. You don't want a bullet that doesn't expand on impact, because it will pass straight through the body.
>
> (quoted in Jefferys, 1994)

According to Diaz, however, Winchester's response to the bad press their bullet was receiving was a little more carefully contrived. 'Industry executives felt that the black talon name "was great from a marketing point of view but bad from a public relations perspective". [Therefore] the gun industry's final answer was to ditch the name but save the technology. … Winchester quietly announced plans to reintr-oduce the ammunition under a new name, Supreme Fail-Safe' (Diaz, 1999: 168).

As a result, although the Black Talon gained a reputation as the deadliest hollow-point ammunition available before being 'withdrawn' it was far from being the only, so-called 'high-performance' hollow-point on the market designed to produce 'fast knockdown' and a 'wide wound channel'. Rather para-doxically, as we shall see later, despite the fact that the dubious qualities of hollow-point ammunition were directly related to its anti-personnel applications, during the early 1990s the British Home Office resisted a German initiative to have the EC prohibit hollow-point ammunition throughout Europe. British handgun shooting enthusiasts argued that the ammunition had a genuine 'sporting purpose'.

Despite the rather unpalatable issues such discussions raise, a number of genuine and practical dilemmas do present themselves in relation to the selection of suitable firearms and ammunition for the use of law enforcement personnel. In another chapter, we discuss these dilemmas in relation to the access of certain British police officers to firearms. Simply put, different specifications apply to military and civilian police ammunition. The Hague Convention of 1899 outlawed the use of hollow-point, expanding or 'dum-dum' ammunition, but no such restrictions apply to civilian use ammunition (Waddington, 1990; Heard, 1997). However, military ammunition – hard, high-velocity or 'fully-jacketed' – is considered entirely unsuitable for law enforcement purposes. Such rounds can either ricochet from hard surfaces or 'over-penetrate' (pass right through their intended targets) thereby increasing the risk to innocent bystanders. As we shall see in a later chapter, in the pages of the *International Police Review* the search for the optimum law enforcement ammunition has become a disturbingly technical and scientific question. With the prohibition of virtually all handguns in the UK, the question of the handgun ammunition available to British civilian shooters is now a rather moot point. Even so, it is worth noting that many of the rounds fired by Thomas Hamilton at Dunblane were of the 'soft-nosed' hollow-point type. In other words, they were bullets designed to incapacitate and/or maximise injury. Given that British civilian handgun shooters were only permitted to shoot their weapons at a variety of targets, the question might remain as to why such inherently lethal ammunition was considered necessary.

Back in the USA, Black Talon ammunition had received much bad publicity even before the recent case – the bullets had been used in several shootings in which police officers had sustained horrific injuries. In turn, the manufacturers expressed sympathy for the victims of the subway shooting but denied any responsibility. 'We sell our products legally to law abiding people. We can't be responsible if they misuse the product. If someone uses a cadillac in a bank robbery, no-one thinks to sue General Motors'. Amy Frederici's parents disagreed. 'A Ruger loaded with hollow point bullets has only one function, to cause horrific injury to the human body. Its design gave my daughter no chance of survival. Those bullets were designed to maim, this is made explicit in the advertising' (quoted in Jefferys, 1994). Karlson and Hargarten likewise draw attention to the influence of the media and firearm advertising in promoting gun sales. Firearm advertising frequently extols such virtues – power, accuracy, concealability, ease and speed of use, even style – in ways which, although perhaps designed with the law-abiding customer in mind, are likely to be no less appealing to the criminally intentioned (Karlson and Hargarten, 1997).

Take for instance the advertising of Smith & Wesson's new Sigma pistol, a .40 mm polymer-framed semi-automatic, in *Guns & Ammo* magazine. According to the magazine's expert, the new semi-automatic pistol was primarily 'designed for the domestic and law enforcement markets'. Its design incorporated the latest research and planning to produce a weapon that was 'low price … lightweight … easy to use and maintain' (Adams, 1994). Examining the gun, Adam noted that the new design, 'meant that S &W could include some features that would not be possible in steel, including light weight, ease of production and low price'. Apparently the production of the gun also marked a near revolution in the Smith & Wesson assembly lines. The new weapon was the first pistol for which Smith & Wesson, in true post-Fordist fashion, had subcontracted the manufacture of most of the components, excluding the barrel. The weapon was only assembled at the factory, where it travelled each stage of the construction process in its own designer box. Having 'tested' the weapon, the reviewer's approval is evident. Handgun technology he noted had to be based upon sound, tried and tested principles and 'had to evolve to the most ergonomic and user friendly standards possible'. That, he continued, was 'pure Darwinism – if the owner survives and buys them for his children. If they don't it could be fatal and a customer could be lost forever'. Scientific principles are neatly sculptured into the weapon's design, 'to make the grip as ergonomic as possible ... [with] a steeper grip angle ... [so] that the pistol would present better, the frontsight coming up first, essential for close range combat shooting'. These, it seems, are the basic requirements of a 'working gun'. Moreover, while 'not quite up to bullseye standard ... accuracy is good enough for combat'. But that, it seems, is the point for, 'while sportsmen shoot their handguns a lot, policemen shoot them very little, but they do carry them for a long time. The light loaded weight of 35 ounces will be a big selling point' (Adam, 1994). Of course, few sporting shooters in the UK require handguns for combat and, as Ayoob notes, 'combat accuracy' is a well-known euphemism, used by firearm correspondents, implying that a weapon is not really particularly accurate at all (Ayoob, 1996).

What could be better, or more bizarre? A post-industrial gun for post-modern society, cheap to buy, requiring minimal skill or maintenance, easy to use, light to carry around, just right for combat and, above all, marketed as 'user-friendly' in the name of social Darwinism. The very features likely to make the weapon attractive to law enforcement officers – or to private citizens desiring their own concealable self-defence handgun – are just as likely to increase its appeal to a wide range of more criminally inclined owners.

Obviously, much more than firearm design and advertising are at stake here. While advertising restrictions are unlikely to give much leverage on the wider gun control question, the product liability complaint in the Frederici case has opened up a range of complex issues. Even though the case was thought to have a slim chance of success by legal commentators, in the longer term, gun control activists hoped it would assist their lobbying efforts by helping foster an unfavourable image of the gun manufacturers. They recognised, however, that with a right-wing republican-dominated Congress already having committed itself to repealing the Brady Law, progress on gun control was not an easy or immediate prospect (Jefferys, 1994). Subsequently, however, a number of pro-gun control political leaders, mayors and city councils, launched their own legal actions against firearms manufacturers, distributors and gunshops within their jurisdictions.

During November 1998, the mayor of New Orleans filed a product liability lawsuit against fifteen gun manufacturers, three trade organisations and a number of gun shops and pawn-shops. Political authorities in Los Angeles, Philadelphia and San Francisco were said to be following suit. Later the same month, the mayor of Chicago launched his city's own $433 million compensation lawsuit against gunshops, manufacturers and distributors in the city. The basis of the Chicago case differed from that of New Orleans in that it alleged that the gun industry had created a public nuisance by knowingly designing, marketing and distributing guns that will be employed in criminal activity in the city. According to reporters, city officials gathered some very compelling evidence as, during a three-month investigation, undercover police officers posing as gang members and would-be criminals bought guns from a series of gunshops outside the city, making it clear to the gun sellers that they intended to use the weapon illegally – or otherwise lacked the authorisation to purchase a gun in the state. In one case, the undercover officer buying the gun hinted that he intended to use it for a retaliation killing whereupon the sales assistant even went so far as to recommend the most appropriate ammunition for the job (*The Economist*, 21.11.1998). According to the coalition of gun control groups, it was hoped that up to sixty cities would eventually file lawsuits against the gun industry. While public lawyers doubt the likely chances of any such cases succeeding in court, all recognised that success in the courts might not be the ultimate objective. Rather, the legal actions were designed to hit the gun industry financially with a view to pressurising it to accept a number of political compromises with the gun control lobbies. Some confirmation of this – and a major breakthrough for the gun control lobby – came in late 1999 when the Colt company announced it was pulling out of handgun production for the American civilian market (Campbell, 1999). Company executives blamed the risk to profits posed by impending lawsuits sponsored by pro-gun control lobbies in twenty-nine American cities, although wider commercial considerations also apply. There are suggestions that the American handgun market is over-supplied and foreign produced handguns now appear to be taking a growing market share (Diaz, 1999).

From a British perspective each of the aforementioned incidents, articles and accounts exposed the, at times farcical and at times tragic, consequences of actual weapon use and misuse in the USA. The sub-text was often very similar. The alien nature of American gun culture remained heavily underpinned by interlocking social, political, historical and economic processes and institutions, powerful vested interests and long-established legal principles. Addressing any single facet of the gun question, however seemingly 'straight-forward' it might appear to a British audience (for instance banning the sale of apparently 'injury maximising' bullets, or military assault weapons, to private citizens), invariably brought about a direct confrontation with a powerful array of political forces whose attachment to the gun (or even to certain types of gun) was often heavily over-determined and at times centrally sustained by core economic interests and emotional attachments. But that was not the end of it. Accepting, at the outset, the need for a gun, the next question concerned the mechanical efficiency and ergonomics of the weapon itself – accuracy, rate of fire, ease of use, speed of reloading, reliability. Ammunition that might appear 'injury-maximising' could, in another light, just be 'effective' or 'maximally incapacitating' while not 'over-penetrating'. In other words, a real 'man stopping' bullet that did not pass right through its unfortunate human target.

The implicit lesson (though no less crucial for being implicit) for a British audience was that the dangerously convoluted legal, political and economic repercussions and implacable social relations of the American armed society could only be overcome with difficulty – if at all. Our best bet was to avoid the gun altogether. Taking up the gun, it followed, was akin to inviting an American tragedy. Tragedy struck on March 13th, 1996.

5 Tragedy, aftermath and politics

From nowhere?

News reporting in the immediate aftermath of Thomas Hamilton's horrific massacre at Dunblane Primary School described the incident as 'unprecedented' and 'an unfathomable horror'. Evil, striking from nowhere, had irretrievably shattered our sense of ourselves and of our community. David Seymour's comments in the *Daily Mirror* on March 14th were typical of many. Dunblane, he said, was:

> the sort of place most people dream of living. An idyllic retreat in which a close-knit community exists in peace. Until yesterday. It is hard to imagine such a cruel massacre in the most deprived inner city area in the world. ... But yesterday the unimaginable happened. The impossible became real ... we cannot even begin to grasp the evil, it is beyond comprehension. ... How anyone could slaughter so many tiny children, to kill and keep on killing those helpless little ones.
>
> (Seymour, 1996)

Furthermore, he continued, the incident suggested a deeper uncertainty at the heart of our very civilisation, 'if we cannot protect five year old children in one of the most peaceful parts of our country, who can we protect?' (Seymour, 1996).

The suddenness of this outburst of violence, striking in the midst of everyday routine rendered the incident all the more 'unreal' and 'unbelievable'. Ordinary domestic life was starkly and dramatically confronted with our worst of nightmares. The violence was so fleeting, yet so permanent. 'It took three minutes to kill sixteen children and their teacher. And tear a community apart'. Steve Boggan, in the *Independent*, captured the mood of incomprehension very effectively: 'Less than an hour before their mothers and fathers were asking if they had cleaned their teeth, telling them to fasten their shoes properly and checking they had packed their gym kit ... a scene played out in hundreds of thousands of homes across the land' (Boggan, 1996). Few readers can have been unmoved by such abrupt tragedy, so brittle seemed our civilising security. Around the country, parents might hug their homecoming children just a little tighter, grateful for having avoided tragedy for yet another day. Millennial anxieties, unimaginable horror and incalculable risks; the wider world offered only uncertainty and fear. In such moments, humanity's reassuring veneer was stripped away and we found ourselves exposed to meaningless fate. We might no longer be standing, hopefully facing the future and ready to realise our collective potential but, rather, just besieged by an oppressive world.

A peculiar detail of the incident was reported by witnesses. During the shooting Hamilton wore ear protectors, supposedly 'to safeguard his hearing' while firing, and before blowing his own head off. Apparently the bulky ear muffs gave him a sinister, almost 'Mickey Mouse' appearance 'that will last forever in the memories of children in the nearby portakabin, at whom he loosed off three shots'. The ear protectors and the familiar cartoon character they resembled render the incident all the more bizarre and unsettling. At the same time they might make his actions marginally more intelligible. He had closed himself off from the world, the school was just a shooting gallery, he didn't want to hear the screams and commotion, he couldn't face the consequences (Ferguson *et al.*, 1996). Later on, interviewed in the *Guardian*, Mick North, father of one of the murdered children, commented that although he tried not to think about Thomas Hamilton too often, 'there is a part of me that wants to think he wasn't seeing children at all, that he was still in that shooting gallery … [with] those humanoid targets. Maybe he thought he was target shooting'. But then he added, raising a question about the values inculcated by shooting at 'humanoid' targets, 'maybe it was the other way around … I would be interested to know what shooters have in their minds when they are shooting at those "humanoid" targets. What was he really seeing when he fired off at those humanoid things?' (Vulliamy, 1996a).

Even before Dunblane, a number of commentators had begun to voice their concerns about the growing popularity of 'practical' or combat-style shooting common in the USA. The weapons employed in such contests, often modelled upon police or military issue weapons and, since the early 1990s, increasingly advertised for the growing American 'concealed-carry' market, pointed towards a markedly different set of orientations towards handgun usage than those usually embraced by target pistol shooting. A brief glimpse of Hamilton's own orientation to handgun shooting emerged in the verbal evidence given on the fourth day of Lord Cullen's Inquiry. Apparently Hamilton would attach 'stickers' and labels to the humanoid targets at which he was firing, sometimes emptying his gun's whole magazine in a reckless twenty-second blast rather than the full two minutes of careful aiming and firing allowed in the 'police pistol' shooting discipline. On occasion, he was even seen to be stroking his weapons, 'as if they were babies'. Unfortunately, it seems that officials at the gun club attended by Hamilton had not seen fit to draw such erratic behaviour to the attention of the police (Clouston, 1996).

Hugo Young, writing in the *Guardian*, argued that Dunblane raised 'many questions' but provided 'no answers'. In the wake of the terror, 'lots of people [were] making suggestions, uttering sincere, shocked, words, [there was] the familiar sound of stable doors being slammed too late and commentators and politicians going through their well-meaning but inadequate motions but … finally, we have to stand, mute, mystified before the enormity of a crime there is no way to stop happening again' (Young, 1996). In the *Guardian*, the following day, the comments of the school's headteacher were given prominence: 'Evil visited us. We don't know why' (*Guardian*, 15.3.1996). Yet if this was the over-whelming initial reaction across the media, it concealed a further, more difficult and unpalatable, question – so unpalatable, in fact, that it was scarcely ever asked. How on earth could we have believed ourselves immune? What compla-cency was it that allowed us to consider ourselves safe? Indeed, for David Mellor MP, writing later in the year, the tragedy had a certain inevitability about it, 'If we import the American way of life, we must expect the American way of death' (Mellor, 1996).

Evil, hope and humanism

Recourse to the language of 'evil' at a point of great despair is an understandable human reaction. In one sense it allows us access to a discourse by which unbear-ably traumatic events may be assimilated into a sphere of human consciousness from which grief, faith, time and memory might eventually redeem them. In another sense, evil points to the uncertainty or, worse, the incomprehensible and uncontrollable nature of events. Evil, in this random destabilising sense, far more than a consistent or predictable malevolent force, runs contrary to every ratio-nalist principle of liberal modernity. Liberal reason, a faith in progress, as it were, gives us hope. It busies us with ideas of planning, prevention, prediction, treat-ment and, if all else fails, cure or rehabilitation. By contrast, evil abandons us to chance and strips our civilised humanity of any vestige of meaning. We are reduced to a desperate visceral struggle less intelligible than a survival of the fittest, more arbitrary than any 'war of all against all' (Putnam, 1981; Hall, 1997). As Porter recognised, 'acknowledging evil goes against every liberal instinct. ... If liberals admit evil ... then we lose hope of explanation and throw from the orbit of human responsibility things that we believe may be improved and controlled to create a better society. ... If we admit Hamilton's actions as evil then we renounce the idea that a society may determine its own enlightenment' (Porter, 1996). More recently, of course, this is precisely what certain theorists, drawing upon notions of 'post-modernity', had been arguing.

Porter's reflective article, written five days after the shootings, drew upon the deliberations about 'evil' of several writers and commentators from the field of crime and criminal justice. John Mortimore QC, insisted we recognise the notions of evil as part of a discourse. Within a religious or spiritual worldview such a discourse might eventually allow redemption or consolation but, on a more worldly plane, he suggested, it simply caused us to deceive ourselves. According to Mortimore, 'a belief in evil is terrifically useful if you want to ignore certain things. If you believe that criminals are evil, you don't have to take responsibility for the society that produces them'. It followed that we should not draw a veil over the shootings at Dunblane as an exceptional and unpredictable evil. Dunblane, the quiet place, nothing like the USA, everyone's safest backyard where atrocities just do not happen, was not just 'unlucky'. Lightning having, against the odds, struck it once, could not be relied upon to pass it safely by. Such rhetorics of naive and misplaced reassurance were, according to Mortimore, a part of the problem. We had been complacent and not resisted the 'gun culture liberalism' within which Hamilton had located himself. 'If this man was allowed to have handguns under licence it is not demonic evil but a failure of resistance' (Mortimore, in Porter, 1996).

Such arguments were to become more forcefully reasserted as a resistance movement emerged in the weeks which followed. In the first few days, however, as we came to learn more about this peaceful town in central Scotland and of its victims, survivors and bereaved, the primary themes in the reporting continued to be underpinned by a sense of disbelief that anything so awful could happen here. In a series of representations we have considered in an earlier chapter, the peace and serenity of Dunblane were contrasted repeatedly with images of reckless, gun-driven carnage in the USA as if these defined, in turn, civilisation and barbarism, opposing poles of humanity.

An editorial in the *Sun* on March 14th commented upon the improbability of such an event in 'the peaceful, safe town of Dunblane ... this was not gun-crazy America nor war-torn Bosnia it was Britain', and even quoted a comment from American lobbyist Mike Beard, President of the American Coalition to stop gun violence, 'It's incomprehensible. We almost expect it here but not in Britain' (*Sun*, 14.3.1996). Other American commentators, reported in the *Guardian* declared their fear that National Rifle Association speakers in the USA would now use Dunblane to 'prove' that strict gun controls, such as in the UK, will not curb gun crimes or similar atrocities (Boseley and White, 1996). *Daily Mirror* journalists drew upon the words of shocked residents and neighbours from Dunblane itself to define the predominant public reaction. 'You think it happens in America – not to someone just across the street' (*Daily Mirror*, 14.3.1996). Later, among a number of background pieces on the shooting in the *Mirror*, Seymour described '*The fear that haunts the U.S.*' arguing that 'school massacres have come to haunt parents in America where no child is safe from the crazed killer' (Seymour, 1996).

Steve Boggan, writing in the *Independent*, took up the theme, 'you can imagine it happening in America, or a city, but not here' (Boggan, 1996). Suzanne Moore, in the *Guardian*, developed the point, 'This is not the USA, after all, not some crack-infested hell-hole but a conservative Scottish town' (Moore, 1996). And Andrew O'Hagan added, 'a world that most thought was somewhere else came home to the people of Dunblane. ... People imagined the world of violence was a world elsewhere: it was on video, it was in New York or Africa, in London and Glasgow and even Edinburgh perhaps. It was miles away in other worlds'. Finally, the comments of Scottish Secretary and local MP, Michael Forsythe, were noted, 'it is the last place in the world where one would expect a tragedy of this kind to occur, if one were to expect it to happen at all'(quoted in O'Hagan, 1996a). But in the uncertainty of Forsythe's final remark: 'if one were to expect it at all', lay a seed of doubt. Our self-defensive disbelief that such things could happen anywhere was having to get used to the idea that apparently widespread and random violence could occur in the most surprising places. As O'Hagan argued, 'many communities are being forced, like Dunblane's, to see the frightening proximity of violence in these times' (O'Hagan, 1996a). And although, for Suzanne Moore, shooting at children was 'unimaginable' (though hardly unprecedented) 'it is not beyond our imagination to picture a man shooting his way out of a crowd … [we have] seen it on the screen. … Only a fool would suggest that no level of desensitisation has occurred because of the imagery we continually see' (Moore, 1996).

No reason, no reasons

If the tendency to see the shootings as evil, isolated, unprecedented and unknowable was one way in which responsibility for it might be abdicated so was the tendency to see Hamilton himself as evil, isolated and unknowable. In the earliest reports in the *Sun*, Hamilton was variously described as 'evil', a 'devil', a 'weirdo', a 'maniac', a 'sick pervert', a 'creepy gun fanatic living in a filthy flat' or as a 'really devious character with weird habits' (14.3.1996). In the *Guardian*'s early reporting he was a 'crazed killer' and a 'misfit' (15.3.1996) and in the *Observer* a 'madman' (17.3.1996). Subsequently, more psychologically informed 'profiles' of this 'gun nut' figure began to emerge just as information presenting a more complex picture began to surface about the real Hamilton. Despite the suggestion of a forensic psychiatrist, writing in the *Guardian*, that spree-killers like Hamilton were typically 'mad, bad and impossible to know' (Eastman, 1996), it soon began to become clear that 'we' – that is, a whole range of public authorities, not least the police – already knew a great deal both about Hamilton himself and about others before him. We will deal with some of these issues, arising in Lord Cullen's Inquiry into the shootings (Cullen, 1996) later in this chapter.

For the moment it is worth acknowledging that ideas about the 'unknowable' or 'unprecedented' character of Hamilton, in telling us nothing, amount to a further abdication of responsibility in the face of 'fate'. Everything is as arbitrary as the explanation offered for her actions by the 16-year-old San Diego schoolgirl who, in 1979, took a gun to school and opened fire on teachers and fellow pupils. Having killed two men and wounded eight pupils and a police officer she told investigators: 'I don't like Mondays' (quoted in Barker, 1996). Reasons can appear at a number of levels. Paul Barker argued that a certain fragmentation of moral community was occurring and he wrote of the 'loners' living 'threadbare realities of life in our urban wastelands'. Even in close-knit communities like Dunblane, 'one of the fastest growing social trends is of single men living alone … there are more of them now'. Lacking both the mutual support and social controls of family and immediate community, such developments carried important implications (Barker, 1996).

A well-established pattern in a time of assassins?

As such reports grudgingly began to acknowledge, the terrible incident was neither unprecedented nor unknowable. Nor was Hamilton alone. It had happened before and, a little over a month later, another 'lone gunman' killed thirty-five people with an automatic rifle in Port Arthur, Tasmania, prompting a further round of speculation about uncertainty and individual motivations.

A short item in the *Guardian* on March 14th headed 'Dunblane joins roll of carnage' commented how: 'Yesterday's tragedy in Dunblane is the latest in a long and bloody line of indiscriminate slaughters in Britain and abroad'. The article went on to cite previous spree killings by apparently extremist or unbalanced men in a range of societies. The problem was an especial concern in the USA (Levin and Fox, 1985) but also a growing problem in the UK, France, Sweden, Australia, New Zealand, South Africa and Canada (Younge *et al.*, 1996). Similar trends were identified by Bennetto: 'Hamilton's spree follows a well-established pattern involving lone gunmen. Similar apparently random killings have occurred throughout the world'. Moreover, a number of the incidents have centred upon schools (Bennetto, 1996). Aside from the killings in Sweden and France, the sequence of incidents pointed a disturbing finger at the culture of Anglo-Saxon societies (Duclos, 1997). School shootings, as we have seen, were hardly unknown in the USA, although a spate of such incidents in late 1997 and early 1998 suggested the problem there might be taking a turn for the worse. For Timmins, the same could be said for the UK's turn for the worse after Hungerford. In 1987, Hungerford could be seen as a 'one-off' – 'but since then it appears that we have [approximately] one person a year going berserk with a gun' (Timmins, 1996). Indeed, after Hungerford, tighter controls were introduced governing the operation of British gun clubs, although later, there is also evidence of some subsequent relaxation of these controls.

For Andrew O'Hagan, writing in the *Guardian*'s 'Friday Review', while Dunblane itself might never have been foreseen, it could be understood. He urged readers to draw an existential lesson from the event. Rather than delude ourselves that such things 'couldn't happen here' and couldn't be prevented, we should accept responsibility for what the event told us about our culture.

> It might have been easier if Hamilton was simply a madman who came out of nowhere, but in fact his casual slaughter comes out of a society which itself is showing signs of deranged and violent breakdown. ... [We are witnessing] a subculture of violence, and an enthusiasm for power and weapons taking a grip in some parts of the UK ... and we can't dismiss it. There are those who seem addicted to screen violence, video horrors and the easy exterminations of the amusement arcades ... can we say this has nothing to do with our experience of seemingly living in a time of assassins?
>
> (O'Hagan, 1996b)

In one sense, he argued, Hamilton in Scotland and Timothy McVeigh in Oklahoma were clearly isolated and embittered figures, 'but there was a world at their backs' (O'Hagan, 1996b). Likewise, *Observer* correspondent Andrew Anthony, giving another American inflection to the interpretation of Dunblane, recalled returning from Texas on the day before the shootings. He described himself 'relieved to see a sign about not taking guns onto planes' and felt 'glad to be coming home to a safer society'. Subsequently, he noted, 'thinking of American gun atrocities, we tend to see them as symptoms of a sick society. So what about ours? We have the ingredients, and enough guns'. He argued that a key theme in people's efforts to understand Dunblane had involved notions of our supposed 'fall from virtue', the final loss of our British 'golden age'. It was said to have occurred at some time in the late 1950s, since when we have been on a one-way trip down a slippery slope into moral turpitude. Perhaps, he remarked, 'approaching the end of a millennium encourages us to interpret these things in terms of an underlying decline, linked to a wider sense of "ontological insecurity"'. Most of all, however, in common with O'Hagan, he urged us to reappraise our cultural assumptions and to stop deluding ourselves. 'One thing about the British culture has been our reluctance to acknowledge our own violent and visceral history ... it undermines our ability to deal with events like Dunblane and, ultimately, our ability to anticipate and prevent them' (Anthony, 1996). Even so, few commentators chose to explore this avenue, fixing instead upon the presumed characteristics of the dangerous individual himself.

Former police chief, John Stalker, writing in the *Observer*, commented, 'We must begin with a basic truth: handguns attract people, invariably men, with personality problems. It is an unhealthy worship of what guns are capable of doing'. Reiterating an argument we have encountered before, the trigger pulling the finger, he added, 'even the most responsible person is transformed when handling guns. ... Police have long recognised the unhealthy nature of a fixation with firearms ... there are sophisticated tests to filter applicants for the post of police marksmen'. He went on to propose stiffer tests of suitability for firearm licence applicants and a more rigorous ongoing scrutiny of applicants, closing what the *Times* called the 'lunatics loophole' in the gun laws, by the establishment of a new licensing authority (Stalker, 1996).

Through the 'lunatics loophole'

Even if, in the UK, the 'spree killer' was seen as a particularly rare occurrence, British commentators clearly thought they knew the type and had seen it before. Tendler, writing in the *Times*, reminded his readers:

> The spree killer was a US phenomenon until Michael Ryan in 1987 ... [he was] often a loner with problems relating to others and carrying embittered grudges. ... Their actions follow a relentless, unfolding path as they ferment an inner rage and then act. ... Often they are living a lie to impress others and draw status. ... They turn to guns because of the feeling of power and the fact that guns made them feel significant. ... Spree killers were more common in USA where guns were more available than in the UK. We have some ... lone embittered gunmen, dressing in macho army gear, or black, and setting out to wreak a bloody revenge for 'society's' treatment of them.
>
> (Tendler, 1996)

Within a day of the incident, psychiatrists were venturing 'profiles' of the type of person (a day before supposedly unknown) who might perpetrate such an outrage (a day before unthinkable). 'Such killers were seldom mentally ill but were often very embittered personalities.' Apparently they were typically 'rejected low achievers' for whom 'the act itself is seen as a final attempt to win fame and recognition'. Their idolisation of the gun was 'a way of grasping power and becoming a soldier-hero' grasping the symbols of power in our culture (Campbell, 1996). By the weekend, forensic psychiatrists were on hand to confirm that 'an obsession with guns is common amongst sexual deviants'. Such characters were apparently 'obsessed with power' and 'driven by jealousy and rage'. These supposed facts neatly embroidered the as yet fairly limited information emerging about Thomas Hamilton's secret life. 'Into adulthood his fascination with guns grew. … He used to have an AK47 until the laws were changed. … He used to say to local boys, "come round and see my guns" ' (Ferguson *et al*, 1996). So, despite ourselves, we knew a great deal about the 'gun-nut', much more than we had imagined. Indeed, after Hungerford, the British Association for Shooting and Conservation (BASC) had been sufficiently concerned about the infiltration of 'unsuitable' characters into the shooting sports that it had commissioned a study to look into the question of psychological screening for would-be gun owners. Likewise, in 1992, the Home Office Firearms Consultative Committee took up the call and recommended that the government investigate the issue of mental illness and firearm licensing. Two years later it expressed its profound disappointment that time had not been found for consideration of the matter.

In the status-conscious world of shooting, however, 'suitability' could be something of a euphemism. Shooting as a 'field sport' (as opposed to agricultural 'pest control') has long had an elitist element, with 'grouse shooting' on country estates on the 'Glorious Twelfth' at its pinnacle. In a similar vein, rifle clubs, partly as a result of the price of the weapons, also tended to be somewhat exclusive. Yet the same was not true of the newer pistol shooting clubs where, according to Barker, a new gun culture 'of would-be Travoltas and Schwarzeneggars' was thought to have taken the sport downmarket by 'allowing in the less stable, great unwashed' (Barker, 1996). Steering clear of anything sounding quite so prejudicial, an editorial in the *Times* (articulating a position in favour of handgun control, which the paper consistently adhered to) tried to draw some crucial lines in the debate.

> It is hard to see why private individuals should be allowed to own handguns. There are some reasons why in some specific circumstances some people (farmers and gamekeepers) should be permitted to possess certain weapons [shotguns]. Game shooting and stalking are vital parts of the rural economy and traditional relaxations of country dwellers. The use of sporting guns is governed by a cultural code that teaches a wary respect for all weaponry as well as legal regulation.
>
> Handguns are, however, wholly different. They are designed to kill human beings, not animals. Pistol shooting is a pursuit altogether more clinical and alien to our society than grouse shooting. The vast majority of gun club members are innocent enthusiasts but the nature of their weapons and the tone of their magazines attract those with an unhealthy interest in violence. Handguns by their very nature are easier to steal and conceal than

rifles or shotguns. The morbid and inadequate have seen these ugly devices celebrated as masculine talismans in popular culture. Yet in a civilised society they have no practical place except on the battlefield or in a police officer's holster.

(Times, 15.3.1996)

BASC's proposed solution to the problem of this 'morbid fascination' on the part of the inadequate and unsuitable was a suggestion for a certificate of psychological fitness for anyone seeking a gun licence. The BMA, however, argued that the idea of pre-emptive psychological testing was very unrealistic and unreliable. The secretary of the BMA made the following argument in evidence to the Home Affairs Select Committee. Doctors are not in a position to judge who will become mass murderers, he said.

> It is not possible from a medical point of view to assist in a reliable way with the prediction of those positively safe with firearms, nor those who are unsafe. … Our conclusion is that until such time as methods are developed to provide reliable predictions, firearms policy needs to be based on the understanding that, from time to time, unpredictable behaviour will occur. … Tragedies such as Dunblane can be seen from this viewpoint as the price to be paid for society's decision to allow legal access to firearms.

Having rejected the possibility of individual psychological assessment, the BMA turned to a collective public health risk argument gaining support among public health professionals in the USA. The best way to reduce firearm deaths and injuries would be to further restrict the types of firearms legally available. 'Bringing doctors in to certify applicants for firearms will not help. It would only offer false reassurance … [doctors] cannot predict the unpredictable. … The evidence is that the more guns there are in society, the more you are likely to die from a gun related killing' (Armstrong, 1996). However, notwithstanding this emphatic rejection of psychological testing, the idea was proposed several more times although few saw much mileage in it in the wake of the medical profession's staunch opposition (Mihill, 1996; Timmins, 1996).

Context and event

Despite the age and vulnerability of the young victims at Dunblane, despite the terrible frenzy of the attack, and despite the death toll, school shooting incidents were not unprecedented. Just how unknowable and unanticipated was it?

The commentary surrounding Dunblane focused initially upon the event and the victims. It then turned to consider the perpetrator. Next the focus of attention settled upon his legally sanctioned access to killing weapons. Finally it came to focus upon the policy process from which tougher gun controls were eventually to emerge. As Hamilton's guns were legally acquired, most conventional criminological discussion was side-stepped. The crime, as it were, fell beyond traditional criminology's more familiar paradigms (Squires, 1997b). Second, the event was discussed as a largely domestic, national tragedy. Later, as the firearms control debate got under way, more critical and challenging commentaries began to surface. They began to question the UK's gun control policies, the very policies hitherto regarded as beyond reproach, the toughest in the world.

With media attention confining itself to questions of legality or the alien nature of the gun in British domestic culture, wider questions, either of a more 'criminological' nature or from a more international agenda – concerning causation, supply and the growing threat posed by illegal firearm trafficking – went largely unasked. Although important, recurring references to the dangers of an American style 'gun culture' taking root in the UK were no substitute for a serious examination back up the lines of firearm supply. In the *Independent* Jason Bennetto reminded readers of Paul Condon's earlier remarks about an 'emerging gun culture amongst teenage gangs' fuelled by weapons 'brought in illegally from Eastern Europe' (Bennetto, 1996). In the same newspaper, Nicholas Timmins commented upon the increasing availability of illegal weapons in Europe. 'Since 1987 border checks have been eased somewhat and borders to former communist states are now less restricted. Consequently the whole of Europe has seen a booming illegal market in guns of all sorts irrespective of new national or European gun control laws' (Timmins, 1996). Yet, in the end, despite the evidence to the contrary, gun control in the UK was treated as a largely domestic matter. We had the strictest gun control legislation in the world but even this appeared to have little significant impact upon the availability of illegal firearms.

The absence of such themes in the press coverage of Dunblane, its aftermath, and the ensuing political debate, is perhaps all the more surprising given a report which appeared in the *Guardian* on March 13th, the day that Hamilton struck. The article concerned issues further up the firearms supply chain describing how weapons smuggling was said to have become 'the single most profitable business in Crete'. According to Helena Smith, 'Despite strict gun laws, Crete has been a weapons-loving culture since ancient times and at least half of households are thought to possess illegal guns. Moreover, many have the very latest in military combat weaponry ... in part a legacy of Turkish occupation.' Apparently, anyone wishing to purchase weapons had only to move out from the usual tourist venues and into back street bars in order to find willing dealers. Officials suggested that most of the newer weapons came, via Italy, from the former Yugoslavia. The article concluded by noting that following recent gunfights between rival gangs, police were attempting to clamp down on the problem. In the schools, apparently, 'children receive lectures on the perils of gun culture' (Smith, 1996). Before March 13th few could have contemplated the need for such lessons in British schools. Nevertheless as we have seen, even in the UK, some of the risks posed by a growing 'gun culture' had been anticipated.

Waiting for Cullen: a political chronology of gun control

As the press reporting of the shooting began to turn into the reporting of its aftermath and the emerging political reactions, attention started to fix upon a wider range of 'gun control' questions. Moore and Kay in the *Sun* set the context with a short article suggesting that 'more Brits now want to carry a firearm'. After Hungerford, there had initially been a fall in the number of licences issued but more recently applications and approvals had begun rising again.

Table 5.1 Shotguns and firearms: England and Wales, certificates and numbers of firearms

Year	Firearm certificates	Number of guns	Shotgun certificates	Number of shotguns
1990	142,500	330,000	802,000	1,500,000
1991	138,600	330,000	724,000	1,250,000
1992	136,800	358,000	689,000	1,200,000
1993	138,400	376,100	681,100	1,320,000
1994	140,200	396,800	670,000	1,330,000
1995	141,700	409,000	653,800	1,290,000

Note: figures for 1990–94 are estimates as complete national records did not begin until 1994

In 1992 there had been 136,800 section 1 firearm licences (excluding shotguns) in England and Wales but by 1994 this had risen to 140,200. Of some 11,700 licences issued or renewed during the year only 120 had been refused. In 1995, licensed handguns accounted for just under half the section 1 firearms in the UK. In the late 1980s there were said to be approximately 8,000 gun clubs but now there were thought to be closer to 10,000, just over 2,000 were handgun only shooting clubs. Shooting, especially handgun shooting, appeared to be undergoing something of a renaissance (Moore and Kay, 1996).

Not to be outdone the *Daily Mirror* boldly announced: 'We find killer's gun shop', at the head of a fairly speculative article which finally revealed that, although Hamilton had contacted the shop four times, there was no actual record of him ever having bought anything there and the staff said they couldn't remember him. The remainder of the piece 'exposed' the little-known world of shooting to readers' scrutiny. The shop was depicted as a virtual Aladdin's cave of lethal firepower. Rows of shotguns were chained to the walls while handguns were locked away in a series of cabinets. Compared to the high cost inflicted by Hamilton's weapons, the journalists expressed journalistic astonishment at the relatively low price of the weapons. 'The weapons of death can cost as little as £140 from dealers who sell an awesome array of handguns ... [furthermore] guns like those used by Hamilton on his killing spree can also be bought by mail order using a credit card. ... About 300 gunshops offer a service by post to Britain's 150,000 licensed handgun enthusiasts'. Turning to the wider shop window of the British gun trade, they added, 'a flick through the pages of gun magazines reveals an astonishing catalogue of handguns ... ranging in power and size from tiny .22 automatic pistols to a six-shot Smith & Wesson .357 which sells for £395. A Glock semi-automatic as used by Scotland Yard's firearms squad can be bought for under £500' (*Daily Mirror*, 14.3.1996). Finally, despite having exposed a number of general concerns about the firearms trade in the UK, the journalists concluded with the observation that 'regulations governing the sale of weapons and the licensing of users in the UK are the tightest in the world'.

The central question of gun control came into clearer and clearer focus. Political party leaders, Prime Minister John Major and Leader of the Opposition, Tony Blair, visited Dunblane together to pay their respects. Major committed the government to a full Judicial Inquiry, chaired by Lord Cullen, and cross-party talks on gun control. He also announced the government's intention to call a firearms amnesty. Several firearms amnesties had taken place since the Second World War, 'soaking-up' some 300,000 unregistered weapons in total, with the most recent, following the Hungerford shootings in 1987, gathering up approximately 48,000 weapons and 1.5 million rounds of ammunition (Prestage and Arlidge, 1996). While no-one actually opposed the idea of an amnesty, there was a general recognition that it was something of a side-issue: neither a solution to the gun control issues already raised nor a response to the illegal firearms already in circulation. Above all, the amnesty was seen as an ineffective political response to the dilemmas generated by both of these (Travis, 1996b). By contrast, Tony Blair's first public statement amounted to a clear policy recommendation for tighter gun controls. He argued that 'gun owners should have to face stricter tests and be investigated as to why they need a gun licence' (Landale and Bowditch, 1996). Later, the Prime Minister was criticised for failing to capitalise upon the mood of cross-party consensus in favour of tighter gun controls. In the months which followed, as the issue became more partisan, the government became increasingly out-manouevred as a result of its commitment to wait for Cullen's report.

The British government – having agreed upon an Inquiry – sought to avoid what it disparagingly labelled 'knee jerk' or 'quick-fix' legislation. By contrast, very soon after the Tasmania killings in April 1996, Australia's Prime Minister announced a significant range of new gun controls. The proposals, for banning automatic and semi-automatic and 'military-style' rifles together with pump-action shotguns were described as 'historic' with Australia's federal, state and territorial governments apparently in agreement, for the first time, on the fraught question of gun control (Zinn, 1996). By contrast, the British government appeared to prevaricate. When John Major reaffirmed that no new gun controls would be considered until the Cullen Inquiry was completed, many MPs took the Australian government's seemingly prompt action as an opportunity to press for similar initiatives in the UK. David Mellor MP, for one, argued for an immediate ban on all handguns above .22 calibre except those used in competitive target shooting noting, 'It is obvious that the Australians don't think it is a knee jerk reaction to act so quickly'. On behalf of the government, Home Secretary Michael Howard replied that Australia had hitherto had fairly lax gun laws and, in fact, the main features of the bans recently announced there had already been introduced into the UK following the Hungerford massacre in 1988.

Guardian leader writers were not convinced and drew a number of lessons from the contrasting responses of the two governments:.

> The prompt response of Australia provides a lesson for Britain, but the point of comparison is not in the detail (our gun controls were already more strict than Australia's) [rather] the decision shows how politicians can seize the moment of public concern to take an initiative from which they might have backed away before ... opinion polls show that an overwhelming majority supports a wide ranging firearms ban. ...
>
> When swift legislative action is contemplated critics are quick to label it knee-jerk, they may be right – but to what end? Blair's initiative was being presented as an attempt to seize the high ground on law and order from the Conservatives. It is a pity to give it such a spin ... this should be an issue on which all main parties could unite. The central aim must be how to shift the onus of justification. The question to ask is not whether an individual should be denied a firearms licence, but whether there is any good reason for the possession of such a weapon at all. Public opinion would accept this: politicians should lead.
>
> (*Guardian*, 13.5.1996, 'Editorial')

The *Times* agreed, while 'legislating in haste is rarely wise', it claimed, 'sometimes one event draws attention to a pressing need. ... Dunblane was such an event' (*Times*, 14.8.1996). Yet as the *Guardian*'s comments made clear, the gun control agenda and the lines of a seemingly unnecessary partisan political conflict were already taking shape. They would centrally dominate political debate and media reporting for the remainder of the year. Indeed, it is fair to say that the political chronology of 1996 both revolved around and was driven along by a number of key events occurring in the aftermath of Dunblane and as part of the political response to it. Significant among these 'key events' were the following, to which we will shortly turn.

In the first weeks after the shooting – soon followed by the Tasmania incident – media reporting addressed the grief and tragedy of the event itself. Next came the funerals and their immediate aftermath, before the focus of attention began to crystallise around a range of issues concerning gun control and firearm licensing. During this time a number of the bereaved parents, their friends and other residents of Dunblane, formed what came to be known as the 'Snowdrop Campaign'. They determined to press for a complete prohibition on handguns.

Although, as commentators later reflected, few of the Snowdrop campaigners had much in the way of previous political or campaigning experience, aided by the tabloid press, they were extraordinarily successful in capitalising upon the public mood. Within only a few weeks of launching their petition, they had amassed an incredible 750,000 supporting signatures. As the gun control debate became, in due course, increasingly bitter and 'political', the simple and uncompromising stance of the Snowdrop campaigners provided both a constant pressure for a handgun ban and an effective and unwavering 'moral benchmark' against which the acceptability of any alternative gun control proposals might be judged. Viewed as an example of pressure-group politics, the Snowdrop Campaign's success was unprecedented. Although the campaigners had the backing of a number of daily newspapers and an enormous reservoir of public goodwill, they lacked many of the usual attributes of successful pressure group campaigning. By contrast their opponents, the gun lobby, although now rather divided and on the defensive, had influence and had successfully exploited their political connections in the past. However, if the success of the Snowdrop Campaign was unprecedented, so was the sense of moral outrage that had prompted its formation.

Many national newspapers quickly threw their support behind the Snowdrop Campaign agenda although, while a number continued to play a supportive role, a degree of ambiguity sometimes crept into the proposal for a 'ban on handguns'. It could, for instance, mean that all handguns, irrespective of calibre, magazine capacity, sporting specification, historical significance or 'military appearance' should be banned. Or it might merely refer to a prohibition on 'private possession' – the idea that working handguns should not be kept in people's own homes. As the debate developed and as the political pressure mounted, politicians and newspaper editors alike came to take refuge in some of this ambiguity. For instance, the *Times* and *Sunday Times* committed their support to the Snowdrop campaigners, as did the *Sun* and, in Scotland, the *Daily Record*. Seven months later, however, the *Sunday Times*, at least, was urging caution and throwing its weight behind the government's planned reprieve for .22 calibre pistols. The *Mail on Sunday* on March 17th led with an article 'Why handguns must be banned' and a piece by David Mellor: 'Handguns have no positive role in society. They merely satisfy the sporting instincts of a coterie of gun lovers. They bring no benefits whatever to a wider public'. In an editorial it added, 'there is no justification for individuals owning powerful handguns like those amassed by Hamilton. These were not small bore target pistols, but military-style killing machines. … Every one is one too many'. So, although the *Mail* argued a case for the prohibition of all handguns, powerful, 'military-style' weapons were singled out as a particular problem. Other newspapers argued the need for tighter gun controls (*Guardian, Observer, Daily Mirror*), for tougher regulation of gun clubs (*Daily Express*) or for measures to address the UK's developing 'gun culture' (*Independent*). By contrast, an editorial in the *Daily Telegraph* (15.3.1996) made no reference to gun control issues at all, simply confining itself to the question of a suitable memorial for the children of Dunblane.

On May 30th the Cullen Inquiry itself opened and, over the next twenty-six days of public hearings, concluding on July 11th, it reviewed both the particular details of Hamilton's outrage as well as the broad background to it. The Inquiry covered Hamilton's own life history, his various attempts to establish boy's clubs, his disputes with the Scout Association and his enthusiasm for firearms. It also covered questions of school security. Finally, the control and licensing of firearms featured prominently in the report, and a great deal of attention was given to a number of apparent shortcomings in the firearm licensing process operated by Central Scotland Police. Each of the issues addressed by the Inquiry gave rise to a set of general or more specific suggestions and recommendations. As the Inquiry progressed, a definitive version of events began to emerge. The Inquiry received submissions of evidence from many different actors involved – representatives of the bereaved families, officers from Central Scotland Police, a variety of local authority representatives, spokesmen representing firearms and shooting interests, those involved in youth organisations, a number of people with more personal experience of Hamilton or his activities, and a range of other more 'technical' experts (pathologists, psychiatrists, ballistics experts and scenes of crime analysts). As new details emerged, in the course of the Inquiry, these were eagerly seized upon by the press but, above all, it was the debate around the emerging gun control policy issues which took centre stage.

The Inquiry concluded in mid-July and Lord Cullen retired to prepare his report. Following the success of the Snowdrop Campaign, a national Gun Control Network was launched. It too declared its aim as the 'elimination of the gun culture', it began to step up its lobbying pressure for a complete ban on handguns. Partly in response and beginning to fear the worst, firearms organisations launched their own appeal to finance a campaign against a ban on handguns. All gun club members and certificate holders were urged to pay £25 into a fighting fund run by the British Sports Shooting Council (BSSC). At a launch of the shooters' campaign – apparently attended by MPs of all parties – firearms enthusiasts and lobbyists described the Gun Control Network as naive and its proposals unworkable. They reiterated an argument that 'knee jerk emotional legislation could make the situation worse' leading to 'non-compliance with [any] new legislation on a massive scale' (Travis, 1996e). This argument rather flew in the face of repeated shooting lobby claims that 'shooters' were invariably law-abiding and responsible. July, however, ended with events taking a more remarkable and unanticipated turn.

In parallel with the Cullen Inquiry into the Dunblane shootings, the House of Commons Home Affairs Committee had announced on March 28th its own inquiry into the possession of handguns. The Committee's deliberations were an aspect of the 'cross-party talks' promised by the Prime Minister but, as it transpired, things rather blew up in his face. Whereas the Cullen Inquiry's brief was to seek to establish what happened at Dunblane and to examine the circumstances leading up to the killings, the Committee's role was 'to consider the wider question of the availability of handguns' (House of Commons, Home Affairs Committee, 1996: iv). The Committee took oral evidence on a single day (May 8th), hearing from the police, BSSC representatives and the Home Office (although no attempt was made to receive oral evidence from anti-gun organisations or victims' families). It received written submissions during April, May and June before meeting to discuss the report and its proposals on July 17th, 22nd and 24th 1996.

We will consider in some greater detail the nature of the actual evidence supplied to the Committee, the substance – as it were – of the UK's gun control debate, in the following chapter. For the moment it is perhaps enough to note the sources of these submissions. Of the twenty-nine written submissions, fourteen were explicitly pro-shooting and a further five were concerned with very specific types of firearms used in particular activities (athletics starting pistols, historical re-enactment societies or veterinary animal destruction). Five submissions came from police or Home Office sources. Of the remaining five submissions, four came from professional associations in medicine, psychiatry or social work and the last described the Canadian government's gun control policies. In stark contrast, no organisations or individuals favouring or campaigning for gun control submitted any evidence at all.

The Committee's 'impartiality' was questioned still further when it became clear that the 'specialist advisor' it had appointed was none other than Colin Greenwood, firearms expert and editor of the magazine *Guns Review*. Greenwood, whose work and opinions we have already encountered, was a former police superintendent and now a firearms consultant. He defended his independence and wide-ranging experience. Nevertheless, as Patrick Wintour argued in the *Observer*, his magazine was currently 'running a vituperative campaign against the police and Opposition parties [and criticising the Snowdrop Campaign] for backing an all-out handgun ban' (Wintour, 1996). In *Guns Review* in July 1994, Greenwood had referred somewhat disparagingly to advocates of tighter gun control as 'hysteria mongers' adding later, in April 1995, that if the shooting sports were to survive, 'we have to stop being nice people and start being as politically dirty as the antis'. Greenwood himself submitted a memorandum of evidence to the Home Affairs Committee, one of the longest it received. Though substantial, well-informed and drawing upon a wealth of research and scholarship, it is difficult to avoid the conclusion that the 'specialist advisor' was particularly keen to dispute any evidence (particularly that supplied by the Scottish Office and Home Office) pointing in the direction of a handgun ban – Greenwood acknowledged as much in his submission (Greenwood, 1996).

It is worth noting that while the oral evidence and most of the written submissions were with the Committee before Cullen's Inquiry opened, the Committee's own deliberations occurred after the Cullen hearings had been completed. This would suggest that, by virtue of the high profile press commentary afforded to the subject, Committee members ought to have been well aware of the emerging issues and developing public debate while they studied their own proposals. Nevertheless, on July 24th the Committee rejected proposals put by its five Labour members that, 'the goal of responsible politicians should be dramatically to reduce the ownership of guns in private hands', and that, 'the private possession of handguns should be banned'. Instead they made a series of more detailed proposals relating to the scrutiny of licence applications and the powers of the police in monitoring licence holders (House of Commons, Home Affairs Committee, Vol. II, 1996).

Having therefore made no significant concessions to the public pressure for a more fundamental review of British gun control policies, the Committee commended its report to the House of Commons, on its Conservative chairman's casting vote. A week later, the content of the Committee's report and its conclusions were leaked to the *Daily Record* in Scotland and the *Sun*. On July 31st the *Sun* gave front page billing to the headline 'Shame on the lot of you. Outrage of parents as Tories snub ban on guns'. An article carried the emotive words of John Crozier, father of one of the Dunblane victims, 'the devil came to Dunblane that day … and he's still at work in the House of Commons. If the deaths of sixteen innocent children and their teacher are not going to change our gun laws I can't see much hope for this country. … We will just go the same way America has gone … a child's right to life is much more important than anyone's right to have a gun'.

In an unprecedented centre page spread, the paper pictured the six Conservative MPs supporting the Committee's recommendations. The MPs constituencies, their listed interests (including any shooting connections) were identified and the paper printed their addresses and phone numbers. 'Tell the six guilty MPs what you think', urged the paper, 'give them a piece of your mind' (Crawford and Lowrie, 1996).

A *Sun* editorial was equally uncompromising:

> The decision of the six conservative MPs flies in the face of the nation's outrage after Dunblane. … The MPs' idea that doctors should sign all applications for firearm certificates is a hopeless fudge that will achieve nothing. The gun culture is not a medical problem, it is one for the government to tackle. … Now we have to wait for Cullen's report and hope that it demands a ban on handguns.
>
> (*Sun*, 31.7.1996)

The Committee's report was officially published on August 14th, but by then its contents had been extensively disclosed and discussed in the media. Sir Ivan Lawrence, Conservative chairman of the Committee, denounced the campaign of 'hate and hysteria' following the leaking of the report and tried to defend the Committee's decision. He argued that his colleagues had tried to find a 'rational' solution to the issue and denied they had been 'nobbled' by the gun lobby. 'No one could give our inquiry any assurances that [a handgun ban] would prevent another Dunblane', he argued in an article for the *Daily Telegraph*. 'The gun debate has produced the most hysterical, ill-informed and vituperative campaign I can ever remember – thanks mainly to the irresponsible tabloid press. Those of us who have opposed a ban have been branded murderers and traitors' (Lawrence, 1996).

But it was all to no avail. Although Sir Ivan's comments prompted a supportive editorial in the *Telegraph*, it found itself alone. The *Guardian* announced the publication of the Report on its front page with a photograph staring into the barrel of a semi-automatic handgun and the headline, 'Telling Scotland to get stuffed' (Vulliamy, 1996b). Scotland's *Daily Record* which was leading a press campaign in Scotland in favour of a total ban on handguns argued that 'the sheer arrogance of those [English] politicians has made this a

Scottish issue'. The words of a gun control campaigner were added for emphasis: 'If those wee children had been killed at Eton or Cambridge then you bet they'd be worried about taking the flak. But [they think they can ignore us] as it's just Scotland bellyaching again' (*Daily Record*, 14.8.1996).

With the government in trouble and seeking to distance itself from the Home Affairs Committee Report, an important ambiguity emerged in Labour's own position on the issue. Labour's earlier submission to the Cullen Inquiry was said to have wrong-footed the Conservatives who had refused to disclose their own proposals prior to the publication of Cullen's report. Labour had proposed restricting the availability of handguns in the following terms:

> We recommend that handguns above .22 calibre should certainly be prohibited. We also believe that the strong case for restricting handguns of .22 calibre and below to those which need to be reloaded after each shot should carefully be examined by the Inquiry.
>
> In general, given the lethal nature of handguns, we see a strong case for banning them altogether. The shooting fraternity must make a case for possession and if they can, they must suggest and accept restrictions and costs necessary to prevent such guns from being used for anything other than target practice.
>
> (Labour Party, 1996, paras 17–18)

Jack Straw, Labour's Home Affairs spokesman was said to have been struck by the Swiss and Japanese contrasts on gun control and rates of firearm homicide. Whereas both countries had internationally low rates of recorded crime, Japan, where gun ownership was almost entirely prohibited, had a gun homicide rate only one-eighth of the UK's, while Switzerland with widespread firearms ownership had a gun murder rate some six times that of the UK. For Straw, therefore, the logic of this was to move gun control in the direction of Japan and towards a complete prohibition on the ownership of handguns (Travis, 1996c).

However, by contrast, Labour members of the Home Affairs Committee had only sought to prohibit the 'private possession' of handguns. Following the publication of the Committee's report, John Prescott (Deputy Leader of the Labour Party and 'in charge' while Tony Blair was away on holiday) and Chris Mullin MP (who had drafted the Labour clauses rejected by the Home Affairs Committee) began to warm to the theme of banning the 'private possession' of handguns rather than the controls implied in Labour's evidence to Cullen (Landale, 1996). Interviewed, in the *Guardian* about Labour's stance Mullin argued, 'It is not our intention to be vindictive towards people who legitimately enjoy target shooting … they could continue to shoot in clubs, but not keep their handguns at home' (Vulliamy, 1996b). In Labour's terms, this was a significant concession to shooting interests and a marked departure from the tough line suggested in Labour's evidence to Cullen and attributed to Tony Blair. In subsequent press commentary the distinction between a complete ban and a ban on 'private possession' was often confused or overlooked. No doubt this was partly due to the firearms lobby regarding a ban on 'private possession' as tantamount to a complete ban (and they vehemently opposed both), but in a rapidly changing political climate, the confusion tended to obscure precisely what was being proposed by whom. While formally 'waiting for Cullen', both parties were obviously feeling their own ways towards a clear and sustainable position on the issue. The ambiguity in Labour's position suggested that they too were willing to compromise, seemingly underestimating the support for more far-reaching proposals.

Speculation continued in the press that the six Conservative MPs had been 'sacrificed' by the government 'testing' public opinion on the gun control issue. As Mills and Arlidge commented in the *Observer*, the government would be committed to going ahead with a handgun ban if that was what Cullen came to recommend. However, some ministers feared that such a policy might alienate many of their 'country sports' supporters and provoke a revolt by MPs with strong shooting links. 'Testing the water' seemed like a sensible precaution, but rather than preparing the ground for pulling the Tory Party together on the issue, the tactic had backfired badly. According to Mills and Arlidge, 'party insiders believed that the Select Committee report would test public opinion and give credibility to any decision falling short of an outright handgun ban'. However, when the report was leaked, aside from prompting a political backlash across the full spectrum of national newspapers, it soon became clear that the Labour MPs on the Home Affairs Committee were gaining support for their suggestion for a ban on the private possession of handguns, irrespective of whatever Cullen might propose. Accordingly, ministers began to distance themselves from the six (Mills and Arlidge, 1996). Tory leaders and Michael Forsythe, the Scottish Secretary, criticised Labour for not abiding by the cross-party agreement to wait until after Cullen had reported before making gun control proposals. Labour replied that the Conservative majority on the Home Affairs Committee had prompted their response by so completely caving-in to the gun lobby (Arlidge and Travis, 1996). In any event the damage to the Conservatives had been done. As Turner, writing in the *Sunday Mirror*, noted: 'The abiding memory will be of self-interested, cynical, huntin', shootin', fishin', Tories who failed to reflect the true national revulsion over Thomas Hamilton's Dunblane massacre. … How does this shabby little sextet, trampling on the memories of the sixteen children murdered at Dunblane, sleep at night?' she asked. 'It is all down to vested interests, nice little outside earners and old fashioned aristo' arrogance', she concluded (Turner, 1996).

Likewise an editorial in the *Mail on Sunday* argued that the government's overall 'law and order' agenda was being lost because of the apparent prevarication on the gun control question:

> In the wake of the Dunblane killings, the government has failed to respond to overwhelming demands for the banning of handguns. Tory MPs [were] voicing the sentiments of Montana backwoodsmen rather than backbenchers. … Labour [were] sensing the divisions [within the Tory party] and about to force the issue … but Dunblane should not become a political

football. A complete ban on handguns is common sense … and a step towards placating the sense of deep injustice now suffered by the parents of Dunblane.

(*Mail on Sunday*, 4.8.1996)

The *Times* was no less critical of the Committee's conclusions. Its editorial, 'Off Target: Tory MPs who oppose gun control are out of touch', on August 14th argued:

[Existing] weapon ownership laws are ill-equipped to cope with the growth of an ugly culture which celebrates the gun as a talisman of masculinity for the morbid and inadequate. There has been a worrying increase in the number of powerful weapons legally held in unsuitable hands. … The Tory members of the Home Affairs Select Committee may have tried not to be swayed by the emotion that Dunblane engendered. Instead they have been influenced by the weak arguments from a powerful lobby.

It summarily dismissed the Committee's claim that controlling legal guns would be fairly pointless given that most armed crime was committed with illegal weapons and found nothing of merit in the arguments about the 'inconvenience' to shooters. Rather, it asserted, 'legislators have a responsibility to act if crimes can be prevented'.

The do-nothing defence mounted by the conservatives is woeful … the fact that illegal guns are mainly used in crime is irrelevant since Dunblane was committed with legally held weapons. … [The] other flimsy straws thrown up by the Tories include problems for starters of races, or people wanting their guns in a hurry and problems of loading guns at tournaments. … Can these MPs really think that the chance of minor inconvenience to sportsmen should come before protecting citizens?

Finally, the *Times* argued, on this fundamentally moral question, a number of more routine political considerations just didn't apply.

The MPs almost wilfully weak position is further undermined by their reference to the cost of the compensation that might be involved. … The appeal to the wallet on an issue that has engaged the public's heart is crass. It reinforces the unhappy impression that Conservatives reduce every moral question to a matter of cash. These MPs support Michael Howard's expenditure on police and prisons to protect the public, they should extend the same logic to restricting ownership of handguns. There is a strong case for an outright ban on weapons designed not for sport or game but to kill human beings.

(*Times*, 14.8.1996)

And the *Guardian* agreed. When the Committee's recommendations were first leaked it argued in an editorial: 'Ban them now, no need to wait. ... The government has the opportunity to make life safer by banning the private ownership of handguns. The Home Affairs select committee has had the opportunity to contribute and has muffed its chance. It should be ignored' (*Guardian*, 1.8.1996). A fortnight later it described the Committee's report, now officially published, as 'contemptible' and argued that the report was better for the firearms lobby than the 'gun freaks' had ever dared hope (*Guardian*, 14.8.1996). Labour's Chris Mullin was more optimistic in his assessment of the situation. At best, he argued, the Select Committee report was a pyrrhic victory for the gun lobby but 'no one should underestimate the power of the gun lobby or its influence within the Conservative party'. All the same, he added, 'we have them on the run' (Mullin, 1996). As it turned out, therefore, the Home Affairs Select Committee achieved the worst of all possible outcomes for the government. Its deeply unpopular report was very damagingly taken to reflect a substantial part of Conservative party opinion on firearms yet its recommendations were effectively ignored.

The scene was now set for the next key events in the UK's political chronology of gun control: the party conference season and the publication of Lord Cullen's Report. Before either, however, further evidence emerged of the Tory Party's predicament on the gun control question. A significant number of prominent Conservative MPs were found to have shooting listed among their 'interests'. A number of these had played an important role in modifying the 1988 Firearms (Amendment) Act introduced after the Hungerford killings and there was a growing concern that such an insider lobby might prove influential in diluting any recommendations from Cullen before they reached the statute book (Travis, 1996a). Indeed, less than a fortnight after the killings at Dunblane, Tory MP and former Olympic athlete Sebastian Coe accepted the Honorary Presidency of the UK National Pistol Association (NPA). Coe was said to be flattered by the invitation although many of his colleagues were appalled by the timing of his decision (*Observer*, 24.3.1996). As the war of words between the gun lobby and gun control campaigners deteriorated, however, the NPA produced a members' bulletin containing a strongly worded personal attack upon bereaved Dunblane parents leading Coe to resign from the organisation (Grey and Burke, 1996).

In 1988, a particular concession won on behalf of the shooting lobby and included in the 1988 Firearms (Amendment) Act had been the establishment of the Firearms Consultative Committee to advise the Home Office on matters relating to the firearms industry and firearms control. Although, as we have seen, the Committee was established in the wake of what was then the UK's worst shooting incident, it was actually dominated by shooting interests. There arose a concern that a similar constellation of firearms lobby interests would prove decisive in deflecting the pressure for more far-reaching gun control changes after Dunblane (Mills and Arlidge, 1996). However what, in other circumstances, might have proved a political advantage came rapidly to appear a disadvantage as the overwhelming weight of public opinion appeared to swing behind proposals for the complete banning of handguns. As the six Tory members of the Home Affairs Select Committee – and anyone else speaking on behalf of an apparent shooting interest – discovered to their cost, they were represented in the press as both unsympathetic and unaccountable, defending an indefensible and dangerous sectional interest. John Crozier, one of the bereaved Dunblane parents interviewed in the *Guardian*, voiced an opinion shared by many:

> My daughter's right to life is more important than anybody's right to shoot guns. ... After Hungerford the same MPs and the same shooting lobby said it was a knee-jerk reaction, an hysterical reaction. If guns had been banned, the children would still be alive with their teacher. ... These MPs appear to be considering the so-called rights of shooters. Instead they should apply their minds to the civil liberties of our babies who were shot dead. What is more important, their right not to be shot dead by a state sanctioned gunman or the right of someone to shoot for fun?
>
> (Boseley, 1996; Arlidge and Travis, 1996)

In this sense, rather than an asset, the Conservative Party's firearm lobbyists were increasingly seen as a liability to a government struggling to achieve a degree of consensus in anticipation of Cullen but rapidly feeling itself overhauled by Labour – and this, perhaps only months from a General Election. Accordingly, a number of senior ministers interviewed in the *Times* and *Daily Telegraph*, including Home Office minister David MacLean, let it be known that they 'would not shirk from doing what was necessary', should Cullen recommend a ban on firearms. By implication, the Tory members of the Select Committee were on their own and their views had not reflected party policy (Webster and Ford, 1996; Hibbs, 1996).

Cullen had been expected to report by the beginning of October but, with a General Election only months away, the government were keen to hold off publication of such a potentially controversial document until after the annual party conference season. However, even on this tactic, the government appeared to come unstuck. As the publication date for Cullen's report drew closer and media sources began to print articles which suggested (as it later transpired, quite accurately) that Cullen's recommendations were going to fall 'some way short of an outright prohibition of handguns', (Squires, 1996b; Watson, 1996), Labour Party conference managers took the unusual step of asking Ann Pearston, a representative of the Dunblane Parents campaign (and not a Party member), to address its conference. Her speech was regarded by all as both impassioned and emotional but no less resolutely committed to the achievement of a ban on handguns. 'Any legislation short of a complete ban on handguns', she argued, 'would mean that we and our children are expendable so that target shooters can retain their right to pursue a sport that uses weapons designed to kill'. Above all, this speech and the overwhelming support for the gun control proposals articulated within it, both inside the Blackpool Winter Gardens where the conference was held and throughout the country as a whole, were credited with convincing

Tony Blair and Jack Straw to adopt the Snowdrop Campaign position – a complete ban on handguns – as its own (Cohen *et al.*, 1996).

Conservative commentators accused Labour of trying to make political capital out of tragedy (Travis, 1996f) but the political damage was done. In sharp contrast to Labour's effective political manoeuvre, an unseemly row erupted at a fringe meeting organised by the British Association for Shooting and Conservation at the Conservative Party conference as gun lobby representatives attempted to put their case. Spokesmen from the BSSC were still sticking to their tired and discredited script that guns were not the problem. The real issue, they argued, was to weed out the risky and unsuitable individuals (Smithers, 1996). Later, Michael Forsythe, the Scottish Secretary, warned his colleagues of the dangers of coming to be seen in the public mind as a 'shooters party'. If the Tories balked at introducing significant new controls on handguns, the 'party of law and order' would be outflanked. Likewise, David Mellor, Conservative MP and former Home Office minister at the time of the Hungerford shootings, but now a firm supporter of a handgun ban, agreed that, 'Labour was outflanking us on law and order and there is a serious danger of the Conservative Party losing the plot on this issue' (White and Travis, 1996). If Cullen recommended anything less than a complete ban, he added, the government would be in real trouble because Labour's campaign had been very effective and a number of Conservative MPs, including himself, would not support anything less than a complete ban.

As public opinion hardened in the run up to the Cullen Report's publication, it became increasingly difficult to see how ministers could avoid adopting more far-reaching gun controls than either they may have originally intended or than Lord Cullen was thought likely to propose. In the last few days of 'waiting for Cullen', events moved particularly fast. In the end, the government was no longer waiting at all. Instead, they found themselves pushed, through stark political necessity, to reach their own conclusion irrespective of Cullen's report (Craig *et al.*, 1996). It might have been difficult for a government to resist this kind of pressure at the best of times, but with an election imminent other considerations undoubtedly applied (Castle, 1996).

The Cullen Report was officially published on October 16th, but had been made available to ministers over the previous weekend, prior to its discussion in Cabinet. In view of the sensitive political situation, and the fact that the Report did not let the government off the hook by recommending a complete ban on the ownership and possession of handguns, senior ministers had to formulate their positions quickly. In a round of hasty negotiations, political soundings and 'off the record' briefings undertaken over the weekend, ministers sought to prepare the ground for a compromise proposal falling short of a complete ban and rather closer, in essence, to Cullen's recommendations. Home Secretary, Michael Howard, had been keen on a less restrictive approach, accepting the thrust of Cullen's suggestion that handguns should not be kept at home, in order to avoid a damaging public clash with around thirty Conservative 'gun lobby' MPs. However, press briefings by 'sources close to the Home Secretary' implying that the Cabinet would agree to no more than a simple ban on the home possession of handguns had prompted a hostile reaction from campaigners.

Howard had voiced his concern that a tougher stance, prohibiting handguns entirely, might risk pushing some weapons into illegality and he justified his preference not to go for a total ban by pointing out that Lord Cullen's main anxiety had been the rapid expansion in the use of the larger calibre handguns 'as symbols of personal power' by shooters who 'don the trappings of combat, such as holsters and camouflage clothing'. The Snowdrop Campaign response was that the tragedy had its roots in the UK's developing gun culture, and rooting this out was an issue on which there could be no compromise (White and Travis, 1996). According to Alan Travis, these 'officially inspired leaks' gave the game away. 'It appeared that ministers had already prepared a compromise to appease the shooting lobby, whatever Lord Cullen said'. Ann Pearston threatened to stand against Scottish Secretary Michael Forsythe (already with the smallest Conservative majority in Scotland) in the forthcoming General Election if the government failed to deliver a gun ban. And, committed to fighting his corner, 'Forsythe went into Tuesday's cabinet meeting with his resignation threat in hand, determined to ensure Dunblane was not fudged'. The Cabinet discussed the Cullen Report for ninety minutes at which the Prime Minister gave his backing to his Scottish Secretary. The resulting proposals, widely seen as a victory for Michael Forsythe, were announced in Parliament the following day. In the Commons, Michael Forsythe explained the government's general approach and Michael Howard detailed the government's legislative proposals for amending the 1968 Firearms Act.

The government had chosen to move far beyond the proposals contained in Lord Cullen's report. While Cullen had suggested, in essence, only that self-loading pistols and revolvers of any calibre should be either disabled when not in use or stored in properly secured shooting club premises, the government had decided upon the complete prohibition of all handguns above .22 calibre. So, after over six months of waiting for Cullen for an answer to the UK's gun question, the government had decided to ignore his advice.

Endings and recriminations

The government's detailed gun control proposals were eventually published on November 2nd in the Firearms (Amendment) Bill. Its main features (bearing a uncanny similarity to the proposals Labour had originally submitted to the Cullen Inquiry back in May – though Labour had subsequently moved on) included a maximum ten-year jail sentence for illegal possession of any handgun. Handguns of .22 in. calibre (or less) could still be legally held on licence but, when not in use, would have to be stored in secure gun club premises. Multi-shot or self-loading handguns of any calibre would also be prohibited. A police permit would be required for permission to transport firearms to other venues, for example, shooting competitions at other ranges. The licensing and inspection of gun owners and the regulation of gun clubs and shooting ranges was to become much tighter (clubs would have to engage in a more thorough 'vetting' of their memberships) and the mail order sales of firearms were to be prohibited. Finally, a number of 'firearm' types were to be exempted from the legislation: 'gas-powered' weapons, starting pistols, veterinary 'fixed-bolt' pistols, heritage weapons and pre-1946 'trophies of war'.

On the basis of these proposals, it was estimated that the owners of some 160,000 larger calibre handguns (approximately 80 per cent of existing licensed handguns) would have to surrender their weapons, leaving some 40,000 .22 calibre pistols 'in circulation'. Although representatives of the shooting lobby declared themselves appalled and horrified, predicting that the proposals would mean the ending of pistol shooting as a sport in the UK, Labour still wanted to go further. Having adopted the Snowdrop Campaign and Gun Control Network objectives of the banning of all handguns, Labour wanted to see .22 in. calibre pistols outlawed as well. The government refused to accept this and indicated that their Bill would carry a three-line whip when debated in the Commons. As a result, the four weeks between October 20th, when the government announced its decisions on the Cullen Report and November 18th when the two-day Commons debate on the Firearms (Amendment) Bill began, saw an acrimonious four-way fight between the government and Opposition and representatives of the shooting lobby and gun control campaign groups.

The government felt itself squeezed from two directions. Some Conservative MPs had already indicated they would only vote for a complete ban on all hand-guns. Others, in particular the twenty-five or so Conservatives with shooting connections, were known to be unhappy with the proposal to ban all higher calibre weapons. While Labour, most of the national press and the gun control campaign groups, were pressing for the government to allow a 'free vote' on the issue, the government reasoned that doing so would probably mean that their own cautiously tailored proposals would be defeated, handing an important propaganda victory to the Opposition.

In view of the political dynamics attendant upon the framing of the government's proposals, it is worth considering briefly the policy option they settled upon and its repercussions. It seems abundantly clear, the proposals were formulated first as a political compromise and only later was an attempt made to 'rationalise' this political settlement as a gun control strategy. The reasons given by Michael Howard for continuing to allow single-shot .22 pistols were, first, to ensure the continuation of .22 pistol shooting as a sport and, second, to lessen the temptation upon shooters to 'go illegal'. Permitting the continuation of .22 shooting would, it was thought, allow shooters to shift down to the lower calibre weapons but still continue with their sport. The third factor in the Home Secretary's reasoning concerned the advice originally given by the Association of Chief Police Officers (ACPO) and the Superintendents' Association) to the Home Affairs Select Committee inquiry, that prohibiting all handguns would be 'impractical' or 'draconian' and 'unfair' (House of Commons, Home Affairs Committee, 1996, Vol. II: 77–79). Intriguingly, both organisations subsequently appeared to reconsider their positions, eroding still further the shaky foundations upon which Howard had built his compromise.

The Superintendents' Association had reconsidered the firearms question at its 1996 Annual Conference and appeared to move closer towards endorsing a complete prohibition on handguns. ACPO later argued that the Home Affairs Committee report, to which it had submitted its original evidence, was 'disappointing' (Webster and Ford, 1996). By August 1996, however, ACPO representatives representatives were reportedly endorsing proposals to ban all handguns bar single-shot .22s, seemingly regarding the prohibition of all handguns 'impractical' but anticipating no similar difficulties in banning only 80 per cent of them (Arlidge and Travis, 1996). Of the police organisations giving evidence to the Select Committee, only the Police Federation had proposed a complete ban on handguns from the outset (House of Commons, Home Affairs Committee, 1996, Vol. II: 80–81).

Howard proffered a final reason for endorsing the government's gun control policy choice. While this reflected rising concerns about firearms, crime and public safety and was consistent with Lord Cullen's own remarks about the changing character of shooting sports in the UK, it rather exposed the flaw at the heart of the government's strategy. In his Report, Cullen had noted:

> Over the last 20 years there has been a considerable expansion in the use of larger calibre and higher capacity handguns. These are based upon military and police models. These are not target guns in the true and original sense, but courses of fire have been evolved for them which make use of their greater power and other characteristics, as well as calling for agility and quick thinking on the part of the shooter. This had led to the growth of combat shooting. It has led some shooters to don the trappings of combat, such as holsters and camouflage clothing. It has caused others to feel uneasy about what appears to be the use of guns as symbols of personal power.
>
> (Cullen, 1996: 115, para. 9.44)

It had been precisely such characteristics, rather than an enthusiasm for the disciplined aesthetic of single-shot .22 target shooting, which had largely been responsible for the significant expansion of handgun shooting in recent years. All the associated paraphernalia of this more 'macho' gun culture were well in evidence – not just the weapons themselves, but the clothing and accessories (speed loaders, quick-release holsters, hi-capacity ammunition clips, human silhouette or moving targets) and above all, perhaps, the American gun magazines (and their British imitators) referred to earlier. Even in the immediate aftermath of the Dunblane killings and anticipating an inevitable backlash against the sport, commentators on shooting had warned that 'behind the claims that shooting is a healthy and responsible sport lurk the sinister figures who fantasise about aiming to kill'. In particular, 'those who cause most concern carry magnums and prefer the run-roll-fire of combat shooting'. After Hungerford a great deal of effort had gone into trying to rebuild the reputation of shooting as a healthy, safe and responsible sport, but this was now left in tatters. Despite proposals emerging to try to 'clean up' shooting once again by more psychological testing and having gun clubs police their own memberships more diligently, such suggestions were probably too little and certainly too late. In any event, it was argued, it would always be difficult 'to separate legitimate sportsmen from the gun nuts ... [for] a considerable grey area existed, encompassing legitimate target shooters and those lurking on the fringe. It is these figures on the edge of the shooting fraternity who [generate] most alarm ... men who have an unhealthy fascination with guns and violence' (Beaumont and Harrison, 1996). Inevitably such shooters preferred the powerful and iconic weaponry popularised by a host of movie warriors or given a certain cultural potency by their associations with the criminal underworld – the 'Dirty Harry' magnum or the new semi-automatic pistols.

So, by proposing to ban the very weapons which had made handgun shooting increasingly popular in recent years, a ban affecting some 80 per cent of the handguns currently licensed, what Michael Howard imagined as a 'compromise' gained the government very few friends in the British shooting lobby – or anywhere else. As David Mellor later argued in the Commons debate: 'The government compromise is not some carefully selected piece of ground, but a piece to which they have been dragged by the pressure of events. I find it difficult to know why they are so attached to a compromise that has no merit beyond the undoubted skill with which it has managed to alienate almost every party to the debate' (House of Commons Debates, *Hansard*, 18.11.1996 cols. 756–757).

In turn, shooting organisations warned the politicians that the shooters about whom they ought to have the greatest concerns were precisely those who had gone into the 'sport' to shoot powerful 'bad' handguns and who, accordingly, were the least likely to change down to the smaller, less powerful .22s. Nor, they argued, did the reprieve for .22s offer the lifeline to pistol shooting that Michael Howard had claimed. Twenty thousand handgunners (shooting their .22s) would be too few participants to sustain the 2,000 or so handgun shooting clubs currently in existence and many would now have to close. Furthermore, many clubs might have to close anyway because they lacked – or could not afford – the secure storage facilities demanded in the new legislation, or because they otherwise fell foul of the new rules. For instance, a representative of the South Downs Rifle and Pistol Club, based in Sussex, claimed in October 1996 that the club would now have to close. Apparently, it had nowhere to store pistols and its members didn't use .22 calibre weapons. Around the country shooting enthusiasts voiced their anger that the handgun ban was taking place 'just to make a political point' despite the fact, they claimed, that it would have only a negligible impact on public safety (White and Travis, 1996). On the one hand, they argued, virtually all armed crime was committed with illegal, stolen, unlicensed or never-licensed firearms (a series of issues to which we will shortly turn). On the other hand, it was argued that the .22 calibre pistol could be just as lethal as other, larger weapons.

Anti-gun campaigners were not satisfied with the reprieve for .22 weapons.

They pointed out that a .22 pistol gun could still kill children, and a police officer interviewed in the *Daily Mail* commented (rather melodramatically) 'a good shot with a .22 could keep a police firearms team pinned down all night' (Hughes, 1996). In the *Guardian*, Boycott drew attention to the fact that Robert Kennedy was assassinated and President Reagan was also shot by gunmen with .22 pistols. Although .22s were smaller and less powerful they could be easily hidden and were just as lethal at close range. Furthermore, even though Cullen specifically expressed concerns about the speed with which a semi-automatic could be fired and reloaded, some .22 revolvers could hold up to twelve rounds and semi-automatic pistols have thirteen round ammunition clips (Boycott, 1996).

Commentators from the gun lobby also poured scorn on the 'spurious logic' of exempting .22 pistols from the ban, arguing that .22s were responsible for a large share of the shooting homicides in the USA. Likewise, Colin Greenwood, specialist advisor to the Home Affairs Select Committee and editor of *Guns Review*, argued that .22s were 'just as dangerous as higher calibre weapons' (Cohen *et al.*, 1996). However, in what was fairly typical of the 'all or nothing' character of the gun lobby's campaigning, every compromise position suggested was rejected as shooters appeared not to recognise that the most likely alternative to a reprieve for the .22 handgun was not a reprieve for all handguns but rather the prohibition of all handguns, including the .22s. Having signed up to the Snowdrop Campaign's call for a complete prohibition on handguns, and supported by public opinion (an NOP poll for the *Sunday Times* on October 20th showed 26 per cent approving the measures announced by the Home Secretary, but 54 per cent supporting a ban on all handguns), this was precisely what Labour promised to do. After the 1997 General Election all handguns (with very few exceptions) were banned in England, Wales and Scotland. To the clear consternation of some commentators, the legislation did not extend to Northern Ireland although, in April 1998, the Northern Ireland Office launched a review of firearms control arrangements throughout Northern Ireland (Northern Ireland Office, 1998).

Despite much pressure, consternation and outright criticism from most of the national press, the government had refused to allow a free vote on its firearms control legislation. This had the effect of turning the issue, first into a party-political matter and subsequently into an election issue. Few had wanted this, least of all the Conservatives, though they were continually outmanoeuvred by Labour raising the stakes. Similarly, the gun control groups were only reluctantly, if opportunistically, partisan, they had a single objective and saw Labour as more likely to help them get it – as Ann Pearston commented – either 'before or after the election'. Likewise, first in an article in the *Guardian* and, second, in the Firearms Amendment Bill debate in the House of Commons, David Mellor eloquently attacked both the government's strategy and its conclusions. 'Public revulsion at the slaughter at Dunblane should have made gun control a tepid potato which no politician feared grasping. Instead the government has shown an almost perverse determination to turn it into a red hot one'. He went on to criticise the appointment of Lord Cullen's Inquiry. 'When will the government learn not to give politician's work to lawyers?', he asked. Judges and politicians worked in different ways, he argued. The former 'operate within a framework of law set by others, precedents and rules of evidence, so nit-picking is inevitable'. For this reason, a judge was the wrong choice for the job. On the contrary, politicians should lead in policy-making. According to Mellor, while Cullen had proposed many detailed recommendations, he had 'missed the big picture', leaving the government having to stitch together a hasty, inadequate and still-controversial compromise. By contrast, an all-party consensus and a free vote in Parliament would have been a far more effective response (not to mention an easier ride for the government) (Mellor, 1996). Later, in the Commons, he argued, by imposing a three-line whip, the government will be seen 'to have won the vote but lost the argument – a pyrrhic victory indeed' (House of Commons Debates, *Hansard*, 18.11.1996, col. 756).

In due course the government did achieve its parliamentary pyrrhic victory after an, at times, emotional debate in the Commons preceded by vociferous lobbies from both sides of the controversy. During the Commons debate, a series of technical amendments relating to particular types of firearms – carbon dioxide powered weapons, muzzle-loading and antique weapons, single-shot weapons – as well as concerning the compensation payable to those surrendering firearms, were all moved. But, finally, with the support of some Ulster Unionist MPs, the government's 'compromise' proposal banning all handguns with the exception of .22 pistols and revolvers was carried by 306 votes to 281. Within minutes of the vote, Labour promised that if it won the General Election it would introduce a complete handgun ban at the earliest opportunity.

In the vote itself, four Conservative MPs had voted with the Opposition and seventeen Labour MPs abstained, although no Labour or Liberal MPs supported the government. A threatened revolt by Tory right-wingers with shooting interests had collapsed, though a number of prominent Conservatives proffered their opinions, criticising the Bill as: 'illogical, ill thought-out and unfair', being rushed through the House with 'indecent haste' (Sir Jerry Wiggin). Similarly, Sir Nicholas Budgeon accused the government of 'banding together like some form of lynch mob, taking away the rights of a significant and honourable minority without proper considerations' (*Guardian*, 19.11.1996). The press and gun control campaigners were accused of demonising the shooting lobby while Tory MP Robert Carlisle attracted much criticism for accusing the gun control campaigners of becoming, 'far too emotional, far too hysterical on what is a very, very important national issue' (MacAskill and Smithers, 1996). Other Tory commentators predicted difficulties for the Bill in the House of Lords where there were, allegedly, many peers 'experienced with guns', many of whom regarded the new laws as nonsensical. However, even this factor was overlain by political considerations, for with Labour contemplating the reform of the House of Lords, few Labour MPs thought the hereditary peers likely to rush to the shooters' aid. According to a Labour Party source interviewed in the *Observer*: 'It would be a dream for us, an absolute dream. ... The hunting, shooting and fishing brigade taking on Dunblane

parents before an election when we are campaigning for reform of the Lords'
(Cohen *et al.*, 1996).

As predicted, the passage of the Bill did not satisfy the gun control
campaigners and it provoked nothing but resentment from the shooting lobby.
Richard Law of the Shooters' Rights Association (SRA) formed after the
Hungerford killings in 1987, compared the new legislation to the actions of an
undemocratic third world dictatorship. 'Picking on shooters and gun clubs is the
easy option', he complained. 'Blame us and everyone's happy, but it won't solve
the problem' (White and Travis, 1996). Later, the SRA went even further. First,
by proposing to stand as a 'shooter's rights' candidate in Stirling in the forthcoming General Election and, second, by issuing a bulletin echoing American
National Rifle Association arguments accusing politicians of trying to undermine democracy by disarming the British people. Foregoing any diplomatic
niceties, the SRA described the new legislation in the following, graphic and
American-sounding terms:

> The spectre of the most pernicious and evil legislation to stalk Europe since
> the reign of the third Reich is about to be forced upon the British Nation.
> … Some people think that this just affects pistol shooters who are dispens-
> able. Some shooters even think that because their particular interest has
> been avoided they have nothing to worry about. This proposed law will
> affect each and every citizen of this once proud country. It paves the way for
> the kind of government that can rule by decree by first disarming the people
> it is supposed to serve.
>
> (cited in Millar, 1996)

Unfortunately, and as Law was soon to discover, while such arguments might
have been persuasive in Texas or Arizona, they cut very little ice in either the
Home Counties or Scotland. Comparing British gun control policies with Nazi
rule prompted a wide spectrum of commentators to criticise the SRA. For
Snowdrop campaigners, the SRA's paranoid outburst underlined the association's isolation from more mainstream shooting organisations. As Ann Pearston
put it: 'The more the SRA come out with, the more irrational they are about the
reasons they hold guns for. They seem to worry about protecting themselves
from some unknown threat, but this only reinforces to the British public that
guns should go – and go now'. For George Robertson MP, Labour's shadow
Scottish secretary, the fact that the gun lobby had 'to stoop to such revolting
rubbish' showed they were losing the argument (Millar, 1996). In the event, the
SRA also withdrew their idea of standing a candidate.

The SRA's main complaint – after Hungerford as well as after Dunblane –
was that shooting organisations had been too defensive and had not taken the
case for shooting to a wider public. As a consequence they felt that shooting had
conceded too much of the principle of the argument. Another pro-shooting
organisation drew the same conclusion but, again, rather too late. Exposing
some of the splits and divisions within shooting's 'fraternity' (an issue reiterated

many times in the British shooting magazines), a newly formed 'grassroots' Sportsman's Association of Great Britain and Northern Ireland criticised other gun lobby groups for being too quiet and inactive since Cullen had reported. They announced a plan to encourage shooters to vote tactically at the coming election in an effort to unseat MPs favouring a gun ban and (unsuccessfully) tried to rally support for a one-million signature petition to outdo the earlier efforts of the Snowdrop Campaign. The chairman of the new association claimed: 'We maintained a dignified silence out of respect for the families of Dunblane, but that dignity has been abused by single issue campaigners and cynical politicians … we believed the government would listen to and accept the recommendations of Lord Cullen's Report' (Watkins, 1996). Later, the *Observer* also reported a leading member of the Sportsman's Association calling for a 'dirty tricks' campaign against the Snowdrop Campaign, 'as part of normal political campaigning to discredit opponents' (Arlidge, 1996). However, both this and the appeal to 'listen to Cullen' had a rather 'last ditch' feel about it for, as Cullen himself had remarked, throughout the Inquiry the shooting organisations had doggedly resisted every gun control proposal floated until the only alternative left was a ban. For their part, gun control campaigners appeared rather unperturbed by the new organisation. A spokeswoman for the Snowdrop Campaign replied that it was too late anyway because the MPs already knew the arguments and the strength of public opinion. 'These people will have to change public opinion, not just lobby MPs', she concluded.

The UK's political chronology of gun control was not finally concluded until 1997 when the newly elected Labour government passed the Firearms (Amendment) (Number 2) Act, delivering on its pledge to add .22 handguns to the list of prohibited weapons. However, the critical political debate came to a head during October and November 1996 and was effectively concluded during the November of that year. The resentment of the shooting lobby that emotion rather than logic had been driving the debate was plain to see. Despite gaining virtually everything they had wanted and certainly much more than they expected, from the Major government in November 1996, the gun control campaigners vowed to fight on to their final objective of a complete ban on handguns – thereby ensuring Labour kept to its word. As many commentators, both inside and outside the campaign, recognised, the collective activity of campaigning and their common purpose was a real source of strength. Above all, the achievement of their objective allowed people to draw some lasting meaning from an otherwise incomprehensible event (Craig *et al.*, 1996).

Yet even as the media celebrated the campaigners' success in what many depicted as a 'David and Goliath' struggle, and barely a month before the crucial House of Commons vote on November 18th, there were distinct signs that some media sources were reflecting on some of the broader questions raised, perhaps even attempting to apply the brakes. While by no means opposing the handgun ban proposed by the government, an *Independent on Sunday* editorial questioned the manner in which it had been achieved, and the apparent ease with which a co-ordinated media campaign could whip up intolerance. Gun club members, it said:

> are a minority with a curious pastime, like many other minorities in a country that prides itself on the diversity of its pastimes. It happens to be a pastime capable of abuse and so it is probably right that they should be asked to give it up or curtail their activities (it is certainly right that they should not be allowed to keep weapons at home). But is it right that their interests and views should be so contemptuously swept aside? ... Much of the reporting of the firearms issue has portrayed gun club members as little better than Hamilton's waiting to erupt.

A more considered approach, it argued, demanded a longer view.

> If we have an established response to great tragedies, with judges and public hearings and parliamentary debate, it is because we have learnt over time that this is a good response. We need ... by and large to be clear-headed in our final judgment. This is not to say that emotions have no part in politics; on the contrary, without them politics could not exist. But they cannot dominate; reason must play its part. ... The circumstances of this firearms debate [were] mercifully extraordinary, not least in that it has occurred so close to a general election. There may be no reason to think that a political issue could be dealt with in the same way in the future; no reason to fear that another minority might find themselves so brusquely swept aside; no reason to imagine that another stricken group, next time less dignified and responsible, could come to dominate the political stage as the Dunblane parents have done. But something unusual and powerful has happened and it is as well that we should recognise that it is a bad model for policy-making in a democracy.
>
> (*Independent on Sunday*, 20.10.1996)

The media had certainly given support and exposure to the Snowdrop Campaign and thereby contributed to its unique success. Perhaps it was this that led editors and media proprietors to feel they also had a role to play in drawing its activities to a close.

An editorial in the *Sun* on October 16th, commented on the Cabinet meeting at which the government had developed its response to Cullen's Report and articulated its own gun control proposals. Major's aim, it declared, is to 'root out irresponsible owners and gun club bosses by pricing shooting out of the market'. 'He wants to make [shooting] an elitist pastime so that only a handful of people would be able to run clubs [and in the process] turn pistol shooting from a casual pastime into a serious sport for only dedicated experts' (*Sun*, 16.10.1996). Implicitly, shooting was to become a privilege of wealth and class. The great unwashed, at times unsuitable or at times unstable, were to be priced out. As a strategy it certainly had its historical precedents but, as we've already seen, the gun control campaigners had not wanted to stop there, their ultimate ambition was a gun free society and the wiping out of the UK's emerging gun culture. Furthermore, both the police and the Labour members of the Home Affairs Committee had begun to express their concerns about the rather more 'liberal' regime under which shotguns were licensed. For many commentators, this was a step too far. Although the *Sunday Times* had supported the gun control ambitions of the Dunblane campaigners from the outset, even sponsoring one of their first campaign visits to London, it tried nonetheless to draw proceedings to a close. An intriguing editorial of October 20th sought to strike a complex balance between praising the achievements of the campaigners, preserving the rights of shooters, finding merit in the government's own proposals and urging the campaigners to now go home.

> The fact is that in all civilised societies people do use handguns for legitimate sporting purposes. ... By allowing handgun enthusiasts an outlet, the government is ensuring that its ban will be workable. ... Public opinion, however, wants to go further. This has become the view of the Dunblane parents. It is also the view, after some opportunistic ground-shifting, of the Labour party. The momentum clearly points towards a total ban. This newspaper's campaign did not go so far. We believe the argument for permitting sporting use of .22 handguns is a strong one. So is the risk that, if a [total] handgun ban was achieved, the anti-gun lobby would move on to shotguns, thus setting town against country.
>
> There is a difference between an appropriate response and a draconian one. This, however, is a matter of individual conscience, not party diktat. Mr Howard should set out his arguments forcefully to the House of Commons and hope to persuade MPs of the logic of his proposals. The issue should then go to a free vote. As for the Dunblane parents, they should accept the verdict of that vote. They have achieved a marvellous victory and, by their actions, will have made Britain safer. But they should also know when to let go.
>
> (*Sunday Times*, 20.10.1996)

However, it soon became clear to government business managers, at least, that the objective desired by the *Sunday Times* could not be achieved by the route it prescribed. A free vote might have seen many pro-gun Conservative MPs rejecting their own party's gun control package, perhaps even gifting victory to Labour's even more 'draconian' total handgun prohibition – with the wider ramifications suggested in the *Sunday Times*. In the event, the Cabinet settled upon a confrontation with the Opposition rather than with its own backbenchers. As it turned out, however, it had rather backed itself into a corner. With the Bill passed, and the general election drawing close, Labour running alongside public opinion and having firmly committed itself to a full handgun ban, the political relations of British gun control largely drew to a close.

As the *Sunday Times* predicted, there were a number of consequences: a 'countryside defence campaign' did later gather momentum but it was as much driven by concerns about fox-hunting and the problems of the rural economy and British farming in particular than with shooting rights as such. A bitter dispute concerning the adequacy of the compensation payable to gun owners, shooting club owners, gun dealers and others working within the firearms business rumbled on long after the handgun ban became law. In December 1996, sixty-three Conservative MPs defied a government three-line whip intended to cap the total compensation package at £150 million. One MP described the compensation payments as 'derisory ... nothing short of legalised robbery' (Travis, 1996g). Later, a group of shooting enthusiasts announced their intention to petition the European Court concerning the adequacy of the government's compensation package (Abrams, 1997). Handgun enthusiasts have been in no mood to compromise. Jan Stevenson, producer and editor of the British magazine *Handgunner* commented, 'we've been robbed of our birthright so we're going to use the compensation as revenge and stuff the government for every penny possible' (quoted in Elliot, 1996). Many gun magazines published in the UK at the end of 1996 or during the early months of 1997 reflected the same sentiments with page after page of angry advertisements describing firearm or shooting-related businesses 'murdered by H.M. government'. By the end of February 1999, the National Audit Office reported to Parliament that 165,353 handguns and 700 tonnes of ammunition, involving an estimated compensation cost of £95 million, had been safely surrendered. Some 25,000 less handguns were surrendered than anticipated by virtue of the exemptions permitted under the legislation (antiques and trophies, for instance) but scrutinies of twenty-six police force areas found (contrary to some predictions) only four cases in which handguns which ought to have been surrendered had been illegally retained (National Audit Office, 1999).

Other concerns emerged during 1997 and 1998 about a number of supposed 'loopholes' in the legislation. Scotland's *Sunday Mail* ran a brief campaign during 1997 to outlaw carbon-dioxide 'gas-powered' handguns which the new legislation had removed from the licensing system. An article claimed that 'gun nuts desperate to beat the post-Dunblane ban are turning to gas powered weapons', which were, allegedly, 'almost as powerful as .22 handguns' and capable of killing (Silvester, 1997). A parallel development had seen the marketing of such air or gas-powered pistols (.22 or .177 calibre) specifically designed to more closely resemble the more 'rugged' and 'macho' pistols popular with the new generation of handgunners.

Furthermore, exemptions granted to 'muzzle-loading' or 'black powder' firearms (considered, essentially, to be 'antique' or 'heritage' weapon types), were exploited by some gun dealers and shooting clubs in order to resurrect a new form of pistol shooting. An undercover investigation by a TV journalist for Channel 4 showed gun clubs evading the handgun prohibitions either by cutting down rifles (exempted from the legislation) so that they could be fired as handguns or by buying (in this case from France) a special type of revolver, the detachable cylinder of which was designed to be separately loaded with powder and shot (Channel 4, 1998). The fact that the cylinder was separately loaded in this way, rather than by using a more conventional sealed bullet cartridge, meant that legally the weapon qualified as a 'muzzle-loader' and was exempted from the legislation. Six shots could be rapidly fired from the weapon and, if the shooter carried several pre-loaded cylinders, clipping each into place as the previous one was emptied (as appeared to be the practice in one of the gun clubs to which the undercover cameraman gained access) a high rate of fire could be maintained. Despite Lord Cullen's concerns about the rate of fire achievable by the semi-automatic pistols used by Hamilton at Dunblane, it had not taken shooting enthusiasts long to find a way around the resulting prohibitions. But of course, once exposed in this way, the loophole might easily be closed (Taylor, 1998).

Less easily tackled but, arguably, less of a concern in the UK, were the plans of a number of British shooting enthusiasts, feeling betrayed by the UK, to take their sport and in some cases their businesses and shooting clubs abroad. According to the police, 1996 had seen an increase in the number of applications for passes to travel abroad with guns, while the Department of Trade had seen a rise in export licenses. In addition, a number of shooters interviewed in the *Guardian* were looking to relocate abroad or transfer their weapons to gun clubs in France or Belgium, 'where people will be able to use the rifles that were taken off them in 1988 and the pistols that were taken from them in 1997' (Elliot, 1996). Finally, as we have seen in an earlier chapter, even the UK's £9 million business in toy firearms experienced something of a dip in sales as a number of prominent stores, responding to the criticism that they were helping foster a childhood fascination with guns, removed toy firearms from their shelves. Judging from more recent, though somewhat casual observations, however, this effect might only have been rather short term.

6 Taking stock of the gun control arguments

The previous chapter sought to describe the process by which the UK came, eventually, to prohibit virtually all handguns. The process was, at every critical stage, irretrievably political. The government sought to maintain control by appointing the Cullen Inquiry, but as we have seen, the pressure was not so easily contained. The shooters, having pinned their hopes upon what they called a 'rational' resolution of the issue, were easily bypassed. Even their limited opportunities for self-presentation had often been badly mishandled, they appeared implacably opposed to any compromise gun control measures arising.

In the immediate aftermath of the killings, shooting enthusiasts had adopted a low profile, but subsequently the BSSC employed a London public relations agency to help them handle the media. At first, 'a determined effort was made to groom the image of gun users … and an internal document … warned against aggressive or hysterical remarks' which might confirm the public's existing suspicions of shooting and shooters. A 'smart, casual appearance, with collar and tie' was recommended for any TV appearances – and absolutely no combat gear (Castle, 1996).

In the event, it was all to no avail and the more their cause appeared to be lost, the more belligerent the shooters became, shifting from pragmatic arguments about improvements in firearms licensing, shooting for sport and the weeding out of the 'unsuitable', to loud American rhetoric about arms and the free man. For instance, echoing the libertarian arguments of the NRA, Jan Stevenson declared, 'there are tens of thousands of people whose pride of citizenship has been taken from them. Arms are the emblem of a free man. The essence of the relationship between the citizen and the state is that you are prepared to fight for it. Now that has been completely reversed: the citizens have been turned into serfs' (Elliot, 1996). Eventually, as we have seen, mere embarrassment turned into a public relations nightmare as gun lobby representatives turned upon the bereaved Dunblane parents and accused them of mounting a witch-hunt and then likened the British government to Nazi Germany.

In view of the overwhelming public and media pressure, however, any careful air-brushing of the image of shooting may not have made much difference. The shooting lobby were to some extent the architects of their own downfall. First they misread the power of the central argument against them. Second, having succeeded 'behind the scenes' after Hungerford they over-estimated their own influence and failed to recognise some important political realities. According to Castle, 'the clever game would have been to put up some reasonable and plausible people. Instead they let loose people who should never have been allowed anywhere near a microphone' (Castle, 1996). Reflecting upon the whole episode almost two years later, at a conference on Gun Control at Leicester University, Bill Harriman of the British Association for Shooting and Conservation, commented that the 1997 Firearms (Amendment) Act was 'a bad law, making no contribution to public safety or crime prevention, rushed through by a weak government desperate for re-election'. There was, as I have shown, rather more to it, but his conclusion that the outcome reflected the influence of certain pre-eminently political factors is hard to dispute. The whole episode was not so much evidence of a consistent policy process at work as an example of 'problem driven' crisis management and political opportunism (Kingdon, 1995; Godwin and Schroedel, 1998). The fact that Dunblane also led to the emergence of a focused British gun control movement and similarly politicised the British shooting lobby has now created a policy environment through which any further firearms legislation must emerge. This effectively forces government and government agencies to address any future gun control questions much more systematically.

As has been argued, notwithstanding the initial sense of horror and outrage, key political forces, including an effectively mobilised public opinion and continued media pressure, shaped the ensuing debate. Around this Labour and the Conservatives played their game of political brinkmanship. For a while, however, one important element of the argument was conducted within the confines of a fairly narrow series of debates about gun control. It is to these particular debates that we now turn. Even though the gun control arguments themselves were not the deciding factors in this episode, they connect us, once again, to our broader themes concerning firearms (legal and illegal) in society, citizenship and 'gun culture' and contrasting perspectives on the management of violence and social disorder. Furthermore, the characteristics of the British gun control debate provide us with a vantage point from which to consider contrasting gun control regimes around the world, predominantly, but not exclusively, those of the USA.

Plugging gaps or changing cultures

Following the shootings, there were immediate calls for tighter laws on gun ownership. That is, tighter laws on gun ownership, but not the prohibition of gun ownership. In the immediate aftermath of Dunblane and with memories of Hungerford, when shooting interests had been able to considerably water-down the emerging proposals, there was no real sense of just how far gun control could be taken. If not exactly 'unthinkable', the idea of a complete ban on all handguns was not thought feasible or practical by many key commentators. Later, however, a number were to shift their ground as the public and media pressure mounted.

Despite the enormity of the incident, an initial reaction in official circles was to see Dunblane within an essentially continuing pattern of policy development.

Licensing arrangements would inevitably have to be tightened up, gaps would have to be plugged, but that might be all. As a *Guardian* editorial, examining the government's options on March 15th, two days after the incident, put it:

> One of the greatest needs of community ravaged in this way is the assurance that steps will be taken to prevent the repeat of such a tragedy. ... There are serious gaps in our firearms control that need plugging. This is what Major should do. plug the gaps that remain even after Hungerford. ... British gun laws are amongst the tightest in the world but that doesn't mean they can't be improved.
>
> (*Guardian*, 'Editorial', 15.3.1996)

While the Hungerford incident in 1987 had led to the banning of automatic rifles and semi-automatic and pump-action shotguns, nothing had been done to strengthen controls over handguns. By contrast, Thomas Hamilton had only used handguns. Even so the immediate emphasis in the developing commentary was upon simply toughening our gun laws still further, outright abolition seemed not yet an option.

According to commentators writing in the first days after the incident, the loopholes that needed closing included a tighter scrutiny of all firearms licence applications. The fact that only 1 per cent of applications were refused was taken to imply an insufficiently discriminating procedure. The rigorous procedures for authorising police officers to carry firearms were compared with the rather more permissive approach taken with civilians. Likewise, it was claimed, the appeals procedure needed rethinking and gun clubs had to be more closely scrutinised. The 'right to own' policy, questioned almost a decade earlier by the Hungerford coroner, had to be reconsidered and the option of storing all guns at gun clubs or other secure premises, with no-one allowed to take them home, had to be examined. It seemed, to some commentators, that there were no circumstances in which personal ownership of firearms could not be effectively replaced by public or organisational ownership. Guns could be kept at gun clubs, or lodged with the police or another agency and booked out for use. Needless to say, such proposals were not welcomed by the police. They regarded the idea as impractical. More scorn was poured upon the idea by shooters themselves who also stressed 'practical' objections. Guns had to be taken home for cleaning and maintenance. Such activities, it was claimed, were an indispensable part of firearm ownership.

Ian Taylor, however, speaking at a gun control conference in Leicester in February 1999, prompted an angry reaction among firearms certificate holders when he hinted at another, perhaps more fundamental, reason for the shooters' reluctance to be separated from their powerful weapons. Many shooters, he noted, owned several weapons. Collecting them, handling them, cleaning them, even customising them, was part of a wider, essentially masculine trait. Both the gun magazine producers and the manufacturers and advertisers of a wide range of firearms accessories, associated paraphernalia and memorabilia also implicitly recognised this. Above all, as we have already seen, gun manufacturers also acknowledge this – guns are designed to be powerful, exciting to hold, attractive, pleasurable. These are, admittedly, aspects of the 'gun culture' that British shooters have usually sought to deny for fear that they implied that shooters shared an essentially unhealthy obsession.

According to Bill Harriman, of the British Association for Shooting and Conservation, speaking at the same Conference as Taylor, for instance: 'There is no gun culture in Britain any more than there is a golf or a fishing culture'. Even so, for some, the precise attraction of guns may lie in their association with the symbolism of powerful masculinity and such a point has often been made in relation to the psychology of the lonely and resentful 'spree-killer'. The point here, however, is not that most gun owners share an unhealthy orientation to their guns but just that it is important to acknowledge the important qualitative and experiential dimensions to the satisfactions that shooters derive from their weapons. Indeed, we have explored some of these issues already. Pleasure in firearms was not just derived from simply shooting them, rather ownership, exclusive possession, even aside from the more abstract arguments from political philosophy about arms and the free citizen, were vital factors in the attachment of men to guns. Despite Harriman's claim, shooting's real equivalent, in terms of ownership, exclusivity, individuality, patriarchy and the gun's unique position as both a commodity with a use value and as itself a determining factor in the social economy of inter-personal power relations, lies with such as car owner-ship. We have less difficulty with the idea of a 'car culture' although similar social relations are involved. As Connell has persuasively argued (Connell, 1995) defending ownership, exclusivity and individuality in relation to almost any valued commodity, be they homes, cars, even computers, but certainly firearms, is part of a wider attempt to sustain a form of hegemonic masculinity. Central to the success of Harriman's denial of the 'gun culture' is a denial of its real foun-dation, the emotional attachment, in this case, of men to guns. Instead, only eminently practical (albeit rather implausible) arguments – shooters' needing to clean and maintain their guns – are permitted to surface.

Such arguments go some way to explaining why shooters displayed such impa-tience with commentators who asked why, if target shooting were simply about composure, discipline and accuracy in marking a target, hadn't some less lethal means of doing so been invented. The answer, of course, was that if shooting were nothing more than a test of the precision with which a person might make a small hole in a cardboard target several metres away, then the greater part of its emotional appeal would be lost. So when the gun lobby in the UK began to echo the argument of the American NRA, that 'guns don't kill, people do', they were denying both the powerful emotional appeal of firearms and the susceptibility of contemporary masculinity to them. Regulating only the shooters themselves, on the premise that the dangerous and unstable could be weeded out in advance, was something of a blind alley that criminology had long abandoned, a poisoned chalice that the medical profession sensibly wanted nothing to do with. Furthermore, overlooking the guns themselves was entirely contrary to the emerging discourses of public safety and crime prevention which stressed the need to remove the proximate causes (in this case firearms) of potential harm (Zimring and Hawkins, 1997).

While one arm of the debate, embracing both shooters and gun controllers, focused upon 'loopholes' in the legislation and personality disorders, the other line of argument, subscribed to only by advocates of greater control addressed the supposed 'gun culture' developing in the UK. The Gun Control Network, a pressure group comprising academics, lawyers, journalists and parents and friends of those killed in Hungerford and Dunblane, and formed during 1996, took the notion of the 'gun culture' as its central campaign priority. The GCN campaign described itself as: 'established to pursue the goal of a gun free environment by fair and reasonable means'. It continued:

> The horrors of Hungerford and Dunblane are powerful evidence of the need for tighter gun controls and have, at the same time, created a climate of opinion in which such reforms can be achieved. Gun crime is growing in this country and is beginning to affect us all. People in inner cities live with it on a daily basis and the dangers of escalation are everywhere. The 'gun culture' surrounds us: through magazines, films and television our young are increasingly exposed to it. We believe it is time we took steps to reverse these trends, to outlaw the most dangerous kinds of guns, to reduce gun ownership and to eliminate gun culture.
>
> (GCN Leaflet, 1996)

As we have seen, the shooting lobby have repeatedly denied that any such culture exists. Harriman has argued that the falling numbers of firearm certificate holders scarcely points to a thriving 'gun culture', but rather one in decline. The argument has been taken up by others. Firearms lobby commentators have even gone further with a claim (made in 1994) that, 'it is Home Office policy to do everything possible to make the private ownership of firearms impossible. There is a positive agenda to eliminate the private ownership of firearms or, at the very least, reduce firearms ownership to those few people whom the establishment can trust' ('Cadmus', *Guns Review*, August 1994). The reasons for the falling numbers of certificate holders or, alternatively, the means by which the alleged policy of public disarmament was being achieved, were said to be a combination of: (1) the rising fees that applicants were charged for the issuing of their firearm licences – pricing people out of the sport, (2) the arbitrary, subjective and obstructively bureaucratic approach taken by different police forces when considering the issue of a licence; and (3) the growing suspicion with which the media tended to treat shooting and shooters. The tarnished image of shooting was, in turn, a factor cited by both police and government as justifying extra vigilance when reviewing firearm licence applications – in order to reassure the public.

Shooters and shooting publications complained bitterly about this alleged mistreatment and Colin Greenwood devoted a good deal of editorial space in *Guns Review* during 1994 and 1995 to angry attacks on the police, the Home Office, the government and the media regarding a range of issues such as: licence fees, the neglect of shooters' rights, the criminalisation of gun owners, arbitrary and incompetent policing, the hypocrisy of politicians, the failure of the Home Office to accept Firearms Consultative Committee proposals and media witch-hunts. In such articles, Greenwood scarcely missed an opportunity to return to a central argument he had been developing since 1972 (Greenwood, 1972: 225–227) that, 'there is a Home Office agenda intended to ensure that the number of lawfully used firearms is progressively reduced until they are virtually eliminated' (*Guns Review*, June 1994: 436). The following month, 'there is undoubtedly a policy within government to remove all privately owned firearms from the hands of the public' (*Guns Review*, July 1994: 518). And, two months later 'it is obvious that the police proposals are intended to facilitate their policy of eliminating private firearms ownership' (*Guns Review*, October 1994: 755).

Even a year before the Dunblane shootings, an article headed 'Public attitudes' drew a picture of the shooting fraternity as a beleaguered and misunderstood minority, 'a minority which is more oppressed than most of the minorities which make all the noise about oppression. Everyone who is not a shooter is against us. Certainly the media is against us individually and collectively' (*Guns Review*, February 1995). The subject matter of the article concerned a telephone poll undertaken by the *Manchester Evening News* about whether to ban all firearms from private possession. The paper had launched the poll in response to a sharp rise in armed crime in the Greater Manchester area, but only 33 per cent of callers agreed that firearms should be prohibited. By contrast 67 per cent were in favour of shooting sports continuing. The result of this local poll contrasts markedly with the abrupt change in public attitudes after Dunblane and certainly suggests the volatile and unformed nature of public attitudes on such questions. For the shooting fraternity, however, such incidents simply confirmed the pernicious influence of the media and paved the way for their argument that public opinion was ruthlessly manipulated by the media after Dunblane.

Yet whatever the particular reasons given, declining popularity, rising costs, unfavourable public attitudes or a policy-led attrition of private gun ownership, it was certainly clear that the past two decades had seen a marked reduction in the number of firearm licence holders. Between 1968, when the Firearms Act was passed, and 1992 the number of firearm certificates issued had fallen by almost a third. This decline accelerated after 1987, a reaction to the Hungerford shootings and the passage of the 1988 Firearms (Amendment) Act (see Figure 6.1).

The distribution, over time, of shotgun certificates shows a different pattern and, as can be seen from Figure 6.2, the impact of the Firearms (Amendment) Act, 1988 is very clear. We should recall that the number of certificates is not the same as the number of actual firearms. Shooters may, and often do, hold several weapons on a single certificate. Indeed, even while the number of firearm licences was still falling in the late 1980s and early 1990s, the actual number of firearms held on those licences was increasing.

Richard Munday, a writer and researcher on firearms, history and culture takes a rather longer view of the 'gun culture' debate. He has argued that, 'Britain is less a "gun culture" today than it was in the beginning of the century when there were rifle clubs in almost every town and large village. … Neither technological changes nor availability of weaponry can have made British

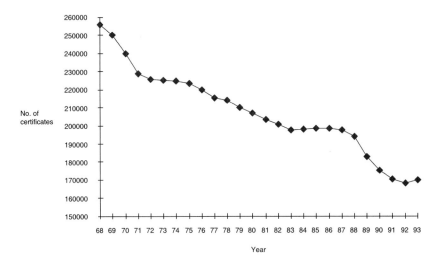

Figure 6.1 Firearm certificates issued in the UK: 1968–1993

Source: *Guns Review,* August 1994

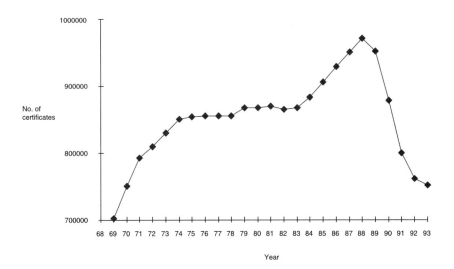

Figure 6.2 Shotgun certificates issued in the UK: 1968–1993

Source: *Guns Review,* December 1994

firearms owners more of a threat today than they were then'. He continued: 'One would be equally hard-pressed to argue that dangers have been enhanced: by greater social or political tensions' (Munday, 1996a). Munday has drawn upon his research on Switzerland's comparatively relaxed (by European standards) firearms control laws, a society where the notion of a legal 'gun culture' might reasonably apply, in order to refute any suggestion of a connection between legally held firearms and levels of firearm-related crime (Munday, 1996a). However, as commentators from within the shooting lobby also recognise, the definition of a gun culture cannot be reduced to a simple question of numbers any more than a monarchy might be in doubt for only having one king. On the contrary, as commentators on both sides of the debate have acknowledged, the real question concerns the extent to which firearms and anything relating to firearms become embedded within cultural relations, influencing attitudes, shaping ideas and suggesting forms of appropriate behaviour.

A significant body of opinion tends to see the UK as inundated with American 'gun culture' influences. Whether these derive directly from the firearms industry itself, or percolate through the publishing industry, the news media or the entertainment industries, matters less than the impact they have in certain sections of society. In the mid-1990s the police began to voice concerns about a weapons culture developing among young, criminally inclined, males in some inner-city areas. Likewise, firearm-related crime appeared to be rising, in particular armed robberies and there were a growing number of shootings related to drug dealing disputes. Finally, education researchers found that 31 per cent of a sample of some 13,000 teenage boys admitted routinely carrying 'offensive weapons', citing a range of reasons including self-protection and confidence boosting (Carvel, 1996).

There is no doubt that the 'gun culture' about which most concern was expressed, both before and after Dunblane, was a criminal – or potentially criminal – gun culture. Even so, aspects of sports target shooting, in particular pistol shooting and especially the more 'practical' shooting disciplines with semi-automatic and higher calibre, military or police specification, weapons were inevitably linked to this more troubling gun culture in the public mind. Though many shooting commentators have sought to deny this connection, emphasising the distinct and responsible character of target pistol shooting, other pistol shooters have from time to time expressed reservations about the growing popularity of some American style combat shooting disciplines. Gun clubs were aware of the problem too when they began to disallow the human silhouette or 'terrorist-style moving targets' and prohibited military style combat gear or holsters at shooting ranges – in order to discourage the 'Rambo' look and avoid, though not always successfully, alarming the public. Unfortunately, many of their efforts in this direction were often undercut by a combination of firearm industry advertising and consumer preferences about the kinds of guns they wanted to shoot. Big 'bad' guns and 'powerful' semi-automatics were enthusiastically promoted in the firearms press and figured significantly in the rising popularity of pistol shooting in the decade before 1996. For instance, Peter Hetherington, writing in the *Guardian* in August 1996, interviewed a pistol shooter whose firearms licence was granted on March 13th that year, the same day as the Dunblane killings. The man's certificate allowed him three guns. One was a .44 magnum, 'the Dirty Harry gun', he explained, which he had long admired.

Similarly, Michael Bracewell, himself a shooter, tried to describe the lure of the big gun in the following terms,

> when it comes to pistols and revolvers, there is such a strong image attached to their use that few people can disassociate the image of Clint Eastwood or John Wayne from the reality of owning and using a gun. Men, for whatever reason, have a strong emotional tug at the sight of a firing gun ... the desire to shoot a serious gun is probably connected to the control of power.
>
> (Bracewell, 1996)

Bracewell sought to dispel some of the negative mythology surrounding guns and the public suspicion concerning 'gun culture':

> There is a popular idea that handguns, by their definition, attract either neo-Nazi military types or deluded survivalists who are preparing for the next Apocalypse – or the next general election. In the UK much of this is an utter falsehood imported from the uglier members of America's gun-obsessed society. ... The belief that sports shooting is politically incorrect is based on an ignorance of its reality. ... The other prejudice against sports shooting is based on society's justified fear of guns being used illegally and becoming more prevalent in muggings and gang warfare. Both of these charges can be repudiated by the sheer diversity of people who own and use guns, and by the necessary restrictions and joining conditions of gun clubs.

But then he concluded: 'It is the unique mythology of guns which gives them their dark reputation, but what this boils down to, in the real world, is the instinctive surge of excitement that guns commend' (Bracewell, 1996). Even as he tried to rationalise his enjoyment of shooting and sanitise its image in the public mind, he was inevitably drawn back to the same powerful cultural factors – power, danger, risk and excitement – responsible for the particular appeal of shooting large calibre handguns, which rather concerned the public. Either way, handgun shooting could not be easily disconnected from its image.

Unfortunately, for shooting's case, other firearms writers and commentators offered relatively little further help in unpacking the notion of a dangerous 'gun culture' developing in the UK. Richard Law and Peter Brookesmith, for instance, in a book published in London shortly after the Dunblane killings, went to some length to outline their view of the continuing basic function of the 'fighting handgun'. Whether employed by the military, the police or by civilians, they argue, the weapon has a primary self-defence role (Law and Brookesmith, 1996: 9, 159). Weapons intended for the military and police may be designed to reflect the different requirements of their intended users. Likewise, weapons designed for civilian use in societies like the USA, where a majority of states have now passed 'concealed-carry' firearms laws, may prioritise other features such as low price, low weight, portability, concealability and convenience of use. These are not characteristics having any real relevance to precision target pistol shooting – nor indeed, are many of the characteristics considered important in military and police weapons (firepower, ease of reloading, large magazine capacity).

Having said this, the mainstream shooting organisations' particular problem with the notion of a 'gun culture', lay in the way the cultural argument connected legal firearms ownership (and the honourable tradition of sports shooting) with the criminal sub-culture of illegal firearms use and the entertainment culture's exploitative glorification of gunpower and paramilitary 'warrior-dom' (Gibson, 1994). Here we will concentrate directly upon the question of the existence of a criminal sub-culture of illegal firearms use. Thus in the wake of Dunblane, commentators rehearsed the grim statistics of British firearms offences. In 1994, the last year for which statistics had been available, there had been some 13,000 firearm offences. In particular, between 1984 and 1994 there had been a 142 per cent increase in the number of cases in which handguns had been employed in crime (from 1,232 to 2,981) (Cullen, 1996: 115). The same year, Metropolitan Police Commissioner Paul Condon had informed the Home Affairs Select Committee of his concerns about an emerging 'gun culture' developing among teenage gangs and a steady increase in the number of offenders willing to turn to guns for power and violence.

Nicholas Timmins, writing in the *Independent* asked whether, given Commissioner Condon's comments about the 'new gun culture on the streets of Britain's inner cities' and Home Office uncertainty as to scale of the illegal gun stock in the UK, British society was becoming hostage to an 'alien gun culture' (Timmins, 1996). Representatives of shooting organisations replied that there was no relation between the number of legally held firearms in a society and crimes committed with illegal weapons. Guns themselves were not the problem, they argued, the police should concentrate their efforts on the criminals who used guns illegally rather than harassing law-abiding shooters (a recurring theme even before Dunblane). The Secretary of the BSSC argued that, 'blaming guns for the shootings [in Dunblane] was like blaming Henry Ford for every fatal road accident. You cannot legislate for one individual act of this nature. The Home Office has been unable to identify any substantial link between lawfully held guns and crime, except in one or two exceptional incidents' (Boseley and White, 1996). Furthermore, shooting correspondents had long found much to fault in the police management of the firearm licensing system and, since 1993, had been confirmed in this view by the publication of a Report of Her Majesty's Inspectors of Constabulary which had found many weaknesses and discrepancies in the police administration of the system (HMIC, 1993). After Dunblane, the shooters argued, it was clear that not only were the police over-bureaucratic, unhelpful and inefficient in operating a licensing system but they were also incapable of weeding out unsuitable characters. In effect, they argued, responsible shooters were being penalised as a result of a two-fold failure in policing: the failure to control the criminal use of firearms and the failure to appropriately restrict and periodically review the provision of firearm licences.

According to the *Times* (15.3.1996), the central focus of Cullen's Inquiry was to be upon how Hamilton actually got his guns. The Inquiry's brief was actually drawn somewhat more broadly than this, and the eventual report included a discussion of the availability of firearms in the UK, yet it was charged with an essentially investigative task – the more explicit policy question being left for the Home Affairs Committee, discussed earlier. At the outset, journalists and informed commentators expressed considerable incredulity that a man such as Hamilton could ever have been granted a firearm licence in the first place. Before the Inquiry opened, newspapers unearthed even more detail pertaining to Hamilton – inviting young boys back to his home to see his guns, being reported to the police for twice threatening a neighbour with a gun, his dismissal from the Scout Association, child abuse allegations made against him to four separate Scottish police forces. All this made the granting of a firearm licence (and its renewal in 1995) difficult to comprehend.

Applicants for firearm licences had to be of 'sound mind' and not of 'intemperate habits', nor likely to pose danger to public safety. They had to have a good reason for wanting firearms and the only acceptable reason was to participate in target shooting as a member of a recognised and regulated shooting club. Further controls should have operated at the club membership level, each new member was supposed to undergo a minimum three months 'probationary' period and appropriate safety training. Handgun shooting clubs, of which there were some 2,300 in the UK as a whole, had to be genuine clubs with written constitutions. Clubs were inspected every six years, their principal officers had to be 'responsible people', and all members had to be of 'good character'. Clubs had to have secure storage facilities for weapons and ammunition. The important role played in the licensing process by the shooting clubs themselves provided an open invitation to investigative journalists interested in seeing just how rigorously the rules were applied. Paul Gallagher, writing in the *Daily Express*, told of a Kent Gun Club he had approached to join. Safety training was apparently minimal and no attempt was made to verify his identity or obtain references. On his first visit, as a new member, he was given a .357 magnum 'to try' and told that within six months he could have one of his own to keep at home. The targets used by the club were the humanoid type and Gallagher described the club as essentially very solitary and non-social – the noise of the gunfire restricted any conversation. Equally, giving a new member a .357 magnum to shoot on his first visit was condemned by weapons experts (Gallagher, 1996).

Nevertheless, having satisfied the requirements of their chosen shooting club, all licence applicants, had to be subjected to a background check and all applications had to be counter-signed by a 'person' of standing well known to the applicant. In fact, very few licence applications were refused or revoked. Out of 2,005 applications in Scotland in 1994 only fourteen were refused (and twenty-three renewal applications revoked), in England, 120 certificates were refused out of 11,700 applications. Even if a certificate was refused or revoked the applicant could appeal to the Crown Court. Police commentators noted that such appeals were invariably successful, so police officers responsible for authorising certificates appeared to set their own agenda, taking a view that applicants with no criminal convictions and against whom there was no clear evidence of 'unsuitability' were very difficult to turn down. This state of affairs appeared to satisfy no-one. Police appeared to resent what they felt were weak enforcement powers while those shooters, against whom these powers were occasionally exercised, criticised the perceived arbitrariness of the police actions. Figures released during May 1996 indicated that only 1 per cent of firearm licence applications were refused. Jack Straw, Labour's shadow Home Secretary, argued that the figures confirmed the need for tighter controls and that police should be given a stronger power of veto over licence applications (Travis, 1996d). The very idea was anathema to shooting organisations. Later, however, Lord Cullen's Inquiry dealt at some length with a series of weaknesses emerging in the licensing and information handling systems employed by Central Scotland Police.

Gun control UK

The first day of Cullen's Inquiry, and the first substantive chapter of his report confined itself to a detailed review of the events of March 13th. Thomas Hamilton had arrived at the school carrying four loaded handguns and 743 rounds of ammunition. In the space of a few minutes he had fired 106 rounds (all bar one from a 9 mm Browning semi-automatic pistol) killing sixteen pupils and their teacher and wounding a further ten pupils and three members of staff. Then he killed himself. In the following days of media coverage the stark details of the terrible event provoked again the simple questions – Why these weapons? Why so many? Why so much firepower? How could such weapons be kept at home? On the second day of the Inquiry, as the 'gun control' debate began in earnest, Scottish Police Chiefs dismayed Snowdrop campaigners and relatives and friends of those killed and injured with evidence arguing that a blanket ban on all handguns was 'unfeasible' (Hardie and Deerin, 1996). Although the Inquiry's role was essentially to investigate the incident itself, Cullen accepted that wider questions concerning the availability of firearms were germane to his Inquiry and effectively invited advocates of firearms control and representatives of the shooting lobby to debate the issue before him (Cullen, 1996: 9). In the event, as we have seen, neither this debate nor its conclusion, nor even Lord Cullen's Report itself, proved decisive in shaping the response of the government. However, insofar as the evidence considered by Cullen and the rather unfortunate Home Affairs Committee engaged in this debate it represented a unique investigation into the firearm and society question within the UK. Consideration of the arguments made in this debate and of the wider discourses and ideologies from which these are drawn allow us important insights into some of the essential value bases of our society. They encourage us to reflect upon our developing conceptions of safety and society, the maintenance of social order, and questions of freedom, rights and citizenship.

Having already considered some of the broader debates concerning the emerging 'gun culture' as well as some of the more specific questions about alleged 'loopholes' in the firearms licensing (and inspection) system, I do not propose to give these issues any more attention here. Furthermore, accepting what appears to be the weight of medical and criminological evidence on predicting the psychological suitability of firearm licence applicants, except to note that various commentators did keep returning to the issue, there seems little further mileage in this question. We now need to consider a number of rather more social-scientific gun control arguments. Even here, however, the debate remains highly charged: what campaigners call 'gun control', many shooters are inclined to call 'civilian disarmament'. Even discussing the issue of firearms control from the perspective of criminology prompted the response that this is not appropriate because the possession of properly licensed firearms is not a crime and licensed shooters are not criminals. However, accepting these caveats about the contrasting definitions of the issue and the creative extension of criminology's own brief, we can proceed.

As we have seen already, one of the interesting issues in the gun control debate developing following the Dunblane massacre was the relative absence of any clear or consistent criminological contributions and the comparative ease with which even those that did emerge were sidelined. What follows, therefore, is less a detailed statistical analysis of rates of firearm ownership and patterns of firearm-related offending than an examination of the contrasting discourses within which the debate itself was largely confined. As Taylor has argued, many participants in the gun control debate frequently appear to lack an appreciation of the nature of 'evidence' and 'explanation' in the contemporary social sciences. Such commentators appear wedded to a rigidly positivistic perspective typical of nineteenth-century scientific thinking. Accordingly they reject any evidence that they believe falls short of demonstrating a strict causal relationship between given factors: for instance, firearm availability in a given society and rates of armed crime (Zimring and Hawkins, 1987; Taylor, 1996, 1998). In this sense, statistical criminology, encounters a very nineteenth-century problem in its analysis of the gun control debate – a problem of the 'missing link' in a supposed causal chain connecting legal firearms with criminal practices. Given that aggregate social scientific data – of even the most reliable kinds – will seldom provide such definitive proofs, an association between guns and crime will be difficult to demonstrate – perhaps especially to sceptics.

Fortunately, contemporary social science embraces a more creative and interpretative approach to social scientific data analysis than its nineteenth-century predecessor. Facts seldom 'speak for themselves' and the interpretation of aggregate social science data is a necessary and appropriate part of public policy analysis, problem solving and law making. A number of important and now largely taken for granted statistical associations underpinning our social and public policies still rely upon such technically unproven 'causal' relationships.

Not to have taken these relationships seriously in public policy circles might have implied that society lacked any basis for establishing policies in respect of smoking and health, the consumption of alcohol and the driving of motor vehicles or, concerning the relationships between social deprivation and educational disadvantage. In similar fashion, it is the contention of gun control campaigners that levels of firearm availability in a given society are linked to levels of gun-related offending in that society. In this vein, Martin Killias, a Swiss criminologist who, in 1989 and 1993, undertook the first cross-national studies of firearm availability and gun-related crime, concluded his 1993 study by voicing his frustration that the most important policy lessons about firearms and crime were going unheeded. 'In terms of the policy agenda', he argued, 'the crucial question is how much time we allow ourselves to wait for more convincing research before we take any steps to curb the ever increasing trend in gun ownership. … Waiting for more convincing evidence risks jeopardising the potential benefits from more rigorous approaches to gun control' (Killias, 1993: 302). We will return to consider Killias's work shortly, for it was the focus of a sharp interchange between the Home Office researchers and firearms lobby representatives during the Cullen Inquiry.

As we have suggested earlier, different ways of interpreting the data are at issue here. One need not prove that legally held weapons 'cause' crime (in any event a peculiar claim) though firearms might, in a variety of ways, facilitate or precipitate offending behaviour by those so inclined. Likewise (another misconception) it is not implied that legitimate owners of firearms are individually or collectively responsible for rates of firearm offending in society (excepting, of course, those who actually commit such offences). In this respect, the kind of conclusion one might seek to draw in relevant policy research would be of a similar order to that arrived at by Zimring and Hawkins in their study of lethal violence in the USA: 'The circumstantial indications that implicate gun use as a contributing cause to American lethal violence are overwhelming' (Zimring and Hawkins, 1997: 199). Having drawn such a conclusion, policy researchers would attempt to establish appropriate and politically feasible risk-reduction strategies. Hence, at issue in the criminological analysis and gun control policy debate after Dunblane, to which we now turn, was a question of the extent to which any similar relationship between firearm availability and firearm-related offending could be established in the UK.

Unfortunately, a policy debate of this order drawing upon the results of research and analysis and informed by reliable evidence was largely absent from the British debate. As commentators have argued, until Dunblane, the UK had virtually no publicly funded research into the criminal use of firearms. In the USA, by contrast, there was an enormous wealth of such evidence contributing to what policy analysts in the USA have termed a 'policy stream' – a body of clear, if not exactly uncontentious, policy and practice, informed by the results of genuine and verifiable research and analysis (Godwin and Schroedel, 1998). Given the increasingly partisan character of the USA's firearms debate over the past decade and a half, however (Spitzer, 1995), it might be more appropriate to refer to two 'policy streams' existing there: the one developing a public safety case for gun control, the other articulating a civil libertarian, individual rights-based case for guns for self-defence. Either way, the situation is markedly different to that of the UK where no such 'policy stream' existed at all. In fact, British firearms correspondents have argued that the UK has had a *de facto* policy of 'civilian disarmament by attrition' for some years. However, civilian disarmament, such as it may be in the UK, appears to be driven less by explicit research and public safety policy than by wider, more obviously ideological factors. These limitations of British gun control policy became particularly apparent in the gun control debate inaugurated by Cullen. For with the exception of the Home Office Research and Statistics Directorate's submission to Cullen – and the critical attention this attracted from firearms lobby commentators – a recognisably criminological perspective was largely absent from the debate.

One has to say *largely* absent. Cullen twice invited the parties to the debate to submit additional material, analysis and arguments relating to the reliability and interpretation of the evidence in the Home Office submission. In due course a kind of – albeit rather narrowly statistical – 'criminological debate' took place between Pat Mayhew of the Home Office Research and Statistics Directorate, researchers from the Scottish Office and a number of representatives of the 'shooting lobby', principally Richard Munday, Jan Stevenson and Colin Greenwood. Their contributions to this debate (some of which were also submitted to the Home Affairs Committee, discussed earlier) are brought together in Munday and Stevenson (1996).

This was a rather uneven debate. The 'official' criminologists of the Home Office and Scottish Office specifically eschewed any comment on the variety of gun control proposals emerging and largely confined themselves to comments regarding the reliability of the evidence from existing comparative research on firearm availability and criminal violence. By contrast, their opponents both criticised the adequacy of the existing research data and what could be derived from it. They also questioned the merits of a range of gun control policies being proposed. This left something of a vacuum in the debate although pressure for stricter firearm controls (or, in the case of the Snowdrop Campaign, a ban on all firearms) was coming from some, but by no means all, police representatives. In fact, the balance of police opinion lay rather in the other direction: ACPO (Scotland), ACPO (England and Wales) and the Superintendents' Association had all, in various ways, initially rejected a complete handgun ban as 'impractical'. The Police Federation was the only police voice proposing a complete handgun ban. In such a context the absence of an independent criminological input to the debate was rather striking.

There are a number of reasons for this vacuum in our recent firearms debate. Analysis of the criminal use of firearms and firearm violence is undoubtedly an under-developed specialism in this country. In part, of course, this is a reflection of the tight controls on firearms operating here since 1920. As a consequence, the use of firearms in crime has been relatively exceptional in the UK and, excluding Greenwood's own work (Greenwood, 1972), there have been very few studies of what had hitherto been regarded as a new and rather un-British crime problem. However, a crucial contextual question raised by many commentators in the wake of the Dunblane massacre (and also, by some, before it – Silverman, 1994; Squires, 1995, 1996a) concerned the extent to which the use of firearms in crime was increasing in the UK.

Yet if British criminology was ill-equipped to get into a debate about firearms and violence it is also fair to suggest that, once the broader public debate began to unfold, conventional criminological approaches were unlikely to have had much impact. As the Home Office sources, referring to American gun control debates, appeared to acknowledge, 'research has had relatively little influence on the political debate about gun control [in the USA] ... one reason for this is that academic debate itself has often been ideologically cast, with some of the litera-ture partisan' (Home Office, 1996: 73; see also, Spitzer, 1995). On this, at least, firearms lobby commentators appeared to agree. Munday and Stevenson also pointed out that many of the submissions to Cullen's inquiry were not evidence at all but rather proposals for changes to the existing firearms control laws on the assumption that these would prove beneficial. Reviewing the American gun control debates, Kleck has also noted that many people support (or oppose) gun control policies on essentially ideological and 'non-utilitarian' grounds. That is, they regard gun control or widespread availability of personal firearms as a 'good thing' irrespective of the impact of such policies on rates of criminal violence (Kleck, 1991: 370–371). Here, though, the issue is not so much the reli-ability of the American data, but rather its questionable relevance to the UK (Squires, 1997a).

According to Munday and Stevenson, the British debate was overtaken by a powerful ideological agenda. They argued, 'over the past months, gun control has been the subject of much sensational sound-bite journalism in the UK; but the simplistic and often ill-informed drama that boosts audience ratings and swells circulation does not necessarily furnish the deeper understanding required to serve the public interest' (Munday and Stevenson, 1996: 7 and 9). Having said this, however, one cannot completely overlook Munday and Stevenson's own agenda. As Stevenson commented in his submission to Cullen: 'it has to be said, realistically, that a constitutional case [for firearms ownership] no longer pertains in this country. ... We believe strongly in the constitutional case, but we do not intend to argue it' (Munday and Stevenson, 1996: 88–89). However, echoing Kopel's earlier arguments about self-defence and civil liberties (Kopel, 1992b) he then went on to refer to a growing body of American evidence about the apparent benefits of widespread firearm ownership in discouraging crime (Stevenson, 1996: 106–113). This 'net benefit' or 'utilitarian' argument was considered very much a side issue by Mayhew (1996: 210) and summarily dismissed by Cullen. 'In this country the possession of firearms for self-defence has not been regarded for many years as a "good reason" for their possession and there never has been a policy of facilitating, let alone encouraging, the acquisition of firearms to discourage crime or limit its effects'. And, he concluded, accordingly. 'I do not see anything in the "net benefit" argument that is relevant to this country' (Cullen, 1996: 112, para. 9.29). Cullen's response was unambiguous. The UK's dominant view on the question, that guns were part of the problem, not part of the solution, remained intact.

Notwithstanding Stevenson's nod towards another agenda, for the most part the 'firearms lobby' commentators confined themselves to an analysis, largely within the parameters of quantitative criminology, regarding the relationships between contrasting gun control regimes, firearm availability and rates of firearm-related crime and violence. Cullen discussed Thomas Hamilton's acquisition of firearms, the control of firearms and ammunition and the licensing arrangements for 'Section 1' firearms in chapters 6 to 8 of his Report. He then turned to the availability of 'Section 1 firearms' by posing the central question concerning the relationships between the 'legal availability of firearms and the incidence of crimes and suicide'. While Cullen evidently drew upon the Home Office evidence (Home Office, 1996), it is clear that he was in no doubt about the limitations of existing international research on this issue. A central plank in the Home Office evidence comprised the research findings of the 1993 study by Martin Killias. Yet although Cullen accepted that the Killias study had to be treated with 'considerable caution', he was 'not persuaded that it should be wholly rejected as unreliable'. For, according to Cullen, 'it shows that there is a relationship between firearm ownership and firearm homicide when considered overall' (Cullen, 1996: 110, para. 9.21).

Quantitative criminology and international comparisons

The Killias 1993 study followed up an earlier work on fourteen countries for the 1989 International Crime Survey. The earlier survey compared rates of gun ownership and patterns of violent crime (Killias, 1989). Overall, the study concluded that higher gun ownership levels were related to higher levels of homicide and suicide in the societies studied although, once the USA was excluded from the data, no relationship was detected between rates of predatory crime (hold-ups, street robberies) and handgun ownership. Killias did not quite claim that high rates of gun ownership *caused* higher rates of homicide or suicide (even though this has been largely how his findings have been interpreted, see for example, Kleck, 1991: 191). Instead, Killias put it as follows.

> It does make sense that gun availability affects the proportion of suicides committed with guns, but one can hardly see how a high rate of suicides committed with guns should motivate people to buy guns. We tend to assume, therefore, that gun ownership precedes interpersonal violence committed with guns, although we admit that the present data do not allow us to rule out the possibility that high rates of violent crime produce high gun ownership rates.
>
> (Killias, 1989: 173–174)

Academic critics attacked Killias's conclusion and, indeed, his final point may be less compelling in the USA where rising fear of crime has been an important factor prompting the purchase of self-defence handguns. By contrast, Killias's point may be much more relevant in societies with a smaller proportionate pool of available handguns in private ownership, or where 'self-defence' is not considered a valid reason for the ownership of a firearm.

Critics also challenged the methods adopted by Killias in his survey and the strength of the relationships he unearthed between guns and homicide. So when his follow-up 1993 study appeared as a central feature of the Home Office evidence to Cullen, this time based upon a wider sample of eighteen countries, dissent was inevitable. A central dilemma in the Killias research concerned the problems inherent in using a random telephone survey methodology to produce a measure of the real availability of firearms in any given society. Even so, between the two survey periods, the rates of firearm ownership ascertained by this method remained fairly constant in the different countries. This would go some way to suggest the reliability of the figures produced.

However, in the UK and a number of other European countries (Nay, 1994), it is widely recognised that the overwhelming majority of firearm-related offences are committed with illegal (never licensed) or stolen firearms. Consequently, serious questions have to be asked about the reliability of data on the distribution of firearms – especially the illegal ones – obtainable from a telephone poll. Germany is a case in point. Before 1972 when comprehensive firearms registration was introduced in West Germany (following concerns about rising violence and terrorism) there were estimated to be up to 20 million licensable firearms in the country. In due course, just over 3 million were registered. Police activity accounted for a small percentage more, although almost 80 per cent of the pre-1972 firearms just 'disappeared' (Munday, 1996b). A poll producing evidence on the guns legally held by German citizens is likely to completely overlook most of the unregistered (and therefore illegal) weapons. This makes any data on legal weapons only a very imprecise measure of actual gun availability – and especially so of the availability of guns to those most likely to use them in criminal and harmful ways.

Similar considerations apply to data on gun availability in the UK, as Mayhew commented in her supplementary submission to Cullen. 'It would be naive to think that the majority (perhaps the vast majority) of offences did not involve illegal firearms [even though] some of the most notorious murders have involved lawfully held ones' (Mayhew, 1996: 202). Firearms lobby commentators obviously agreed (Greenwood, 1996). Leaving aside, for the moment, many of the broader cultural and ideological factors which influence both the demand for firearms and the relative levels of violence in a society, quantitative criminology exposes a crucial question which, on the available data, we are unable to answer satisfactorily. This question concerns the connection – if any – between legally held firearms and the size, scale and distribution of illegal guns. An answer to this question might provide us with the definitive 'missing link' in a causal chain connecting legal and illegal weapons. Unfortunately, such evidence is intrinsically hard to come by and, as a variety of gun control advocates referred to earlier have noted (Killias, 1993), a potentially fruitless search for more definitive 'evidence' may merely serve to delay the introduction of policy responses. None of this, however, is to suggest that there is no direct evidence of legal firearms either filtering into the illegal pool or being used in the commission of offences – at Hungerford and Dunblane, for instance. A range of issues arise here. These concern: (1) the scale of this 'leakage' of legal firearms into criminal hands, (2) whether the leakage is largely exceptional or more commonplace, (3) the scale of the criminal harms resulting from either the misuse of legal (or illegal) weapons and, (4) whether the 'leakage' or misuse can be effectively controlled or prevented. We will turn to these questions shortly. Before that it is important to review just what the 1993 Killias survey discovered.

In the absence of definitive and irrefutable evidence of a firm 'causal' connection between gun availability and gun crime, however, we are drawn back to rather more circumstantial evidence of the aggregate associations produced by researchers such as Killias. Even here, however, the evidence available is, as Cullen acknowledged, somewhat limited. Moreover, it requires careful interpretation. Killias concluded his 1993 survey in the following terms. 'The present study … confirms the results of previous work. … Substantial correlations were found between gun ownership and gun-related violence as well as total suicide and homicide rates. … More guns usually means more victims of suicide and homicide' (Killias, 1993: 301). Figure 6.3 presents the results of Killias's survey into the rate of ownership of firearms alongside the firearm homicide rates in those same countries. The data derived from the study has been presented in a variety of ways in different places. The original study compared eighteen societies although in Figures 6.3 and 6.4 the range of comparison has been restricted to fifteen countries in Europe and North America. The graph's left hand axis combines a percentage scale (the percentage of households with guns) and a numerical scale (the gun homicide rate per million of the population).

There are undoubtedly difficulties with the data and its interpretation. Unfortunately, a number of these were exacerbated in the debate surrounding the Cullen Inquiry by virtue of certain errors in the original Home Office submission which drew upon the Killias study.

The striking variation between high gun-ownership, high gun-homicide in the USA and the figures from England and Wales, Scotland and the Netherlands overwhelm the somewhat more complex picture which emerges if the USA is omitted (see Figure 6.4). However, there are further problems common to all the graphs. First, the data on homicides and suicides do not always relate to the same period for each country. For most countries, the data are drawn from 1983 to 1986, although for Italy the dates are 1986 to 1989 and Sweden 1987 to 1990. In itself this may not pose a major problem, homicide rates do not fluctuate so very dramatically – though they do change. The latter point is borne out by data from a later international study of firearm availability and firearm homicide undertaken by the Canadian Department of Justice in 1995. This study

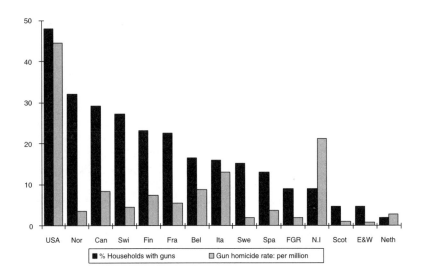

Figure 6.3   Rates of firearm ownership (percentage of households with guns) and gun homicide (rate per million) in Europe and the USA
Source: Derived from Killias (1993)

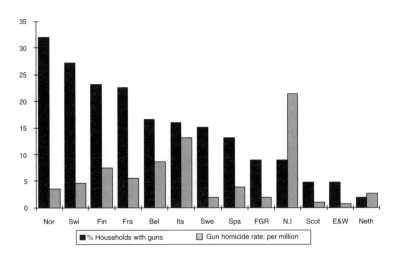

Figure 6.4   Rates of firearm ownership (percentage of households with guns) and gun homicide (rate per million) in Europe
Source: Derived from Killias (1993)

compared more recent data on seven countries (this time including Japan) using a wider and not altogether consistent definition of 'homicide', resulting in figures rather at variance to those produced by Killias (Canadian Department of Justice, 1995). For instance, the Canadian study produced a gun homicide rate for the USA which was 43 per cent higher, an Australian rate 45 per cent lower and a British rate 75 per cent higher than the figures established by Killias. Obviously, one is bound to be cautious when comparisons are being drawn between data sets which appear to vary so substantially.

A second problem concerns the figures of gun availability themselves. Killias measured 'households owning guns' whereas the Canadian study examined the actual number of firearms, registered. There is a real question about the most appropriate measure to take. In the USA, where some 48 per cent of households report owning firearms, the average number of actual guns owned is five (Kleck, 1991), so different measures of 'gun availability' can throw up quite different figures. When the USA and Northern Ireland were considered within the range of countries a stronger correlation was found between 'gun availability' and gun homicide; however when these countries were excluded (Figure 6.4) a rather weaker relationship appeared.

As Figure 6.4 shows, without the USA the relationship between firearms and gun homicide appears rather less clear-cut. Rather paradoxically, there appears to be an inverse relationship between the percentage of households with guns in a society and the problem of gun homicide for the six European societies with the highest rates of firearms ownership. Overlooking, for the moment, the special circumstances of Northern Ireland, the cases of Italy and Belgium (mid-range rates of firearms ownership, high rates of gun homicide) and Norway and Switzerland (highest rates of ownership but more typically 'European' rates of gun homicide) rather complicate the picture. In fact, as Munday and Stevenson have pointed out (1996) the figures for firearm availability in Switzerland (where militia service responsibilities imply that a large proportion of adult males keep weapons at home) are themselves rather problematic. Nevertheless, the firearm homicide rate in Switzerland is still around six times that of England and Wales. Finally, even on Killias's figures, heavily armed Norway shares a similar gun homicide rate with the Netherlands, the least armed of all. Apparently, gun availability alone does not seem to dictate the patterns of firearm homicide found across this range of countries. Even so, it still remains to be seen whether restricting the availability of firearms might represent a sensible policy choice.

Accepting the limited and rather problematic data available in the Killias survey, it is clear that the relationship between firearm availability (however measured) and homicide is neither simple nor straightforward and a range of socio-economic and cultural factors need adding to the equation. Commentators on either side of the gun control debate have suggested the existence of a cluster of factors – tradition, social disorganisation, crime patterns, racial conflict – which might increase relative 'population lethality' (Kleck, 1991) and as Killias shows, societies with high gun homicide rates tend to have higher overall homicide rates. Accordingly, he concludes, 'guns may increase homicide rates beyond a country's "natural" propensity to killings' (Killias, 1993: 297). Furthermore the role of some more broadly 'cultural' factors, is suggested in Figure 6.5.

Figure 6.5 combines information from both the Killias (1993) survey and the Canadian Department of Justice study of 1995. The graph presents data on rates of firearm availability, and on homicides and suicides using guns.

In one sense the particular selection of countries in Figure 6.5 might be used to illustrate, albeit rather crudely, the general 'gun availability' thesis, although that is not its purpose here. Rather, it demonstrates the importance of cultural variations in rates of firearm availability and in homicide and suicide rates in different types of 'new', individualist and 'frontier' societies as compared with older, more traditional and collectivist societies. While the gun ownership rate in the 'new' or 'frontier' societies is still dwarfed by the American figure, for all four societies it is still upwards of 20 per cent. By contrast (though with notable exceptions) rates of firearm ownership in Europe tend to fall below 20 per cent of households and, even by comparison with other European societies, British rates of firearm ownership are low. Japanese rates of firearms ownership are lower still, for a combination of cultural, traditional and legal reasons. Japanese firearms controls are reportedly strict, with a virtual prohibition on the private possession of handguns (Tonso, 1982; Kopel, 1992a), but enforcement of gun control policy is said to be complex and inefficient (Cho, 1994). The low number of firearms in private hands in Japan also translates into a low gun-related death rate (homicides and suicides). However, the case of Japan illustrates both the importance of cultural variation and a more general weakness in the available data. While, relatively speaking, Japan has one of the highest overall suicide rates

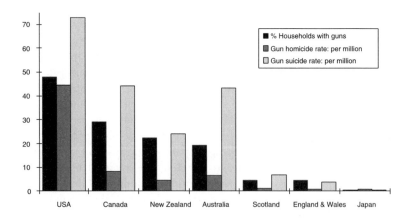

Figure 6.5   Rates of firearm ownership (percentage of households with guns) and gun homicide and suicide (rate per million) in selected countries

Source: Derived from Killias (1993) and Canadian Department of Justice (1995)

among the countries studied, it has by far the lowest gun suicide rate. As Figure 6.6 reveals there is a much stronger correlation between firearms ownership and gun suicide. More guns do seem to mean more gun suicides.

Yet the case of Japan also points to a broader problem. The surveys undertaken have only produced data on the availability of 'legal firearms' and total firearm homicides so, at face value, it can appear that the smallest pool of legal weapons in the world is also the most lethal (estimate of available guns divided by number of gun homicides). The conclusion is obviously nonsensical. The legal gun stock of Japan is not in any way more lethal than that of the USA (in fact, quite the contrary). Rather, Japan (and the UK for that matter) have problems with *illegal* weapons (Greenwood, 1996; Munday, 1996b). Illegal weapons are responsible for virtually all of the firearm homicides these societies experience. Japanese criminal justice statistics indicate that of sixty-nine handgun homicides in 1991, sixty-five were committed by 'gangsters' (professional criminals or terrorists) (Cho, 1994). Similar proportions are thought to prevail in the UK although, hitherto, no systematic record has been kept of the legal status of firearms used in crime (Mayhew, 1996). Nonetheless, figures collated by the Scottish Office for the years 1990 to 1994 showed that only 8.1 per cent of a total of 943 firearm-related incidents (in which the offender was identified) involved a firearm licence holder.

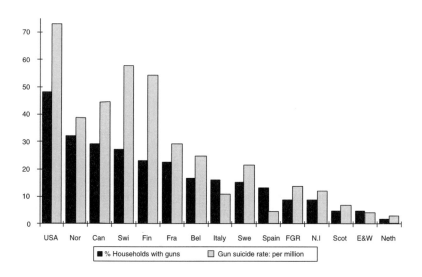

Figure 6.6   Rates of firearm ownership (percentage of households with guns) and gun suicide (rate per million) in Europe and the USA
Source: Derived from Killias (1993)

Accordingly, Greenwood concluded his submission to both the Home Affairs Committee and to the Cullen Inquiry in the following terms:

> the Home Office advice [drawing upon Killias] that there is a direct correlation between the numbers of firearms in the hands of members of the public and the rate [of] homicide or other violent crime with firearms is, at best, controversial and unhelpful. There is nothing in the statistics, or in any of the material which the Home Office has selected, which suggests that further reductions of legally held weapons will be in any way beneficial. They do not suggest how illegally held firearms might be reduced or even quantify their role.
>
> (Greenwood, 1996)

His argument went a little further than the evidence allowed. Restricting handguns might have prevented the seventy-six (8.1 per cent of 943) firearm incidents involving licensed weapons in Scotland during 1990–1994 and might have made it impossible for Thomas Hamilton to gain access to the weapons he used to such terrible effect in Dunblane. Even so, the more general point might be upheld. Whatever the *overall* relationship between measures of the availability of legal firearms and armed crime across a range of societies, the findings seem to have only limited application to the UK – unless, of course, clear connections could be established between legal firearms and the pool of illegal guns.

As Figure 6.6 demonstrates there does seem to be a stronger correlation between firearm availability and gun suicide considered overall. With the USA and Northern Ireland included, a strong correlation is produced between households with guns and gun suicide. Despite this, even in the USA where the gun suicide rate is highest and more people commit suicide with guns than commit murder with them, the public health issue surrounding gun availability attracts much less attention than the issue of armed crime.

The problem of handguns

The heat generated by these issues during the Cullen Inquiry might appear rather disproportionate to the fairly tentative conclusions to be drawn from the limited cross-national research available. Yet, while the conclusions may have appeared fairly tentative, the policy direction they suggested was clear both to Killias and his detractors. This might account, in part, for the vehemence with which the latter sought to discredit both Killias's work and the Home Office's seeming reliance upon it.

The international research had not distinguished between types of firearms (handguns, rifles) but the Home Office evidence to Cullen drew attention to what it called the 'particularly dangerous nature' of handguns. The point reflected a good deal of research (much of it American) on the portability, concealability, ease of use and rate of fire possible with many modern handguns. Equally of concern was their apparently growing popularity, on both sides of the

Atlantic, as the criminal firearm of choice. The point was also covered in the verbal evidence given to the Home Affairs Committee by the minister of state, David Maclean MP. Rather perversely, the Committee chairman, Sir Ivan Lawrence MP, appeared to consider the government's failure to legislate against handguns after Hungerford in 1988 to be a reason for doing likewise in 1996. As the Committee chairman put it to the minister:

> In your memorandum you regard handguns as 'of a particularly dangerous nature' … [but] pistols were not considered to be so dangerous as to be listed in the Firearms (Amendment) Act of 1988 which followed the Hungerford shooting. Why not? … Presumably exactly the same reasons [for banning handguns] were advanced in 1988 and they must have been rejected by the government … what were the reasons for the rejection in 1988 of pistols to be prohibited and if those reasons were good then, why are they not good now?'
> (House of Commons, Home Affairs Committee, 1996: 25, paras 177–178)

There are, perhaps inevitably, problems concerning the available data, but regarding the growing threat apparently posed by the criminal use of handguns, we might be on firmer ground. Greenwood devotes a few paragraphs to the question, attempting to refute the claim that handguns represent a specifically increased level of risk. Although he acknowledges that handguns were reported to have been used in many more offences than any other firearms, handguns were fired less often and resulted in less killings than, for instance, offences involving shotguns. Interestingly, the frequency of handgun robberies and homicides appears to increase sharply after 1988.

Figure 6.7, detailing figures for England and Wales only, treats 1980 as a base year and represents each subsequent year as a percentage of the 1980 figure. In order to appreciate the actual numbers of offences involved, there were 308 armed robberies with shotguns in 1980 and 1,030 in 1993, the peak year. Likewise there were 529 handgun armed robberies in 1980 but 3,605 in 1993. The comparable figures for homicides are, respectively, twelve shotgun homicides in 1980, thirty-nine in 1993; eight handgun killings in 1980, thirty-five in 1993. For each category of armed offending the trend is invariably upwards although handgun robberies indicate the most dramatically rising profile. By the end of the fifteen-year period all homicides with a firearm occur three times more often than in 1980, robberies with shotguns seem twice as common as they were in 1980 but declining as a proportion of all robberies. Handgun robberies, however, appear almost five times more prevalent in 1994 compared to 1980. How many of these 'handgun robberies' involve real firearms is difficult to assess, although work by Morrison and O'Donnell (1994) discussed later, and Rix *et al.* (1998) suggests that as many as 40 or 50 per cent of these supposed weapons may only be imitations or replicas incapable of firing.

Homicide figures, with each type of weapon, show the more variable pattern while offences involving shotguns indicate more stable trends over the period,

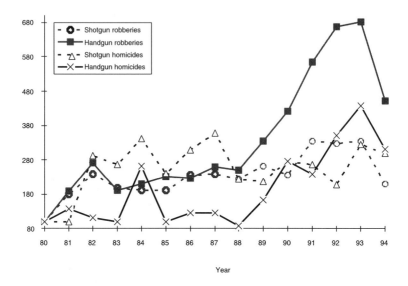

Figure 6.7   Index of robberies and homicides using handguns and shotguns: 1980–1994

apparently little affected by the Firearms (Amendment) Act 1988 which prohibited certain types of shotguns. Indeed the sharpest increases in handgun offending (homicides and robberies) occurred after 1988 and all offence trends appeared to peak in 1993, falling sharply the following year. According to Matthews, except for the use of handguns, which rose again by 4 per cent, the decline in firearm use in robbery continued during 1995. Reports of handguns accounted for 63 per cent of the weapons used in armed robberies that year (Matthews, 1996).

Unfortunately, as we have seen already, the criminal statistics describing firearm involvement in crime are scarcely an exact science. If only we knew how many of the 3,000 or so criminal uses of handguns involved real, loaded and working handguns, the true 'lethality rate' of handguns may be considerably higher (and much closer to shotguns). Greenwood's view, however, is that restricting handguns might result in 'weapon displacement' as offenders opt for more available or more dangerous firearms (shotguns and rifles) with which to commit offences. He then examines the differing impacts of handgun bullets or shotgun loads on their unfortunate victims. Despite the fact that the analysis is detailed and undoubtedly reliable, it surely fails to convince in the manner its author intended. By the time that discussion turns to a weapon's impact upon the human body, all firearms seem dangerous enough to warrant stricter control (Greenwood, 1996, paras 113–116).

Beyond these detailed questions regarding the interpretation of the criminal statistics, however, deeper concerns were triggered by the apparent growth in firearm-related crime in the UK. Crimes involving handguns appeared to be growing fastest of all (by 142 per cent in the decade to 1994 – Cullen, 1996: 115, para. 9.45) and especially in armed robberies (Morrison and O'Donnell, 1994). More to the point, however, none of the firearms used in serious, organised or drug-related crime (handguns being by far the most popular) recovered by the police during 1992–1994 had been legally held (Cullen, 1996: 116, para. 9.46).

At the time of the Cullen Inquiry, few commentators appeared to believe that any alterations in the regulation of legal firearms would have much impact upon the distribution of illegal firearms. There was thought to be no real link between legal and illegal weapons. Yet this claim was advanced in the context of widespread claims on the part of 'firearms lobby' analysts that the pool of illegal firearms far exceeded that of legal firearms. While everyone agreed that the number of illegal (unregistered) firearms was impossible to determine precisely, estimates varied, putting the illegal weapons pool at between one million and eight million guns (Greenwood, 1996; Stevenson, 1996; Yardley, 1996). However such figures were arrived at, they were seldom little more than informed 'guesstimates'. One important factor concerned whether the weapons were in active criminal circulation or, rather, formed part of some more 'benign' pool of weapons acquired long ago and now largely neglected or forgotten.

Proposing, even on the basis of rather circumstantial evidence, that the pool of illegal weapons was very large was a very convenient tactic for the firearms lobbyists. A large pool of already illegal weapons made any control efforts directed at the legal pool appear rather marginal and of limited potential benefit. Tighter regulation of legal weapons was presented as a classic case of closing the stable door after the horses had bolted. Furthermore, leakage of a few weapons into the illegal pools (for instance through theft) could seem a rather minor question by comparison with the large already-existing pool of illegal weapons. As the shooting lobby would have it, police efforts ought to be directed towards more effective control of illegal weapons rather than continually 'harassing' law-abiding shooters.

However, if, as some more recent evidence and analysis seems to suggest (Hallowes, 1999), the illegal pool is much smaller than indicated by the estimates recycled for the benefit of Lord Cullen, then different factors apply. Any leakage, either from the pool of legally held firearms or criminally diverted from legal channels under the cover of legal firearms dealing (Paul Condon's claim in 1994) would inevitably assume a greater relative significance. An important link, as it were, between legal firearms (and activities associated with the distribution of legal weapons) and illegal firearms would have been established. The fact that few weapons used in crime were traceable back to legal sources proved only that few could be traced back to their source.

In one of the few studies of this question, only a small number of firearms used in the course of a crime were ever recovered and only a small proportion of these could be traced back to a legal source (3.6 per cent of all the firearms recovered). Yet rather than indicating the absence of a link between criminal use and (once) legal weapons, the study might simply confirm the difficulty of tracing the provenance of a weapon. The efforts of the criminally inclined to remove serial numbers and conceal the sources of weapons to which they had access were often successful. In the study referred to, the researcher, an inspector in the Metropolitan Police, acknowledged the difficulty of establishing whether firearms had been stolen or otherwise illegally obtained. Such an acknowledgement rather undermines the confidence one might have in the results obtained (Maybanks, 1992). The suggestion that less than 4 per cent of firearms used in crime were ever part of the licensing system implies only a very marginal link between legal and illegal firearms and strengthens the moral force of the shooting lobby's argument. However, accepting that we know very little about the vast majority of firearms used in crime – because most are never recovered – implies there is little reassurance to be derived from this. The relatively low proportions of criminally employed firearms traceable back to legal sources identified in work by either Maybanks or the Scottish Office researchers (Scottish Office, 1996) indicates, above all, how little we know about the subject. What is more, firearms actually recovered by the police may not be typical of criminally employed firearms in general.

Conversely, the fact that Morrison and O'Donnell (1994) found that 6 per cent of the armed robbers they interviewed claimed to know that the gun they had used had come from a residential burglary, tells us little about the origins of the firearms used by the other 94 per cent of offenders. And, as the authors noted, many of their interviewees implied that they tended not to enquire too closely about the sources of the weapons they used. Similarly, Corkery's Home Office study (1994) found that at least 9 per cent of the stolen firearms recovered by the police had been used in crime (mostly robberies). Unfortunately, it was impossible to draw any conclusions about the uses to which the vast majority of stolen firearms were put because so few of them were ever recovered.

As Figure 6.8 reveals there are significantly more thefts of shotguns reported to the police. This would be expected, there are roughly seven licensed shotguns for every licensed handgun. On average, some 600 shotguns are stolen each year. There was a significant fall in the numbers stolen in the four years after 1986 which may be attributable to the Hungerford incident and the introduction of the 1988 Firearms (Amendment) Act which prohibited some types of shotguns and led to tighter controls on others. After 1990, shotgun thefts appear to rise once again. Similarly, the years after 1987 indicate a rising profile of handgun thefts. In fact, during the early 1990s, handgun thefts were rising faster than any other types of weapons theft. Over the entire twenty-year period, 1976 to 1996, in excess of 13,604 shotguns, 4,215 handguns and 2,705 rifles were stolen. That is, at least 20,524 firearms were stolen over the course of twenty years, just over a thousand a year. Stolen weapons represent a continuing criminological problem for, as American research bears out, firearms are generally very durable, do not 'wear out' quickly and have a long active life (Kleck, 1991). The actual numbers of weapons stolen are undoubtedly higher than represented in the graph for, until 1995, the statistics recorded simply the numbers of offences in which firearms were reported stolen. After 1995 the numbers of actual firearms

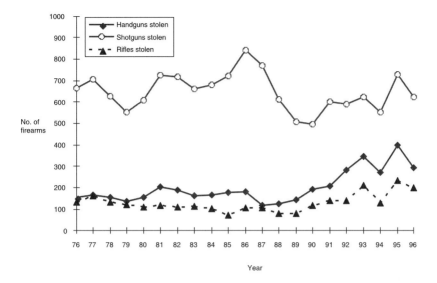

Figure 6.8   Firearms stolen or misappropriated: 1976–1996
Source: Home Office, Criminal Statistics

stolen were recorded. Police also separately record thefts of air weapons, starting guns, replicas and imitations but, for the sake of clarity, these are omitted from the graph.

Implicit in the graph is a further issue. Despite the fact that there are considerably more shotguns in the country a significantly higher proportion of handguns are stolen. After 1990 handguns were approximately twice as likely to be stolen as shotguns. Furthermore, because, prior to 1995, the figures only reveal the numbers of incidents in which a firearm was stolen (rather than the actual number of firearms stolen) the number of handguns stolen are almost certainly under-represented. Firearm licence holders often held more than one weapon on their certificate. During 1994–1995, for instance, there were over 45,000 firearm certificates in force allowing the holder to possess more than one handgun and a total of some 200,490 handguns were held on an overall total of 57,510 firearm certificates in England, Wales and Scotland, that is approximately four handguns per certificate (Home Office Memorandum of Evidence, Home Affairs Committee, 1996, Volume II: 59). Consequently when considering the attraction of handguns to offenders, in addition to concerns about their portability, concealability, ease of use and rate of fire, one also has to consider their 'stealability'. A rising profile of handgun thefts in the early 1990s does suggest a clear and direct link, albeit a small one, between legal and illegal firearms. Even so, over the past twenty years the theft of firearms and shotguns from their legal owners has contributed upwards of twenty thousand firearms to the illegal weapons pool. All of these weapons pass through criminal hands – they are stolen, 'received' and illegally passed on – relatively few are intercepted by the police, fewer still are traced and we have few reliable ways of estimating how many come to be used in the course of criminal activity.

We return to these issues shortly. Above all, they indicate some of the weaknesses in the UK's firearm registration system and underscore the argument made by the Gun Control Network that a national firearms register should be introduced. The argument has since been adopted by many police commentators. A national register would have facilitated intelligence gathering and would have permitted some analysis to be made of firearms surrendered, either following the 1996 amnesty or following handgun prohibition in 1998. Research on the sources of firearms surrendered might have allowed a clearer picture to be drawn of the real scale of the UK's illegal weapons pool. Likewise it might have allowed some statistical 'clearing up' of recent years' firearm thefts and might have allowed either the police or the customs services to identify weak points in the systems of production, distribution, sale and exchange where firearms were more likely to slip into the illegal pool.

In retrospect, the Dunblane killings and the ensuing gun control debate starkly exposed the inadequacies of the UK's supposedly strict licensing system. There were problems in the way the policy was implemented, shooters had felt themselves subject to arbitrary police decision-making for many years. More importantly there appeared to be serious weaknesses at the intelligence gathering, analysis and strategic policy development levels. Deep suspicions of the 'civilian disarmament' agenda allegedly being pursued by the Home Office and the police and their experiences of the way the licensing system was managed seemed to dissuade many within the shooting fraternity to co-operate in strategic firearms control or public safety policy development. Instead, commentators from within the firearms lobby sought chiefly to defend their own corner.

For instance, Firearms Consultative Committee, introduced at the eleventh hour into the Firearms (Amendment) Bill in 1988, after successful lobbying by a number of Conservative MPs with shooting connections, has primarily been seen as a forum for the representation of shooting interests. Kopel revealingly described the Committee in the following terms, 'gun owners see the committee as a partial shield against the Home Office or police misapplication of the law' (Kopel, 1992b: 45). In due course, this was precisely the somewhat partisan role that the FCC went on to play – much to the apparent displeasure of police commentators (*Police Review*, 10.8.1990). Similarly, Greenwood, in his 1996 submission to the Home Affairs Select Committee, went rather beyond the role of an impartial advisor and sought, instead, to defend a principle. He cited the 1688 'Bill of Rights' which, he argued, underpinned the right of citizens to have firearms (Greenwood, 1996, para. 13). Later he added: 'shooting is said to be the second largest participatory sport in the country' (para. 149), 'no other democratic country in the world [has] sought to impose a ban [on handguns] ... all human activity involves some risk' (para. 150), and 'no other country in Europe bans the recreational use of handguns' (para. 155). Even Cullen, in his final Report was moved to criticise what he called the 'entrenched attitude' of British shooting's representatives. By their continued rejection of any control measure falling short of a ban, he argued, at every turn, they had raised the stakes (Cullen, 1996, para. 9.110). The British gun control debate has been much more 'American' and confrontational than we cared to admit. This has clearly inhibited effective policy development and, beyond reacting to tragedies or periodic concerns about rising levels of violence, governments have not generally been too interested in the issue.

The acceptability of risk

No-one giving evidence to Cullen claimed that a licensing or controlled access system could ever be made absolutely watertight. Thus the real criminological or public safety policy issues for Cullen concerned, first, what he called the 'acceptability of risk' of the relatively small percentage of offences, mainly domestic or acquaintance homicides. Yet among such incidents are also numbered Dunblane and Hungerford, and a series of smaller-scale 'amok killings', typically perpetrated by mentally unbalanced individuals, using legally held firearms. A second issue concerned the extent of the slippage of firearms from the legal to the illegal pools, the result of thefts, the activities of illegal dealers, the reactivation of 'deactivated' firearms or weapons smuggling. Also related, although not directly addressed by Cullen, were questions relating to replica, imitation and deactivated weapons which, on the face of it, appeared responsible for a significant proportion of the increase in recorded firearm-related offences, especially robbery.

The former issue, the 'acceptability of risk', contrary to David Mellor's eloquent and powerful intervention in the House of Commons gun control debate on November 18th, Cullen had already conceded fell among those 'questions which are peculiarly within the province of the Government and Parliament to decide' (Cullen, 1996: 130, para. 9.111). The latter issue seemed less clear cut but both Cullen and the Home Affairs Committee (Home Office, 1996: xiii, para. 33) commented upon the absence of reliable statistical information and the lack of routine research into the sources of firearms used in crime in Great Britain. In response to this observation, Cullen was provided with further data by the Home Office and Scottish Office and undertook his own assessment of the available evidence on legally held firearms stolen and subsequently employed in the commission of crimes.

Cullen concluded his discussion of this evidence in the following terms: 'While illegal firearms are used in the great majority of firearm-related crimes, and especially robberies, the existence of legally held firearms leads to their use in crime in a significant, though relatively small, number of cases' (Cullen, 1996: 108, para. 9.12). Supplementary evidence supplied to Cullen by the Home Office covering the years 1992–1994 showed firearm homicides totalling 196 (9 per cent), with handguns responsible for some 40 per cent of these and legally owned handguns for only 14 per cent of these (once again, mainly domestic incidents). Of fifteen handguns used in domestic murders, six were legally held by the perpetrator (Home Office, 1996; Cullen, 1996, paras 9.10 and 9.46).

The fact that firearms appeared most vulnerable to theft and also most vulnerable to misuse by their legal owners when kept in residential premises formed the central thread to Cullen's control proposals. As we have seen, Cullen drew, in particular, upon the Home Office evidence which itself featured the 1993 Killias study. Supplementary work by Pat Mayhew then developed an earlier comparative study (Clarke and Mayhew, 1988) which had attempted to compare British and American firearm homicide rates (Mayhew, 1996). In the original Home Office evidence, comparative homicide statistics revealed that between 1985 and 1990 the annual average handgun homicide rate in England and Wales was 0.26 killings per million population. In the USA, by contrast, the rate was 38.97 killings per million. In other words, the USA's handgun homicide rate was some 150 times higher than that of England and Wales – the figure made for a good headline in the press. Expressing the ratio this way infuriated the firearms correspondents. Without some qualification, they argued, it was a fairly meaningless figure, for the USA had at least 100 times the handgun ownership rate of the UK and it would be unusual not to expect a significantly higher gun homicide rate in the USA. The 'all firearms' homicide rate in the USA was fifty-one times that of England and Wales, and the non-gun homicide rate only three times higher. The overall homicide rate (11.3 in England and Wales, 85.48 in the USA) was similarly almost eight times higher in the USA (Home Office, 1996). Overall, Mayhew's work reinforced a perception of the role of widely available firearms in increasing rates of firearm-related violence and crime. This is an important point to emphasise given that critics have often pointed to general notions of 'population lethality', a 'culture of violence' and 'weapon-choice displacement' to explain away high rates of firearm violence.

Data comparing the rates of various crimes in the USA and England and Wales (between 1990 and 1994) do suggest that the USA may be, in some respects, a more violent culture. 'Non-gun robbery' and 'non-gun homicide' rates in the USA exceed those of England and Wales by 1.7 to 1 and 2.4 to 1 respectively. On the other hand, a slightly higher rate of 'non-gun assaults' is reported for England and Wales and the rate of acquisitive property crime (burglary and theft of motor vehicles) is higher in the UK. Yet while the 'non-gun' offence ratios do differ, they remain recognisably similar as the crime rates of modern, liberal capitalist societies. By contrast, the gun-related offences ratios are massively disproportionate and it is scarcely plausible to attribute such huge differences to cultural factors while overlooking the means by which such offences are committed – firearms, especially handguns.

Weapons of choice and doubtful motives?

The question of weapon choice displacement is difficult to address though it has a long academic pedigree. Zimring and Hawkins in *The Citizen's Guide to Gun*

Control, first published in 1987, reviewed versions of the weapon displacement argument reaching back to 1958. In their book, however, they quote a more recent version of the argument: 'it definitely does not follow that in the complete absence of handguns, crimes now committed with handguns would not be committed. The more plausible expectation is that they would be committed with other weaponry' (Wright *et al.*, 1983; Zimring and Hawkins, 1987). That said, however, it would be an extremely violent culture indeed that would expect to see the 13,000 Americans killed in handgun homicides to be killed by other weapons in the absence of an offender's weapon of first choice. For instance, as Zimring and Hawkins put it 'firearms are not only the most deadly instrument of attack but also the most versatile. Firearms make some attacks possible that simply would not occur without firearms' (Zimring and Hawkins, 1987: 15).

A more plausible explanation of high rates of handgun crime, rejecting the weapon displacement argument, might be found in the circumstances of the crimes themselves. Thus, most homicides are committed in moments of rage and frustration and are not usually the result of a single-minded intention to kill. They are, as Zimring put it in 1968, 'ambiguously motivated' (Zimring, 1968). Planned, cold-blooded murders tend to be the exception. While some researchers, notably Kleck (1991), have criticised these arguments claiming that, in certain circumstances, crimes committed with firearms can be safer for victims. For instance, gun robbery victims are less likely to resist and as a result they are less likely to be killed or injured by persons whose primary motivation is robbery. (Of course, when guns are used as part of an attack rather than simply to intimidate, they are far more likely to result in the death of the victim.) Once again, however, Kleck insists that one must take account, not simply of 'weapon lethality' but also of 'attacker lethality' and he disputes Zimring's argument regarding the 'ambiguous motivations' of killers. In this sense, the notion of 'attacker lethality' in relation to individual offending corresponds to the notion of 'population lethality', considered earlier, which was raised by Killias's critics. In either case, the argument is the same. Guns are not the problem – murderous people or murderous societies are the problem. As we have seen however, the massive disproportion between British and American gun and non-gun murder rates make exempting the contribution of the firearm as a crime facilitator and risk multiplier somewhat implausible.

Zimring and Hawkins' evidence regarding the contexts of lethal homicide stress four general conclusions, (1) most killers and victims know one another prior to the killing or are family related (77 per cent of cases where the relationship was known to the police), (2) a large proportion of killings result from arguments (44 per cent of cases where the precipitating factors were known), (3) most gun homicide victims are killed by a single shot, (4) alcohol was a precipitating factor in most homicides. Zimring and Hawkins returned to these themes in their more recent study of *Crime is Not the Problem: Lethal Violence in America*, published in 1997. In this work they argued that

> when the precipitating factors are known, the bulk of all homicides stem
> from conflicts that emerge from social relations, [only] fifteen percent of

homicides are by-products of felonies. ... The social processes that generate arguments that result in homicides are not distinctively criminal in most cases. Many of the same conflicts that produce non-life threatening outcomes in most cases also lead to homicides.

(Zimring and Hawkins, 1997: 61)

They go on to note that arguments about money, sexual jealousy and male honour are a daily occurrence in the USA – as well as in every other modern society. The crucial difference, turning arguments into lethal encounters, is the widespread availability of firearms in the USA.

The foregoing arguments about firearms as crime facilitators and the widespread availability of firearms increasing rates of gun-related crime in a given society draw us directly back to Cullen's central questions concerning the overall relationships between firearms and crime. The issues are complex but very important. They are worth spelling out because recent years have seen the publication, in the USA, of a number of academic texts, which have sought to question the, hitherto generally pro-gun control, orientation of American criminology. Prominent among these have been works by Wright *et al.* (1983), Kates (1984) and especially Kleck (1991 and 1997) discussed earlier. The conclusions reached in such works have filtered down into the often heated and highly partisan political debates about gun control. Typically, the reception of these ideas into the public domain has occurred in the absence of the qualifications (the 'ifs' and 'buts') which are a normal part of academic research and analysis. The issue is important because Kleck's work, in particular, was used in the British gun control debate to support a case against restricting handguns and to refute evidence of any association between guns and gun-related crime emerging from the few international surveys so far undertaken. Yet, in the USA, Kleck's work has been criticised and it is important to briefly consider these criticisms.

Kleck's work is impressively thorough, scholarly and detailed. His central argument is that the positive and negative consequences of widespread gun ownership more or less cancel one another out. In one sense this puts us in a seemingly 'utilitarian' equation relevant only to the USA where firearms are said to have a self-defence and crime prevention role. On this score, as I have argued elsewhere, much American (academic and otherwise) commentary on the gun question is probably quite irrelevant for British public policy development (Squires, 1997a). More important, however, for our present purposes are a number of questions regarding research on firearm availability and firearm-related offending.

Kleck's overall argument is largely developed around four related propositions. First, he argues that in the USA guns are used for defensive purposes about as often as they are used for criminal ones. Second, he claims that widespread gun availability has had little net impact on overall rates of violent crime. Third, it is claimed that crime committed with firearms is, on the whole, no more risky than any other types of violent crime. Finally, he suggests that most gun control laws are pretty ineffective while others are likely to make matters worse by disarming the law-abiding – hence the NRA slogan: 'when guns are outlawed, only the outlaws will have guns'. The first and the final propositions are not relevant to the British context. Firearms are not permitted for citizen self-defence in the UK although, on the back of wildly varying estimates of the size of the illegal gun stock in the UK, a number of firearms lobby commentators have questioned the efficacy of British gun control policies.

Kleck's second and third points, however, do have some relevance to British debates, referring as they do to firearm availability and lethality. On the question of availability, despite sophisticated statistical modelling Kleck remains in a similar difficulty to researchers like Killias whose work he criticised. The problem is that surveys do not reveal the true level of gun availability. Only legitimate owners tend to disclose their possession of a firearm and we do not know the extent of firearm possession among the most problematic (criminologically speaking) groups in society. Kleck's solution to this dilemma was to develop a proxy measure of gun availability derived from a range of associated variables. Most of the measures he adopted involved firearms use in crime. Yet relatively high rates of firearm-related offending tended to prompt the purchase of firearms for self-defence purposes by law-abiding citizens (thereby increasing the overall gun supply). Consequently, areas where guns are widely available will be areas where guns are more frequently employed in illegal activities (Alba and Messner, 1995). Of course, only some of these guns will be involved in crime. On this point at least, Kleck concurred, 'where non criminal gun ownership is higher, criminal gun ownership is also higher, and where criminal gun ownership is higher, the *percent* of crimes which are committed with guns is higher' (Kleck, 1995: 413; emphasis in original). Kleck concedes that the proportion of crimes committed with a gun is higher in high gun-availability areas but argues that overall levels of criminal violence are not higher. This point corresponds to his conclusions that high rates of firearm homicide simply reflect weapon choices by criminally inclined persons and that, where gun ownership is widespread, guns are used to prevent or deter attacks about as often as offenders use them to initiate attacks. A characteristic of Kleck's perspective appears to be his fixed conception of aggressive criminal motivation. Violence does not emerge from defective social relations but rather it reflects a more classical conception of criminal motivation – offenders make choices. Criminal aggressors simply exist – 'out there'. The perspective is similar to that implied in the more 'situational' crime prevention paradigms. The vital issue is seen to be less a matter of pondering the motivations of offenders and much more a question of stopping them. In effect, shooting first and asking questions later.

We have considered these issues earlier. Drawing upon Zimring and Hawkins' (1997) work, we noted that such arguments simply do not square with the available information on the precipitating 'causes' of homicidal conflicts or the existence of prior relationships between offenders and victims. Most killings are not premeditated actions by persons who carefully choose their weapons, but angry outbursts by persons who seize what comes to hand. Thus the gun is a violence facilitator, and by far the most lethal.

One central theme of Alba and Messner's (1995) critique of Kleck concerned the problematic statistical modelling by which Kleck derived his estimates of firearm availability. Because these models placed a strong emphasis upon a, somewhat reciprocal, relationship between criminal firearms and non-criminal firearms, the entire mode of analysis is scarcely relevant to the UK. Firearms are not permitted for self-defence purposes in the UK and it has always been the utmost aim of the UK's shooting lobby to refute any connection between the legal and illegal gun stocks.

The fact that Kleck's form of assessing firearm availability is not applicable to the UK (despite whatever merits it may have in the USA) is exposed in his brief treatment of almost the only British study of firearm availability and firearm-related crime in England and Wales. Greenwood's 1972 study, *Firearms Control*, considered this question. Although Greenwood's statistical analysis in no way matched the sophistication of Kleck's own work, he concluded, 'the rate of armed crime is in no way connected with the density of firearms in the community. Indeed, if anything, the reverse appears to be true. The legitimate use of firearms is largely a rural pursuit, and crime is a city pursuit' (Greenwood, 1972: 219). Greenwood's data is now over three decades old and it relates to a time when the criminal use of firearms was far less common than today. A time when the shotgun had not yet been eclipsed by the handgun as the offender's weapon of choice. Even so, in Greenwood's rural and urban divisions it is clear that we are considering not just separate cultural communities but, very largely, two distinct weapon stocks.

Kleck's re-analysis of the data confirmed Greenwood's conclusion, he then supplemented the point with rural/urban data from the USA on crime rates and weapon availability (Kleck, 1991: 201–202). Overall, the conclusion reveals little more than we already knew. Legal firearms are generally not a criminal problem. Available British data, considered earlier, suggests that something like 6–9 per cent of them may be involved in criminal activity. Of course, with a large stock of firearms that could spell a great deal of firearm-related crime. Likewise, a proportion of these firearms will be stolen and might make their way into criminal hands. Acknowledging the variable effects of a wide range of social and cultural factors, increased firearm availability does appear to increase firearm involvement in offending. In a society with low levels of firearm availability, the interests of public safety would suggest we keep it that way. Despite the formidable challenge Kleck's work poses to the pro-control argument in the USA and the interesting issues his research raises concerning the analysis of firearm availability, it falters when one seeks to apply it in the British context.

Kleck's second key point, regarding firearm lethality in violent encounters is more directly dealt with, even in the American context. He undertook an individual level analysis of violent criminal incidents involving firearms and a variety of other weapons and concluded that incidents involving firearms can be less likely to result in injury or death. The firearm discourages victim resistance by enhancing the ability of the offender to control the incident. This outcome is, to some extent, offset by those occasions when a gun is actually used (i.e. fired) rather than merely pointed to intimidate, for then the likelihood of the victim's death is substantially greater. However, Kleck's data on this are derived from a rather unrepresentative sample of violent incidents – conflicts involving strangers. As we have seen, most homicides involve acquaintances. Stranger homicides are untypical and may be more likely to arise in situations where homicide is not the main objective of the aggressor (e.g. a robbery). Compared to a violent domestic argument where a gun clearly acts as a homicide facilitator, an armed robber may only intend that his weapon be a means to an end.

Notwithstanding the untypical sample Kleck bases his conclusions upon, Alba and Messner further criticise his claim that the presence of a gun does not increase the lethality of conflicts. They re-examine his data finding that, even in conflicts between strangers, when a gun is present the conflict is 2.8 times more likely to result in homicide than when a knife is present, 5.8 times more likely than when any other weapon is present and 43.7 times more likely when no weapon is present. They conclude, 'the presence of guns … makes incidents much more lethal than they otherwise would be' (Alba and Messner, 1995: 400). The conclusions of Alba and Messner anticipate the findings of Zimring and Hawkins in their sweeping study of lethal violence in the USA (Zimring and Hawkins, 1997). In this work, the authors argue that the USA's research and policy priority has to rest upon the 'proximate causes of death and serious injury'. Rates of property crime and even those of many interpersonal crimes are comparable to those reported by other Western industrialised nations, 'but rates of lethal violence in the USA are much higher than can be found elsewhere' (ibid. p. xii).

Such violence appears a unique feature of American life. It cannot be dismissed as some overarching cultural experience for it appears as a particularly focused and specific American phenomenon even though, considered overall, it represents a relatively small proportion of all recorded crime in the USA. As the authors acknowledge, however, it is the violence that causes the 'special destruction and disorganisation' and, they might add, the levels of fear and insecurity, produced by American crime. Likewise, they continue, lethal violence, considered as an outcome of a specific set of behaviours, appears to be influenced by different factors than those which generate more routine lawlessness. Thus, 'a particular focus on the instruments that make violent crime more likely to kill and on the willingness to use them are more plausible explanations than either the quantity of crime … or the willingness of criminals to use personal force'. Foremost among these 'proximate causes' influencing and apparently facilitating record levels of lethal violence is the widespread availability of handguns (Zimring and Hawkins, 1997: 15, 19, 32, 35, 106–124).

Zimring and Hawkins' work was not published when Mayhew drafted her second submission to Cullen. Even so, Mayhew's evaluation of the markedly differing proportions of gun-related crime in the UK and the USA undoubtedly pointed in the same direction. In view of Mayhew's findings, Cullen felt confident in endorsing the Home Office Research and Statistics Directorate's conclusion, 'the availability of guns increases both fatal and non-fatal gun-related crimes considerably in excess of what might be expected from differences in recorded crime levels for other offences' (Mayhew, 1996: 196; Cullen, 1996: 110, para. 9.20).

Cullen accepted that, 'there is a relationship between firearm ownership and firearm homicide when considered overall', (para. 9.21) but this did not in any sense dictate his final policy recommendations. He was convinced of the need for a substantial enhancement in the security arrangements attached to the private possession of handguns. However, in the interest of preserving target shooting, he recommended that the availability of working handguns could be appropriately restricted by partly dismantling them, by fitting lockable barrel blocks or by requiring the storage of weapons at appropriately licensed and secured shooting clubs (para. 9.112). But he added a rider, 'if such a system is not adopted [the government should consider] the banning of the possession of such handguns by individual owners' (para. 9.113). Even these proposals went significantly further than the shooting lobby interests were willing to accept and they raised numerous objections to both the principle and the practice of such recommendations. Inevitably, the more they rejected any compromise proposals the more they raised the stakes.

As it turned out, of course, the stakes were much higher anyway. In the end, Cullen's cautiously pragmatic and detailed recommendations on gun control were swept aside (virtually none of them making it into the Commons debate or the subsequent legislation) by a tide of public sympathy, anger and indignation at times crucially abetted by the media. Towards the end of its term of office, as we have seen, the Conservative government voted to prohibit all handguns exceeding .22 in calibre. And then, newly elected, Tony Blair's new Labour government honoured its election pledge and extended the prohibition to virtually all handguns.

This is unlikely to be the end of the criminology of the gun, however. At best it just marks the closure of a particular chapter on the UK. On the cautiously positive side, serious firearms offences – the use of guns in murder, robbery and drug dealing appear to be falling slightly from a peak in 1993. On the other hand, against a generally declining trend, the proportion of robberies and homicides involving a gun seems to be rising. More troubling still, there continue to be thriving international markets in illegal weapons and large-scale smuggling and illegal dealing of small arms in many parts of the world. Firearms still play a key role in sustaining the chronic political and military instability of many underdeveloped countries (Naylor, 1995; Smith, 1999). There is now evidence of a growing commitment on the part of international agencies, the UN included, to address the problem of illicit small arms trafficking and the social and political instability to which this contributes. Unfortunately, few commentators entertain any illusions about the scale of such a task (Bonner, 1998; Peters, 1998; Margue, 1999).

By contrast with the international situation, there appears to be little evidence of large-scale importation of illegal firearms into the UK from abroad. During the thirteen years before 1997 HM Customs and Excise seized in the region of 5,800 illegally imported handguns, the number fluctuating considerably from year to year. Over the same period some 2,000 rifles and some 700 shotguns were seized. It is obviously difficult to draw any conclusions about the scale of successful arms smuggling from the seizures (Customs and Excise, *Annual Report*, 1997).

According to one intelligence officer with Customs and Excise, with the exception of a few renowned anti-terrorist seizures, 'UK Customs have no evidence of wholesale smuggling of commercial or large scale quantities of firearms' (Crossley, 1999). Yet, as the 1998 'Arms to Africa' controversy revealed, British and European arms brokers may still be heavily implicated in the illicit distribution of firearms world-wide. Fortunately for British citizens, however, few of these weapons appear to be turning up in the UK itself. Even so, there appear few grounds for complacency.

7 Conclusions

Culture and ricochets

Almost every stage in the writing of the book was accompanied by yet more news of the havoc wrought by firearms in society and continuing controversy as to their role in helping keep the peace. In 1999 there came news of thirteen people, students and a teacher, shot and killed at a school in a quiet, middle-class suburb near Denver, Colorado (Ellison, 1999; Nelson, 1999). In the UK, shots were fired and bystanders were injured during a high-speed car chase through the outskirts of Manchester as armed offenders tried to elude the pursuing police. In London, a popular TV presenter was shot and killed on her own doorstep by an unknown assailant with a 9 mm semi-automatic handgun. Also in London, the Metropolitan Police launched 'Operation Trident' following growing evidence of a return to hostilities among drug and protection-racket gangs which, during the first part of 1999, led to thirteen killings and over thirty other shootings (Hopkins, 1999). Public awareness of the issue leapt significantly following a drive-by shooting in which a Radio One disc-jockey was wounded when a man on a motor-bike sprayed bullets into the Range Rover he was driving from a hand-held sub-machine gun. The episode focused attention upon the weaponry, Uzis and Mach 10 sub-machine guns, to which gang members appeared to have access. The event prompted the organisation of an anti-gun rally in the capital (Thompson and Wazir, 1999). Throughout 1999 in Northern Ireland, continuing doubts about the decommissioning of paramilitary weapons appeared ever likely to derail the 'peace process'. Handguns may have been prohibited on the British mainland, but they are seldom very far from our headlines.

The USA was said to be stunned (once again) by the Denver school shootings and, once more, media violence rather than firearms, was blamed for cultivating a disrespect for life among the young. In the wake of the latest shooting, the Clinton administration attempted, once again, to introduce legislation which sought to restrict the sale of guns to persons aged under 21, restrict private gun sales and require the sale of security locks with all handguns. The Bill was defeated in Congress, although an amendment requiring the display of notices bearing the ten commandments in schools and public buildings was carried. American politicians now require schools to display posters reminding pupils that 'Thou shalt not kill', while doing nothing to restrict the availability of the one item with which young people undertake the most of their killing. In the

UK, by contrast, despite figures indicating falling levels of firearm-related offending, it was becoming clear that, whatever a prohibition on the private ownership of handguns contributed to public safety, it certainly did not remove the problem of the gun.

Problems of the gun: realism and relativism

It should, by now, be clear that the problem of the gun is no simple matter. Depending upon the standpoint of the viewer the problem might be variously described as a problem that guns are too freely available, or too freely available to the wrong people or that the 'wrong people' are insufficiently discouraged from using firearms for criminal purposes. By contrast, the problem of the gun might equally be described in terms of them being insufficiently available or, following the logic of Lott's examination of the 'concealed-carry' laws in the USA (Lott, 1998) insufficiently available to the right people. By this token, if only there were more guns, there would be even less crime, a conclusion emphatically denied by Handgun Control Inc. (1999).

Alternatively, the problem may be that the right people with the guns fail to use them appropriately or take insufficient precautions, leaving them unlocked and loaded where curious childish hands might find them. It may also be a question of the 'wrong guns' or of 'bad guns' although, as Kleck has argued, the search for 'bad guns' which often appears to animate the gun control movement might result in contradictory and self-defeating policy conclusions (Kleck, 1991, 1997). A number of gun lobby commentators have been known to argue that, 'there is no such thing as a bad gun, just bad people', a slogan from the same stable as the NRA's 'guns don't kill – people do' rhetoric.

Yet if guns are to be judged on more utilitarian grounds, it follows that some 'fitness for purpose' test might suggest that some guns are less well suited to certain purposes. The extensive field-testing of police and military weapons and the endless articles in the gun press comparing virtually identical new semi-automatics indicates very clearly that serious shooters have a marked sense of the advantages and disadvantages of different types of guns. The marketing of guns for the domestic American market in recent years has seen the virtues of reliability, speed of use and concealability strongly promoted. Likewise as the size of the weapon has been reduced to aid concealability, their calibre and magazine capacity – respectively, 'stopping power' and 'firepower' – have been increased. Rather like the weapons carried by the crime warriors of recent Hollywood blockbusters, a self-defence handgun may be a problem if it doesn't do its job.

Equally, the firepower and capacity of firearms is a law enforcement issue. The FBI began to query the standard issue 9 mm semi-automatic after a Florida shoot-out in which a fatally wounded felon still managed to kill two agents. Something with a little more first-shot 'stopping power' was called for, although, no sooner were such weapons and ammunition adopted in law enforcement circles, than they became available on the civilian market and started turning up in criminal hands (Diaz, 1999). More typical manifestations of the problem of the gun in law enforcement circles, however, concern, on the one hand, the enforcement effort put into 'gun control' and the prosecution and custodial incapacitation of gun-using offenders. On the other hand, the unwarranted, perhaps over-zealous, use of lethal force against suspected persons is a recurring issue in the USA and not an unknown problem in the UK.

It follows that the identification of a problem with guns is contextually, culturally and ideologically determined. This is not a retreat into relativism, but simply a recognition that there is unlikely to be a single truth, a single solution or right answer to the problem(s) of the gun. As good realists, we need to begin by reviewing the lessons learned during the preceding chapters very much from the point of view of those most directly involved or affected. That is to say, starting from where we are but without overlooking other, more holistic perspectives given by discourses on human rights and justice. These considerations provide a framework through which we can consider the lessons derived.

Chapter 1 sought to set a context for 'taking guns seriously' by considering some of the ways in which they have come to influence our personal, social and cultural lives. The more neutral term 'influence' is employed here in order to embrace the full range of gun-related social relations, from problems of gun prevalence (persons living in constant fear of guns and violence who never leave their homes) to those of gun scarcity (people who would not dream of leaving home unless 'tooled up'). In the UK the influence of guns flows through a range of channels. These include trends in the criminal use of firearms, encounters with armed police officers, media reporting of firearm incidents and a wide range of cultural influences (films to video games) in which firearms are invariably depicted as a means to human ends. Finally, incidents such as Hungerford and Dunblane result in bursts of concern which, as in the UK, can fundamentally alter the shape of public policies in hitherto unexpected ways. Similar influences operate in the USA although there a far more substantial pro-gun influence exists. A 'gun culture' is not only mediated throughout American history and institutions, but is reinforced through effective political lobbies (representing shooters themselves and also the firearms industry) which are able to shape political priorities, promote or frustrate legislative and policy change and, generally, keep 'gun rights' high up the agenda. In more recent years, however, gun control groups have begun to challenge the hegemony of organisations such as the NRA. In both societies, the highly partisan nature of the debates has meant that academic contributions – still less sociological or criminological ones – have tended to play only a fairly marginal role. Even then, academic work is often adopted or discarded according to the conclusions it has reached or the prior affiliations of its authors, rather than employed to enhance the general level of the debate.

Having set out such a contested context, we might want to conclude, either, that the spectre of the gun is looming ever larger, or, that the utility of the personal defence handgun is becoming increasingly important in a fragmenting, insecure, world. That said, chapters 2 and 3 explored the contrasting cultural realities of firearms within British and American historical discourses centring upon guns, society and firearms control. Chapter 4, on the other hand, examined a series of themes reflected in contemporary news media reporting of firearms. Two particularly prominent perspectives were revealed in these related discussions. They concerned contrasting notions of firearms as *civilising* or, conversely, as *decivilising* influences. This distinction is sometimes confused with notions of historical progression. In this, I would argue, erroneous, view, firearms once played a role in the creation of a modern, industrial capitalist, world order but then, with the advent of peace and prosperity, a universal franchise and the rights of modern citizenship, firearms have become dangerously anachronistic and decivilising. This is a view that both revisionist historians and Charlton Heston, the NRA President in 1999, both appear to agree upon – though from differing ends of the historical scale. The civilising potential of the Maxim gun is unlikely to have been apparent to the African tribesmen upon whom Europe's industrialised weaponry was first tested in the late nineteenth century. Even though the machine gun's first inventor and sponsors appeared to believe that weapons so terrible would reduce casualties by encouraging men to think twice about the folly of warfare, history appears to have proven otherwise (Ellis, 1976). Likewise, Charlton Heston, addressing his closing remarks to a beleaguered NRA Annual Convention in Denver, held in the wake of the school shooting only a few days earlier in the same city, saw nothing anachronistic in concealed handgun carrying. Indeed, he welcomed it as a reaffirmation of American freedoms and a positive contribution to crime prevention:

> Tyranny in any form, can never find footing within a society of law-abiding, armed, ethical people. The majesty of the Second Amendment ... guarantees that no government despot, no renegade faction of armed forces, no roving criminals, no breakdown of law and order, no massive anarchy, no force of evil or crime or oppression from within or without, can ever rob you of the liberties that define your Americanism. ... That's why you and your descendants need never fear fascism, state-run faith, refugee camps, brainwashing, ethnic cleansing, or especially, submission to the wanton will of criminals.
>
> (Heston, 1999a)

Neither the tone nor the content of Heston's commentary sets it apart from a wide range of other contributions to the gun rights debate (Hornberger and Ebeling, 1997). The alleged 'right to bear arms' appears to safeguard Americans from all manner of social and political misfortunes, with the exception, perhaps, of historical amnesia – a complaint shared, to some extent, with the American film industry. It is, perhaps, no mere coincidence that a former Hollywood actor came to chair an organisation which sees itself as the last defender of American armed tradition and it was another former actor who held the USA's most progun presidency of recent times.

Regarding history and culture through the lenses of Hollywood, the civilising then decivilising 'genres of the gun' can seem particularly emphatic. We move from narratives focusing upon *The Gun that Won the West*, defeating the Indians, taming the frontier, rescuing the girl and making the man (Slotkin, 1992) to *Robocop*, the self styled 'future of law enforcement' dealing out swift 'justice' in a post-apocalyptic city-scape by invariably shooting first. So when Marshall Will Kane (Gary Cooper in *High Noon*) walked alone down the town's dusty street to face his would-be killers, his gun was undeniably a force for law and order and the future. Its function, in the hands of a good and strong man, was the elimination of the renegade elements from the USA's past who might unsettle the new social contract. Much the same is true of John Wayne's ageing gunfighter John Books (in *The Shootist*), settling some old scores, and closing the book on the USA's past. The theme of historical closure is a central component of the film. Riding into town, Books buys a local newspaper which reports the death of Queen Victoria, the end of another era and the beginning of a new century. Both *High Noon* and *The Shootist* echo another central theme of the gun debate in the way they represent the frightened and belittled private citizens of the different communities. These people, while grateful of the protection brought by the guns of the righteous, lack the responsibility or moral courage to confront evil, assert their beliefs or face the consequences of their actions. In Charlton Heston's terms, speaking as NRA President at the organisation's 1999 Annual Convention, such people lack the courage to stand up and be counted against tyranny.

On the contrary, according to Snyder, also from the pro-gun camp, the USA has become 'a nation of cowards and shirkers' too fearful to confront and therefore willing to tolerate, compromise or negotiate with those who oppress. 'Crime is rampant', he argues, 'because the law-abiding, each of us, condone it, excuse it, permit it, submit to it. We permit it and encourage it because we do not fight back, immediately, then and there, when it happens' (Snyder, 1976). Real men, it seems will refuse to be victims and want no part of victim culture.

> One who values his life and takes seriously his responsibilities to his family will possess and cultivate the means of fighting back, and will retaliate when threatened ... he will never be content to rely solely on others for his safety ... he will be armed [and] trained in the use of his weapon and will defend himself when threatened with lethal violence.
>
> (ibid.)

Women too were offered this version of the American dream of armed citizenship and urged to 'fight fire with fire' (Wolf, 1994). Accordingly, the NRA's self-defence and handgun training programme for women was called 'Refuse to be a Victim' (Quigley, 1989). Unfortunately, such assertions of uncompromising vigilance can also be the basis of a new intolerance. This is not 'zero tolerance', the latest in a line of questionable policing strategies inherited from the USA, but maximum intolerance of a kind which licenses the kind of avenger character depicted in Michael Winner's *Death Wish* films.

In one sense, however, there may be nothing much to distinguish the virtuous firepower of one genre's movie heroes from those of more recent times. Charles Bronson, Clint Eastwood or Mel Gibson, lethal weapons all, protect the universal 'citizen-victims' of the late modern era just as the cowboy heroes did of old. Their guns remain 'peacemakers', as essential in the modern era as they were when the Colt revolver was first produced over a century ago. In this sense, the civilising gun is not so much associated with a former stage of historical development but, in contemporary history and the cinema, the gun is always essential as a tool with which to hold the forces of disorder at bay. The same is evidently not true of other guns in other contexts. In the early decades of twentieth-century USA, the zip-guns and 'nigger-town Saturday night specials' were not viewed in the favourable light which large sections of the USA now bestow upon small, cheap and concealable handguns – primarily because of their jaundiced views about who owned such weapons. Likewise, the Thompson sub-machine gun, *The Gun that Made the Twenties Roar* (Helmer, 1970), hardly gained the 'respectable' political support that military assault weapons have achieved over the past two decades, again, primarily, because of perceptions of the Tommy gun's criminally destabilising influence during and after the prohibition years.

The same might be said of the shocking return of decivilising firepower in a new generation of gun dramas. Here the protagonist heroes blast their way through a 'war of all against all' narrative in much the same way as players progress through the programmes of 'shoot-em up' video arcade or computer games. Involvement is restricted to a simple process of aiming and pulling the trigger. Survival is about winning. Everything about the narrative is, in the true sense of the words, 'gun-driven'. Armed, there is nothing one might not accomplish, disarmed there is nothing one can achieve. Guns become the major players; they confront, intimidate, stand-off, give life and take it away. Men become no more than the carriers of this firepower, like the factory 'hands' of the industrial system they are now but 'guns'. Yet, for these men, being 'dressed to kill' is being ready and able, looking the part, a matter of confident masculine style. Self-respect and dignity are everything, insults are not taken lightly; a code of honour, of sorts.

In similar fashion a code of honour began to deplete the junior ranks of the militarised hierarchies of seventeenth- and eighteenth-century Europe as methods of dispute resolution failed to adapt to the increasingly accurate, powerful and lethal technologies available to disputants. Duelling had once served several vital, even civilising, functions in maintaining privilege, resolving disputes, testing the true worth of a man and providing 'satisfaction', if not justice. However, it became socially counterproductive when social changes and newer and more reliable weapons made the duel both a more lethal and more 'democratic' exchange, when gentlemen of name and standing could be cut down in their prime by a lucky shot from a *nouveau riche* pretender (Kiernan, 1988). The civilising power of arms in older European societies, in hunting, duelling and military hierarchy, was founded upon class and social exclusivity until these social structures themselves began to fragment. Even then, the disciplinary power of arms continued to be a vehicle for the defence of empire and the control of domestic populations right up until the early decades of the twentieth century. Paternalistic conceptions of ordered hierarchy had been essential to the British state's enthusiasm for militarising and training the working class (and its youth). Military discipline was about learning citizenship. Firearms trained the man. Paradoxically, essentially similar paternalistic conceptions of social order that conferred firepower on the British people, contrived to take it away again, beginning in 1920.

It follows that there seems no simple 'historical' connection between 'civilising' or 'decivilising' gun power. Social contexts and social purposes remain important. This is not a version of the NRA argument that there are no 'bad guns', there clearly are, but it is a reminder that, even overloaded as guns are with ascribed qualities, social contexts can be at least as important as any supposed qualities of guns themselves. This lesson, in particular, appears also to derive from discussions of firearms in law enforcement. The British police force (or service) remains one of the few law enforcement agencies maintaining a very largely unarmed approach to its routine, operational patrol activity.

Order and routine

For the British police (and the British public) the unarmed model of policing is said to embody principles of policing by the consent of the public in an accountable, non-militaristic fashion. Over recent decades, a number of incidents have knocked a few dents in this model of policing and, particularly during the 1980s, the armed response capacity of the police was enhanced. Specialist units began to receive extensive training in armed response tactics and then, in the early nineties, responding to pressure following the fatal shooting of a number of police officers, patrol officers in armed response vehicles were authorised to carry firearms on routine uniformed duties. Even though officers at international airports had been openly carrying weapons for some time and the policy of more routine arming was to be accompanied by a reduction in the overall number of authorised firearms officers, the press reported the decision as a major departure from traditional British policing philosophy. The Commissioner of the Metropolitan Police explained the policy change as 'event driven' and, although subsequent surveys showed serving police officers not to favour generalised arming, other forces came to follow the lead taken in London.

Clearly the suitability and appropriateness of armed law enforcement will depend upon a range of factors, not least the situations encountered by the police and the roles they might be expected to perform. However, a policy described as 'event driven' suggests few inherent limits. In effect, 'event driven' becomes 'gun driven', the police always responding, ratchet-like, to criminally raised stakes (McKenzie, 1996). To avoid this, strategies of criminal disarmament, including Customs and Excise and inter-agency 'intelligence-led' policing, need to precede attempts to deal with armed offenders on the ground. However, accepting that some illegal firearms are always likely to slip through any net (particularly if there were many holes in that net) officers might at any time encounter armed offenders. A second aspect of the 'gun driven' dilemma reveals itself. Although the development of police operational tactics with firearms has traditionally emphasised containment first and foremost – and the avoidance of confrontation – the more widespread deployment of armed officers and an increasing emphasis upon rapid deployment makes confrontation more likely. Events in the 1980s suggested an increase in confrontational policing tactics. Once in a confrontational situation, the options available to the armed officers become somewhat more limited. The media generally tend to have a field day with notions of 'shooting to kill', although the legal framework established by the 1967 Criminal Law Act is intended to reinforce the conservative, last resort, nature of any police decision to shoot (Waddington, 1991). However, while the law in the books and the training given to police officers might be clear cut, practice and the interpretation of the law by the courts has occasionally been more than a little ambiguous.

Ultimately, the arming of (some – or all) police officers, much like their adoption of defensive equipment, is based upon a series of judgments about the roles they have to perform. Yet it is also a question of reassuring the public without whose consent effective policing could scarcely begin. One of the vital factors influencing the growing demand for self-defence handguns in the USA is fear, and a widespread public perception that the police cannot be relied upon to provide protection. Surveys suggest that this perception varies by geography, neighbourhood, ethnicity, age and social class. In some American cities, a growing dissatisfaction with policing responses to urgent calls helped coin the saying: 'Dial a cop, dial an ambulance, dial a pizza; see which comes first'. If things are not so bad in the UK and firearms are no longer an option for private citizens it need not follow that the 'tooling up' of police officers necessarily brings (in and of itself) the desired social benefits – public reassurance and violence control. In this context an emphasis upon more traditional policing strategies seems paramount: proactive efforts to control the stock of illegal weapons and tighter restrictions to prevent the slippage of weapons into illegal circles. In this light, after Dunblane, in the context of a substantially unarmed society where armed self-defence scarcely presents itself as an issue, the prohibition of the private ownership of handguns might seem by far the lesser evil.

After the Acts

Since the 1997 Firearms (Amendment) Acts prohibiting the private ownership of virtually all types of handguns, members of the shooting fraternity have scarcely missed an opportunity to condemn the decisions taken. This has involved relatively little change of attitude in respect of the control of firearms in the UK. Throughout the early 1990s, a continuing theme in shooting journalism had involved gloomy predictions of shooting's imminent demise. We have already considered Greenwood's thoughts on this topic, and his oft-repeated suspicion – confirmed somewhat by the 1973 Green Paper on the control of firearms – that the Home Office would not be satisfied until the objective of a gun-free society had been achieved.

Greenwood was not alone on this issue, however. Jan Stevenson, editor of the

British-published *Handgunner* magazine, devoted many pages during 1994–1995 to an analysis of the issue of firearm licence fees. Matters were not helped, according to Stevenson, when the Charity Commission took a decision late in 1993 to remove charitable status from rifle and pistol clubs. Whereas 'rifle and pistol clubs had always been recognised as charitable on the basis of their purpose of promoting the skills of marksmanship among Her Majesty's subjects in the interests of the defence of the realm' (Stevenson, 1994a) the question before the Charity Commission, was whether this was still a worthwhile social purpose deserving of favourable tax status. In the end, they decided it was not, arguing that, 'the ownership, possession and ability to use guns is popularly seen as being injurious to the public interest. The ease of availability of firearms is becoming increasingly unacceptable to the public' (quoted in *Guns Review*, Volume 34, Number 6, 1994: 436).

Politicians and Home Office officials, argued Stevenson, were being entirely duplicitous in their justification of fees increases and in their more general penalising of shooting. Fees were being used to price shooting out of existence, Stevenson claimed. He characterised the Home Office perspective in the following terms, firearms licence fees, 'formed a spiral staircase to some celestial bureaucratic utopia where no-one had guns and the docile, servile, indeed, helpless inhabitants did cheerfully as they were told' (Stevenson, 1995b: 60). Showing a degree of prescience, six months earlier in an article in another British shooting magazine, he had remarked that the Home Office's latest licence fee order 'is the death knell of private firearms ownership in this country' (Stevenson, 1994b: 102). He went on to berate a number of shooting organisations, principally the British Association for Shooting and Conservation and the British Field Sports Society (primarily shotgun organisations), for failing to use their credibility, connections and numerically greater memberships to come to the aid of the other shooters (essentially handgun shooters). Others also criticised the fragmented series of special interests representing shooting and lamented the lack of a 'single powerful association like the NRA of America ... in place of the present mosaic of fractious special interests groups' (Yardley, 1995b: 5). Likewise, John Cook, manager of a shooting range company in Kent, writing in *Guns and Shooting*, while agreeing that the sectional interests running British shooting did the sport few favours, had the following concerns about the tactics of some groups. 'What worries me is that we don't want to be too political and some of the stands made by the SRA seem to be creating arguments for the sake of them and to over-fight issues' (Cook, 1994).

As we have already noted, divisions within the shooting lobby and internal feuding have tendered to hamper its effectiveness as a political lobby although, for Stevenson, neither 'nanny state' paternalism nor cultural elitism had much to offer. Even so, both attitudes lay firmly rooted in British approaches to firearms and these were noticeably incompatible with the American orientations to guns reflected in firearm discourses (publishing and marketing) emerging during the early 1990s.

Despite the forewarnings of Greenwood and Stevenson, the period following the 1997 prohibition on the private ownership of handguns has seen shooter's websites bristling with indignation. The government is repeatedly portrayed as either exploiting the Dunblane tragedy for a prior political purpose or punishing thousands of responsible and law-abiding shooters for the actions of one crazed individual. A number of commentators, both individuals as well as representatives of shooting organisations, have continued to assert a defence of shooting in terms of 'rights', character training and self-discipline, economic benefit and an argument for cultural autonomy (although many are at pain to deny that the UK has a 'gun culture'). None of these arguments, however, address the central dilemma involved in proposing gun rights in the context of the UK's own largely gun-free cultural perspective. Shooters believe themselves a persecuted and misunderstood minority but make few concessions to the society that, they themselves acknowledged, viewed them with suspicion. The more perceptive of shooting commentators appeared to recognise the problems that this entailed. According to Yardley, writing in 1995, 'our public image at present could be much improved. We shooters are seen essentially in two ways in the outside world: either as chinless wonders who enjoy killing animals or as pot-bellied, camouflaged obsessives who like big guns to make up for other inadequacies'. He went on to argue that the image had to be changed, 'for like all modern wars, this one – the struggle for the survival of the shooting sports – is essentially a war of perception' (Yardley, 1995b: 5). However, if shooting's general image was poor before March 1996, how much worse did it appear after? Nevertheless, it was not so much perception as intransigence that irritated Lord Cullen when he criticised the evidence given by shooters during his Inquiry. They were, apparently, unwilling to acknowledge the possibility that any additional precautions in the control of firearms might contribute to public safety. As we have seen, this seems to be an attitude they share with American opponents of gun control. And here, of course, lies the issue.

In a chapter on the media reporting of firearms-related issues in the UK we have seen how a dominant perspective informing the discourse of the British news media has concerned the apparent dangers of the US gun culture. Whatever guns might have meant for the USA's past they appeared to create a large degree of havoc in its present. American gun culture was perceived as a profoundly alien world. The repercussions of the contemporary gun culture, for crime control and law enforcement, for poor communities in deprived inner-city neighbourhoods, for accident and emergency centres and in terms of the perceived risks and actual fears of large sections of the USA's population, at times appeared almost overwhelming. Moreover, there are tortuous legal and political processes associated with managing the consequences of freely available firearms; 20,000 different laws, armed police officers, concealed-carry statutes, public safety and product liability lawsuits, and metal detectors in schools. Nevertheless, British journalists and commentators became most animated of all by a fear that this American gun culture – with rising firearm-related offending, armed drug gangs, 'hit-men', armed police, 'shoot-outs', new 'combat-style' semi-automatic weapons, and its wider paraphernalia of attitudes and accessories – was coming to the UK.

British shooting organisations appeared unable to recognise the concerns that such developments might generate. A number of factors militated against them doing so. On the one hand, there were the divisions in the shooting fraternity itself. The more 'traditional' field sports were less affected by the newer American influences. On the other hand, the increasingly popular discipline of 'practical' handgun shooting – firing the newer, higher calibre revolvers and semi-automatic pistols, using humanoid targets and mimicking 'combat-style' conditions – was largely being taken up by shooting enthusiasts who were much more in thrall to American gun culture itself. Therefore, they were far less inclined to question it.

Lethal practices?

Practical shooting, based, to a degree, upon police firearms training exercises, had grown increasingly popular in the USA. According to Walker, writing in *Guns and Shooting* magazine, 'practical shooting has evolved from combat-based scenario shooting to a world-wide sport enjoyed by shooters in some fifty countries. Guns and equipment', he added, rather tellingly, 'have progressed so much that it seems at times as if the guns are running the shooters instead of the other way around' (Walker, 1995: 12). In the practical shooting discipline, the shooter 'shoots a course' by moving through a series of obstacles during which potential targets will appear, requiring the shooter to make snap 'shoot/don't shoot' decisions. Accuracy is important but so are speed and agility as the events are timed. Firepower is also a factor, as we shall see later. In some of the more elaborate shooting courses, participants are given additional problems to deal with, awkward obstacles to negotiate, ladders to climb, vehicles to exit, objects to carry. Enthusiasts argue that the practical shooting contests represent genuine athletic and sporting events. Participants are 'tested' having to solve real shooting problems and dilemmas while on the move. Given all this, shooting commentators express resentment at the *de facto* media boycott of shooting sports – combat scenario shooting is considered 'anti-social' and straight target shooting is considered 'too boring' to attract viewers.

In 1994 Cook even suggested new viewer-friendly shooting competitions derived from 'practical shooting' but borrowing rather more from TV's *Gladiators* (Cook, 1994). Another American import gaining popularity in the UK during the early 1990s and which might also have revived the media fortunes of British shooting was 'Western-style' shooting using revolvers based upon their predecessors from the 1870s. Competitors, expected to dress in cowboy costumes, participated in man against man fast-draw contests, pitting speed and accuracy against one another. Commentators have regarded it as a form of practical shooting in fancy dress (Moore, 1994).

As its name suggests, the discipline of practical shooting originated in the very practical training of police officers and security personnel in self-defence and combat handgun techniques. Consequently the handguns originally used were the standard issue handguns carried on a daily basis by law enforcement officers (or equivalent weapons). In other words, these were standard, production model, firearms, the kind that it might be 'practical' to carry around all day. Over the years, the newer semi-automatics came to dominate the revolvers, largely due to their magazine capacity, rate of fire and the ease and speed with which they might be reloaded (though separate, revolver-only, competitions still exist). At the same time, a new kind of handgun, the 'race gun' was developed. Specialised and customised for practical 'race-style' competitions the new guns were often far from practical and led purists to complain that practical shooting was moving away from its roots. In the event, separate competitions were developed for the newer specialist weapons and for differing grades of 'standard issue' weapons. While not all British handgun shooting competitions were of the 'practical' combat type, British shooting magazines *Handgunner, Guns and Shooting, Guns Review* and *Target Gun* gave prominent coverage to the new discipline. They frequently discussed its growing popularity, the latter devoting space each month to reports from the United Kingdom Practical Shooting Association.

From the British perspective a number of issues followed from the growing popularity of this kind of shooting. In the USA, with its armed police and (potentially) armed citizenry, the rigours of practical shooting bear a certain connection to American society, a connection which was almost entirely absent in the UK. Equally, the development in the UK of a sport, the essential elements of which were modelled upon combat and killing, raises at least a few questions. Reading the magazine coverage given to this shooting discipline, it takes relatively little scrutiny to uncover both its American credentials and its inherent preoccupation with firepower and weapon lethality. Take, for instance, the following introduction to a review of the SIG P226 9 mm semi-automatic pistol in the British *Guns and Shooting* magazine.

> The popularisation of various American-led shooting disciplines has transformed both the competition semi-automatic and revolver almost beyond recognition ... what the hell has happened to the 'standard' handgun? It is something of a paradox that competitions designed to simulate combat rely so heavily on custom shops to produce the winning hardware. Out in the real world, where the difference between a hit and a miss is survival rather than points, guns like the P226 fare considerably better.
>
> (Robinson, 1994: 58)

Notions of the 'real world' tend to refer, inevitably, to an American 'real world' with product development in the world's biggest handgun market shaping purchasing trends in the British shooting community. The idea of there being a 'real world' for handgun use beyond the shooting range is explicitly denied in British firearm licensing and, most of the time, an issue avoided by shooters themselves. On the other hand, several gun writers have commented upon the way the American market has tended to lead while a rather fickle, seemingly impressionistic, British shooting community has tended to follow. According to Parker, the average shooter is quite fickle in terms of product loyalty. ... When the American market came out with the high capacity pistols, a lot of shooters followed the market trends and moved over to these new guns. It seemed to me as a case of, 'we don't care what it is but as long as the Americans have got them we must have them too'.

(Parker, 1994)

Although, as other commentators noted, many of the newer features demanded in a modern semi-automatic pistol (such as high-capacity magazines) derived from weapon specifications dictated by military or police needs. The suitability of such weapons for police use (high capacity handguns were said to encourage a 'spray and pray' approach to shooting among American police officers), let alone their suitability for sports marksmanship, remains open to question (*Guns Review*, June 1994: 433, October 1994: 768).

Elsewhere, the 1995 *Guns and Shooting* guide to firearm licensing described the attitude of newly qualified shooting applicants in the following terms. 'OK, so you've joined a club, done your six months probation and are now ready to apply for that all-important first ticket. Every night your dreams are full of all the exotic and wonderful guns you are going to buy just as soon as the fat brown envelope lands on your mat' (Tarling and Suffling, 1995: 43). Neither attitude, neither the fickle American 'wannabe' nor the dreamer after exotic guns, suggests a particularly responsible or detached perspective on the part of shooters or shooting journalists toward the specific context of pistol shooting in the UK. As we have noted already, the only legal purpose for which a handgun could be privately possessed in the UK (before the legislation of 1997) was for target shooting at an approved shooting club. This was, indeed, the only legal purpose to which handguns could be put. Accordingly, it might be pertinent to ask why no further restraints were considered necessary for the weapons and ammunition employed for no other purpose than making holes in cardboard targets (or similar) at a variety of distances.

To take a particular instance, the Home Office firearm licensing form, Form 101, allowed applicants to nominate six handguns, specifying both type and calibre. A suitably qualified applicant was simply seeking permission to purchase the weapons he or she had listed. The permission to purchase lasted for the five-year duration of the licence, applicants did not have to purchase all the guns they had listed at once. In itself this may have been a realistic concession, although the *Guns and Shooting* guidance was for applicants to fill in all the available spaces to safeguard future choices and because permissions for certain weapons might have been refused anyway by the police. However, a comment by the *Guns and Shooting* editor gave a different emphasis.

Most shooters seem to have at least one revolver and a semi-auto pistol in one of the more popular centre-fire calibres, but if you were to look at your average gun owner's collection, one imagines you would be quite surprised to discover what else they have. Shooters are akin to pack rats and are loathe to get rid of anything they might want to shoot one day. And a lot of their hardware is often bought on a whim or simply their inability to turn down a bargain. ... Consider the Desert Eagle, many is the shooter that has one of these big buggers tucked away, but how often are they used? Not a lot. ... I am as guilty as the next person and have some lovely guns in my collection I never use. ... In truth they get an airing about twice a year if they are lucky. For the type of shooting I do they are no longer competitive.

(Moore, 1995)

Aside from what such a comment reveals about shooters orientations to their weapons ('lovely guns') and their tendency to hoard, or collect, several types, there remains an issue about the firearm licensing requirement. As we have seen, the only legal purpose for which a handgun could be privately possessed was for target shooting at an approved shooting club. If guns were not regularly employed in this manner (perhaps because they had become somewhat 'obsolete' for competition purposes), might there not have been a case for these guns being surrendered, or at least deactivated. Moore's view was that there ought to be a greater diversity of shooting contests to accommodate the diversity of 'weird and wonderful' guns that shooters had 'tucked away' – in essence, that shooting competitions should continue to follow the American market's product development lead. An alternative British gun control perspective, on the other hand, which emphasised public safety might have required a tighter specification of competition standard weapons on firearm licences and the withdrawal or surrender of other guns that did not meet these criteria or which were not regularly used.

The paradox of 'practical shooting' in a disarmed society is something of a key to understanding both the peculiarly acquisitive habits of the British shooter and his enthusiasm for the latest American weaponry. The firearms industry in the USA has continuously worked to augment the calibre, power and magazine capacity of newer weapons and ammunition. Each innovation seemed to bring greater lethality, but with few compensating safeguards (Diaz, 1999). As new weapons and ammunition have been produced and marketed in the USA, shooters in the UK have wanted them despite, often, their unsuitability for British shooting purposes. For instance, as American firearms companies geared up their production lines for the expanding American 'concealed-carry' market, they developed a language through which to rationalise these guns and sell them to the American public. In time, these same notions, parading the peculiar virtues of any particular gun, filtered through to the UK, there becoming part of a wider, but quite insular, shooting fraternity discourse through which the rival merits of different guns could be compared.

Having no reference back in the 'real world' of the UK, as it were, where self-defence handguns were not permitted, the only reality for such weapons lay either in the USA (hence the tendency to draw heavily upon American firearm experts in British magazines). Alternatively, it lay in the synthetic world of practical shooting. Thus, weapons or ammunition reviews in British shooting magazines, addressed to the UK's target shooters, frequently deployed 'code' words which tended to suggest rather different purposes in quite other worlds. For instance Massad Ayoob, *Handgunner*'s American correspondent, a police captain and combat handgun specialist, explained his view that a newly marketed .357 magnum round, 'was not only the only load that made the mid-bore revolver a viable proposition, but was the most demonstrably effective load, round for round, of any in use' (*Handgunner*, Number 64, June/July 1995: 51). Here, 'viability' and 'effectiveness' have nothing to do with punching a hole in a paper target or 'practical shooting', they refer to the bullet's lethality, or its 'stopping power'. The same coded language emerged in Northmore's 1995 review of the new Taurus semi-automatics, 'if you like the Taurus but are not keen on 9 mm, the company make the PT101, which is exactly the same gun but in the larger and more effective .40' S&W calibre' (Northmore, 1995). Again, the larger the weapon calibre, the greater the lethality, the more 'effective' the weapon's 'stopping power'.

Similarly, 'effectiveness' was an issue in many of the ammunition feature articles. The magazines carried advertisements and test results for 'hollow-point', 'expanding' or 'high-penetration' ammunition. None of these ammunition types have much difficulty in passing through the card or paper targets used in most British shooting contests. Indeed, the ammunition is explicitly designed with other, more obviously anti-personnel, purposes in mind. This rather suggests that something with a little less inherent lethality might have been considered more appropriate for the purely 'sporting' uses to which British target ammunition could be put. Thomas Hamilton used hollow-point ammunition in Dunblane, a type explicitly prohibited for military use by the Hague Conventions of 1889–1907, although the Conventions have never been applied to ammunition used either by the police or private citizens. During the early 1990s, Germany unsuccessfully attempted to outlaw expanding, hollow-point, ammunition throughout the European Union. In February 1995, a *Guns and Shooting* article explained that expanding and hollow-point ammunition were not normally available in the UK, but then went on to describe how applicants could request that an extra condition be added to their licence allowing them to hold such ammunition 'for sporting purposes' (Tarling and Suffling, 1995). The decision to permit British shooters to use hollow-point ammunition – that is, bullets purposefully designed to produce large wound channels in body tissue – for sporting purposes, was celebrated enthusiastically by Ayoob. It was, he suggested, a victory over the 'fascist tendencies' of the Home Office, and an issue worth defending in order that hollow-point bullets did not 'wind up as a minor trinket on the scrap heap of expired liberties' (Ayoob, 1996: 29).

Under the guise of 'practical shooting' seemingly any gun or ammunition type, however unsuitable its design specification for target shooting, could find a place. There is a strong sense, as the editor of the *Guns Review: Summer Pistol Supplement* acknowledged, that in practical pistol shooting, 'the match is tailored to the gun, rather than the gun to the match' (*Guns Review Pistol Supplement*, Summer 1994: 14). Following this logic, a 'sporting purpose', in the terms of British firearm licensing, might be claimed for any handgun however otherwise unsuitable for civilian use. In 1994 the UK Action Pistol Association launched a new competition for the compact 'pocket-rocket' semi-automatics sold in the

USA for citizen self-defence. Such pistols are not intended for accuracy classes, but for last resort defence at close range. This may, indeed, be very practical shooting – in the USA, but it has no equivalent relevance to the UK. The same might have been said for a new 'pocket semi-automatic', the Taurus PT22 reviewed in *Guns and Shooting* in January 1995.

The reviewer began by outlining the context and market for the Taurus PT22. 'A lot of guns in the States are bought by people who would not normally consider themselves shooters. Most of these guns will see limited use and probably spend most of their time in bedside drawers in case something goes bump in the night. Their small size, light recoil and affordable price are important factors in their being chosen' (Milner, 1995: 66). Although the reviewer did not mention it, the gun was a 'Saturday Night Special' in all but name. If the Brazilian Parent company, Taurus, had not set up a production plant in Miami, the gun would almost certainly have fallen foul of the 1968 Gun Control Act's handgun importation restrictions. However, now manufactured in the USA, the gun could be legally sold in the USA. It could also be sold in the UK too, despite the fact that, as the reviewer himself conceded, the weapon's accuracy at twenty yards would be unlikely to prove attractive to shooters who wanted to hit the centre of a target. Clearly there really was no place for such a weapon in British shooting sports. As Milner concluded his review. 'It is a shame that there really is not much of a role for this pistol on the British shooting scene. Competitions for pocket pistols are scarce which is a pity as these little guns possess a lot of charm ... still, if you are looking for a fun gun contact ... your nearest dealer' (Milner, 1995: 68). In short, then, the PT22 is a highly concealable, charming, 'fun-gun' designed for the American self-defence market with no realistic place in the British shooting scene but sold in the UK only by reference to some unspecified 'potential' role in practical shooting contests which still had to be devised. On this basis, a more rigorous scrutiny – a 'genuine sporting purpose' test – might have led to the prohibition of a number of such weapons.

In this way, the discipline of 'practical shooting' provided something of a flag of convenience under which particular classes of weapons and more generic attitudes and discourses pertaining to firearms, deriving from the USA, were imported and became part of our own nascent gun culture. David Thomas, reviewing for *Handgunner* magazine, a book entitled *The 100 Greatest Ever Combat Pistols* (Mullin, 1994) implicitly acknowledged a similar point when he described the rationale of the book as, 'to provide pointers for those who find themselves with a strange pistol and a possible need to use it' (Thomas, 1995). One can only speculate on the relevance of such a rationale to handgun shooting in the UK – or, indeed, how such a reason might look on a firearm licence application. Later in his review, Thomas also considered the different criteria applied by military or police purchasers of handguns as compared with 'private citizens' or 'sporting shooters' when buying weapons. While no purchaser would want an 'unsafe' or 'unreliable' weapon, somewhat different considerations applied. There were trade-offs between efficiency, speed of use, accuracy, firepower and safety that would render certain guns more or less suitable for different purposes.

Waddington (1991), for instance, discusses at some length the differing considerations brought to bear concerning the selection of firearms (and ammunition) to be used by authorised firearms officers within the Metropolitan Police. In the case of the police, however, it was also apparent that factors other than those intrinsic to the weapon itself (such as public acceptability) were also a consideration. Thomas suggests that efficiency and reliability might be the primary considerations in a military specification handgun, whereas self-defence weapons might need to prioritise ease and speed of use – 'rapid first shot capability'. None of these factors, however, would be a priority for a sports target shooter, except, that is, one who participated in speed events or certain types of 'practical shooting'.

Given the differing characteristics of different weapons with a variety of trigger, firing, safety and reload mechanisms, it would have been entirely possible to attach a tighter 'shooting sports' weapon specification to the grant of a handgun licence. In the USA, although the attempt to outlaw certain types of military specification 'assault rifles' was much derided by the gun lobby there was a relatively clear legislative intention at work. In the years before 1996, the British government might have adopted a similar approach in seeking to restrict the types of (military specification) handguns available to British shooters. Since the Hungerford massacre in 1987, conscious of its public image, British shooting had begun to address the issue of its 'militaristic' overtones – ranges were forbidding 'combat-style' clothing and debates erupted about humanoid silhouette targets or concerning the 'aggressive' look of competitors openly carrying firearms in holsters at shooting events. Reflecting the shooting fraternity's new-found sensitivity to these issues, the National Pistol Association's chairman noted in 1994, 'a stubborn refusal to accept that our continuing enjoyment of our sport depends in part upon public opinion on the civilian use and ownership of firearms is dangerously naive' (Love, 1995: 65). Nevertheless, firearms manufacturers continued to advertise weapons in British gun magazines on the strength of successful military and combat service or contracts with police or military purchasers.

For instance, first among the claims made by Beretta when advertising their 92F 9 mm semi-automatic in *Handgunner* magazine during 1994, was the fact that it had been 'chosen as the official side-arm of the US military and for numerous military and police forces around the world'. The advertisement obviously neglected to mention that a Beretta semi-automatic was the weapon used by Michael Ryan to kill several of his victims in Hungerford in 1987. Similar issues pertain to the Colt 1911A1 .45, designed by Browning, by repute one of the best and most prolific semi-automatics ever made. Examined and customised, in 1995, by Rob Adam, for *Guns and Shooting*, the 1911A1 was described in the following terms: 'This was a military pistol, remember. ... Its job was to work when used as a last resort weapon, probably at short range, when covered in mud, sand and sweat. It was not originally destined to become a sporting handgun. We would see what we could do to change that' (Adam, 1994). Perhaps it would have been just as well if he had not bothered. It was a 'well-tuned competition model' Browning semi-automatic, chambered for 9 mm ammunition, that Thomas Hamilton used to kill all of his victims in Dunblane.

In December 1994, *Handgunner* carried an advertisement for the SIG/Sauer P228 semi-automatic. The headline on the advertisement was that the gun had recently been adopted in the USA by both the FBI and DEA. Key characteristics of the weapon, revealed following gruelling agency tests, were 'ruggedness, operational suitability, firepower, rapid first shot potential and a lightning magazine change'. Whether such characteristics were equally relevant to the sporting context of British shooting, was an issue that the advertisement rather overlooked. The features that make a handgun serviceable for regular operational use, easy to carry and swift to use, apparently 'work against pure accuracy' (*Pistol Supplement*, Summer 1994: 22). Law and Brookesmith agreed, the problem with .40 calibre semi-automatics was accuracy. 'They were hard hitters', a characteristic important only where the target – a criminal aggressor – needed to be 'hit hard' and 'put down', 'but lacked the pinpoint accuracy of 9 mm' (Law and Brookesmith, 1996: 158). Ayoob, the doyen of American combat shooting experts, went even further. His retrospective assessment of the .40 calibre semi-automatics makes clear that while power – 'stopping power' – was a vital factor in their adoption throughout American law enforcement circles from the late 1980s, target accuracy was considered rather lacking.

> In the ultimate arena, gunfight reports were coming in. ... Bad guys were going down, usually with no more than four solid hits and most of the time with a lot less than that. The bullets were opening up because [they were] designed to mushroom at subsonic velocities. ... [However] there is the problem of accuracy. ... It is the near universal observation of owners that the .40 S&W is simply not match accurate. One is likely to get three to four inch groups at 25 metres from the bench. This is mediocre at best, akin to what gun writers call 'acceptable combat accuracy'.
>
> (Ayoob, 1996: 28–32)

Likewise, although the Beretta (but not the SIG/Sauer) advertisement was careful to include 'safety' among the weapon's attributes, a still pertinent question remains (as in the USA) about the advertising and sale of military or police specification weapons in civilian markets. The issue is more complicated in the USA where, as Diaz has noted, manufacturers supply weapons to police and military buyers (often as virtual loss leaders) precisely in order to gain leverage in the much more lucrative civilian market (Diaz, 1999).

One does not have to probe 'practical shooting' too far to discover how closely the discipline was premised upon a 'combat-kill' philosophy or how directly the rules and scoring of the competitions actually promoted a number of characteristics contributing to enhanced weapon and ammunition lethality. For instance, practical shooting had major and minor divisions. In the major division the weapon calibre had to be at least .40 in. Competitors could shoot smaller calibre weapons (for example, 9 mm semi-automatics, easier to control because of reduced recoil) in the same contests. Provided they hit the target in the 'A zone' – the central area in the torso of a humanoid silhouette target – they scored the same points as persons firing a heavier calibre weapon. However, lower calibre shots outside the 'A zone' scored fewer points. Hence contestants were very unlikely to win a practical shooting competition shooting a lower calibre weapon – unless they were consistently more accurate (Sharman, 1995). The formulation of such rules clearly reflects ideas about the stopping power of different weapons. Nine millimetre semi-automatics were widely adopted by American military and police departments throughout the 1980s. However, stories of offenders hit by 9 mm rounds but continuing to fight dented the reputation of these weapons. This led to a process of the ratcheting-up of calibres and weapon lethality described by Diaz (Diaz, 1999; *Guns Review*, February 1995: 112). Although many shooting correspondents argue that 'shot placement' (accuracy) is the best guarantee of 'stopping' an opponent, the equation between higher calibre and greater lethality was imported wholesale into the rules of British practical shooting. The silhouette target's 'A zone' represents the location of vital body organs. Any shot in this area would be likely to prove fatal to a human being and would certainly 'stop' an opponent. Lower calibre hits in the less vital body areas were considered less likely to achieve this and so, in practical shooting, they scored less points.

Proper targets?

A final insight into the preoccupation with lethality and firepower in practical shooting might be gained from the debate about target types which developed in the shooting fraternity in the late 1980s and early 1990s. Stevenson, writing an opinion piece in *Guns and Shooting* in January 1995, condemned what he called the wave of political correctness which had led to the gradual transformation of the human silhouette target originally used in police and military training. In Stevenson's own words, 'the UIT Silhouette, in its original version, had hands and feet. By the time I was competing these had been amputated and the head made square … later in the 1970s they decapitated it, yielding a target that looked like a coffin lid. It was not that the UIT were necrophiliacs; they were cowards'. For Stevenson, such retreating, even in the face of a public opinion concerned about sports shooters using images of people as targets, was a betrayal of shooting and 'the escutcheon of a mentality that is fundamentally opposed to the shooting sports' (Stevenson, 1995a: 82). By comparison with other correspondents, however, even Stevenson's comments were fairly mild. If shooting had to deny its raison d'être and its honourable roots in combat, self-defence and hunting just to appease an uninformed public, they asked, was there much point in continuing? Shooting's appeal, they argued, lay in the physical and psychological challenges it imposed; the controlled aggression, the power and the responsibility to deploy it effectively. Remove these essential elements, they claimed, and shooters might as well swap their weapons for something altogether less harmful. In the heavily ironic words of one correspondent to *Guns and Shooting* in 1994:

When will you learn that you cannot ever appease the anti-shooters … following your arguments, why should we use nasty, dangerous firearms at all? We could all use laser guns or simulators as they have in amusement arcades. Of course, they wouldn't be shaped like guns, the media wouldn't approve. This would have its plus points though. No more long hours reloading ammunition or cleaning guns, instead we could collect and arrange flowers or something else equally limp wristed and non aggressive.

(Hartnell, 1994)

On the other side of the debate, were those who argued that unless the sport could show greater responsibility and pick up more participants and more sponsorship, shooting would continue to struggle. The key, many claimed, lay in wider public acceptability. However, they queried, 'how can we shoot at targets that are in the shape of human beings and then complain when people criticise us for being Rambos?' (Baxindale, 1994). Gun control campaigners posed similar questions during 1996, as they struggled to comprehend the motivations of shooters. By then, however, the entire debate about the shape of the targets had become rather academic. The shooting fraternity were embroiled in a losing struggle to retain anything to shoot at their targets with.

Even before Dunblane, therefore, despite a resurgence of interest in the combat, action and practical shooting disciplines, the British shooting sports were already facing something of a crisis. There were potentially serious divisions emerging on a number of issues and clearly contrasting schools of thought about the best way to take shooting forwards, to improve and popularise the sport, achieve greater sponsorship and reassure the public. Some within shooting were willing to make concessions in order to safeguard what they saw as the long-term interests of the sport. Others, suspicious of the government's underlying ambitions for the private ownership of firearms and highly critical of both the fees charged and the overall operation of the licensing and control systems, seemed prepared to fight tooth and nail to defend, on principle, existing British sports shooting.

As we have seen, however, a series of shooting disciplines were developing on the British sports shooting scene, which were increasingly difficult to defend within the traditional discourse of British sports shooting. They were modelled upon practical, military or combat-style, scenarios. The new shooting disciplines privileged types of guns and ammunition never designed for sports shooting and which lacked a traditional British sports shooting pedigree. They encouraged the adoption of American weapons (designed either for military use, law enforcement or civilian self-defence) and increasingly American orientations towards them. They incorporated the preoccupation with 'firepower' and lethality, which had lately been driving the American handgun market, into the structure of British shooting events and harbouring an aggressive 'kill' focus within aspects of the sport. Equally, the least compromising of British shooting's advocates always acknowledged that there was more to handgunning than just sport and often reminded their readers that the handgun was, after all, a combat weapon – designed to kill.

The new shooting disciplines tested the elasticity of the 'sporting purpose' crite-
rion at the heart of British firearms licensing. 'Practical shooting' had become
something of a 'Trojan Horse' as far as the UK's developing gun culture was
concerned. Inextricably linked with the importation of American firearms and
American discourses on firearms, there emerged a series of attitudes premised
upon the supposedly 'natural' relationship between man and firearm in an increasingly risky world. In the UK, the more ideologically militant of the pro-shooting
pressure groups and magazines, for example the Shooters' Rights Association and
Guns Review, have sought to advance a utilitarian case regarding the shooting sports
as a 'national asset' (Munday, 1988b: 121–122). From this argument are derived
both a military national interest in civilian marksmanship (based upon the Swiss or
Israeli models), a needs-based assessment of firearms for personal protection (the
police cannot be everywhere to protect everyone) and more generic claims
concerning civil liberties and democratic freedoms ('Cadmus', 1995a, 1995b).

In the thinking of the SRA and its supporters, such claims formed the basis
for a renewed British 'right to bear arms'. In 1988, the SRA proposed that
consideration be given to the 'deregulation' of firearms controls and adopted, in
all but name, the 'right to bear arms' as a campaign philosophy (Munday, 1988b:
132). The same line of argument could be found in Lyall's article, in *Target Gun*
magazine in April 1997, as the Firearms (Amendment) Act received its royal
assent. Why an article in *Target Gun* magazine should address itself to the citizen
self-defence issue is rather unclear. Shooting writers usually tried hard to confine
their comments to 'sporting firearms'. In Lyall's argument, however, such fine
distinctions had disappeared, although, by then, the game was up. Bitterly
condemning the 'criminal traitors who seek to destroy our national self-respect
and with it Britain's third line of defence', Lyall's words could have come straight
from the American NRA. 'In Britain', he argued, 'Police, Home Office establishment and the anti-gun, rent-a-mob would rather die than let people defend
themselves against criminal violence ... we are defenceless, but that's all part of
the 20th century death wish currently destroying our country' (Lyall, 1997: 25).

The same point was developed in the conclusion of a *Gun Review* article in
September 1995. The author rejected the collectivist and consensual notions that
there was any kind of social contract between the citizen and the state, whereby
the state guaranteed protection allowing citizens to surrender the means of
protecting themselves. 'In fact', it was argued,

> that has never been true, but even if there had been such a pact in the past,
> and evidence shows that both parties came to accept it in this country
> between the wars, the State has broken that pact. The State has lost all
> control. The citizen is not safe in his home or anywhere else for that matter.
> The right to keep arms for defence is now a necessity and the arguments
> must be addressed. ... It is now time to start exerting pressure on Parliament
> ... so that we may all sleep more soundly in our beds.
>
> ('Cadmus', 1995a: 670; 1995b: 751)

As Law and Brookesmith have argued, 'there is a pistol out there for everyone', a corollary being, perhaps, that anyone might need one. Their book, however, was published in 1996, a year in which even the most enthusiastic advocate of shooters' rights might have conceded that there ought to be some exceptions to this maxim. Indeed, Law and Brookesmith went even further, arguing the case for self-defence handguns in the UK, because 'the police cannot be everywhere to protect everyone' (Law and Brookesmith, 1996: 170). Shooters tried to depict the legislative response to Dunblane as the hysterical, uninformed scapegoating of a law-abiding and eminently responsible section of the community. The pro-control lobby and the Home Office were said to have seized upon the tragedy in order to do what they had always wanted: disarm the public. Yet the foregoing commentary does suggest that there was rather more to it. Different sections of the shooting fraternity were indeed pursuing different agendas. Some of these, evidently, had rather more than just sports shooting in mind. This much at least was implicit in Law and Brookesmith's eulogy for the 'fighting handgun'. Handguns, they argued, were essentially fighting weapons and should be available for self-defence purposes in the UK. It followed that the real function of target shooting was no more than training for the 'real thing', protecting our homes and families. The spectre of the 'gun culture' that many shooting commentators had tried long and hard to keep at arm's length was precisely Law and Brookesmith's solution for the UK's law and order problems (Law and Brookesmith, 1996).

Others, even if motivated primarily by an interest in target shooting, appeared unwilling to acknowledge their sport's lethal orientations and aggressive, even anti-social, combat philosophy. It may only have been a question of inanimate objects fired at inanimate targets, but the handgun had a very particular historical pedigree. It sat at the centre of an entire matrix of values, attitudes, discourses, ideologies and fears that, in the USA, comprised an entire 'gun culture'. Such issues did not always surface so explicitly in the UK but, beyond the direct legislative response to Dunblane, it would seem we abolished the handgun in order to help thwart the onset of this 'alien' gun culture.

In the USA, often described as a 'gun culture', a different perspective seems to prevail. There, gun culture is not understood as an attribute only of the weaponry itself but also, significantly, a tradition of the people, an aspect of history and ideology. Contemporary Britain has seen the gun as an external force to be regulated while the USA, awash with guns anyway, has sought to control the people in order to control the gun. American enforcement approaches, especially those backed by the pro-gun movements, prioritise tough sanctions against firearm offenders rather than gun control per se (LaPierre, 1994). In the UK, addressing the 'societal impact' of the gun – a collectivist principle – has prompted British gun control since the 1920s. Although to shooters this has been seen as a futile exercise in attacking symptoms rather than causes, we have generally believed (though with certain exceptions) that the less firearms in private hands, the better.

By contrast, an American view has argued, often quite explicitly, that, the more firearms in private hands, the better. It is frequently suggested of the USA, in complete seriousness, that an armed society is a polite society. Whether expressed this way, the claim is simply an exercise in non sequitur logic or just wishful thinking, it need not detain us long. Kleck has argued that, 'much of the social order in America may depend on the fact that millions of people are armed and dangerous to each other' (Kleck, 1991: 143) implying an essentially individualist foundation to the maintenance of law and order. Pro-gun American commentators argue that libertarian foundations create a more democratic and responsible citizenry. Training in the safe handling of guns encourages respect and self-discipline, they argue. A greater familiarity with weapons generates a greater confidence in them, removing the fear and mystique often surrounding them. In turn, it requires law-makers to concentrate upon the person, not the weapon. Firearm-related crime is therefore seen as a fault of the gun-owner, not the gun, a point relentlessly driven home by Gottlieb in his satirical book, *Politically Correct Guns* (Gottlieb, 1996). In this viewpoint, individual ownership of firearms is seen as a foundation of order. Firearm ownership promotes individual responsibility and the criminal law should deal with individual transgressors. On the other hand, those individuals not owning firearms are seen as free-loaders on the efforts of others, much in the same way that fare-dodgers or tax-avoiders are seen. They are not merely getting something for nothing but increasing the burden borne by others.

Sketched here only in outline, this pro-gun stance nevertheless embraces an entire ideological perspective resting upon the self-sufficient, armed individual. Where it begins to fall down, however, even on its own terms, is in respect of the collective costs borne by some individuals largely as a result of the widespread availability of firearms among criminally inclined persons. A key premise of the individualism which sustains the libertarian core of the pro-gun argument, much like the notion of the 'rational economic man' to which it is closely related, is that the responsibility of gun ownership promotes a disciplined citizenship. By contrast, the USA's million or so gun-related offences each year, imply that often it does not. Furthermore, the prevalence of gun-related crime in some of the USA's pluralistic and divided communities has major consequences for people's quality of life. Alba and Messner, in their review of Kleck's work conclude by asking:

> we wonder about the quality of life in the kind of society where routine social order depends upon the massive armament of the citizenry. ... What is the psychological effect on a community's residents of the knowledge that many guns are in its homes, on its streets, and even in its schools. These are the conditions in many inner-city, minority communities in the USA, and a great deal of persuasive personal testimony ... indicates that fear is the dominant emotion inspired by the pervasiveness of guns and gun crime.
>
> (Alba and Messner, 1995: 208–209)

Pro-gun commentators tend to retort by suggesting that, without so many guns in private hands, things could be much worse.

Unfortunately, resolving the complex dilemma of American gun control appears to depend upon learning the lessons of history and grappling with a number of seemingly irreconcilable 'truths' articulated by the rival camps in order to find some workable and politically feasible middle-ground options. Success is not ideological purity but a safer society. Handgun Control Inc., the USA's major gun control lobby organisation, no longer considers the prohibition of the private ownership of handguns among its objectives. Kopel, on the other hand, having argued that a gunfree USA is not possible, goes on to suggest that a serious effort has to be made to change gun culture for the better by encouraging social responsibility and civic virtue in gun ownership (Kopel, 1992a). But still there is much suspicion, dishonesty and distrust, with gun controllers questioning the very concept of responsible gun ownership and (perhaps because of that) gun owners seeing the thin end of a long wedge in every measure of control.

However, in the USA, a workable strategy that does not make the mistakes of earlier measures is sorely needed. There is little sense in passing tough sounding laws if they are not effectively enforced. Gun production, distribution and ownership must be considered together. There is little sense in having restrictive laws in one jurisdiction if neighbouring jurisdictions are more relaxed. Firearm buy-back programmes which work to the advantage of the gun trade by removing older weapons (thereby creating a demand for newer ones) probably need rethinking. Making legal purchase or ownership more difficult for 'law-abiding citizens' without addressing the problem of 'kitchen-table', private or 'black-market' sales may well be counter-productive. Generally, gun controls that appear ineffective undermine the credibility of other initiatives so progress in this field is necessarily cautious. Yet it must proceed in two directions at once. On the one hand, practical effect has to be given to the notion of 'responsible gun ownership', on the other, the collective public safety issues arising from widespread weapon availability need addressing.

Kleck has attempted to sketch the outlines of a workable gun control policy. His suggestions include: instantaneous national background records checks, tighter regulation of private firearm transfers, more rigorous disqualifications and more effective routine enforcement of gun carrying laws (Kleck, 1991, 1997). If the gun lobby's goal really is a more responsible gun ownership, it is difficult to see this as incompatible with national firearms licensing, a national firearms database and a national forensic database. Even so, the proposals fall a long way short of handgun prohibition. Nevertheless, Kleck acknowledges that unless the policies he suggests are accompanied by measures 'reducing the economic inequality, injustice and the social disorder these generate ... [and] ... improving the life chances of the underclass that contributes the bulk of both the victims and the perpetrators of violent crime', they might still only nibble at the edge of the USA's firearm violence problems (Kleck, 1997: 396). Despite their limitations, Kleck's suggestions do go some way beyond the gun lobby's simple advocacy for rigorous enforcement and tougher, mandatory, sentencing of firearm using offenders.

Having said that, the social measures to promote individual responsibility require complementing with public interventions to address the collective harms resulting from gun availability. Tighter regulation of gun production and marketing would seem a first step. Equally, firearms need to be incorporated within product safety legislation and, before a gun is made available on the civilian 'self-defence' market, efforts should be made to enhance its safety features. For instance, although designed to overcome problems relating to police use of firearms, the technology incorporated into so-called 'smart guns' might suggest a way forwards – but not without problems.

Around 10 per cent of American police officers killed or injured by firearms are shot with their own guns (taken from them by offenders). Accordingly the National Institute for Justice was testing a so-called 'smart gun', incorporating a micro-chip recognition system, which meant that the gun could only be fired by its owner. Unfortunately, any interest shown by weapons manufacturers in this development reflects not so much the requirements of law enforcement or public safety but, above all, the industry's assessment of such a weapon's market potential. Selling 'smart' self-defence handguns to vulnerable or fearful citizens which remain safe even in the wrong hands has some obvious attractions. The weapons cannot be fired by children if picked up in the home and cannot be turned against their owner. Nevertheless, others in the firearm industry are not so sure. The additional cost of the micro-chip technology within the gun is seen as a likely disincentive to most gun buyers. By the same token, the new guns have divided the gun control lobby, many of whom simply want less guns not more of them with additional safety features (Peterson, 1998).

Even so, designing in new safety features for civilian handguns might be one way of beginning to sever the links between military and law enforcement weapon specifications and civilian weapon types. Likewise, efforts to address the 'lethality spiral' in weapons and ammunition during the 1980s and early 1990s, described by Diaz (1999) might be pursued by the identification of acceptable weapon and ammunition types, calibres, magazine capacities and so on. This could also be a consideration in respect of the weapon types made available to law enforcement officers. Following a spate of school shootings in recent years, and a debate arising in the wake of the 'concealed-carry' issue, the idea of making schools 'gun-free zones' could be extended to other public or social amenities. American communities have variously restricted the consumption of alcohol in public places and have established 'smoke-free' zones, making it not unthinkable to extend the idea to firearms. On the other hand, measures to restrict the production, marketing, ownership – and therefore the availability – of firearms, would seem unlikely to succeed unless accompanied by measures to address the fears and concerns of those sections of the American public motivated, over recent decades, to purchase firearms for their own self-defence.

Measures such as those sketched above do not even begin to approach a goal of comprehensive firearms control but they might be a start. Perhaps for too long, the ideal of comprehensive gun control, confronted by an effective gun-rights lobby, has hindered the development of more incremental strategic gains. Instead the combatants in the debate have fought themselves to a standstill. In contrast, the measures identified above take the notion of a 'socially respon-

sible' gun culture and attempt to further underpin it with public policy interventions. To do so is to assert a 'societal' interest in restricting irresponsible
firearm production, advertising, distribution, exchange and ownership with a
view to promoting collective interests – safety, fear reduction, crime prevention,
diminishing fatality – if not in a gun free society, then at least in a more collectively responsible gun-owning one. It is inevitable that such a process will be
slow and will take a long time, it is equally inevitable that progress in such an
endeavour will bring gun law reformers into conflict with powerful vested interests. Not least among these will be the gun manufacturers themselves, and their
apologists in the variety of 'gun media' discussed by Diaz (1999) whose trans-
parently economic motives and relentless marketing strategies over recent
decades have been perhaps the foremost influence behind the entire 'gun question'.

Needless to say, it would not be the first time, that asserting a broader 'social'
or societal interest involved confronting the irresponsibility of short-term
economic interests (Titmuss, 1987). In this case, however, it also involves
confronting the entire host of social, psychological and cultural values and attitudes circulating around a commodity of almost unparalleled real and symbolic
significance. The gun is, always and everywhere, overloaded. Suitably armed and
with a smattering of libertarian ideology a man might consider himself
complete: individual and independent, a master of his own universe, beholding
to none and untrammelled by obligations to strangers. As author Tom Clancy
emphatically puts it in his Foreword to LaPierre's, *Guns, Crime and Freedom*,
'Having a gun today still gives the individual a degree of personal autonomy. ...
I submit that the actions of criminals and lunatics are irrelevant to my own right
to own and use firearms in pursuit of my own personal enjoyment, or in pursuit
of my legitimate right to self-defence' (Clancy, 1994). Paradoxically Clancy's
argument contrasts with the substance of NRA President, Charlton Heston's
speech, 'Truth and Consequences' to the Yale Political Union in 1999 (Heston,
1999b).

For Clancy, seemingly, the actions of others have no socially relevant consequences for us. Likewise, our individual rights have no bearing upon them. It
was, seemingly, entirely a question of us and them or, more accurately, each
against the world. And, in this 'war of all against all', Chris Bird's *Concealed
Handgun Manual* has a few handy hints to help you get through. Bird advocates a
colour-coded approach to street survival citizenship. In 'Condition Yellow' you
are alert to potential threats, in 'Condition Orange' you have identified a threat
and in 'Condition Red' your gun has to be coming up. Helpful to the last, Bird
imparts one final piece of advice:

> The color code ratchets up your readiness and willingness to shoot. Another
> approach that may help you pull the trigger on another human being is to
> dehumanize him. Think of your assailant as a target rather than as a
> person. ... When we go to war with another nation we try to dehumanize
> our enemy. We talked of 'Gooks' or 'Japs' in an attempt to make killing

them easier. It may help you to pull the trigger if you look on your attackers as 'trash' … or 'scumbags'.

(Bird, 1997: 172)

Clearly there is no such thing as society, after all. There is only me, and mine, and a whole bunch of 'scumbag' targets.

Bibliography

Abrams, F. (1997) 'Shooters to sue over gun ban', *Independent*, August 26th.

Adam, R. (1994) 'Project .45', *Guns and Shooting*, January: 26–28.

Alba, R.D. and Messner, S.F. (1995) '*Point Blank* against itself: evidence and inference about guns crime and gun control', *Journal of Quantitative Criminology*, 11 (4): 391–410.

Anderson, J. (1996) *Inside the NRA: Armed and Dangerous, An Expose*, Beverly Hills, CA, Dove Books.

Anthony, A. (1996) 'Hysteria repeats itself', *Observer*, March 17th.

Appleyard, B. (1996) 'Staring down the barrel of an American icon', *Independent*, May 30th.

Arlidge, J. (1996) 'Pro-gun plot to smear snowdrop', *Observer*, November 3rd.

Arlidge, J. and Travis, A. (1996) 'Ministers disown MPs who oppose handgun ban', *Guardian*, August 1st.

Armstrong, E.M. (1996) *Memorandum by the British Medical Association to the Home Affairs Select Committee on the Possession of Handguns*, HC 293, Volume 2, House of Commons.

Asmal, K. (1985) *Shoot to Kill: International Lawyer's Inquiry into the Lethal Use of Firearms by the Security Forces in Northern Ireland*, Dublin, Mercier Press.

Ayoob, M. (1996) 'The .40 S&W: six years on', *Handgunner*, 67, May/June: 22–33.

Bakal, C. (1966) *The Right to Bear Arms*, New York, McGraw-Hill.

Ball, G. (1996a) 'Dunblane drives toy guns out of Selfridges', *Independent On Sunday*, October 20th.

—— (1996b) 'Bang, bang, toy guns aren't dead', *Independent On Sunday*, October 28th.

Ball, J., Chester, L. and Perrott, R. (1978) *Cops & Robbers: An Investigation into Armed Bank Robbery*, London, André Deutsch.

Bar Association of New York (1982) *To Keep and Bear Arms*, Report of the Sub-Committee on the Constitution of the Committee on the Judiciary, US Senate, Washington, Government Printing Office.

Barker, P. (1996) 'Loner in our midst', *Guardian*, March 15th.

Barnett, R.E. (1995) 'Guns, militias and Oklahoma City', *Tenessee Law Review*, 63 (2).

Bauman, Z. (1989) *Modernity and the Holocaust*, Oxford, Polity Press.

—— (1993) *Postmodern Ethics*, Oxford, Blackwell.

Baxindale, T. (1994) 'Correspondence', *Guns and Shooting*, September: 86.

Beaumont, P. and Harrison, D. (1996) 'Outlaws will defy rules, warn gunmen', *Observer*, March 24th.

Beckley, A. (1995) 'Biting the bullet', *Police Review*, January 20th.

Behr, E. (1997) *Prohibition: The Thirteen Years That Changed America*, London, Penguin/BBC Books.

Benn, M. and Worpole, K. (1986) *Death in the City*, London, Canary Press.

Bennetto, J. (1994) 'Condon calls for laws that stop criminals getting guns', *Independent*, August 2nd.

—— (1996) 'Fears of a new gun culture beyond the law', *Independent*, March 14th.

Bigony, M-L. (1995) 'Ethical choices', *Texas Parks and Wildlife*, November: 48–53.

Bijlefeld, M. (ed.) (1997) *The Gun Control Debate: A Documentary History*, Westport, Greenwood Press.

Billacois, F. (1990) *The Duel: Its Rise and Fall in Early Modern France*, New Haven, Yale University Press.

Bird, C. (1997) *The Concealed Handgun Manual: How to Choose, Carry and Shoot a Gun in Self Defense*, San Antonio, TX, Privateer Publications.

Blackman, P.H. (1994) 'The federal factoid factory on firearms and violence', in Bijlefeld (1997): 136.

Blackstone, W. (1793) *Commentaries upon the Laws of England*, 4 Volumes, E. Christian (ed.), London.

Blumberg, A.S. (1973) *Law and Order: The Scales of Justice*, New Brunswick, Transaction Books.

Boggan, S. (1996) 'Massacre in class P1', *Independent*, March 14th.

Bonner, R. (1998) 'US, in a shift, backs UN move to curb illicit trade in guns', *New York Times*, April 25th.

Boseley, S. (1996) 'Ban guns say Dunblane parents', *Guardian*, July 10th.

Boseley, S. and White, M. (1996) 'Who licensed him to kill?', *Guardian*, March 15th.

Bottoms, A.E. (1990) 'Crime prevention facing the 1990s', *Policing and Society*, 1: 3–22.

Bowditch, G. (1995) 'Police buy firearms from underworld to reduce offences', *Times*, March 17th.

Boycott, O. (1996) 'The small but deadly .22 guns that will stay legal', *Guardian*, October 18th.

Bracewell, M. (1996) 'In the line of fire', *Men's Health*, 2 (3) April.

Bromhead, P. (1988) *Living in America*, London, Longman.

Brown, R.M. (1975) *Strain of Violence: Historical studies of American Violence and Vigilantism*, New York, Oxford University Press.

—— (1991) *No Duty to Retreat: Violence and Values in American History and Society*, Norman, University of Oklahoma Press.

—— (1994) 'Violence', in C.A. Milner *et al.* (eds) *The Oxford History of the American West*, Oxford, Oxford University Press.

Bruce, J.M. and Wilcox, C. (eds) (1998) *The Changing Politics of Gun Control*, New York, Rowman & Littlefield.

'Cadmus' (1994) 'The Firearms Amendment Bill 1994', *Guns Review*, 34 (8): 579.

—— (1995a) 'Arms for self-preservation and defence', *Guns Review*, 35 (9): 750–751.

—— (1995b) 'Arms for self-preservation and defence: part II', *Guns Review*, 35 (10): 668–670.

Campbell, B. (1992) *Goliath: Britain's Dangerous Places*, London, Methuen.

Campbell, D. (1996) 'Fantasies turn to awful reality', *Guardian*, March 14th.

—— (1999) 'Colt bites the bullet and stops production of handguns', *Guardian*, October 12th.

Campbell, D. and Travis, A. (1995) 'Top policemen resist rank and file call to arms', *Guardian*, April 20th.

Canada, G. (1995) *Fist, Stick, Knife, Gun*, Boston, Beacon Press.

Canadian Department of Justice (1995) *A Review of Firearms Statistics and Regulations in Selected Countries*, Department of Justice, Canada, April.

Capers, J. (1994) 'Act now and you can stop horror of New York happening here', *Sun*, April 14th.

Carter, G.L. (1997) *The Gun Control Movement*, New York, Twayne Publishers.

Carvel, J. (1996) 'A third of boys aged 15 "carry arms" ', *Guardian*, May 15th.

Castle, S. (1996) 'The parents, the government and the gun', *Independent on Sunday*, October 20th.

Cho, S.Y. (1994) 'Japanese firearms controls, in R.L. Nay (ed.) *Firearms Regulation: A Comparative Study of Selected Foreign Nations*, Report for Congress, Law Library of Congress, Washington DC.

Christie, N. (1993) *Crime Control as Industry*, London, Macmillan.

Clancy, T. (1994) 'Foreword' to LaPierre (1994).

Clarke, R.V. and Mayhew, P. (1988) 'The British Gas suicide story and its criminological implications', in M. Tonry and N. Morris (eds) *Crime and Justice: A Review of Research*, Volume 10, Chicago, University of Chicago Press.

Clouston, E. (1996) 'Gun club ignored Hamilton "evidence": 4th Day, Cullen Inquiry', *Guardian*, June 4th.

Coates, J. (1987) *Armed and Dangerous: The Rise of the Survivalist Right*, New York, Hill and Wang.

Cohen, D. (1994) 'On the way to school: Johannesburg', *The Observer, Life Magazine*, April 17th.

Cohen, N., Arlidge, J. and Wintour, P. (1996) 'An accomplished mission', *Observer*, October 20th.

Connell, R. (1995) *Masculinities*, Cambridge, Polity Press.

Cook, J. (1994) 'Gladiators and not gunmen', *Guns and Shooting*, February: 16.

Cook, P.J. (1981) 'The effect of gun availability on violent crime patterns', in P.J. Cook, (ed.) *Gun Control. The Annals of the American Academy of Political Science*, Thousand Oaks, CA, Sage, pp. 63–79.

Cook, P.J. and Blose, J. (1981) 'State programs for screening handgun buyers', in Cook (1981): 80–91.

Cooper, J. (1989) *Principles of Personal Defence*, Boulder, CO, Paladin Press.

Corkery, M. (1994) *The Theft of Firearms*, London, Home Office.

Cottrol, R.J. and Diamond, R.T. (1995) 'The Second Amendment: towards an Afro-Americanist reconsideration', in Kopel (1995).

Courtwright, D.T. (1996) *Violent Land: Single Men and Social Disorder from the Frontier to the Inner City*, Cambridge, MA, Harvard University Press.

Craig, O., Shields, J. and Grey, S. (1996) 'A victory for sense and sensibility', *Sunday Times*, October 20th.

Cramer, C.E. (1994) *For the Defense of Themselves and the State: The Original Intent and Judicial Interpretation of the Right to Keep and Bear Arms*, Westport, CT, Praeger Publishers.

Crawford, S. and Lowrie, H. (1996) 'Shame on the lot of you. Outrage of parents as Tories snub ban on guns', *Sun*, July 31st.

Cress, L.D. (1984) 'An armed community: the origins and meaning of the right to bear arms', *Journal of American History*, 71 (1): 22–42.

Critchley, T.A. (1970) *The Conquest of Violence*, London, Constable.

Crossley, B. (1999) 'Firearms control and the role of customs', unpublished paper presented to a Conference on Gun Control, Scarman Centre, Leicester University, February.

Cullen, Lord W.D. (1996) *The Public Inquiry into the Circumstances Leading up to and Surrounding the Events at Dunblane Primary School on Wednesday 13th March 1996*, The Scottish Office, Cm. 3386, HMSO.

Cumberbatch, G. and Howitt, D. (1989) *A Measure of Uncertainty: The Effects of the Mass Media*, London, John Libby Publisher.

Cunningham, H. (1975) *The Volunteer Force: A Social and Political History 1859–1908*, Hamden, CT, Archon Books.

Currie, E. (1996) 'Is America really winning the war on crime and should Britain follow its example?', NACRO, 30th Anniversary Lecture, London, NACRO.

—— (1997) 'Market, crime and community: toward a mid-range theory of post-industrial violence', *Theoretical Criminology*, 1 (2).

Customs and Excise (1997) *Annual Report: The Protection of Society*, London, HMSO.

Darbyshire, N. (1994) 'Angry gun trade challenges police over crime claim', *Daily Telegraph*, August 3rd.

Davidson, B.R. (1969) *To Keep and Bear Arms*, New York, Arlington House.

Davidson, O.G. (1993) *Under Fire: The NRA and the Battle for Gun Control*, New York, Holt.

Davis, M. (1991) *City of Quartz: Excavating the Future in Los Angeles*, London, Verso.

Davis, M. and El Nasser (1994) 'New ammo for the gun debate', *USA Today*, December 28th.

Davison, J. (1997) *Gangsta: The Sinister Spread of Yardie Gun Culture*, London, Vision Paperbacks.

Defensor, H.C. (1970) *Gun Registration Now – Confiscation Later*, New York, Vantage Press.

Delbruck, H. (1990) *The Dawn of Modern Warfare*, London, Bison Books and University of Nebraska Press.

Deutsch, S.J. and Alt, F.B. (1977) 'The effect of Massachusetts' gun control law on gun related crimes in the city of Boston', *Evaluation Quarterly*, 1 (4): 543–568.

DeZee, M.R. (1978) 'Gun control and federal legislation', in J.A. Inciardi and A.E. Pottiger (eds) *Violence and American History*, London, Sage.

Diaz, T. (1999) *Making a Killing: The Business of Guns in America*, New York, The New Press.

Drinan, R.F. (1990) 'The good outweighs the evil', in L. Nisbet (ed.) *The Gun Control Debate*, New York, Prometheus Books.

Duclos, D. (1997) *The Werewolf Complex: America's Fascination with Violence*, Oxford, Oxford International Publishers.

DuRant, R.H. *et al.* (1995) 'The association between weapon carrying and the use of violence among adolescents living in or around public housing', *Journal of Adolescence*, 18 (5).

Eastman, N. (1996) 'Mad, bad and impossible to know', *Guardian*, March 14th.

Edel, W. (1995) *Gun Control: Threat to Liberty or Defense Against Anarchy?*, Westport, CT, Praeger Press.

Edwards, C. (1988) 'Was Hungerford a basic failure of the police?', *The Listener*, January 14th.

Ehrman, K.A. and Henigan, D.A. (1989) 'The Second Amendment in the twentieth century: have you seen your militia lately?', *University of Dayton Law Review*, 15: 5–58.

Einstadter, W.J. (1978) 'Robbery-outlawry on the US frontier, 1863–1890: a re-examination', in J. Inciardi and A. Pottiger (eds) *Violence and American History*, New York, Sage.

Elias, N. (1982) *State Formation and Civilisation: The Civilising Process*, Volume 2, Oxford, Blackwell.

Elliot, C. (1996) 'Guns aim abroad', *Guardian*, November 23rd.

Ellis, J. (1976) *The Social History of the Machine Gun*, London, Croom-Helm.

Ellis, W. and Foster, H. (1994) 'Mean streets', *Sunday Times*, February 13th.

Ellison, M. (1999) 'The massacre that challenges America's love affair with the gun', *Guardian*, April 22nd.

Emery, L.A. (1915) 'The constitutional right to keep and bear Arms', *Harvard Law Review*, 28: 473–477.

Fagan, J. (1996) 'Gangs, drugs and neighbourhood change', in Huff (1996a).

Farrell, M. (1983) *Arming the Protestants*, London, Pluto Press.

Feller, P.B. and Gotting, K.L. (1966) 'The Second Amendment: a second look', *Northwestern University Law Review*, 61, March–April: 46–70.

Ferguson, E., Harrison, D. and McKay, R. (1996) 'Dunblane: a story that need never have been told', *Observer*, March 17th.

Firearms Tactical Institute (1998) 'Wound ballistics', Firearms Tactical Institute Website, <http://www.firearmstactical.com/wound.htm>

Flynn, K. and Gerhardt, G. (1989) *The Silent Brotherhood: Inside America's Racist Underground*, New York, The Free Press.

Foucault, M. (1977) *Discipline and Punish: The Birth of the Prison*, London, Allen Lane.

Freedland, J. (1994) 'Adolf's US army', *Guardian*, December 15th.

—— (1995a) 'Guns, plots and warlike poses', *Guardian*, May 6th.

—— (1995b) 'Right in disarray as Bush quits gun lobby', *Guardian*, May 12th.

—— (1996) 'Siege at the little house on the prairie', *Guardian*, April 22nd.

Freedman, W. (1989) *The Privilege to Keep and Bear Arms: The Second Amendment and its interpretation*, New York, Quorum Books.

Fry, C. (1989) 'Dangerous imitations', *Police Review*, September 29th.

—— (1991) 'Real or replica: do you shoot first?', *Police Review*, September 13th.

Furedi, F. (1997) *Culture of Fear: Risk-Taking and the Morality of Low Expectation*, London, Cassell.

Gallagher, P. (1996) 'It's so easy to be a gun man', *Daily Express*, March 22nd.

Gardiner, R. (1982) 'To preserve liberty – a look at the right to keep and bear arms', in the Second Amendment Symposium: Rights in Conflict in the 1980s, *Northern Kentucky Law Review*, 10 (1).

GCN (Gun Control Network) Leaflet (1996) 'Working towards a gun-free environment', PO Box 11495, London.

Gerrard, N. (1996) 'We are the law', *The Observer*, January 7th.

Gibson, J.W. (1994) *Warrior Dreams: Violence and Manhood in Post-Vietnam America*, New York, Hill and Wang.

Giddens, A. (1981) *A Contemporary Critique of Historical Materialism*, London, Macmillan.

Gilmour, I. (1992) *Riot, Risings and Revolution: Governance and Violence in Eighteenth Century England*, London, Hutchinson.

Gingrich, N. (1995) *To Renew America*, New York, Harper Collins.

Glendon, M.A. (1991) *Rights Talk: The Impoverishment of Political Discourse*, New York, Free Press.

Godwin, M. and Schroedel, J. (1998) 'Gun control politics in California', in Bruce and Wilcox (1998).

Gottlieb, A. (1986) *The Gun Grabbers*, Bellevue, Washington, Merril Press.

—— (1996) *Politically Correct Guns*, Bellevue, Washington, Merril Press.

Gould, R.W. and Waldren, M.J. (1986) *London's Armed Police*, London, Arms & Armour Press.

Gramsci, A. (1971) 'Americanism and Fordism', in *Selections from the Prison Notebooks*, London, Lawrence & Wishart.

Green, G.S. (1987) 'Citizen gun ownership and criminal deterrence: theory, research and policy', *Criminology*, 25 (1): 65–81.

Greenwood, C. (1972) *Firearms Control: A Study of Armed Crime and Firearms Control in England and Wales*, London, Routledge & Kegan Paul.

—— (1996) 'Memorandum of evidence, Appendix 21 in Volume II of the House of Commons: Home Affairs Committee', *The Possession of Handguns*, Minutes of Evidence, HMSO, HC 393-II.

Grey, S. and Burke, J. (1996) 'Gun lobby smears Dunblane father', *Sunday Times*, September 8th.

Grey, S., Craig, O. and Shields, J. (1996) 'Police press for shotgun control', *Sunday Times*, October 20th.

Haight, G.I. (1941) 'The right to keep and bear arms', *Bill of Rights Review*, Fall: 31–42.

Halbrook, S.P. (1982) 'To keep and bear their private arms: the adoption of the Second Amendment 1787–1791', *Northern Kentucky Law Review*, 10 (1).

—— (1984) *That Every Man be Armed: The Evolution of a Constitutional Right and Social Philosophy*, University of New Mexico Press.

—— (1989) *A Right to bear Arms: State and Federal Bills of Rights and Constitutional Guarantees*, New York, Greenwood Press.

—— (1994) 'The right of the people or the power of the state: bearing arms, arming militias and the Second Amendment', *Journal on Firearms and Public Policy*, Second Amendment Foundation, 6, Fall: 69–163.

Hall, A. (1994) 'Dirty Harriet', *Daily Mirror*, February 8th.

Hall, S. (1997) 'Visceral cultures and criminal practices', *Theoretical Criminology*, 1 (4).

Hallowes, M. (1999) 'Developing a dynamic approach to firearms intelligence', unpublished paper presented to a Conference on Gun Control, Scarman Centre, Leicester University, February.

Handgun Control Inc. (1999) *Carrying Concealed Weapons: Questions and Answers*, HCI Website <http://www.handguncontrol.org/gunlaw> June 1999.

Hardie, A and Deerin, C. (1996) 'Why does anyone need guns at home?', *Daily Mail*, May 31st.

Harding, R. (1979) 'Firearms use in crime', *Criminal Law Review*: 765–774.

Harris, R. (1968) 'If you love your guns', *The New Yorker*, April 20th.

Hartnell, M. (1994) 'Correspondence', *Guns and Shooting*, October: 86.

Haswell, J. (1973) *Citizen Armies*, London, Cox & Wyman.

Hay, D. (1975) 'Poaching and the game laws on Cannock Chase', in D. Hay *et al.* (eds) *Albion's Fatal Tree: Crime and Society in Eighteenth Century England*, Harmondsworth, Penguin.

Hayek, F. (1976) *The Mirage of Social Justice*, London, Routledge.

Hays, S.R. (1960) 'The right to bear arms, a study of judicial misinterpretation', *William and Mary Law Review*, 2 (2): 381–406.

Heard, B.J. (1997) *Handbook of Firearms and Ballistics: Examining and Interpreting Forensic Evidence*, New York, Wiley.

Hellman, J. (1986) *American Myth and the Legacy of Vietnam*, Columbia, Columbia University Press.

Helmer, W.J. (1970) *The Gun that Made the Twenties Roar*, New York, Macmillan.

Hemenway, D., Solnick, S.J. and Azrael, D.R. (1995) 'Firearms and community feelings of safety', *Journal of Criminal Law and Criminology*, 86 (1).

Henigan, D.A. (1989) 'The right to be armed: a constitutional illusion', *San Francisco Barrister*, December: 11–14.

Heston, C. (1999a) *Closing Remarks to Members*, NRA Annual Convention, Denver, Colorado. NRA Website <http//:nrahq.com/transcripts/denver/>

—— (1999b) *Truth and Consequences: Speech to the Yale Political Union*, NRA Website <http://nrahq.com/transcripts/yale.html/>

Hibbs, J. (1996) 'Minister insists handgun ban is in prospect', *Daily Telegraph*, August 14th.

Hill, C. (1997) 'Guns are the tools by which we forge our liberty', reprinted in J.E. Dizard, *et al.* (1999) *Guns in America*, New York, New York University Press.

Hillyard, P. and Percy-Smith, J. (1988) *The Coercive State: The Decline of Democracy in Britain*, London, Fontana/Collins.

Hitchens, P. (1994) 'Lessons from the land where law grows from the barrel of a gun', *Daily Express*, May 18th.

HMIC (1993) (Her Majesty's Inspectorate of Constabulary) *Report into the Administration of the Firearm Licensing System*, Home Office, November.

Hoare, M. (1980) 'The pattern of experience in the use of firearms by criminals and the police response', unpublished MA thesis, Cranfield Institute of Technology.

Hofstadter, R. (1970) 'America as a gun culture', *American Heritage*, 21 (6).

Home Office (1934) *Report of the Departmental Committee on the Statutary Definition and Classification of Firearms and their Ammunition* (The Bodkin Report), Cmnd. 4758, London, HMSO.

—— (1973) 'Green Paper: *The Control of Firearms in Great Britain: A Consultative Document*', Cmnd. 5297, London, HMSO.

—— (1986) *Report by the Home Office Working Group on the Police Use of Firearms*, London, HMSO.

—— (1987) *Firearms Act 1968: Proposals for Reform*, London, HMSO.

—— (1989) *Firearms Law: Specifications for the Adaptation of Shot Gun Magazines and the De-activation of Firearms*, London, HMSO.

—— (1996) *Criminal Statistics*, London HMSO.

Home Office, Research and Statistics Directorate (1996) 'Annex G: gun availability and violent crime: research evidence', Appendix 21 in Volume II of the House of Commons: Home Affairs Committee, *The Possession of Handguns*, Minutes of Evidence, HMSO. HC 393-II. Also reprinted in Munday and Stevenson (1996).

Hopkins, N. (1999) 'Turf wars', *Guardian G2*, July 8: 2–3.

Hornberger, J.G. and Ebeling, R.M. (eds) (1997) *The Tyranny of Gun Control*, Future of Freedom Foundation, Fairfax, Virginia.

House of Commons: Home Affairs Committee (1994) *Video Violence and Young Offenders*, Fourth Report, Session 1993–1994, HOC 514, London, HMSO.

—— (1996) *Fifth Report: The Possession of Handguns*, Volume I, Report and Proceedings, Volume II, Minutes of Evidence, HMSO, HC 393-I/II.

House of Commons Debates: Hansard (1996) *The Debate on the Firearms (Amendment) Bill*, HMSO, November 18th.

Huff, G.R. (1996a) *Gangs in America*, 2nd edn, London, Sage.

—— (1996b) 'The criminal behaviour of gang members and nongang at-risk youth', in Huff (1996a).

Hughes, D. (1996) 'Almost every handgun will be banned', *Daily Mail*, October 16th.

Hunt, A. (1996) 'Postmodernism and critical criminology', in J. Muncie, E. McLaughlin and M. Langan, *Criminological Perspectives*, London, Sage.

Ingleton, R. (1997) *Arming the British Police: The Great Debate*, London, Frank Cass & Co.

Jackson, T. (1988) *Legitimate Pursuit: The Case for the Sporting Gun*, Southampton, Ashford Press.

Jefferson, T. (1990) *The Case Against Paramilitary Policing*, Milton Keynes, Open University Press.

Jefferys, D. (1994) 'Shoot to kill', *Independent*, November 21st.

Jenkins, S. (1994) 'Gun law in the firing line', *The Times*, May 18th.

Jennings, A. (1990) 'Shoot to kill: the final courts of justice', in A. Jennings (ed.) *Justice Under Fire: The Abuse of Civil Liberties in Northern Ireland*, London, Pluto Press.

Jones, E.D. (1981) 'The District of Columbia's "Firearms Control Regulations Act of 1975": the toughest handgun control law in the United States – or is it?', in Cook (1981): 138–149.

Joseph, K. and Sumption, J. (1979) *Equality*, London, John Murray.

Josephs, J. (1993) *Hungerford: One Man's Massacre*, London, Smith Gryphon Publishers.

Kaplan, J. (1981) 'The wisdom of gun prohibition', in Cook (1981): 11–23.

Karlson, T. and Hargarten, S. (1997) *Reducing Firearm Injury and Death: A Public Health Sourcebook*, New Brunswick, Rutgers University Press.

Kates, D. (1983) 'Handgun prohibition and the original meaning of the Second Amendment', *Michigan Law Review*, 82 (2): 204–273.

—— (1984) 'Handgun banning in the light of the prohibition experience', in Kates and Kaplan (1984).

—— (1986) (ed.) 'Gun control', Special edition of *Law and Contemporary Problems*, 49 (1).

Kates, D. and Kaplan, J. (ed.) (1984) *Firearms and Violence: Issues of Public Policy*, Pacific Institute for Public Policy Research, Cambridge, MA, Ballinger Publishing.

Kates, D., Schaffer, H.E., Lattimer, J.K., Murray, G.B. and Cassem, E.H. (1995) 'Bad medicine: doctors and guns', in Kopel (1995).

Katz, I. (1996) 'Subway vigilante prepares for his next showdown', *Guardian*, April 8th.

Kavanagh, D. and Morris, P. (1989) *Consensus Politics from Attlee to Thatcher*, Oxford, Blackwell.

Keegan, J. (1993) *A History of Warfare*, London, Hutchinson.

Kellerman, A.L. and Reay, D.T. (1986) 'Protection or peril', *New England Journal of Medicine*, 314 (24).

Kellerman, A.L. *et al.* (1993) 'Gun ownership as a risk factor for homicide in the home', *New England Journal of Medicine*, Volume 329, October.

Kennett, L. and Anderson, J.L. (1975) *The Gun in America: The Origins of a National Dilemma*, London, Greenwood Press.

Kiernan, V. (1967) 'Foreign mercenaries and absolute monarchy', in Aston (ed.) *Crisis in Europe: 1560–1660*, New York, Anchor Books.

—— (1988) *The Duel in European History*, Oxford, Oxford University Press.

Killias, M. (1989) 'Gun ownership and violent crime: the Swiss experience in international perspective', *Security Journal*, 1 (3): 169–174.

—— (1993) 'Gun ownership, suicide and homicide: an international perspective', in A. del Frate, U. Zvekic and J.J. van Dijk (eds) *Understanding Crime and Experiences of Crime and Crime Control*, Rome, UNICRI Publication No. 49.

Kingdon, J. (1995) *Agendas, Alternatives and Public Policies*, 2nd edn, New York, Harper Collins.

Kleck, G. (1984) 'Handgun-only gun control: a policy disaster in the making', in Kates and Kaplan (1984).

—— (1986) 'Policy lessons from recent gun control research', in Kates (1986).

—— (1988) 'Crime control through the private use of armed force', *Social Problems*, 35 (1): 1–21.

—— (1991) *Point Blank: Guns and Violence in America*, New York, Aldine De Gruyter.

—— (1995) 'Using speculation to meet evidence: reply to Alba and Messner', *Journal of Quantitative Criminology*, 11 (4): 411–424.

—— (1997) *Targeting Guns: Firearms and their Control*, New York, Aldine De Gruyter.

Kleck, G. and Bordua, D.J. (1983) 'The factual foundations for certain key assumptions of gun control', *Law and Policy Quarterly*, 5: 271–298.

Koop, C.E. and Lundberg, G.D. (1992) 'Violence in America: a public health emergency', *Journal of the American Medical Association*, June 10th: 3,075–3,076.

Kopel, D. (1992a) *The Samurai, the Mountie and the Cowboy: Should America Adopt the Gun Controls of Other Democracies?*, New York, Prometheus Books.

—— (1992b) *Gun Control in Great Britain: Saving Lives or Constricting Liberty*, Chicago, Office of International Criminal Justice, University of Illinois Press.

—— (1995a) *Guns: Who Should Have Them*, New York, Prometheus Books.

—— (1995b) 'Background checks and waiting periods', in Kopel (1995a).

—— (1995c) 'Assault weapons', in Kopel (1995a).

Labour Party (1996) *Control of Guns: The Labour Party's Evidence to the Cullen Inquiry*, May 1996, London.

Landale, J. (1996) 'Tory committee members defend decision on guns', *Times*, August 14th.

Landale, J. and Bowditch, G. (1996) 'Blair calls for tougher laws on the issue of gun licences', *Times*, March 20th.

LaPierre, W. (1994) *Guns, Crime and Freedom*, New York, HarperPerennial.

Larson, E. (1994) *Lethal Passage: How the Travels of a Single Handgun Expose the Roots of America's Gun Crisis*, New York, Crown Publishers.

Law, R. and Brookesmith, P. (1996) *The Fighting Handgun: An illustrated History*, London, Arms & Armour Press.

Lawrence, I. (1996) 'Why I said "no" to a ban on handguns', *Daily Telegraph*, August 14th.

Leff, C.S. and Leff, M.H. (1981) 'The politics of ineffectiveness: federal firearms legislation, 1919–1938', in Cook (1981): 48–62.

Lentz, K.M. (1993) 'The popular pleasures of female revenge (or, Rage bursting in a blaze of gunfire)', *Cultural Studies*, 7 (3): 374–405.

Leppard, D. (1994a) 'Police set to use machine guns to fight UK crime', *Sunday Times*, May 15th.

—— (1994b) 'Who agreed to armed police?', *Sunday Times*, June 26th.

Letwin, O. (1983) *Against Equality*, London, Macmillan.

Levin, J. and Fox, J.A. (1985) *Mass Murder: America's Growing Problem*, New York, Plenum Press.

Levinson, S. (1989) 'The embarrassing Second Amendment', *The Yale Law Journal*, 99: 637–659.

Little, C.B. and Sheffield, C.P. (1983) 'Frontiers and criminal justice: English private prosecution societies and American vigilantism in the 18th and 19th centuries', *American Sociological Review*, December, 48: 796–808.

Lizotte, A. and Zatz, M.S. (1986) 'The use and abuse of sentence enhancement for firearms offences in California', in Kates (1986).

Loftin, C. and McDowall, D. (1981) '"One with a gun gets you two": mandatory sentencing and firearms violence in Detroit', in Cook (1981): 150–167.

Lott, J.R. (1998) *More Guns, Less Crime: Understanding Crime and Gun Control Laws*, Chicago, University of Chicago Press.

Love, H.G.M. (1995) 'National Pistol Association News', *Handgunner*, 66, December/January.

Lyall, W. (1997) 'To make the world a safer place – but for whom?', *Target Gun*, April: 25.

MacAskill, E. and Smithers, R. (1996) 'MP slated for Dunblane remarks', *Guardian*, October 18th.

Macauly, T. (1850) *Critical and Historical Essays*, Leipzig, The Edinburgh Review.

McCaghy, C.H. and Cernkovitch, S.A. (1987) *Crime in American Society*, 2nd edn, New York, Macmillan.

McClain, P.D. (1984) 'Prohibiting the "Saturday Night Special": a feasible policy option?', in Kates and Kaplan (1984).

McDowall, D. and Loftin, C. (1983) 'Collective security and the demand for legal handguns', *American Journal of Sociology*, 88 (6): 1,146–1,161.

McDowall, D., Wiersma, B. and Loftin, C. (1989) 'Did mandatory firearm ownership in Kennesaw really prevent burglaries?', *Sociology and Social Research*, 74 (1): 48–51.

McDowell, D. and Wiersma, B. (1994) 'The incidence of defensive firearm use by U.S. crime victims, 1987 through 1990', *American Journal of Public Health*, 84, December: 1,982–1,984.

McKenzie, I. (1996) 'Violent encounters: force and deadly force in British policing', in F. Leishman, B. Loveday and S. Savage (eds) *Core Issues in Policing*, Harlow, Longman.

McSmith, A. (1994) 'Deadly weapons slip through legal loophole', *Observer*, June 19th.

McVeigh, T. (1999) 'Toy guns create violent adults', *Observer*, November 21st.Macaulay, T. (1850) *Critical and Historical Essays*, Leipzig, The Edinburgh Review.

Mainwaring-White, S. (1983) *The Policing Revolution*, Brighton, Harvester.

Malcolm, J.L. (1994) *To Keep and Bear Arms: The Evolution of an Anglo-American Right*, Cambridge, MA, Harvard University Press.

Mann, M. (1986) *The Sources of Social Power*, Volume 1, Cambridge, Cambridge University Press.

Mannheim, H. (1941) *War and Crime*, London, Watts & Company.

Margue, T.L. (1999) 'The EU and the international perspective in the fight against trafficking in firearms', paper presented to a Conference on Gun Control, Scarman Centre, Leicester University, February.

Martinek, W.L., Meier, K.J. and Keiser, L.R. (1998) 'Jackboots or lace panties? The Bureau of Alcohol, Tobacco and Firearms', in Bruce and Wilcox (1998).

Mason, G. (1988) 'When communications fail: the HMI's report on the lessons of Hungerford', *Police Review*, August 5th.

Matthews, R. (1996) *Armed Robbery: Two Police Responses*, Home Office, Police Research Group, Crime Detection and Prevention Series, paper 78.

Mawby, R. and Walklate, S. (1994) *Critical Victimology*, London, Sage.

Maybanks, A. (1992) 'Firearms controls: an examination of the effects of present legislation and the provenance of firearms used in armed robberies in the Metropolitan Police District', unpublished MA dissertation, University of Exeter.

Maybanks, A. and Yardley, M. (1992) 'Controls are not bullet-proof', *Police Review*, September 25th.

Mayhew, P. (1996) 'Comments on the research note in the Government evidence, Home Office Research and Statistics Directorate', in Munday and Stevenson (1996).

Mellor, D. (1996) 'No guns in the house', *Guardian*, October 14th.

Mestrovic, S. (1993) *The Barbarian Temperament*, London, Routledge.

Mihill, C. (1996) 'Gun licence tests "are pointless" ', *Guardian*, May 3rd.

Millar, S. (1996) 'Gun group says curbs are "Nazi" ', *Guardian*, October 24th.

Miller, B.R. (1975) 'The legal basis for firearms controls', *Report to the American Bar Association*, New York.

Miller, J.G. (1996) *Search and Destroy: African-American Males in the Criminal Justice System*, Cambridge, Cambridge University Press.

Mills, H. and Arlidge, J. (1996) 'Labour pledges gun ban after Tory ruse backfires', *Observer*, August 4th.

Millward, D. (1994) 'Hungerford massacre led to quick change in the law', *Daily Telegraph*, August 3rd.

Milner, N. (1995) 'Blow back baby: the Taurus PT22', *Guns and Shooting*, January: 66–68.

Moore, M.H. (1981) 'Keeping handguns from criminal offenders', in Cook (1981): 92–109.

Moore, J. and Kay, J. (1996) 'More Brits now want to carry a firearm', *Sun*, March 14th.

Moore, P. (1994) 'Packin' iron', *Guns and Shooting*, November: 16–17.

—— (1995) 'Wasted opportunity: editorial', *Guns and Shooting*, February: 6.

Moore, S. (1993) 'They shoot tourists don't they?', *Guardian*, September 17th.

—— (1996) 'A tragedy in our midst', *Guardian*, March 14th.

Morris, N. and Hawkins, G. (1970) *The Honest Politician's Guide to Crime Control*, Chicago, University of Chicago Press.

Morris, T. (1989) *Crime and Criminal Justice in Britain Since 1945*, Oxford, Blackwell.

Morrison, S. and O'Donnell, I. (1994) 'Armed robbery: a study in London', occasional paper number 15, Oxford, Centre for Criminological Research.

—— (1997) 'Armed and dangerous? The use of firearms in robbery', *Howard Journal of Criminal Justice*, 36 (3).

Morrison, W. (1995) *Theoretical Criminology: From Modernity to Post-Modernism*, London, Cavendish.

Muir, K. (1992) *Arms and the Woman*, London, Coronet Books.

Mullin, C. (1996) 'Gun lobby on the run', *Guardian*, August 14th.

Mullin, D. (1994) *The 100 Greatest Ever Combat Pistols*, Boulder, CO, Paladin Press.

Mullin, J. (1996) 'The hit', *Guardian*, March 7th.

Munday, R. (1988a) 'The right to bear arms', in Yardley and Stevenson (1988).

—— (1988b) 'The civilian use of military firearms', in Yardley and Stevenson (1988).

—— (1996a) *Most Armed and Most Free*, Brightlingsea, Essex, Piedmont Publishing.

—— (1996b) 'Does the level of firearms ownership affect levels of violence? An appraisal of the evidence', in Munday and Stevenson (1996).

Munday, R.A. and Stevenson, J. (eds) (1996) *Guns and Violence: The Debate Before Lord Cullen*, Brightlingsea, Essex, Piedmont Publishing.

Mungo, P. (1996) 'A power in the land', *Guardian Weekend*, June 1st.

Murray, D.R. (1975) 'Handguns, gun control laws and firearm violence', *Social Problems*, 23 (91): 81–93.

Nash, T. and Weston, K. (1992) 'Fatal flaw', *Police Review*, May 22nd.

National Audit Office (1999) *Home Office: Handgun Surrender and Compensation*, House of Commons HC 225, Session 1998/99, London, HMSO.

National Commission on the Causes and Prevention of Violence (1969) *To Establish Justice, To Insure Domestic Tranquillity*, Washington, US Government Printing Office.

Nay, R.L. (1994) *Firearms Regulation: A Comparative Study of Selected Foreign Nations*, Report for Congress, Law Library of Congress, Washington DC.

Naylor, R.T. (1995) 'Loose cannons: covert commerce and underground finance in the modern arms black market', *Crime, Law and Social Change*, 22: 1–57.

Nelson, Z. (1999) 'Gun nation', *Observer Magazine*, June 6th.

Newark, P. (1989) *Firefight: The History of Personal Firepower*, Newton Abbot, David & Charles.

Newsinger, J. (1997) *Dangerous Men: The SAS and Popular Culture*, London, Pluto Press.

Newton, G.D. and Zimring, F.E. (1968) *Firearms and Violence in American Life. A Staff Report to the National Commission on the Causes and Prevention of Violence*, Washington, US, Government Printing Office.

Nicholl, C. (1994) 'Ease off the trigger we don't want to be armed', *Observer*, August 7th.

Nicoll, R. (1995) 'Gang babes love to kill', *Observer*, November 12th.

Nkagbu, N. (1996) 'Trigger happy', *Maxim*, April.

Northam, G. (1988) *Shooting in the Dark*, London, Faber & Faber.

Northern Ireland Office (1998) *A Review of the Firearms (Northern Ireland) Order, 1981*, Belfast, Northern Ireland Office, HMSO.

Northmore, J. (1995) 'Three way split: the Taurus PT99 AF/S', *Guns and Shooting*, February: 20–22.

Nozick, R. (1974) *Anarchy, State and Utopia*, London, Blackwell.

Nye, R. (1998) 'The end of the modern French duel', in P. Spierenburg (ed.) *Men and Violence: Gender, Honour and Ritual in Modern Europe and America*, Ohio, Ohio State University Press.

O'Hagan, A. (1996a) 'A darkness falls on the disbelieving town', *Guardian*, March 14th.

—— (1996b) 'Scotland's damaged heart', *Guardian Friday Review*, March 15th.

Paddock, R. (1994) 'Guns for shrinks', *Guardian*, October 6th.

Parker, S.L. (1994) 'Personal view', *Guns and Shooting*, November: 14.

Passmore, J. (1994) 'More police guns on the streets of London', *Evening Standard*, May 16th.

Patterson, S.C. and Eakins, K.R. (1998) 'Congress and gun control', in Bruce and Wilcox (1998).

Paux, R. (1994) 'Arms find linked with drugs', *Times*, February 8th.

Pearson, G. (1983) *Hooligan: A History of Respectable Fears*, London, Macmillan.

Peters, R. (1998) 'Measures to regulate firearms', *7th Session of the UN Commission on Crime Prevention and Criminal Justice*, April, 27. <http://www.soros.org/crime/peters-un.htm>

Peterson, R. (1998) ' "Smart" guns blaze a trail for improved safety', *Guardian*, October 23rd.

Pick, D. (1993) *War Machine: The Rationalisation of Slaughter in the Modern Age*, Connecticut, Yale University Press.

Pierce, G.L. and Bowers, W.J. (1981) 'The Bartley-Fox Gun Law's short-term impact on crime in Boston', in Cook (1981): 120–137.

Pilgrim, R. (1996) 'SWAT techniques: shooting on the move', *Guns and Weapons for Law Enforcement*, November.

Pogrebin, L. (1989) 'Neither pink nor cute: pistols for the women of America', *The Nation*, No. 248, May 15th.

Polsby, D.D. (1986) 'Reflections on violence, guns and the defensive use of lethal force', in Kates (1986).

Poole, R. (1993) 'Making shopping safer', unpublished paper to the Annual Conference of the Association of Town Centre Managers, Wolverhampton, February 16th.

Porter, H. (1996) 'Reason eclipsed by evil', *Guardian*, March 18th.

Potok, M. (1996) 'Texan says gun law saved his life', *USA Today* (international edition), March 25th.

Potter, K. (1997) 'Female perception', *Police Review*, January 31st.

President's Commission on Law Enforcement and Administration of Justice (1967) *The Challenge of Crime in a Free Society*, Washington DC, Government Printing Office.

Prestage, M. (1994) 'PCs powerless as gangland makes its own gun laws', *Observer*, May 22nd.

Prestage, M. and Arlidge, J. (1996) 'Gun handovers rise fivefold after Dunblane', *Observer*, June 2nd.

Putnam, H. (1981) *Reason, Truth and History*, Cambridge, Cambridge University Press.

Quigley, P. (1989) *Armed and Female*, New York, Dutton.

Raynor, R. (1992) 'Los Angeles', *Granta Magazine*.

Reiner, R. (1992a) *The Politics of the Police*, 2nd edn, Hemel Hempstead, Harvester/ Wheatsheaf.

—— (1992b) 'Policing a post-modern society', *Modern Law Review*, 55 (6): 761–781.

Reynolds, G.H. (1995) 'A critical guide to the Second Amendment', *Tennessee Law Review*, 62: 461–508.

Richards, J. (1997) *Films and British National Identity: From Dickens to Dad's Army*, Manchester, Manchester University Press.

Rix, B., Walker, D. and Ward, D. (1998) *The Criminal Use of Firearms*, Home Office, Police Research Group.

Robinson, S. (1994) 'The SIG P226', *Guns and Shooting*, June: 58–60.

Rohner, R.J. (1966) 'The right to bear arms: a phenomenon of constitutional history', *Catholic University of America Law Review*, 16: 53–84.

Rose, D. (1994) 'Police forced into the firing line', *Observer*, May 8th.

Sanders, W.B. (1994) *Gangbangs and Drive-Bys: Grounded Culture and Juvenile Gang Violence*, New York, Aldine De Gruyter.

Sargent, S., Brown, J. and Gourlay, R. (1994) 'Who wants to carry a gun?', *Policing*, 10 (4).

Schlesinger, P., Murdock, G. and Elliott, P. (1983) *Televising Terrorism*, London, Commedia Publications.

Schulman, J.N. (1994) *Stopping Power: Why 70 Million Americans Own Guns*, Mill Valley, CA, Centurion Books.

Schwarz, T. (1999) *Kids and Guns: The History, the Present, the Dangers and the Remedies*, New York, Franklin Watts.

Scottish Office (1996) *An Evaluation of Serious Incidents Involving the use of a Firearm*, Scottish Office Central Research Unit, Edinburgh.

Scraton, P. (1987) 'Unreasonable force: policing, punishment and marginalisation,' in P. Scraton (ed.) *Law, Order and the Authoritarian State*, Milton Keynes, Open University Press.

Seymour, D. (1996) 'How can we have spawned such evil?', *Daily Mirror*, March 14th.

Shalhope, R.E. (1982) 'The ideological origins of the Second Amendment', *Journal of American History*, 69 (3): 599–614.

Shalhope, R.E. and Cress, L.D. (1984) 'The Second Amendment and the right to bear arms: an exchange', *Journal of American History*, 71 (3): 587–593.

Sharman, N. (1995) 'Boxing Day: what is standard division?', *Guns and Shooting*, January: 74–75.

Shaw, S. (1989) 'Give me a gun', *Police*, 21, May 13th.

Sheley, J.F. and Wright, J.D. (1993) 'Motivations for gun possession and carrying among serious juvenile offenders', *Behavioural Sciences and the Law*, 11 (4).

Sherrill, R. (1973) *The Saturday Night Special*, New York, Charterhouse.

Short, J.R. (1996) 'Personal, gang and community careers', in Huff (1996).

Shubert, A. (1980) 'Private initiative in law enforcement', in Bailey (ed.) *Policing and Punishment in 19th Century Britain*, London, Croom Helm.

Silver, A. (1967) 'The demand for order in civil society', in A. Bordua (ed.) *The Police: Six Sociological Essays*, New York, Wiley.

Silverman, J. (1994) *Crack of Doom*, London, Headline.

Silvester, N. (1997) 'Ban the gun of death', *Sunday Mail*, October 8th.

Skogan, W.G. (1978) 'Weapon use in robbery', in J.A. Inciardi and A.E. Pottiger (eds) *Violence and American History*, London, Sage.

Sloan, J.H. *et al.* (1988) 'Handgun regulations, crime, assaults and homicide', *New England Journal of Medicine*, 319, November: 1,256–1,262.

Slotkin, R. (1973) *Regeneration through Violence: The Mythology of the American Frontier, 1600–1860*, Middletown, CT, Wesleyan University Press.

—— (1992) *Gunfighter Nation: The Myth of the Frontier in Twentieth Century America*, New York, Athaeneum.

—— (1996) *Regeneration Through Violence: The Mythology of the American Frontier: 1600–1860*, New York, HarperCollins.

Small, G. (1995) *Ruthless: The Global Rise of the Yardies*, London, Warner Books.

Smith, C. (1999) 'Illegal firearms trafficking', paper presented to a Conference on Gun Control, Scarman Centre, Leicester University, February.

Smith, H. (1996) 'Bullets fly as Crete swaps tourism for gun running', *Guardian*, March 13th.

Smith, T.W. and Smith, R.J. (1995) 'Changes in firearms ownership among women, 1980–1994', *Journal of Criminal Law and Criminology*, 86 (1).

Smithers, R. (1996) 'Gun lobby pleads case', *Guardian*, October 9th.

Smoler, F.P. (1994) 'They shoot policemen don't they?', *The Observer*, Reviews, August 7th.

Snyder, J.R. (1976) 'A nation of cowards', *The Public Interest*, 113 (Fall): 40–56.

South, N. (1988) *Policing for Profit*, London, Sage.

Sparks, R. (1996) 'Masculinity and heroism in the Hollywood blockbuster', *British Journal of Criminology*, 36 (3).

Spierenburg, P. (ed.) (1998) *Men and Violence: Gender, Honour and Ritual in Modern Europe and America*, Ohio, Ohio State University Press.

Spillius, A. (1996) 'Teen gunmen terrorise blacks in Birmingham', *Observer*, February 25th.

Spitzer, R.J. (1995) *The Politics of Gun Control*, New Jersey, Chatham House.

Sprecher, R.A. (1965) 'The lost amendment', *American Bar Association Journal*, 51, in two parts, June and July: 554–557 and 665–669.

Squires, P. (1982) 'Beyond the thin blue line: policing and political change in Britain 1970–1981', in *ACTES; Cahiers D'Action Juridiques*, No. 38, Paris.

—— (1995), 'Siege mentality: firearms, violence and social disorder', unpublished paper to the Conference of the British Criminology Association, Loughborough.

—— (1996a) 'The social control of deadly technology: a case study of firearms and society', in R. Gill (ed.) *Information Society*, New York, Springer Verlag.

—— (1996b) 'Shooters aren't sexy: gun control must be accompanied by an assault on gun culture', *New Statesman*, September 27th.

—— (1997a) 'The irrelevance of America', paper to the British Criminology Association Conference, International Symposium on Gun Control, Queen's University, Belfast, July.

—— (1997b) 'Reviewing the firearms control debate', *British Journal of Criminology*, 37 (4).

—— (1999) 'Criminology and the "community safety" paradigm: safety, power and success and the limits of the local', in M. Brogden (ed.) *British Criminology Conferences: Selected Proceedings*, Volume 2. <http://www.lboro.ac.uk/departments/ss/bsc/bccsp>

—— (2000) 'Firearms: driven to it?', *Criminal Justice Matters*, 38, Winter 1999/2000.

Stalker, J. (1996) 'Why gun laws must be changed', *Observer*, March 17th.

Stange, M.Z. (1995) 'Arms and the woman: a feminist reappraisal', in Kopel (1995).

Stell, L.K. (1986) 'Close encounters of the lethal kind: the use of deadly force in self-defence', in Kates (1986).

Stevenson, J.A. (1994a) 'Editorial', *Handgunner*, 60, May/June: 5.

—— (1994b) 'One last push', *Guns and Shooting*, December: 102.

—— (1995a) 'Look to the future not the past', *Guns and Shooting*, January: 82.

—— (1995b) 'The curious history of firearms fees, part IV', *Handgunner*, 64, June/July: 56–63.

—— (1996) 'Evidence into issues concerning the control of firearms arising from the Dunblane tragedy', in Munday and Stevenson (1966).

Stobart, R. (1989) 'Gunning for justice', *Police Review*, January 6th.

Stourton, E. (1994) 'Teenage gangsters shoot down the American Dream', *Sunday Telegraph*, October 9th.

Suter, E.A. (1994) 'Guns in the medical literature – a failure of peer review', *Journal of the American Medical Association of Georgia*, 83, March: 133–147.

Swanton, O. (1998) 'Gangchester and gang law', *Mixmag*, February.

Tanner, M. (1995) *The Armed Citizen Solution to Crime in the Streets: So Many Criminals, So Few Bullets*, Boulder, Paladin Press.

Tarling, S. and Suffling, K. (1995) 'Just the ticket: form 101', *Guns and Shooting*, February: 43–47.

Taylor, I. (1996) 'Firearms crime at the time of the Cullen Enquiry', Salford Papers in Sociology, No. 20, University of Salford.

—— (1997) 'Respectable, rural, masculine? The politics of the English gun lobby', unpublished paper presented at the International Symposium on Gun Control, British Criminological Association Conference, July, The Queen's University, Belfast.

—— (1998) 'Behavioural science and firearms', *Theoretical Criminology*, 2 (4).

—— (1999) *Crime in Context: A Critical Criminology of Market Societies*, Cambridge, Polity Press.

Tendler, S. (1994a) 'Drug seizures trigger warning over armed gangs', *Times*, January 1st.

—— (1994b) 'Police step up gun patrols to protect London officers', *Times*, February 21st.

—— (1994c) 'Police could show guns on the street', *Times*, March 28th.

—— (1994d) 'Police chiefs seek more firepower', *Times*, May 16th.

—— (1994e) 'Public happy to see police armed', *Times*, May 18th.

—— (1994f) 'Condon calls for new laws to curb gun culture', *Times*, August 2nd.

—— (1996) 'Grim toll of killers who seek power from the gun', *Times*, March 14th.

Thomas, D. (1995) 'Review of *The 100 Greatest Ever Combat Pistols*, by D. Mullin', *Handgunner*, 64, June/July: 55.

Thomas, L. and Leppard, D. (1994) 'Fear stalks the beat of Britain's unarmed bobby', *Sunday Times*, March 13th.

Thompson, E.P. (1963) *The Making of the English Working Class*, Harmondsworth, Penguin.

—— (1975) *Whigs and Hunters: The Origins of the Black Act*, Harmondsworth, Penguin.

Thompson, T. and Wazir, B. (1999) 'Fear keeps black stars from anti-gun rally', *Observer*, July 25th.

Timmins, N. (1996) 'Are we hostage to a gun culture?', *Independent*, March 14th.

Titmuss, R. (1987) 'The irresponsible society', in R. Titmuss and B. Abel-Smith, *The Philosophy of Welfare*, London, Allen and Unwin.

Tonry, M. (1995) *Malign Neglect: Race, Crime and Punishment in America*, New York, Oxford University Press.

Tonso, W.R. (1982) *Gun and Society: The Social and Existential roots of the American attachment to Firearms*, Lanham, University Press of America.

Trachtenberg, A. (1982) *The Incorporation of America: Culture and Society in the Gilded Age*, New York, Hill and Wang.

Travis, A. (1994a) 'Gun crime linked to cocaine deals', *The Guardian*, July 2nd.

—— (1994b) 'Armed patrols loom, says police chief', *The Guardian*, July 7th.

—— (1995) 'Police hold referendum on carrying firearms', *Guardian*, March 21st.

—— (1996a) 'Who's who in the gun lobby?', *Guardian*, March 19th.

—— (1996b) 'Amnesty expected to net thousands of guns', *Guardian*, April 25th.

—— (1996c) 'Labour proposes guns crackdown', *Guardian*, May 13th.

—— (1996d) 'Police "lack power" to veto requests for gun licences', *Guardian*, May 22nd.

—— (1996e) 'Gun groups set up a fighting fund', *Guardian*, July 17th.

—— (1996f) 'Don't weaken guns pledge pleads Dunblane petition organiser', *Guardian*, October 6th.

—— (1996g) 'Howard ups gun payouts but fails to quell revolt', *Guardian*, December 5th.

Tredre, R. (1995) 'Crime falls as city's gangs hold their fire', *Observer*, May 14th.

Turner, L. (1996) 'Six-gun suicide of Tory baddies', *Sunday Mirror*, August 4th.

Twomey, J. (1994a) 'The Old British Bobby now a cop with a gun', *Daily Express*, May 17th.

—— (1994b) 'Protect us from the gunmen on our streets', *Daily Express*, August 2nd.

Uglow, S. (1988) *Policing Liberal Democracy*, Oxford, Oxford University Press.

Uniacke, S. (1994) *Permissable Killing: The Self-Defence Justification for Homicide*, Cambridge, Cambridge University Press.

Urban, M. (1992) *Big Boys' Rules: The Secret Struggle Against the IRA*, London, BCA, Faber & Faber.

Van Alstyne, W. (1995) 'The Second Amendment and the personal right to arms', *Journal on Firearms and Public Policy*, Second Amendment Foundation, 7, Fall: 1–20.

Vergara, J.L. (1994) 'Fortress mentality', *New Statesman and Society*, February.

Vizzard, W.J. (1997) *In the Crossfire: A Political History of the Bureau of Alcohol, Tobacco and Firearms*, Boulder, Lynne Rienner Publishers.

Vulliamy, E. (1994a) 'Sheriff Clinton spikes guns of the first lady of firepower', *Observer*, May 8th.

—— (1994b) 'Kill for God, America and fun', *Observer*, September 18th.

—— (1995) 'Clinton tackles the mighty right', *Observer*, April 30th.

—— (1996a) 'Dunblane's long good-bye', *Guardian*, August 7th.

—— (1996b) 'Telling Scotland to get stuffed', *Guardian*, August 14th.

—— (1998) 'Young guns: slaughter in America's playgrounds', *Guardian*, March 23rd.

Waddington, P.J. (1988) *Arming an Unarmed Police: Policy and Practice in the Metropolitan Police*, London, The Police Foundation.

—— (1989) 'Beware the shot in the dark', *Police*, 22 (6).

—— (1990) 'Overkill or minimum force'?, *Criminal Law Review*: 695–707.

—— (1991) *The Strong Arm of the Law: Armed and public order policing*, Oxford, Clarendon Press.

—— (1994) 'How can we stem the tide of gun crime?', *Daily Mail*, August 4th.

—— (1995) 'Both arms of the law', unpublished paper to British Criminological Association Conference, University of Loughborough.

Waddington, P.J. and Hamilton, M. (1997) 'The impotence of the powerful: recent British police weapons policy', *Sociology*, 31 (1): 91–109.

Walker, M. (1994) 'Clinton wins ban on "deadly assault weapons" ', *Guardian*, May 6th.

Walker, T. (1994) 'Concealed carry – stateside', *Guns and Shooting Magazine*, August: 14.

—— (1995) 'Walkersville', *Guns and Shooting*, January: 12.

Waters, R.A. (1998) *The Best Defence: True Stories of Intended Victims Who Defended Themselves With a Firearm*, Nashville TX, Cumberland House.

Watkins, A. (1996) 'Gun fans fight higher calibre ban threat', *Guardian*, November 1st.

Watson, P. (1996) 'Dunblane inquiry will ban handguns at home', *Sun*, September 30th.

Weatherhead, A.D. and Robinson, B.M. (1970) *Firearms in Crime: A Home Office Statistical Division Report on Indictable Offences Involving Firearms in England and Wales*, London, HMSO.

Weatherup, R.G. (1988) 'Standing armies and armed citizens', *Journal on Firearms and Public Policy*, Second Amendment Foundation, 1 (1).

Webster, P. and Ford, R. (1996) 'Government will support ban on handguns despite Tory MPs vote', *Times*, August 14th.

Weil, D.S. and Hemenway, D. (1992) 'Loaded guns in the home: analysis of a national random survey of gun owners', reprinted in J.E. Dizard *et al.* (1999) *Guns in America*, New York, New York University Press.

Weiss, R. (1978) 'The emergence and transformation of private detective industrial policing in the United States, 1850–1940', in *Crime and Social Justice*, 9, Spring/Summer.

Wheen, F. (1999) *Karl Marx*, London, Fourth Estate Publishers.

White, M. and Travis, A. (1996) 'We will not compromise', *Guardian*, October 17th.

Williams, D.C. (1991) 'Civic republicanism and the citizen militia: the terrifying Second Amendment', *Yale Law Journal*, 101: 551–615.

Williams, S.J. and McGrath, J.H. (1978) 'A social profile of urban gun owners', in J. Inciardi and A. Pottiger (eds) *Violence and American History*, New York, Sage.

Wilson, C. (1996) 'Police seize gun maniac', *Daily Mail*, April 29th.

Wintemute, G.J. (1987) 'When children shoot children: 88 unintended deaths in California', *Journal of the American Medical Association*, 257: 3,107–3,109.

Wintour, P. (1996) 'Gun report advisor is arms lobbyist', *Observer*, August 18th.

Wolf, N. (1994) *Fire with Fire: The New Female Power and how it will Change the 21st Century*, New York, Vantage Books.

Wright, A. (1998) 'Slippery slopes? The paramilitary imperative in European policing', *The International Journal of Police Research and Management*, 2 (2).

Wright, J.D. (1984) 'The ownership of firearms for reasons of self-defence', in Kates and Kaplan (1984).

—— (1988) 'Second thoughts about gun control', *Public Interest*, 91: 23–39.

—— (1995) 'Ten essential observations on guns in America', *Society*, 32 (3) March–April.

Wright, J.D. and Marston, L.M. (1975) 'The ownership of the means of destruction: weapons in the United States', *Social Problems*, 23 (1): 93–107.

Wright, J.D. and Rossi, P.H. (1986) *Armed and Considered Dangerous: A Survey of Felons and Their Firearms*, New York, Aldine de Gruyter.

Wright, J.D., Rossi, P.H. and Daly, K. (1983) *Under the Gun: Weapons, Crime and Violence in America*, New York, Aldine de Gruyter.

Wright, J.D., Sheley, J.F. and Smith, M.D. (1992) 'Kids, guns and killing fields', *Society*, 30, November/December: 84–89.

Yardley, M. (1988) 'Hitting the wrong targets', *Police Review*, January 15th.

—— (1995a) *The Shooting Sports and the Firearms Bill*, Shrewsbury, The Sportsman's Association.

—— (1995b) 'Editorial', *Handgunner*, 65, August/September: 5.

—— (1996) 'Shooting and the law', *Gun Mart*, November: 24–27.

Yardley, M. and Eliot, P. (1986) 'The case for special units', *Police*, 18, June: 26–31.

Yardley, M. and Stevenson, J. (1988) *The Firearms Amendment Bill: A Research Report*, 4th edn, Brightlingsea, Essex, Piedmont Publishing.

Young, H. (1996) 'Many questions, no answers', *Guardian*, March 14th.

Younge, G., Duval Smith, A. and Tran, M. (1996) 'Dunblane joins roll of carnage', *Guardian*, March 14th.

Zimring, F.E. (1968) 'Is gun control likely to reduce violent killings?', *University of Chicago Law Review*, 35: 721–737.

—— (1981) 'Handguns in the twenty-first century: alternative policy futures', in Cook (1981): 1–10.

Zimring F. and Hawkins, G. (1987) *The Citizen's Guide to Gun Control*, New York, Macmillan.

—— (1997) *Crime is Not the Problem: Lethal Violence in America*, New York, Oxford University Press.

Zinn, C. (1996) 'Australian states bury differences to agree tough crackdown on guns', *Guardian*, May 11th.

Index